Augsburg College
George Sverdrup Library
Minneapolis, Minnesota 55404

Bonapartism after Sedan

Bonapartism after Sedan

BY JOHN ROTHNEY

Cornell University Press
ITHACA, NEW YORK

Copyright © 1969 by Cornell University

All rights reserved. Except for brief quotations in a review, this book, or parts thereof, must not be reproduced in any form without permission in writing from the publisher. For information address Cornell University Press, 124 Roberts Place, Ithaca, New York 14850.

First published 1969

Library of Congress Catalog Card Number: 68-9752

PRINTED IN THE UNITED STATES OF AMERICA
BY THE VAIL-BALLOU PRESS, INC.

For

F. P. R.

Acknowledgments

One reason that the history of Bonapartism after Sedan has not been thoroughly explored has doubtless been the inaccessibility of sources. Published memoirs are rare and sometimes untrustworthy; the documentation available in public archives is fragmentary and dispersed. The historian is therefore compelled to seek out new material which may still be in private hands. Two sets of papers that were thus discovered have provided the foundations upon which much of this study is based.

The unpublished "Mémoires" of Baron Eschasseriaux have been my single most important source. My gratitude to Baron Paul de Chaubry, Eschasseriaux's great-grandson, for allowing me to consult them at length at his château of Oyré is quite beyond expression. It is equally difficult to express adequately my thanks to M. Edgar Raoul-Duval, who allowed me to use the papers of his grandfather, preserved at his château of Le Vaudreuil. I am happy to pay tribute not only to his hospitality and generosity, but also to the stimulation of his keen historical interest.

It is a pleasure to acknowledge my special obligation to Professor H. Stuart Hughes, of Harvard University, under whose direction I began my work on this subject, for his unfailing encouragement. I am also indebted to Professor David Pinkney, of the University of Washington, for his stimulating criticisms.

Acknowledgments

I must particularly thank M. Marcel Delafosse, Archivist of the Charente-Maritime, Mme. Geneviève Gille, of the Archives Nationales, and Mme. Hélène Tulard and her staff at the Archives of the Prefecture of Police, for their aid and suggestions.

I am grateful also to a number of persons who took time to search their memories or their libraries for information which might help me: the Comte de Suarez d'Aulan; the Marquis d'Ayguesvives; M. A. Belanger; the Marquis de Candolle; M. Paul de Cassagnac; Général Comte de Cossé-Brissac; the Duc de Dalmatie; the Duchesse de Feltre; M. Maurice Hennessy; Mme. Suzanne d'Huart; Colonel J. Le Marois; Mme. Alfred Leroux; the Duc de Mouchy; Baronne de Ravignan; Baron Reille; M. René Rémond; Dr. Rouher; Baron de Saint-Paul; Professor Alexander Sedgwick; Baron de Septenville.

Finally, I must record my thanks for the award of a Fulbright fellowship, which financed the year in France during which my research was begun. I am similarly obliged to the Research Council of the University of Missouri.

JOHN ROTHNEY

Portland, Oregon
May 1968

Contents

	Acknowledgments	vii
	Abbreviations	xiii
	Introduction	1
I	Chislehurst	9
II	Paris	
	Rue de l'Elysée, Rue Montmartre, Belleville	53
III	Versailles	104
IV	"Pyrénées-Occidentales"	158
V	Prangins and Brussels	230
	Conclusion: The Limits of Authoritarian Democracy	292
	Appendix	321
	Bibliography	329
	Index	345

Illustrations

Chart of organization of the Bonapartist party   55

MAPS

1. Subscriptions to Bonapartist or sympathizing newspapers as a percentage of subscriptions to all Parisian *journaux d'opinion*, April–June 1872   78
2. Net change in the provincial circulation by mail of seven Bonapartist Parisian dailies, 1872–1876   79
3. Mid–1872 circulation by mail of local Bonapartist papers as a percentage of total subscriptions   84
4. January–March 1876 circulation by mail of local Bonapartist papers as a percentage of total subscriptions   85
5. Platforms of candidates endorsed by the *Comité national conservateur* for the general elections of February 20, 1876   197
6. Percentage by *département* of independent and opposition deputies in the *Corps législatif* in 1870   205
7. The Bonapartist popular vote in the elections of 1876: Percentage, by *départements*, of votes cast February 20   208
8. *Arrondissements* electing Bonapartist candidates on February 20 and March 5, 1876   209

Abbreviations

The following abbreviations have been used throughout in the citation of manuscript sources:

ACM Archives Départementales de la Charente-Maritime, La Rochelle
AN   Archives Nationales, Paris
APP Archives de la Préfecture de Police, Paris
BN   Bibliothèque Nationale, Paris

Bonapartism after Sedan

Introduction

The first responsibility confronting anyone writing the history of the Bonapartist party after September 4, 1870, is to explain why it should be done. Historical scholarship might seem to have little time to spare on the fortunes of a minority party representing the regime which had just led an illprepared France into a disastrous war with Prussia. Why then violate the dramatic finality of Sedan, and pursue the story of the Empire at a moment when France was entering upon the longest-lived of her modern regimes, and with it a new chapter in her political and social history?

The events of the period between the proclamation of the Republic in Paris at the news of the Emperor's defeat and its consolidation with the resignation of Marshal MacMahon in 1879, well known to every student of modern French history, can be summarized as an astonishingly rapid succession of ups and downs in a see-saw battle between Left and Right for control over the nation's future. The heroic but futile efforts of Gambetta, as "dictator" of the Republican Government of National Defense, to prolong resistance to the invader, were rebuked by the election, in 1871, of a National Assembly with a Monarchist majority. The Assembly, at first dominated by Thiers, the subduer of the Paris Commune, overthrew him in 1873 because he espoused the Republican cause, and attempted to unite Orleanists and Legitimists for the restoration of the Bourbon pretender, the Comte de Chambord.

Bonapartism after Sedan

After that failed, the Monarchists, to stall for time, could only extend the term of MacMahon as President of the Republic, but in 1874 their leader, the Duc de Broglie, was in his turn overthrown. Finally in 1875 Gambetta and Thiers seemed to have won, when by one vote the Assembly passed the Wallon Amendment consecrating the Republic. Hardly had the electorate ratified this solution in the general elections of 1876, however, when MacMahon and the Orleanists attempted to avenge the defeat by dismissing the Republican government of Jules Simon and holding new elections; but the failure of this coup of *Seize Mai*, 1877, put the Republicans more firmly in the saddle, so that MacMahon, challenged by Gambetta to "give in or get out," chose to get out in 1879. The vicissitudes of this decade of struggle are, then, familiar; need the Bonapartists be investigated in order to explain them?

Comparative history, that perilous but fascinating mode of inquiry, suggests why the answer must be affirmative. The year 1870 was not the only time in modern European history when a military and authoritarian regime succumbed after a defeat on the battlefield to a coalition of liberal *Frondeurs* and radical demagogues (to employ the terminology of the regime's defenders.) Yet far from collapsing within fifteen years, the Third French Republic, spawned in a national humiliation in which some saw treason, proved to be more enduring than any of its predecessors, despite economic setbacks, prolonged diplomatic isolation, a succession of sordid scandals, and a political system which assured preference to mediocrity and mistook stagnation for government. Many variables, of course, explain the difference, not least the self-assurance of the victorious Republicans. But what, comparatively, was the role of the Republic's opponents?

Considered in this light, a study of the party of the Empire will be seen to be indispensable for explaining the origin and survival of the Third Republic. Directly and indirectly, by

Introduction

their achievements and by their failures, the men of the regime for which six million Frenchmen had voted in 1870, the only Rightist regime which boasted of mass support, exercised a crucial influence upon the course of events. Yet thus far relatively little of substance has been known about this bogey of both Thiers and Broglie, though general accounts seldom fail to mention that it was the off-stage thunder of Bonapartist electoral victories in 1874–1875 which frightened the Orleanists into accepting a Republican constitution.

The first objective of this study is to remedy this deficiency by telling, as fully as possible, the story of Bonapartism's initial resurgence and eventual eclipse after Sedan. The form is that of a drama in five acts, focusing on the 1870's when the Bonapartists still seemed to represent a serious challenge to the new regime, but continuing in the last act into the 1890's in order to confirm the persistence of the weaknesses that undid them.

Although in the first act the principal characters enter engaged in a fateful debate on how Frenchmen could best be persuaded to restore the Empire, the action is dominated by the possibility that the exile of Chislehurst would seek to regain his throne by force rather than persuasion. Historically, Bonapartism had frequently been not only a party but a plot; its power was not always won at the polls. Could it again bring off a *coup d'etat* with the complicity of elements, at least, of the army and the bureaucracy? There is good reason to think that Napoleon III underwent the surgery that killed him early in 1873 in order to prepare for a "return from Elba." But the evidence available suggests that France's functional elites did not feel themselves sufficiently imperiled by the advent of a regime hitherto revolutionary to violate their traditions by entering into conspiracy against the Republic.

Without a *coup de main*, the Empire could only be restored by a successful appeal of the Bonapartist "party" to the electorate. But what was implied by the word "party" in the 1870's? How was a party to be led and organized? What propagandistic methods must it employ? How should it collect and budget its funds? Could it appeal simultaneously to mutually hostile social classes? The scene for the second act of our drama is Paris, where the Bonapartists struggled unavailingly to find effective answers to all these questions. Their eventual admission of the inferiority of their party on all these counts, an admission which this study has amply confirmed, suggests that the superiority of Gambetta's political *technique*, as much as his message, may have given him victory.

The scene shifts in the third act to Versailles, to follow the Bonapartists' tortuous course among the rival factions of the National Assembly and to clarify their part in its closely spaced crises. It was the Bonapartists, neglectful of the interests of their party, who provided the votes necessary to overthrow Thiers and thus open the way to a Legitimist restoration, just as later they enabled MacMahon to carry out his coup, though they had not conceived it and derived no benefit from it, and their leaders had been desperately anxious to avoid it. The fatal incongruities of their parliamentary performance reveal, in fact, that there is little truth in the image of them as a well-disciplined phalanx with their dynasty's hopes always clearly in mind.

With the general elections of 1876, the fourth and climactic act of the drama arrives. Analysis of the election results indicates the real dimensions of the threat the Bonapartists posed. The enumeration of their candidacies and victories, the explanations of where they won and why, make it clear that the Orleanists had taken needless alarm in 1875; the Second Empire had not left behind it a party capable of successfully facing a democratic electorate.

It is the historian's responsibility not only to tell what hap-

Introduction

pened, but also to try to explain why it happened. Analysis of this failure of the Bonapartist revival does more than illuminate the formative years of the Third Republic. It also enlarges our understanding of the interaction of social groups and political institutions in the broader context of nineteenth-century French history, thus achieving the second objective of this study. For the defective electoral campaign of the Bonapartists in 1876, like their organizational weaknesses and their mistakes at Versailles, must be explained by analyzing the party's structure and composition. To do this requires re-examining the social and political history of the Second Empire.

Nineteenth-century French history is not a series of watertight compartments separated by revolutions telegraphed from Paris. It was the ruling class of the Empire which became the party under the Republic. The successes and failures of the Bonapartists after 1870 were due, in large part, to what they had learned or failed to learn of democratic politics during the preceding two decades. What, then, were the relations among the Imperial regime, the politicians who supported it and were supported by it, and the masses of universal suffrage? Did the Imperial political elite differ significantly in outlook and attributes from the other groups of notables who had successively ruled France since the Revolution? How are the emergence of a strong popular Bonapartism in some regions and its absence in others to be explained?

Everyone, of course, knows about the pressure applied to the electorate by Imperial officials. Too little attention has been paid, on the other hand, to another group of managers of universal suffrage who emerged under the Second Empire. These were notables who had come to grips with the problem of winning support for their traditional tutelage from a democratic electorate by developing a quasi-feudal relationship with the population of their domains, and maintaining it with political machines which American politicians of the Gilded Age might have envied.

There is a high degree of correlation between the foci of popular Bonapartism under the Third Republic and these baronial fiefs of certain deputies of the Empire, none higher than in the Charente-Inférieure, where Baron Eschasseriaux, the "King of the Charentes," held sway. To explain this phenomenon and to show how it had always represented a theoretical anomaly and in the end became a practical obstacle for the Imperial government, much of the fourth chapter is devoted to the politics of this *département* during the generation before 1876. For if we know how the Baron laid the foundations of Charentais Bonapartism, and how and why he was able to sustain it triumphantly after 1870, we shall know by contrast the reasons for the failure of so many of his fellow Bonapartist politicians.

Bonapartism is often alluded to as a kind of intermittent fever endemic in the French body politic, or at least in certain regions or classes, the Fifth Republic representing merely the latest outbreak of the contagion. In line with this reasoning, explanations for patterns of voting have tended to stress the sociological and economic characteristics of the various regions and their idiosyncratic habits of thought over a long historical span. An effort has been made in this study to take account of these factors in the explanation of how Bonapartism came back after Sedan and why its renascence was limited. But it must be pointed out as well that, like any other political movement, Bonapartism to become effective had to become more than a state of mind. Its fate depended on the way its leaders construed its meaning for the benefit of the voters, and on the practical steps they took to enroll those voters for the cause.

Considered abstractly, Bonapartism is a remarkably protean political concept. Even in the 1870's different members of the

Introduction

Imperial party interpreted it as implying everything from socialism to an extreme clerical reaction. Similarly, some thought that their party's task was the intensive organization of the peasant, or even the urban working-class, vote, and others believed the aim should be the formation of a coalition of all who stood to lose from any further democratization of French life. It was the politicians of the party, however, the former official deputies of the Empire, who now gave Bonapartism its effective meaning by their parliamentary votes, their electoral platforms, and their campaign methods. Unfortunately for its revived hopes, the Second Empire had not designed a political system which produced very many men like Eschasseriaux. In practice, supporters after 1870 construed Bonapartism in a manner which did not enable them to counteract the appeal of Gambetta.

After the failure of the *Seize Mai*, Bonapartism fell into a decline which was immensely accelerated in 1879 when the Prince Imperial, who had succeeded Napoleon III as pretender, was killed while serving with the British army in Africa. Rather than submit to the leadership of the Emperor's cousin Prince Napoleon, the notorious "Plon-plon," the Bonapartist party disintegrated. Unable to accept the constructive role within the Republic which more than once was offered them, the Bonapartist politicians were doomed eventually to experience that humiliating defeat by their social inferiors which Daniel Halévy has dubbed the *fin des notables*. Even for Eschasseriaux this last act of the Bonapartist drama was a tragic one; Charentais Bonapartism gradually dwindled until the new century found the Baron almost isolated in a land of which he had once been the unquestioned master.

The eviction of such an established elite from the seats of power is often cited as a prime cause for the emergence of twentieth-century "Fascist" movements, of which Bonapartism is sometimes taken to be the distant but direct

Bonapartism after Sedan

French precursor. The third objective of this book is in conclusion to decide whether the Bonapartism of the Republic in fact foreshadowed these movements or differed radically from them.

This study therefore seeks not only to heighten our understanding of the origins of the Third Republic, but also to explain the place of Bonapartism in the society and politics of the Second Empire and in the development of the Right in modern French history.

Chapter I

Chislehurst

When Paris, on hearing of Napoleon III's surrender to the Prussians at Sedan, rose up on September 4, 1870 and overthrew the Second Empire, the end appeared to have come for Bonapartism in France. Yet in January of 1873 it seemed to many Frenchmen that only the Emperor's sudden death in exile had averted a reenactment of Napoleon I's triumphal return from Elba. In the course of two and a half years it had become obvious that at least in parts of France, Bonapartist politicians possessed the will and the means to maintain strong popular support for the Imperial government. The Bonapartist party remained as ideologically diversified as ever. Encouraged by their growing confidence in the possibility of a restoration, Bonapartists argued whether it could better be accomplished by a *coup de main* or a plebiscite. Cutting across this argument was another, no less acrimonious for being premature, over what *kind* of Empire they would restore: authoritarian or liberal? clerical or socialistic? These arguments had by no means been resolved by January, 1873. Their very urgency, however, revealed how strongly Bonapartism had revived since the fatal day when the Republic was proclaimed at the Hôtel de Ville.

On September 5, 1870, the Rothschilds' Paris correspondent reported, "Less than four months ago, the Second Empire, by a plebiscite that gave it a majority of 5,800,000 votes, believed itself to be impregnable. We now see it disappear without a single protesting voice." [1]

This report was no exaggeration. At the confused night session of the Legislative Body on September 3, not one deputy opposed the Republican Jules Favre's proposal to depose the captive Emperor;[2] a Bonapartist journalist who reproached several of the Imperialist majority for this dereliction was answered by shrugs of cynical resignation.[3] The conduct of the former government press was no more praiseworthy; only three papers, among them Paul de Cassagnac's *Pays*, defended the fallen regime or protested the advent of the Republican Government of National Defense.[4]

Thus the Paris of Rochefort's *Lanterne* dismissed the Empire and, in the person of her deputies, took over the destinies of France. In the volatile city the government of "Badinguet" and December 2 had been considered an intruder by both the Faubourg Saint-Antoine and the Faubourg Saint-Germain. Its disappearance had been long hoped for and was taken as a matter of course.

Such was not always the case in the provinces. The story of how the Republic came to La Rochelle offers an illuminating comparison. On September 5, the Imperial mayor, M. Charles Fournier, was asked by the entire municipal council to remain at his post. Thus reinforced, he concurred with the Imperial Prefect in refusing the plea of a small deputation of Republicans that the Republic be proclaimed. The new government in Paris, he declared, was provisional; only a demo-

[1] Robert Henrey, ed., *Letters from Paris 1870–75* (London, 1942), 65.
[2] E. Hermant, "La régence de l'Impératrice Eugénie," *Revue des Questions Historiques*, CIV (1926), 354–355.
[3] Jules Richard, *Le Bonapartisme sous la République* (3d ed.; Paris, 1883), 6.
[4] Eugène Balleyguier (Fidus, pseud.), *Journal de Fidus* (Paris, 1889), I, 74.

cratic vote could decide its definitive form. Thus the Republic was blithely ignored at La Rochelle for two days, until the disappointed deputation had its plea granted by Gambetta's newly-appointed Prefect. There is no reason to doubt Fournier's comment that the new Prefect's proclamation "offended the character and sentiments of our fellow citizens. . . . The recent elections held in complete freedom . . . had made the will of the Rochelais sufficiently known." Nor did the citizens react favorably to such an initiative at a moment of national danger. In Fournier's eyes and theirs the Prefect had entered into an "alliance with the perpetual conspirators."

Therefore there was all the more reason, Fournier thought, to remain at his post. He decided to resign only when he learned that Gambetta had empowered Prefects to dismiss mayors and dissolve municipal councils. Before resigning he had the bitter satisfaction of refusing the Prefect's plea that he stay on, for Gambetta's appointee had soon realized that the support of Republicans alone would be more compromising than useful. Fournier pointed out that, with the Republic proclaimed, he could not remain without betraying his oath of office. "Leaving the Prefecture I read on the walls of the town the proclamation of the Prefect; it contained insults against the Emperor and his government. I thus had immediate proof that I had acted rightly." [5]

Clearly, then, there were places in France where it was not the Empire which slipped out the back door, but Gambetta's Republic which slipped in, to confront the reserve or the actual hostility of the populations and their accustomed leaders. Moreover, there must have been many men who, like Fournier, felt that events at Sedan or in Paris had in no way lessened their responsibility for leadership. If they stepped

[5] Famille Fournier, "Mémoires," twelve manuscript volumes numbered I–VI, VIII, X–XII, XVI–XVII (ACM 4J1509), X, 312, 316–324.

Bonapartism after Sedan

down rather than serve the Republic, it was because they felt that the Republic, the government of the "perpetual conspirators," could not long endure.

It was easy to overlook these facts, however, for when France, in the respite granted after the capitulation of Paris, voted massively for peace in the general elections of February 8, 1871, Bonapartism played a nearly unnoticeable part. The contrast with the plebiscite of May, 1870, was absolute.

Admittedly the circumstances of the vote worked against the Bonapartists. With more than forty departments occupied by the enemy, normal campaigning was out of the question. War or peace was the overriding issue on which hastily composed, motley lists of candidates were elected. A decree of Gambetta's declaring all servants of the Empire ineligible had been annulled, but not until a few days before the poll. This concession to freedom of opinion could be the more confidently granted because the system of voting—*scrutin de liste* on a departmental basis—was designed to hamstring the former "official" deputies.[6]

Such precautions proved however, wasted effort; at this low point of Imperial fortunes, most Bonapartists had gone to ground. Altogether they polled throughout France a mere 100,000 votes; the nucleus in the National Assembly of the future Imperial party, the *Appel au peuple*, was composed of only nineteen deputies, though a half-dozen future fellow-travelers had also been elected.[7] Meanwhile the East and Southeast had chosen Republicans, while most of the rest of the country returned Orleanists and Legitimists.[8] France seemed to have confirmed the verdict of the Parisian boulevards.

---

[6] Jacques Gouault, *Comment la France est devenue républicaine: Les élections générales et partielles à l'Assemblée nationale 1870–1875* (Paris, 1954), 33–36, 41–44, 52–75; Charles Seignobos, *Le déclin de l'Empire et l'établissement de la Troisième République* (Paris, 1921), 279–284.

[7] Gouault, *Comment*, 191, 197–237.   [8] Seignobos, *Déclin*, 284.

Chislehurst

How and where had the handful of Bonapartist survivors managed to hold their ground? The explanation of one of them, Baron Eschasseriaux of the Charente-Inférieure,[9] is worth following, for success in this darkest hour may afford clues to the greater triumphs of better days to come. In only one department, he recalled in his memoirs, had they displayed their Imperial colors openly; four of the five Corsican deputies were Bonapartists "thanks to the influence which Gavini,[10] former prefect of Nice, had always exercised in that island, cradle of the Imperial family." But Corsica was always a special case; the reasons—not wholly sentimental—for its persistent Bonapartism are discussed in a later chapter.[11]

In southwestern France, some isolated candidates were elected because of their personal reputations and influence, without having made any sort of *profession de foi*. In the Lot, Count Murat was elected though he was on no electoral list and had printed no ballots. "The popularity of his name had elected him by simple handwritten ballots." [12] In the Tarn-et-Garonne, Prax-Paris "an independent deputy, pugnacious, very popular, had won alone."

Such men possessed sufficient political power to win unaided. In other departments, Bonapartists of local pre-

[9] Eugène, Baron Eschasseriaux, "Mémoires," twenty manuscript volumes preserved in the library of the château of Oyré (Sarthe), V, 373-374.

[10] Denis Gavini, Corsican-born, member of the Constituent Assembly in 1848 where he voted with the Left, rallied to the Elysée after the *coup d'état*, Prefect of the Empire, deputy for Corsica 1871-1886. For biographical details consult Félix Ribeyre, *Biographie des sénateurs et des députés* (new ed.; Paris, n.d.), 422, a useful compilation by a Bonapartist, and A. Robert, E. Bourloton, and G. Cougny, eds., *Dictionnaire des parlementaires français* 1789-1889 (Paris, 1891), III, 142-143 (hereinafter cited as RBC).

[11] See below, 221-223.

[12] Joachim, Comte Murat, grand-nephew of the King of Naples; son of a deputy; himself deputy 1854-1870, sitting first with the majority, then with the *Tiers Parti*, and deputy under the Republic 1871-1889 (Ribeyre, *Biographie*, 524-525; RBC, IV, 461-462).

eminence were elected as "men of order" on lists which included representatives of the monarchical parties. This was true in the Charente, as well as in the Sarthe, where "Haentjens, who had at Le Mans fought courageously against the dictatorship [of Gambetta] with his paper *La Sarthe*, was alone elected of his party, with Orleanists and Legitimists." [13]

In many places, however, the Bonapartists, while not altogether inactive, preferred to exercise the influence they still wielded very discreetly; thus the three former deputies of the Landes, among them Eschasseriaux's brother-in-law,[14] "who had been official candidates agreeable to the government, did not dare risk their candidacy and worked to elect moderate lists composed in the majority of enemies of the Empire."

Such an expedient was unnecessary in the Charente-Inférieure, where Eschasseriaux in 1869 had sustained an epic battle against seven opponents including the official candidate. In 1871 he and three other Bonapartists were among the ten deputies elected—the greatest success of his party, Corsica excepted. His explanation should be carefully noted:

It had been necessary to possess a powerful electoral organization, to enjoy great popularity in the district, and to have fought with a newspaper against the candidacy of the men of September 4. . . . Success came to those who had shown independence before September 4 and who afterwards had turned their efforts against the dictatorship of Tours and Bordeaux.

Two dozen-odd former Imperial notables had possessed these formidable multiple advantages, but "everywhere else, either

[13] Alfred-Alphonse Haentjens, son of a rich shipowner of Nantes, Protestant; Imperial deputy 1863–1870, a member of the *Tiers Parti* who voted against war; again deputy from 1871 until his death in 1884 (Ribeyre, *Biographie*, 441–442; RBC, III, 303–304).

[14] Louis-Adhémar, Marquis de Guilloutet, of a rich family of ancient lineage, landed proprietor and *bouilleur de cru*, deputy 1863–1870 and 1876–1886 (RBC, III, 285).

Chislehurst

through lack of organization or . . . of courage," the Empire had gone unrepresented, even covertly or on coalition lists, at the polls.[15] The years to come would reveal to what extent its spokesmen could overcome deficiencies of organization or courage.

The results of the numerous by-elections held on July 2, 1871, were even less impressive. Bonapartists ran in only a few departments, and though three were elected, only one would later become a reliable member of the party of the *Appel au peuple*.[16] A "conservative, free-trade" list headed by Rouher, the former "Vice-Emperor," was soundly beaten both in the Gironde and in the Charente.[17] The euphemistic title of this ticket is significant, for nowhere did a candidate breathe a word of sympathy for the deposed regime, far less avow himself its partisan.[18]

The prudence of this calculated equivocation was undeniable, for the National Assembly had solemnly declared the Bonaparte dynasty responsible for "the ruin, invasion, and dismemberment of France," and a propagandistic counteroffensive had yet to be mounted. There was, however, in the candidacies of July, 1871, a deeper, *un*calculated equivocation which represented a dangerous portent for the future of Bonapartism.

One of the most distinguished notables of the Dordogne was Pierre Magne, former Imperial Minister of Finance. Urged to put his name in nomination at the February elections, he had refused, declaring that "all division would compromise the success of the men of order, which is the first requirement of the moment," and had supported a list of

---

[15] Eschasseriaux, "Mémoires," V, 373–374.
[16] Gouault, *Comment*, 111–112, 116.
[17] Robert Schnerb, *Rouher et le Second Empire* (Paris, 1949), 292; Gouault, *Comment*, 126.
[18] Gouault, *Comment*, 111–112.

such men untarnished by Imperial associations. Now, in July, he obeyed the same principle in accepting a candidacy patronized by the "conservative-liberal party," and publishing a *profession de foi* which asserted that "when a house is on fire is not the best moment to discuss the best system of pumps." France was still shuddering at the spectacle of the Commune; in such an hour the "men of order," the "conservative-liberals" must unite against the "social peril" regardless of their dynastic preferences.[19] This was not merely a vote-catching tactic. It faithfully reflected Magne's state of mind; he was dubious of a Bonapartist restoration and in any case much more preoccupied by the threat of "Communism," against which M. Thiers, soon to be named President of the Republic, seemed the only bulwark.[20]

Ex-mayor Fournier at La Rochelle would have been glad to recapture his political role under the same auspices. He wanted, he thought, to "remain outside the parties"; he had not had "any particular connection with the family of Napoleon"; so he confided to his diary on June 18 while awaiting the results of the deliberations of an interparty committee authorized to compose a conservative ticket. Alas for conservative unity! "In this *committee of fusion* the candidacy of the *Duc de Chartres* was proposed and accepted. . . . Thus the committee is henceforth an *Orleanist committee*; everyone resumes his own persuasion." Fournier in particular resumed his so quickly that by June 23 he had become convinced that only the Constitution of 1852 could protect France from "the conspirators and the International." [21]

This broadmindedness of two former devoted servants of the Empire was disturbing. Of course in the glare of the

---

[19] Joseph Durieux, *Le ministre Pierre Magne 1806–1879* (Paris, 1929), II, 270–272, 279–280.

[20] Henrey, ed., *Letters*, 161.

[21] Fournier, "Mémoires," XI, 301–303, 305, 311.

Chislehurst

flames of Paris a lively fear of the imminent subversion of organized society was only to be expected, and in the Imperial heritage the repression of the "Communists" was an essential theme. But it could not be the *only* theme, else what reason (aside from the partisan exclusivism Fournier had encountered) was there for conservative men to divide their allegiances among three separate dynasties? If the representatives of the Empire could label themselves as "conservative-liberal" —that *appellation contrôlée* of Orleanism—how would they define and practice Bonapartism, and Bonapartism in opposition at that?

The answer to this question was not to be determined, unfortunately, by the aging and careworn figure who had in March quitted his German captivity to rejoin his wife and son at Camden Place, a modest country house overlooking the Kentish village of Chislehurst. It seems undeniable that, though Napoleon III unceasingly reiterated that Strasbourg and Boulogne had been youthful escapades which he would never think of repeating, the possibility of a return to France was never out of his mind, and he followed the course of events there with keen attention. The calvary of Sedan had briefly shaken his belief in himself, certainly; on September 2 he had written the Empress: "I feel that my career is broken, that my name has lost its lustre. I am in despair"; his one desire was "to go to live in England with you and Louis [the Prince Imperial] in a little cottage." [22] But the almost torpid fatalism which was so marked a feature of his character reasserted itself within a few weeks; if the wreck was not complete, if circumstances raised the possibility of a Return, he would accept that as he had accepted so much—without real excitement, but also without hesitation. While still a captive, he had written to his cousin Prince Napoleon: "We have *for*

[22] Napoleon III, "Lettres à l'Impératrice Eugénie 1870–1871," *Revue des Deux Mondes*, 7th period, LIX (1930), 7, 10.

the moment nothing to do. The reaction in our favor will come of itself, since the anarchy which reigns in France cannot last." [23]

As he settled at Chislehurst, his policy was still to wait upon events. Meanwhile he passed his time in listening noncommittally to a host of self-appointed emissaries who braved the Channel to come propound their views on what the restored Empire should be like.

One of the more assiduous of these was the clerical journalist who used the nom de plume Fidus, whose imaginative memoirs have unduly influenced too many historians. Fidus, a friend of Veuillot, was a true "prophet of the past." He left Chislehurst convinced that the Emperor had endorsed every particular of a program which was essentially a trumpet-call for retreat to the *ancien régime*, though his own account of the interview comically belies his conviction. He spoke of the "necessity of constituting an aristocracy." "That will be very difficult in France," remarked the Emperor. A reinforced constitution of 1852, authoritarian and Christian education free of state control, strict sabbatarian observance—"the Emperor told me it was not as easy as I thought." On and on went Fidus: reconstitution of the former provinces, decentralization to allow them to conduct their affairs independently of Paris, elimination of universal suffrage and a return to the *régime censitaire*, and of course the restoration of the temporal power of the Papacy. "That will be very difficult," said Napoleon III.[24]

If the aspirations of Fidus—shared by many Frenchmen who hoped for an Imperial restoration—had really been approved by an Emperor chastened by his reverses, one would have to conclude that Napoleon had made an almost com-

[23] Ernest d'Hauterive, ed., *Napoléon III et le Prince Napoléon: Correspondance inédite* (Paris, 1925), 317.
[24] Fidus, *Journal*, III, 123–129.

Chislehurst

plete volte-face on many of the central issues in French political life, and that a Third Empire would have made Henri V's monarchy seem dangerously libertine by comparison. The Emperor's own writings [25] and the testimony of other visitors to Chislehurst, however, reveal that his musings on the problems of France and on the Imperial mission had changed little in adversity.

The essential aim after as before September 4 was somehow to achieve that delicate balance between authority and individual liberty which he felt had been attained in England: "How I wish the French would follow the example of this country! Here everyone is free, absolutely free, but everyone submits to the law."

But France was not England, and Napoleon frankly acknowledged that the Empire had not thus far been able to strike the balance: "All the forms of government have been tried and not one has worked. I also tried . . . and I failed. . . . Just the same, this revolutionary situation cannot go on forever. . . . Dictatorship can only be a temporary regime, and yet a parliamentary system destroys the government which founds it. So then what do you do?" [26]

Characteristically, Napoleon still hoped to solve this fundamental dilemma of French political life by ingenious if chimerical mechanical expedients. He spoke, for example, of granting "absolute parliamentary liberty," but reserving to the government an equally absolute right of veto over the election

---

[25] Comte Alfred de la Chapelle, ed., *Oeuvres posthumes et autographes inédites de Napoléon III en exil* (Paris, 1873). In 1878, when debate on the direction the party should take had been sharpened by two electoral defeats, the Count intervened with *Déclarations des Napoléon* (Paris, 1878), which he declared to be based on Imperial private papers not used in preparing the posthumous collection first cited.

[26] Alfred Magne, "Deux visites à Chislehurst en 1872," *Revue hebdomadaire*, VIII (August 17, 1912), 306–307.

Bonapartism after Sedan

results in order to exclude deputies whose aims were subversive, though he admitted that this plan was "only a dream." [27] It is most important, however, to underline his insistence that the balance was essential, and that the system of 1852 could not possibly be more than an interim solution. These statements demonstrate his basic, unaltered convictions.

These had as their starting point his evaluation of the great Revolution of 1789, which in the bitterness of defeat many Frenchmen now saw as a terrible mistake, the great fountainhead of all their woes. For Napoleon III, however, Republic and Empire remained its twin democratic offspring. To preserve the Revolution's "moral and social" conquests, Frenchmen had turned to a form of government which "while establishing heredity in the family of the new monarch, offered guarantees of liberty and consecrated the rights of the people; thus they created the Empire based on democracy." Its function was to make democracy practicable and workable; the Empire "finds an element of force and stability in . . . democracy . . . because it knows how to discipline it; it follows neither the uncertain path of a party nor the passions of the crowd, it leads by reason." [28]

These "Napoleonic ideas" are familiar enough, of course, yet they are significant for that very reason. The Emperor who had seen the overthrow of his dynasty follow closely upon the surrender of many of his arbitrary prerogatives remained at heart a man of the hopeful springtime of 1848. He still believed that his government's function was not merely repressive, but beneficent. He still wanted to help the working classes, though he did not see very clearly how to do it. (He attributed social upheaval to the prevalence of such bad literature as the works of Sue and Dumas and thought that the

[27] Magne, "Deux visites," 307.
[28] La Chapelle, *Déclarations*, 13–15.

remedy was to "moralize" the masses.) [29] Therefore a Third Empire, to the extent that he could effectively have directed it, would have been not a regime of reaction, but a renewed attempt to place the maximum possible authority on a basis of political democracy.

The preceding eighteen years had painfully shown, however, the variety of practical conclusions at which Bonapartist exegetes might arrive in departing from Napoleonic dogma. There had also been schools of heresy and potential schism which rejected some part of the dogma while vehemently insisting upon the purity of their Bonapartist faith. Their rivalries had been of vital importance in determining the course of the fallen regime, and it was already clear in the summer of 1871 that their collective defeat had not stilled their polemic. On the contrary, the apportionment of blame for the final disaster was now an added element of division, and the Emperor was an even less effective arbiter at Chislehurst than he had been on the throne.

The most recent occasion for conflict among Bonapartists had of course been the experiment of the Liberal Empire. It would be temptingly easy to divide Bonapartists according to their attitude toward the government of Emile Ollivier: on the one hand those who had supported him and a whole panoply of characteristically "liberal" reforms, either out of conviction or opportunism; and on the other, those unyielding reactionaries, like Baron Jérôme David [30] and his "Mamelukes" of the rue de l'Arcade, who had regarded the new dispensation as total apostasy, a ministry "lacking only d'Aumale and Join-

[29] Magne, "Deux visites," 307.
[30] Jérôme-Frédéric-Paul, Baron David, protégé of King Jerome; deputy of the Gironde 1859–1870 and 1876–1881; founder with Granier de Cassagnac of the Arcade group; ardently pro-war in 1870 and a minister in the Palikao government (Ribeyre, *Biographie*, 360–369; RBC, II, 275–276).

Bonapartism after Sedan

ville," [31] prepared to demolish all the distinctive works of the regime and open the gates to revolution.

Unfortunately the task of the taxonomist of Bonapartism is not nearly so simple. The divisions of the party in 1871 were multiple, not dual, and long antedated the last years of the Empire. They reflected not merely a quarrel over the merits of a "half-turn to the left," but the play of economic interests, the influence of individuals, and sometimes even profoundly different philosophical convictions about some of the basic problems of human existence.

Yet for the historian the task of classification is essential, since the history of the party from 1870 to 1879 was significantly influenced by the balance of power and influence among these rival schools, while their almost continuous public wrangling demoralized the faithful and provided an easy target for Republican pamphleteers.[32]

Using the traditional language of the *hémicycle*, one could speak of a Bonapartist spectrum ranging from extreme left to extreme right. Yet this method of classification is beset by troubling ambiguities; for example, Jules Amigues, the spokesman of Bonapartist "socialism," would certainly have been placed by contemporaries on the extreme left—yet insofar as his concern with the solution and exploitation of the social question was shared anywhere in the party, it was on the extreme right. This raises the perplexing question of whether a proponent of an authoritarian regime with a social conscience is to the right or to the left of a champion of a "liberal" regime which provides parliament as a forum for the defense of vested interests.

On the whole, therefore, it seems wiser to adopt another less conventional but less confining set of metaphors, drawn

[31] Seignobos, *Déclin*, 86.
[32] Paul Beurdeley, *Petite histoire du parti bonapartiste* (Paris, 1875), 27.

from the Revolution whose issues were still vital, and to speak, for example, of a Bonapartist "Mountain," a Bonapartist "Plain," even a "Coblence." Only in this way can the ideological diversity of Bonapartism be accurately depicted. In fact, in the ranks of the party—though not in its higher councils—were to be found spokesmen for all the schools of political philosophy among which the revolutionary decade 1789–1799 had divided Frenchmen.

If pride of place is to be awarded among these Bonapartist schools for the promptitude with which their faith was reasserted or the volume of noise they could generate in relation to their numbers, the Bonapartist "Coblence" must come first. The outlook of these men could be broadly characterized as a kind of practical neo-Legitimism; they had accepted the Empire as a satisfactory device for reconstructing the traditional, hierarchical society which had seemed irretrievably ruined by the revolutionaries of 1789, but openly admitted that, lacking a Bonaparte, they would prefer the monarchy of the *ancien régime*.[33]

In extreme cases, this outlook formed the foundation for a program of pure reaction. The pithy aphorisms of Fidus are instructive:

4. . . . The principle of the Bonapartes is the reestablishment of order. Their banner is not that of the Revolution, but of victory and authority. . . .

29. Whoever does not scorn the people and men in assemblies is incapable of governing. . . .

42. There was no democratic revolution made for the people; all are made for the bourgeois.

---

[33] Ernest Merson, *Confessions d'un journaliste* (2d ed.; Paris, 1890), 291. Merson headed the provincial press syndicate of the party. Significantly, he was from the clerical West of France—his paper was the *Union bretonne* of Nantes.

Bonapartism after Sedan

So are Fidus' "ideas and plans" for the restored Empire:

1. *Question of the Working Class.* There is none; it can be resolved in one word: suppression of cabarets. . . .

11. Religious festivals: Reestablish the procession, etc. . . .

18. One of the first measures to adopt: name eighty-nine executioners, one to a department; the number of crimes will diminish immediately.

19. . . . To pay these . . . executioners, eliminate eighty-nine deputies, one from each department—if there is a chamber. . . .

20. No Jews in high positions. . . .

42. *Agriculture.* Attract industrial workers to cultivation of the land. . . .

51. *Protestants.* Do not employ them in high positions. On principle they are revolutionaries. . . .[34]

Not everyone of the Bonapartist "Coblence" would have approved Fidus' violence—or at least his candor. Nevertheless all shared to a degree his radically pessimistic view of human nature, which had its source in profound religious convictions. Like all the Bonapartist schools, they talked of the principle of "national sovereignty"—the plebiscitary confirmation of dictatorial authority—but they interpreted it to mean that "the people have the right to be led—gently—as much as possible; they have only that right, but they have it."[35]

For men of this breed, more Bonapartist in their own fashion than the Emperor, the drive to restore the dynasty much resembled a crusade, and it was altogether in keeping that to lead them against the infidel they looked to a Gascon champion who had proved a score of times on the field of honor that his sword was as dangerous a weapon as his pen. This was M. Paul Granier de Cassagnac, *enfant terrible* of the party

---

[34] Fidus, *Journal*, IV, 349–360.   [35] Fidus, *Journal*, I, 350.

(he was thirty in 1871), editor of the uncompromising *Pays*, and with his father absolute master of the department of the Gers.

As the personification of intransigence, "built like a sixteenth-century soldier, with a large moustache turned up *en panache*," he provoked unqualified reactions in all who had to reckon with him. In many of the party's rank and file, particularly the young, he inspired unalloyed admiration. When he exhorted the Corsican colony of Marseille, his fervor brought "tears to the eyes of the most skeptical"; he seemed "a handsome giant, . . . a Hercules, redresser of wrongs." [36]

Most of the official leaders of the party regarded Cassagnac and his vituperative, clericalist *Pays* in a different light. For them he was the irresponsible spokesman of a turbulent fanaticism. They felt that he had forgotten not only that the Concordat was an Imperial achievement, but also "that in the ballot box of universal suffrage the Faubourg Saint-Germain carries little weight." [37] They found particularly obnoxious the unshakeable self-righteousness with which time after time he meddled in the management of the party's affairs.

His intellectual patrimony had well fitted him for the leadership of the Bonapartist "Coblence." His father had published in 1851 a work which sought to demolish the myth of the Revolution of 1789 by undermining the theory of its spontaneous generation and proving that it was rather the result of the machinations of "the ambitious, intriguers, and Utopians." [38] Such was the authoritarian lineage of this volatile character who had fought a duel with Rochefort in de-

[36] Paul Corticchiato, *Les Corses et le parti bonapartiste à Marseille en 1870 et pendant les premières années de la République* (Marseille, 1921), 168; Richard, *Bonapartisme*, 54.

[37] Richard, *Bonapartisme*, 53–54.

[38] A. Granier de Cassagnac, *Histoire des causes de la Révolution française* (Brussels, 1851), I, v–vii; II, 386–387.

Bonapartism after Sedan

fense of the honor of Joan of Arc. His bold romanticism, when contrasted with the prudence of older, less colorful leaders, seemed to illustrate the superiority of *mystique* over *politique* and often won him a hearing among authoritarian Bonapartists who themselves did not share his sympathy for the Jesuits [39] or his hankering for an alliance with Legitimism. For the *politiques*, however, Cassagnac was a constant thorn in the flesh, untalented, politically ignorant, and remarkable only for his brutal inventive.[40]

This was the judgment of a man who might be called a "Brumairean" Bonapartist, who in August 1871 returned from Chislehurst invested with the leadership of the party within France. The Emperor's choice of Eugène Rouher for this crucial post was virtually inevitable. From the practical standpoint, the indefatigable mayor of the palace, with his unrivaled knowledge of the Bonapartist personnel, appeared indispensable if France's presumed enthusiasm for the Empire were to be mobilized by a systematic party organization pursuing a coherent policy. Rouher's selection was also symbolically appropriate. Now that Morny and Persigny were gone, it was he who incarnated the successful years of the Second Empire, the authoritarian years which many Bonapartists hoped would come again, enabling the Empire to "dam up revolution for a third time while borrowing from it those of its conquests which could aid the country's prosperity." [41]

In 1851, Rouher had been no Napoleonic enthusiast. If he had been a caller at the Elysée, he had by no means been

[39] Fidus, *Journal*, IV, 308.
[40] Rouher to Raoul-Duval, August 9, 1877; in dossier "Correspondance Rouher" of Raoul-Duval papers, château of Le Vaudreuil (Eure).
[41] Richard, *Bonapartisme*, 32, 34–35.

unfamiliar with the rue de Poitiers. Provincial lawyer, *arriviste*, he had been elected in 1848 in the Puy-de-Dôme as the candidate of the old ruling circle of notables into whose ranks he was seeking to break, that *grande bourgeoisie* which honored the memory of 1789, when its hegemony had begun, but which sought to ensure that there would be no further displacement of political power.[42] His years as virtual prime minister of an authoritarian and popular regime had, however, estranged him from a class he now found "frondeuse" and "ungrateful" [43] to the savior of the social order, and his credo had become that of a Caesarean democrat, though with nuances that reflected his origins.

Unlike the men of the Bonapartist "Coblence," Rouher felt no nostalgia for the Old Regime, and shared the Gallican sentiments of most *gens de robe*. He believed that the era of progress begun by the Revolution could not continue unless the conflicting demands of order and liberty, of equality and strong government, could be reconciled. Only the Napoleonic regime could effect this reconciliation; on the grounds of efficiency and political realism alike, parliamentary government by the bourgeoisie in conclave stood condemned as incompatible with the "immense sovereignty of ten million voters." [44] Insofar as so eminently practical a man possessed a faith, it was in the response of the masses to the Napoleonic idea. Even under the Republic, he would tell aspiring Bonapartist candidates:

As soon as you come into your district you must first of all go direct to the people, and you can leave the bourgeoisie alone. The big landowner, the notary, the influential men of the higher classes . . . are most reluctant to have their peace disturbed and

[42] Schnerb, *Rouher*, 20. Cf. Jean Lhomme, *La grande bourgeoisie au pouvoir* (Paris, 1960).
[43] Schnerb, *Rouher*, 166.   [44] Schnerb, *Rouher*, 42–43, 56, 163.

have a terrible fear of compromising themselves. . . . Seek out the little people, go to the simple man, with him you will know at once where you are.[45]

He was, of course, referring to the peasants. The June Days and the Commune had indelibly demonstrated how different were the problems and politics of the urban masses. Rouher's Caesarean democracy was not that of a *déclassé*; even to conciliate the working classes he envisioned no real changes in an economic system which he accepted as unquestioningly as did the bourgeoisie he now scorned.[46]

He might well seem ideally fitted for his new post, representing as he did a middle position between the Gothic fancies of men like Fidus on the one hand, and the rhetorical platitudes of "Liberalism" or, worse, the red radicalism of the Bonapartist "Montagnard" wing on the other. Rarely, however, has a leader been less gladly followed. His supporters and critics agreed that "he . . . found himself powerless on most decisive occasions, systematically thwarted by intrigue, by the desertion of his followers and by the impolitic acts of inexperienced personages . . . who sought to snatch command from his grasp."[47]

This ineffectiveness of Rouher's leadership resulted partly from his own reputation, partly from the role he had played in the days of power, but most of all from the characteristic outlook of the men at the top of the party he strove to lead. Like the members of the Revolutionary Convention, most Bonapartist politicians were not uncompromising adherents of any ideological school. Rather, within limits dictated by their instinctive prejudices, they hesitatingly followed now

[45] Théophile Gautier, "Herr Rouher," *Deutsche Revue* (September, 1886), 286.

[46] Schnerb, *Rouher*, 89–92; but cf. 65, where his interest in *sociétés de secours mutuels* is discussed.

[47] La Chapelle, *Déclarations*, 23. Cf. Richard, *Bonapartisme*, 160.

Chislehurst

one school, now another, attentive above all to the preservation of their own individual interests. Bonapartism, in other words, had its "Plain."

It may be inevitable for a man in Rouher's position to be blamed simultaneously for doing too little and too much. When one of his spies within the party reported to Thiers' Prefect of Police that the Vice-Emperor did not really believe in an Imperial restoration and was more concerned with reestablishing his own political credit,[48] he was only repeating what many Bonapartists whispered. Whatever Rouher's leadership lacked in thoroughness and continuity many ascribed to the basic cynicism of the lawyer who will plead any case for a fee. The occasions when, disgusted by the party's internal wrangling, he simply threw up his hands altogether [49] lent some color to these allegations. Yet at the same time it was felt that the "Rouhernement" was still in adversity attempting to perpetuate the domination of the party by a "camarilla which . . . had come to consider the Empire as its property." To combine the two grievances in one sentence: "He did not like others to take charge of doing what his *jemenfichisme* prevented him from doing himself." [50]

The reader will be able to judge for himself how accurate was this unflattering reading of the Vice-Emperor's character. Had he been far more patient and persevering than he was, enmities dating from his years in power would go far toward explaining the constant nagging undertone of distrust and dislike directed at him. Moreover, a resentment of high-handed dictation (whether fancied or real) typified the attitude of many Bonapartist politicians who had been or were now dep-

[48] Renault to Thiers, December 6, 1871 (BN Cabinet des manuscrits: Nouvelles acquisitions françaises 20658, "Rapports journaliers du Préfet de Police"; hereinafter cited as BN Naf 20658-20660).

[49] Richard, *Bonapartisme*, 128.

[50] H. J. Dugué de la Fauçonnerie, *Souvenirs d'un vieil homme* (2d ed.; Paris, n.d.), 33, 254.

uties, or who would be needed to seek a mandate again to swell the ranks of the party in the Assembly.

The anomalous position of the deputy under such a regime as the authoritarian Empire has not often been remarked. His existence between Caesar and the democracy was barely justifiable in theory, particularly since Caesar's minions (Prefects and Sub-Prefects) were everywhere visible. Yet in many cases the deputy was, by force of accomplishments, income, or energy, the leading man of his region, a *grand bourgeois* in good standing in every respect save his commitment to the Imperial regime.[51] It would have been too much to expect all such men forever to endure a system under which their only possible check upon the central authority was through backstairs influence—the backstairs, as likely as not, of M. Rouher himself. When a prophet had appeared suggesting that it was possible without risk to conservative interests to "liberalize" the Empire and to give their personal influence institutional confirmation, by reinforcing the parliamentary system which Rouher scorned, many had been quick to heed.

After 1870 Bonapartist politicians of this turn of mind lacked a real leader, for the man who might have played such a role bore the most hated name in a France to which he dared not return. Emile Ollivier remained merely an off-stage voice in the postwar decade. While the principal actors anathematized him as a matter of policy, from the wings, in a surprisingly catholic correspondence he firmly upheld the idea of the Liberal Empire, and warned that the deviation from it which he watched from day to day would ultimately make a restoration impossible.

The men of the Bonapartist "Coblence" and the journalistic henchmen of Rouher had lost little time in trying to make Ollivier—and all that he stood for—the scapegoat for

---

[51] Theodore Zeldin, *The Political System of Napoleon III* (London, 1958), 44–45 and *passim*.

the fall of the regime.⁵² So virulent did their denunciations become that he finally protested, through Prince Napoleon, to the Emperor. Napoleon III characteristically replied: "I forever repeat, God preserve me from my friends, I will deal with my enemies. E. Ollivier should certainly know that I do not approve of these impolitic diatribes, and I shall not conceal the fact from their authors." ⁵³

For Ollivier there was bitter irony in the charge that the liberalization of the Empire had been its undoing. He insisted that the regime had already been in desperate straits when he took office. It was "the irreparable mistakes hidden under the false glories of the authoritarian period" which had made the Liberal Empire inevitable, but then prevented its effectiveness. "It is too strange to see a party which went to Sedan by way of Mexico and Sadowa accuse liberty. This false view of the past is pregnant with catastrophe for the future of the Bonapartist cause." ⁵⁴

For he was convinced that the same defenders of authoritarianism, in seeking to discredit the liberal experiment, were preparing to subject the cause again to their own fallacious interpretation. He was particularly shocked by the language of the men of "Coblence": "To let it be supposed that they deny the French revolution, what an aberration! . . . If the Imperialist party becomes . . . counter-revolutionary, retrograde, an enemy of Democracy, it is finished." Nor had he much confidence in Rouher, who sometimes appeared to be following their lead.⁵⁵ Again and again he warned that the Bonapartists must not cut themselves off from the people. Their propaganda must be measured: "Order, yes; but not reaction . . . respect for the Church, not enslavement to its

⁵² Emile Ollivier, *Lettres de l'exil 1870–1874* (n.p., n.d.), 40.
⁵³ D'Hauterive, ed., *Correspondance*, 322–323.
⁵⁴ Merson, *Confessions*, 286; cf. Ollivier, *Lettres*, 54.
⁵⁵ Ollivier, *Lettres*, 112, 127, 142.

domination; war on the lawyer, the revolutionary scribbler, not on the suffering plebeian." [56]

These salutary admonitions reflected a clear understanding of the necessities of Caesarean democracy. Caesarean democrats, however, remembered Ollivier as the man who, in forming a government in 1870 with the Orleanist "burgraves," had preferred an oligarchic "liberalism" to a democratic, truly Bonapartist program of practical reform.[57] Chafe as they often did under the leadership of Rouher, they could never have accepted Ollivier as an alternative even had he not been the man who "with a light heart" had sent France to war. Thus they were long doomed to the frustration of their hopes for a really progressive Empire, represented by a new standard-bearer who would carry out Ollivier's injunction "to show the nation something other than red Jacobins and white Jacobins, and to give the Napoleonic tradition its real visage." [58]

Above all, though, no Jacobins! The Bonapartists of the "Plain," torn though they might be between parliamentary, conservative liberalism and Caesarean democracy, viewed the small but vociferous faction of the Bonapartist "Mountain" with no more sympathetic an eye than did the men of "Coblence." It was small wonder that they were annoyed by an eccentric like the prolific polemicist Marcus Allart, who might even be called a Bonapartist "Hébertiste" because of the especial ferocity of his anticlericalism, the distinguishing feature of all the "Mountain." Allart poured forth brochures on the theme that the Republic was too weak to withstand the wiles of Rome and only the Bonapartes could do for France what Henry VIII had done for England. (In a national church there would be no rule of celibacy and hence no more of the pastoral abuse of youthful parishioners, with ac-

[56] Ollivier, *Lettres*, 152.
[57] Dugué, *Souvenirs*, 44, 89–90, 116, 139.
[58] Ollivier, *Lettres*, 189.

Chislehurst

counts of which Allart often rounded out his pamphlets.) [59] Rouher's newspaper promptly disavowed Allart when he presumed to run in Paris as a Bonapartist candidate on a platform of "marriage of the clergy, suppression of confession, etc." (He got 792 votes.) [60]

It was a good deal more embarrassing to be compelled to disavow the leader of the "Mountain," for he was a prince of Imperial blood, the Emperor's cousin, in fact, though perhaps not much less an eccentric than was Allart. Yet almost from the first, Rouher had to contend not merely with the skirmishing within the official party, but also with a sort of Jérômiste guerrilla, whose harassing tactics included proposals so demagogic that even Ollivier, the friend of Prince Napoléon-Jérôme, was aroused to protest: "However much I sympathize with an alliance with democratic ideas, I find just as repugnant a rapprochement with the personnel of the demagogic party. . . . I do not like mixing clericalism in political questions." [61] For the conventional bourgeois mind even the "Mountain" was not the worst; there were also rumors of Bonapartist activity among the former Communards, of a school of Imperialist socialism led by a dramatically sinister figure, perhaps a latter-day *Enragé*.

"Emigrés" of "Coblence," "Brumaireans," a "Plain" tempted by conservative liberalism, "Montagnards," even an "Enragé," all claimed that their slogans, however tainted with Legitimism or Orleanism or Republicanism or Socialism, conformed to the real ideas of the "august exile of Chislehurst." But Napoleon III in reality had little control over the ideas of his party. He was unable to get his own self-justifying

---

[59] Marcus Allart, *Nos frontières morales et politiques* (Paris, 1872); *Contre-fusion! Réforme! Empire et revanche!* (Paris, 1873); *Appel aux électeurs de France* (Paris, 1874); *Appel au peuple: Gouvernement et église nationals* (Paris, 1874).

[60] *L'Ordre*, April 22, 1873; May 4, 1873.

[61] Ollivier, *Lettres*, 198.

Bonapartism after Sedan

pamphlet published by one of the Bonapartist houses in Paris without a struggle, and was reduced to his familiar tactic of having separate confidants, none knowing the whole story, in his search for the "new, liberal, independent" men who might eventually supplant the too-familiar Rouher.[62]

The schools of Bonapartism presented an array as confusing for the contemporary Frenchman [63] as it may seem to the reader. Of course any attempt at retrospective classification by a historian has inevitable hazards. Vocabulary is not a sure guide to the issues which divided these men, for few persons in any society would care to come out unequivocally against either "liberty" or "order," even presuming they were entirely certain what such words meant. The Bonapartist factions naturally overlapped one another on some issues, yet verbal agreement might not presage united action in a showdown. (Verbal disagreement, however, was apt to become hyperbolic.) Moreover a Bonapartist politician of the "Plain" might succumb successively to the attractions of each of the ideological schools. Haentjens of the Sarthe had been in 1869 an enthusiastic supporter of the Liberal Empire, unafraid even of liberty of the press; in 1876, he was speaking out for a conservative alliance behind MacMahon "in his work of social preservation"; by 1880, he was counted a Bonapartist of the extreme right, yet he rallied, unlike many so characterized, to Prince Napoleon, supporting the latter's attack on the Republic by denouncing its failure to solve the problems of the working man.[64]

---

[62] Comte de la Chapelle in *Le Spécial*, December 8, 1887; quoted in Comte d'Hérisson, *Le Prince Impérial* (4th ed.; Paris, 1890), 179–181, 183.

[63] Albert Duruy, *Comment les Empires reviennent* (Paris, 1875), 14–15.

[64] A. Haentjens, *Discours et lettres politiques* (Le Mans, 1886), I, 6–9, 204–211, 305–307; II, 119–134 and *passim*.

Chislehurst

Despite these difficulties of classification, the reader must have some feeling for the various factions within the Bonapartist party if he is to understand its fate after 1870. Would any spokesman for one of these points of view establish ascendancy over that vital "Plain" and thus be able to impose strategic unity on the crucial issue of where, among the strata of French society, it was most important to kindle enthusiasm for a restoration, even at the risk of alienating others? Or would the individual candidate have always the tactical disadvantage of representing a movement seemingly incapable, because of its internal turmoil, of presenting an alternative government to the Republic? If, as both the Bonapartists and their opponents firmly believed, the voter's exercise of political choice in nineteenth-century France was actually related to what the candidate professed and what sort of group he represented, the answers to these questions were vital.

They were, however, answers which the future still concealed as, in 1872, the Bonapartists began gradually to pick their way back into political life. During that year, modest but encouraging results were scored in by-elections to the Assembly, though in some of these contests there were disturbing portents.

In January, two former Prefects of the Pas-de-Calais battled for the right to represent that department. One had been Gambetta's appointee; the other was a son of the region, Charles Levert, who on September 4, as Prefect in Marseille, had been wounded resisting the mob. In a department which had endorsed the Empire by a four-to-one margin in 1870, Levert beat the Radical by 18,000 votes (mostly rural) and hastened to the Assembly, where he would remain until 1889, to found the party of the *Appel au peuple*.[65]

The next month, a leader for the party was elected in Cor-

[65] Gouault, *Comment*, 144; RBC, IV, 147–148.

sica, where a fellow Bonapartist had resigned to provide Rouher with a safe seat.⁶⁶ In the Eure, the home department of the new leader of the Monarchist majority, the Duc de Broglie, the going was not so smooth. The Duke and his friends had refused to accept a compromise anti-Republican candidate because of his Bonapartist sympathies, though he was a sure winner. Another Bonapartist, the former official deputy, had then entered the race only a week before the poll and despite this handicap had outdistanced Broglie's own candidate, though losing to the Republican. Rouher's newspaper severely drew the moral for the Monarchist party: "If it claims the right to exclude us, instead of forming the Conservative Union with us, it will be beaten everywhere."

Concerning the election in the Côtes-du-Nord, the *Ordre's* reproaches were directed at the local Bonapartist leaders, for in a region where the masses were eager to see the issue tested, no Imperialist candidacy had materialized. Commented the editorialist: "In all parties, the leaders have duties to carry out; the most important is to advance, at the risk of defeat." ⁶⁷ This would become a frequent complaint, for in 1872, in a total of twenty-eight by-elections, only seven Bonapartists ran.

The score at the end of the year stood: Nine Radicals elected, eleven conservative Republicans, five Monarchists, and three Bonapartists.⁶⁸ This not very impressive total would be greatly exceeded in later years; everywhere Bonapartists had run, however, they had done remarkably well considering that they were the guilty representatives of a condemned regime, and, where inertia or Monarchist obstructionism had kept them from running, they congratulated themselves that the large numbers who failed to vote belonged to them.⁶⁹

⁶⁶ Gouault, *Comment*, 148. ⁶⁷ *L'Ordre*, February 14, 1872.
⁶⁸ Gouault, *Comment*, 141–151. ⁶⁹ *L'Ordre*, October 24, 1872.

Chislehurst

For that matter the fear generated throughout the country by nine Radical victories might be more useful to the Bonapartists than their own gain of three seats. While Thiers' conservative Republicans were merely talking, warned the *Ordre* in October, "the revolutionaries are striding ahead . . . the *jacquerie* is drawing near." [70]

Earlier that same month, the Prefect of the Nord had sent an urgent dispatch to the Minister of the Interior, reporting that in obedience to his orders, "the most active measures of surveillance along the coasts" had been applied and would be "continued until further orders." [71] With the politics of the provisional government at an obvious impasse, Thiers at irreconcilable odds with a conservative majority, itself divided, in the Assembly at Versailles, and with Gambetta making a noisy tour of the provinces as the "traveling-salesman" of Radicalism, the time might have come for the Emperor to intervene decisively.

The psychological problems which a life in exile poses for a regime might merit comparative study. The Return as an ideal supplies such a regime its whole continuing *raison d'être*, but the Return as a practical problem calling for deliberate planning is painful to think about.[72] Waiting on events, so eminently sensible, is attended by the great risk of becoming mere wishful thinking, but forcing the hand of Fate might win all at one throw, or lose all. The career of the Comte de Chambord well illustrates this dilemma. Bonapartists who tried to read the omens looked back upon a dynastic past rich in varying historical precedents. There had been, for example, the return from Egypt of young General

[70] *L'Ordre*, October 23, 1872.
[71] Prefect of Nord to Minister of Interior, October 11, 1872 (AN F^{7}12428, "Police générale—Agissements bonapartistes"; hereinafter cited as AN F^{7}12428–12429).
[72] Richard, *Bonapartisme*, 24.

37

Bonapartism after Sedan

Bonaparte: 1879 would see a pathetic *pastiche* by the Prince Imperial end in disaster.

In 1872, however, the first precedent that came to mind was of course the "return from the isle of Elba" (*never* called the "Hundred Days")—the feeble and failing government, the indifferent or indignant population, the Emperor suddenly landing and advancing unopposed on Paris, the cheering army falling into ranks behind him. The hotblooded reactionary Fidus for a decade continued to urge that cold reason argued for an "Elban" solution; he raged at every failure to follow up a crisis in public affairs with a *coup de main*, particularly since he had often been given the impression (or so he says) that action was contemplated.[73]

Napoleon III had long firmly refused to give the "Elban" enthusiasts any encouragement. As late as May of 1872, he told a visitor to Chislehurst, "I am too old to attempt that kind of adventure, and what means would I have? What chances of success? I shall only return if recalled. The country better enlightened will decide." [74]

For if the return from Elba was one glittering memory of the dynasty, another was the plebiscite which restored to unity a despairing and chaotic France. It was true that the events which had preceded the plebiscites of 1851–1852 and ensured their success could not be reproduced in 1873, and the Emperor admitted the difficulty. Nevertheless a start could be made by accepting every opportunity afforded by by-elections: "Because they [the National Assembly] do not want to consult the country, let us try to increase the number of [our] supporters in the Chamber." [75] Every effort must also be made to find newspapers and journalists to broadcast

---

[73] Fidus, *Journal*, III, 206–207, 284, 311, 339, 346–347; IV, 20, 221–222.
[74] Magne, "Deux visites," 309–310.
[75] Magne, "Deux visites," 295, 301.

the call for a new popular consultation.[76] Throughout most of 1872 Napoleon III remained more interested in the possibilities of ballots than in those of bullets.

As experienced a politician as Rouher himself never entirely abandoned his belief that conservative, peasant France would ultimately perceive the inability of bourgeois parliamentarism to contain the "Reds" and would turn once more to the security of Caesarism. In 1871 he had declared flatly that "the Empire would obviously have no chance except through an appeal to the country." A plebiscite was bound to come, whatever institutions were adopted. He would not, in 1874, be "very worried about the duration of the Republic even if it is definitively proclaimed." In 1876, he would find that "republican institutions are not taking root." In 1878, he would insist that "we are condemned to pass through the revolutionary crisis." It was always the same note, however discouraging the news of the day might be: "The past shows us identical situations which all collapsed under the mistakes of the governments." [77]

It is not surprising, given such authority, that the readers of Bonapartist newspapers were often exhorted to patience with this postulate of the historical inevitability of a plebiscite. Not all were willing to accept it. The Corsicans of Marseille, for example, so receptive to Paul de Cassagnac, had little enthusiasm for Rouher whom they thought "obsessed with legality." Failing to understand that the Republicans would never repeat their mistake of 1848 by permitting a free consultation of the country, he weakened Bonapartism by allowing it to become "embogged in plebiscitary demands." [78]

[76] Richard, *Bonapartisme*, 63.
[77] Mme. Eschasseriaux to the Baron, June, 1871 (Eschasseriaux, "Mémoires," VI, 105); Rouher to Eschasseriaux, October 28, 1874, VII, 425; September 23, 1876, VIII, 427; June 26, 1878, IX, 346; July 11, 1878, IX, 356. Cf. Schnerb, *Rouher*, 291.
[78] Corticchiato, *Corses*, 75.

Bonapartism after Sedan

Pronunciamento or plebiscite? Each had its firm partisans among the Bonapartists throughout 1871 and 1872, the former enough to provoke a rumor of an imminent landing as early as August, 1871.[79] M. Thiers' Prefect of Police, Léon Renault, was kept well enough informed of the Emperor's visitors, health, and intended journeys by the concierge, valet, and groom at Chislehurst who were in his pay [80] to be able generally to reassure his master of the groundlessness of such rumors.[81] Confident though Renault was that an attempted landing would permit the government to "finish off" the Bonapartists, even he had his moments of nervous apprehension, one of which produced a bill in the Assembly for its protection and that of the executive.[82] But by the beginning of July 1872, he was again reporting that Napoleon III and his principal advisers had chosen a waiting game.[83]

By autumn, however, the wind was up again, and the Channel coasts under surveillance. In December, Renault's reports betrayed a real anxiety. Rouher had hurried to Chislehurst, where the sister of General Bourbaki was in attendance; a loan was being negotiated from Barings'; "a great deal of attention is being paid to the health of the Emperor; an attempt is being made to enable him to move around easily. . . . There must be something urgent." [84]

Even today, the historian cannot prove that this was not another false alarm—that the Emperor had finally fallen in with the proponents of a *pronunciamento*. Circumstantial

---

[79] Henrey, ed., *Letters*, 164.

[80] Police report of August 8, 1872 (APP B^A417, "Famille impériale—Affaires bonapartistes 1865 à 1872").

[81] Renault to Thiers, December 1, 1871; December 4, 1871 (BN Naf 20658).

[82] Renault to Thiers, February 4, 1872 (BN Naf 20658); Seignobos, *Déclin*, 341–342.

[83] Renault to Thiers, July 3, 1872 (BN Naf 20659).

[84] Renault to Thiers, December 13, 1872 (BN Naf 20659).

Chislehurst

evidence, however (for example, Napoleon's decision to submit to the long-deferred surgery), suggests that in all probability the October alert to the Prefect of the Nord was geographically misplaced and somewhat premature—but not a false alarm.

Certainly a dramatic transformation in Bonapartist morale had taken place during the year. Baron Eschasseriaux later recalled:

> The country . . . seeing the confusion of the Assembly, was rapidly returning to the Empire. . . . At the end of 1872 I felt myself master of [my] department. . . . The year . . . was also that of the reawakening of the Bonapartist idea throughout France. The election of M. Rouher . . . the formation of the party of the deputies of the *Appel au peuple* . . . the *comité de comptabilité* which collected funds, budgeted for their use and assured the means of propaganda. . . .

all had been steps toward the regrouping of the forces shattered by the debacle. "Hope was reborn at the end of 1872; some decision on the part of the Emperor was expected." [85] During the holiday season 700,000 cards and letters of greetings were conveyed to Chislehurst. "A rapid denouement was needed in such a situation, since a long delay would have been a confession of impotence." [86]

As the strength of the once prostrate party was apparently waxing, moreover, that of its mutually hostile opponents seemed on the wane. Proclaiming the Empire's readiness to restore a definitive government to France, Bonapartist propaganda stood in stark contrast with "the prudent phraseology of the Orleanists who wouldn't, the Legitimists who couldn't, and the clericals who did not know what they wanted. To say to the people that one is prepared is half the battle. . . .

---

[85] Eschasseriaux, "Mémoires," VII, 18–20. See also Léonce Dupont, *Les deux démocraties: République—Empire* (Paris, 1878), 6–7, 11.

[86] Richard, *Bonapartisme*, 83–85.

Bonapartism after Sedan

Confidence ran from one to another . . . the current was there." [87] Even the cautious Rouher apparently was swept off his feet. He told Fidus in December that within three months a crisis following the overthrow of Thiers could be expected, and that the Emperor would take action.[88] Already, indeed, a rumor that he was actually in the city had electrified Paris.[89]

Exactly what Napoleon III proposed to do once he was again able to mount a horse remains a matter of surmise. The plan may have been for him to quit Cowes, where he would be ostensibly convalescing, and to proceed swiftly and secretly through Belgium and Basel to Prince Napoleon's estate at Prangins near the Swiss border. From there he would enter France in uniform, lead the cavalry regiment at Annecy to Lyon, where Bourbaki commanded, and march with his troops on the capital. "It would be learned in Paris, and by all France, in the midst of the confusion provoked by the resignation of Thiers, that the Emperor was marching . . . at the head of 30,000 men. Then it would suffice for a regiment . . . at Versailles to disperse the Assembly." [90] March 1873 was believed by many to be the target date,[91] although since Thiers did not fall until May and the final German evacuation would not begin until July (the two indispensable preconditions), the "return from the isle of Elba" might not have been attempted until late summer.

In any event, the return was postponed indefinitely, if not precluded, by tragic news from Chislehurst in January, and the historian has neither a triumph nor a fiasco to record. Nevertheless it is worth inquiring what support such a plan

[87] Richard, *Bonapartisme*, 66.
[88] Fidus, *Journal*, III, 129–130. See also Richard, *Bonapartisme*, 82.
[89] Gabriel Hanotaux, *Histoire de la fondation de la Troisième République* (new ed., Paris, 1925), II, 217; Richard, *Bonapartisme*, 83.
[90] Richard, *Bonapartisme*, 64–65.
[91] Alfred d'Almbert, *Le Bonapartisme: son passé, son avenir* (Paris, 1873), 88; Henrey, ed., *Letters*, 186.

Chislehurst

might have rallied, and to what extent the young Republic had reason to go in fear of its own police and army.

There can be little doubt that, as Republicans hotly charged and Imperialists complacently acknowledged, Bonapartism enjoyed the passive sympathy of some of the "forces of order." "The magistracy, the army, the police and the administration were never very hard on Bonapartism while Napoleon III and Napoleon IV were alive. An Imperial restoration was a possibility which consoled them under the incessant threats of a purge." [92] The story was even told that in Paris an investigation disclosed that "the *Garde Républicaine*, the *Légion Mobile*, and the police were composed of absolutely nothing but Corsicans or veterans of the Guards." [93]

Yet it may have been more dangerous for the Republic to discharge than to retain such men. Unemployed, they might join a private Bonapartist police under the orders of M. Piétri, the notorious former Prefect of Police,[94] while remaining in touch with their former colleagues or subordinates who were still in official service. The usefulness of such contacts was demonstrated by the business manager of the *Ordre*, a former captain of *gendarmerie*, who compiled a list of the Empire's supporters throughout France. When the survey was completed at the end of December, 1872, the *Ordre's* editor took to Chislehurst "lists . . . of more than 1800 cantonal correspondents on whose devotion and cooperation we could surely count." [95]

[92] Richard, *Bonapartisme*, 49.

[93] Richard, *Bonapartisme*, 137–138; Renault denied to Thiers that there was any truth in these stories. What Bonapartists there were were "isolated and without influence." (Renault to Thiers, February 12, 1872; BN Naf 20658.)

[94] André Daniel, ed., *L'Année politique—1875* (Paris, 1876), 70–71, 206. Cf. Extracts of police reports of April 12, 1872; June 24, 1873; March 23, 1874; and Barthelémy-Saint-Hilaire to Renault, May 7, 1872 (dossier "Joachim Piétri," APP B^A1634).

[95] Dugué, *Souvenirs*, 254.

Bonapartism after Sedan

The policeman's old habit of deference to the local Bonapartist leader in the departments was not easy to break, particularly since the Bonapartist usually stood for many of the things in which a policeman believed, which was often more than could be said of his Republican rivals. Consider the private letter written just before the 1876 elections to Baron de Saint-Paul, leader in the Ariège, by the local *brigadier de gendarmerie*:

The hour has struck when all the men of order must group ourselves around you to crush flat the vile reptile which scatters its venom in our countryside.

For my part, I swear it on my honor and on my personal responsibility: I have served and shall serve your cause, which is that of the preservation of the family, property, and public security. . . .

You should . . . prescribe to your agents to tell the voters and make them understand that when we need protection, where do we go? to M. de Saint-Paul's; there we need not have a 200-sou piece in hand, nor a basket on the arm, on the contrary we are asked to come into the kitchen; that this is not the way of the partisans of M. Gambeta [sic] and the allies of the men of the 40 [sic] centimes.

As far as I am concerned, I shall not fail on any point, although meanwhile remaining within the limits of my rights.[96]

"Within the limits"—this indeed is always the rub for any prospective putschist. After the election of Levert, the Prefect of Police had sent a special agent to investigate the loyalty of the local authorities in the Pas-de-Calais. His report proved reassuring; it was true that the customs-men, Imperial army veterans for the most part, had "favorable memories" of the fallen regime, but they were not "party men." They were serving the Republic as well as they would any government,

[96] *Brigadier de gendarmerie* to Baron de Saint-Paul, February 15, 1876; in the Saint-Paul papers at the château of Poudelaye (Ariège).

Chislehurst

"and it seems certain that none would be found among them to run the risk of active complicity in an attempt of Napoleon to return to France." [97] When it is borne in mind that the difference between a return from Elba and a return to Ham might rest with just such men, one can measure the problematical character of any landing on the Channel coast. But what of the Lyon adventure? Would there have been a momentous shout from Bourbaki's soldiers of "Vive l'Empereur"?

Bonapartism had lost no time in seeking to reestablish its hold on the army, which had been, since 1852, perhaps the most favored social group. As early as November, 1870, *Le Drapeau,* a paper intended for the captive French troops in Germany, had been founded in Brussels by the elder Cassagnac. This initial effort proved more damaging than useful, for the paper's violent campaign of denigration against a Government of National Defense which was endeavoring to prolong resistance could not fail to arouse patriotic resentment even among men attached to the Imperial regime, and their protests were collected and publicized by the Emperor's enemies.[98]

A later, subtler attempt to appeal to the soldiery was effectively thwarted by the Republican authorities, who were determined in this sphere above all others to nip any Bonapartist initiatives in the bud. In early February of 1872, Jules Richard, the party's leading military journalist, launched a paper called *L'Armée.* His first editorial claimed that politics would be kept out of its columns: "We are not the spokesman of a party; we shall try to be the reflection of the needs and instincts of the army and of military France." He made an effort to sustain this professional tone, although, now that the National Defense had proved a failure, he could delicately

[97] Renault to Thiers, February 11, 1872 (BN Naf 20658).
[98] Georges Girard, ed., *La vie et les souvenirs du Général Castelnau* (Paris, 1930), 266–268; Richard, *Bonapartisme,* 15–16.

Bonapartism after Sedan

flatter the army's amour-propre by suggesting that that Government, and not the high command, had caused France's defeat. "Whatever the café generals and bar-room dictators may say, our army was betrayed only by fortune . . . honor remains intact." [99]

Reading this sort of thing, commented the Prefect of Police, "one quickly perceives that M. Richard . . . knows in what form the lie ought to be presented in order to make its way in the Army's ranks." Within three weeks, during which it had attracted some 700 military subscribers, the publication of L'Armée was prohibited by decree.[100]

This marked the end of attempts to create a journal especially for military readers. There were, however, other means of propaganda: the ordinary trooper was the recipient of Imperialist brochures and portraits; the officer got a free subscription to one of the regular Bonapartist papers, and found in its columns a sustained effort to demonstrate that the party was the only one with a real comprehension of his desires and grievances. The party's spokesmen in Parliament seconded the efforts of its press. They became the army's vociferous champions, quick to interpret any budgetary haggling by the Republicans as the expression of a desire to humiliate or punish the nation's defenders.[101]

The fascination of historical analogy as well as practical calculation can be detected in all of this activity. Bonapartists remembered the political harvest that had been reaped from the Restoration's humiliation of the Grande Armée.[102] This

---

[99] L'Ordre, February 4, 1872.

[100] Renault to Thiers, February 14, 1872 (BN Naf 20658). Richard, Bonapartisme, 46–47.

[101] Renault to Thiers, May 24, June 1, 1872 (BN Naf 20658). Renault to Thiers, July 23–24, 1872 (BN Naf 20659). Daniel, ed., Année politique—1875, 71. L'Ordre, February 25, 1874.

[102] Adolphe Caillé, L'Empereur et ses détracteurs (Niort, 1872), 38–40.

Chislehurst

memory of an army whose dutiful patience masked an inexpressible attachment to the Emperor and his line was now a consoling dream for the party. Nor was it entirely an illusion. A young Marseillais remembered how in 1874 he took letters from the Prince Imperial to a regimental mess which had pledged him its fidelity:

> "Gentlemen, letters from the Little Prince!" At these words, two or three officers, of about twenty, took their *képis* and hastily withdrew. The others surrounded me to receive the replies addressed to them. They devoured them with their eyes rather than read them, and offered me champagne. I raised my glass to "the exile." They cried "Vive l'Empereur!" like real *demi-soldes*.[103]

Even officers less sentimental than these might feel a strong pull toward the fallen regime when they reflected that out of the uncertainty of a provisional government might spring the triumph of Radicals whom they dreaded and loathed. The presence of Thiers as chief of state afforded the army some reassurance,[104] but as the provisional government outlasted him and threatened to become permanent, the Bonapartists' dream remained a nightmare for their opponents.

The Duc de Broglie was convinced that the War Ministry was "strongly tinged" with Bonapartism,[105] and saw to it that the numerous officers on active duty who applied for leave to attend the celebration of the Prince Imperial's coming-of-age were publicly forbidden to go; any who attempted to reach England secretly were to be instantly reported.[106] Broglie's successors were no less careful. In 1875, when Vice-Admiral La Roncière Le Noury, commanding the Mediterranean fleet, sent a letter of greeting to a Bonapartist

---

[103] Corticchiato, *Corses*, 52.
[104] Renault to Thiers, January 23, January 26, 1872 (BN Naf 20658).
[105] Duc de Broglie, *Mémoires* (Paris, 1941), II, 226.
[106] Daniel, ed., *Année politique—1874*, 114.

banquet in his native department, he was summarily dismissed.[107]

It must be emphasized, however, that the La Roncière affair was a sensation, though it involved nothing more ominous than a letter, precisely because overt political commitments by military men were so rare. The Prefect of Police was somewhat optimistic in assuring Thiers that every officer with any real influence over the army scorned the Empire;[108] it was nevertheless true that finding a general who would not shrink from backing a restoration might have proved impossible. Fidus in his diary over the years conjured with many names, including those of some of the commanders of *corps d'armée* like Bourbaki, but only to express the hope that this time, at last, their indecision would be overcome.[109] However prodigal the generals might be with private expressions of devotion, they had nothing to offer when the question of action was brought up.[110]

The Imperial generals who had retained their commands distrusted Bonapartist politicians almost as much as they detested Republican ones. General Pajol, who sometimes served as an intermediary between the party and his comrades-in-arms, told Fidus that his consultations with Rouher and his advisers left him "stupefied by the useless chatter he had heard, the indecision of that little parliament."[111] When a general who was running such risks despaired of his party's nerve and sense of purpose, how much the more understandable was the skeptical reserve of a less committed officer,

[107] Daniel, ed., *Année politique*—1875, 269–271.
[108] Renault to Thiers, February 6, 1872 (BN Naf 20658).
[109] Fidus, *Journal*, III, 42, 115, 270, 312; IV, 20, 123–124, 218–219, 222.
[110] Renault to Thiers, November 22, 1872 (BN Naf 20659).
[111] Fidus, *Journal*, III, 312. On Pajol, cf. his police dossier (APP B^A1213).

particularly when he could see how spasmodically and unsystematically the Bonapartists faced the task of preparing for "Elba." The fact is that the admittedly enormous job of subverting the army through selected personal contacts was never satisfactorily carried out.

It was Napoleon's intimate, General Fleury, who was given this task, and the Prefect of Police took him seriously enough to have him kept under constant surveillance and to procure a minutely detailed plan of his house in Paris. Unfortunately for the Bonapartists, he was not taken so seriously either by the generals, who regarded him as a uniformed Imperial procurer, or by Rouher, with whom he was in frequent political disagreement.[112] Nor was he very persevering in his labors, to judge by several desolate letters which Baron Eschasseriaux received in late 1877 from the general who commanded his son's regiment.

This officer was convinced that Bonapartism was "the resurrection and the life" for France, yet he had returned from a recent visit to Paris "profoundly saddened," partly by the party's factional strife, but above all by "many lacunae in organization and tactics." He had urged Rouher to find a military mentor for the Prince Imperial, who would link him to the army by maintaining "constant relations with each unit . . . through several sure officers known to him," and thus keep Bonapartist sympathies alive. It was a matter of desperate urgency that such a man be found, since "the Napoleonic legend, the very legend of the Fatherland, is diminishing every day. . . . For seven years I have been deploring the isolation which I am pointing out to you, and nothing has been tried to bring it to an end." Nothing, again, came of the

[112] Extracts from police reports of April 11, April 17, August 5, 1873; February 26, 1875; May 3, 1876; May 30, 1877; March 19, 1878; July 18, 1879 (in Fleury's dossier, APP B^{A}1078).

general's suggestion, and he was left to lament the way in which the Republic was getting an ever-firmer grip on defeated France.[113]

Torn in their dreams of Return between the visions of 1815 and of 1848–1851, the Bonapartists were easily tempted to neglect practical preparations for either, and to hope instead for miracles. Meanwhile the average superior officer, foreseeing that if the politicians did screw up their courage to attempt a coup, it would certainly divide the Army, prudently confined his Bonapartism to the mess and contented himself with the most platonic of pledges. In doing so, moreover, he conformed to a pattern customary in an age of repeated revolutions. The historian of the nineteenth-century French officer has written: "His device remained *Cedant arma togae*. After the overthrow of legality, after changes of regime, he is seen to pass with a dull fatalism to the side of the former rebels. . . . No one is more docile or more submissive to established power than the officer." [114]

It would be a foolhardy historian, however, who would assert on the basis of the negative evidence cited that the Lyon enterprise, for example, was bound to fail. He cannot dismiss as hysterical the nervousness and precautions (which in 1872 included changes in the Paris command) [115] of the various governments of the Republic. What he can do is to point out the unknowns the "Elban" equation would have contained. Could Bourbaki have been persuaded to take the plunge? Would his men (who, the Prefect of Police reported, were well-disciplined, uncontaminated by Bonapartist propaganda, and inclined to Republicanism) [116] have followed

[113] General Archinard to Baron Eschasseriaux, December 11, December 14, 1877; Eschasseriaux, "Mémoires," IX, 236–238, 244.
[114] Pierre Chalmin, *L'Officier français de 1815 à 1870* (Paris, 1957), 362.
[115] Renault to Thiers, March 11, 1872 (BN Naf 20658).
[116] Renault to Thiers, February 11, 1872 (BN Naf 20658).

Chislehurst

him? The large element in the calculations left to chance would have made such an attempted *pronunciamento* a formidable gamble, comparable to Strasbourg and Boulogne—or, perhaps, to the return from Elba itself.

Therefore one suspects that in the hearts of some officers, relief was mingled with regret when early in January, 1873, the news came from Chislehurst that the Emperor had succumbed to complications following surgery. The Prefect of the Aube telegraphed to the Minister of the Interior:

The army showed . . . rather great regret. The majority of the officers have hardly concealed . . . the fact that the death of the Emperor cut short their hopes. . . . They have all . . . remained within the limits of the strictest correctness. . . . I think that today, like everyone, they recognize that chimerical restorations must be abandoned. They are perhaps beginning to take satisfaction from an event which completely releases them, if they felt somewhat committed by their past services.

"The bonds . . . are broken, and . . . it will be hard to replace them," wrote Léon Renault.[117]

With the death of Napoleon III, indeed, the history of the Second Empire, recalled to life after Sedan, came to an end. While he was alive, his own personality had been the best—or worst—argument for Bonapartism, and hopes for a restoration had depended as much on the decisions in a crisis of well-placed men personally devoted to him as on appeals to the electorate. There had even been debate over whether it was desirable for the party to be represented in the National Assembly.

Now Bonapartists found themselves confronted with a new set of problems, requiring new modes of action. Whether the dreams of a *Third* Empire would become reality would be

[117] Prefect of Aube to Minister of Interior, January 13, 1873 (AN F⁷12429). Renault to Thiers, February 6, 1873 (BN Naf 20660).

Bonapartism after Sedan

decided not at Chislehurst, nor in headquarters messes, but in Paris, where Rouher struggled to construct, from recalcitrant elements, an ideologically cohesive political party, and to endow it with effective means; at Versailles, where a slowly increasing number of deputies confronted and consorted with the spokesmen of Henri V, the heirs of Louis Philippe, and the various possible Third Republics; and, not least, in the towns and hamlets below the horizons of the capital, where men like Mayor Fournier and Baron Eschasseriaux, recalled by proscription to Bonapartism or unflinching in its defense, bore the prime responsibility for generating the mass enthusiasm which alone could raise the Prince Imperial to his father's throne.

Chapter II

Paris

Rue de l'Elysée
Rue Montmartre
Belleville

"The fact is that the Bonapartist party has no organization properly so called. It exists, it lives, it develops of itself, without any kind of cultivation, drawing its strength from the very bowels of the country."[1] This assertion in one of the innumerable cheap pamphlets which poured out of the several Bonapartist publishing houses in 1875 represented a fundamental article of faith of the party. The more practical Bonapartists, however, recognized that the spontaneous creation of the Empire by the masses in 1852 had been carefully prepared and that such preparation was even more necessary now that the pretender was an exiled youth of seventeen.

Therefore Bonapartists had to become effective suitors for the favors of a democratic electorate, sustaining the instinctive preferences of the apolitical masses and attempting to persuade the politically conscious classes of the superiority of their system of ideas. They would have to develop an effective headquarters in Paris, and a complete chain of command[2] to

[1] *Les complots d'Arenenberg* (Paris, 1875), 20.
[2] The reader may find the "Chart of organization of the Bonapartist party" helpful, though he should bear in mind that in many regions

Bonapartism after Sedan

ensure that all possible means of propaganda were effectively deployed throughout France. For this effort they would somehow have to find money. If it ran short, they would have to assign priorities in expenditure, and this would raise again in the most practical way the doctrinal question of which groups in French society must be most assiduously cultivated. In a literal sense, the assertions of the pamphlet-writer of 1875 were false. The party did have an organization. This chapter will reveal how Bonapartism's severed head did in fact regenerate a trunk, creating an organism very occasionally capable of coordinated movements and endowed with a certain faculty of communication. Whether or not it represented a species sufficiently evolved for survival is another question. In an ironic sense the pamphlet's author never intended, he may have been telling no more than the truth.

Forging a chain of command required building, almost clandestinely, an organization which could transmit political intelligence as effectively and exercise command as firmly as had the whole hierarchy of *fonctionnaires* who had kept the Empire going. These men had now retired into private life, or had even accepted service under the Republic. Thus no structure of the sort had existed for the elections of 1871, and the few Bonapartists then elected had owed their victories to their own resources.

When Rouher returned to Paris in the summer of that year, charged by the Emperor with finding "men of considerable importance to group the others around and . . . to give direction,"[3] he was therefore starting virtually from scratch. Yet when he moved into number 4, rue de l'Elysée (a small

---

the ranks indicated below the *Missi dominici* were quite hypothetical.

[3] Napoleon III to Prince Napoleon, August 21, 1871, in Ernest d'Hauterive, ed., *Napoléon III et le Prince Napoléon: Correspondance inédite* (Paris, 1925), 321–323.

Chart of organization of the Bonapartist party

CHISLEHURST
The Emperor; the Prince Imperial

RUE DE L'ELYSÉE
Rouher

COMITÉ DE COMPTABILITÉ
(Mansard, secretary)

Réunion of the deputies of the *Appel au peuple*

RUE MONTMARTRE
(*Correspondance Mansard*; pamphlets and photographs)

Departmental press syndicate (Merson)

Provincial newspapers

REGIONAL MISSI DOMINICI
(e.g. Eschasseriaux)

(Leaders or committees in a department)

(Leaders or committees in an *arrondissement*)

(Leaders or committees in a canton)

(Leaders or committees in a commune)

THE ORDRE
(Dugué de la Fauçonnerie)

OTHER PARIS PAPERS
(e.g. the *Pays* of the Cassagnacs and the *Gaulois* of Tarbé)

Bonapartism after Sedan

house tantalizingly close to the Palace itself), it quickly became obvious that the mere provision of a rendezvous more convenient than the Café de la Paix was an important first step in organization. Here politicians and journalists could reestablish contact, and visitors from the provinces, calling to pay their respects, could be asked their impressions of the state of opinion in their respective regions and even be invited to assume local leadership.[4]

The small salons soon became the haunt of a picturesquely variegated throng:

> Next to the Emperor's former adjutant-general stood the ex-gendarme, discharged before his time for political reasons. The journalist, who under the Empire had worked at Liberalism, but who had now been enlightened by the force of facts and circumstances, conversed here in friendly fashion with the Imperial prosecutor who once had tried him before the police court. Here a former chamberlain with a resounding name and title exchanged political opinions with a simple shopkeeper, while a deputy full of hope for the success of the good cause convinced a crowd of spellbound listeners, on the weightiest grounds, that the Empire would be restored within three months.[5]

Certain of the visitors who called most often and penetrated beyond the antechamber for the longest private interviews with the Vice-Emperor formed a kind of embryonic and quite unofficial "general staff" of the party—men like Piétri, Duvernois of the *Ordre*, General Fleury. By May of 1872, however, it was becoming clear that their informal, *ad hoc* decisions were not adequate guidelines for a party which was growing sufficiently optimistic to aspire to a properly hier-

---

[4] Jules Richard, *Le Bonapartisme sous la République* (3d ed., Paris, 1883), 31–37.
[5] Théophile Gautier, "Herr Rouher," *Deutsche Revue* (September, 1886), 279.

archical direction. A former Prefect, noting that amid the "anarchy" of these irregular consultations even direct orders from Chislehurst were not being carried out, proposed to the Emperor the creation of a directing committee in Paris and subordinate committees in each department to be headed by the Imperial deputies and Prefect. This plan received Napoleon III's enthusiastic assent.[6]

The Prefect's criticisms were merely the first notes of what was to become a weary refrain among thoughtful Bonapartists in the years to come. Nevertheless, steps were taken both to designate precisely those responsible for decision-making in Paris and to maintain an effective liaison with the party chiefs in the provinces. During the last week of May, Baron Eschasseriaux attended two meetings which decided on a number of important initiatives. A parliamentary party (or *réunion*) was to be formally organized, a propaganda campaign for the sending of pamphlets to all departments was to be launched. "We also decided . . . to reconstruct the organization of the party in the departments, by seeking correspondents in the *arrondissements* and cantons." And, presumably to coordinate all these activities, there would be created at the top "a party committee destined to act outside the Assembly under the presidency of M. Rouher."[7]

This latter body was the so-called *comité de comptabilité*, destined for notoriety in the Republican press. It is not possible to reconstruct its membership with complete accuracy, although it is clear that the initial summons to about a dozen people "provoked the discontent of those who were not admitted without much satisfying those who were."[8] Rouher,

---

[6] Renault to Thiers, July 14, July 30, 1872 (BN Cabinet des manuscrits: Nouvelles acquisitions françaises 20659, "Rapports journaliers du Préfet de Police"; hereinafter cited as BN Naf 20658–20660).

[7] Eugène, Baron Eschasseriaux, "Mémoires," twenty manuscript volumes in the château of Oyré (Sarthe), VI, 332, 334.

[8] Richard, *Bonapartisme*, 45.

of course, presided at the Tuesday and Friday meetings, and copious minutes were sometimes taken by the secretary, M. Mansard, "who was also syndic of the Bonapartist departmental press, which facilitated the execution of the decisions . . . with regard to certain party newspapers."[9] Others in more or less frequent attendance were men with a real or presumed special competence, like Piétri and Fleury, or stalwarts of the parliamentary party who held bastions of Bonapartism in the provinces, like Eschasseriaux himself, as well as a few who had not yet recouped the losses of September 4, former ministers like the Duc de Padoue and Ernest Pinard, or former Prefects like the brothers Chevreau.

After the death of Napoleon III, Paris headquarters bore even heavier responsibilities,[10] balanced though they were by an even greater freedom from interference from the pretender, since a youth was hardly thought equipped to supervise the decisions of experienced politicians. Thus in 1874 the committee was enlarged to an unwieldy eighteen, still carefully within the limit of twenty dictated by the law.[11] Some of the newcomers may have been purely ornamental, like Palikao, but a practical concern with the increasing danger of prosecution was reflected in the appointment of some of the party's best legal talent.[12]

It is a question whether the deliberations of a plenum of eighteen were any more ineffective than those of the original dozen. For the performance of the *comité de comptabilité*, which had been instituted with the idea of taking some of the burden of decision and supervision from Rouher's shoulders, was certainly no better and perhaps rather worse than the performance of committees in general, though its member-

---

[9] Eschasseriaux, "Mémoires," VII, 61–62.
[10] Renault to Thiers, January 30 ,1873 (BN Naf 20660). Cf. Robert Schnerb, *Rouher et le Second Empire* (Paris, 1949), 297.
[11] André Daniel, ed., *L'Année politique*—1875 (Paris, 1876), 202.
[12] Eschasseriaux, "Mémoires," VII, 330–331.

Paris

ship was rent by no great dogmatic differences. (There were no Cassagnacs, no Prince Napoleons on it to raise troubling questions of principle, and the original membership at least was of a rather *Rouheriste* cast.) Nevertheless outsiders who were afforded the honor of sitting in on its proceedings were seldom flattering in their appraisals of its effectiveness. The reader will recall the military impatience of General Pajol. The journalist Richard discovered that it was precisely those members most insistent on receiving their due as former Imperial dignitaries who were most lacking in boldness and intelligence, and that all were principally preoccupied with escaping blame in case of defeat.[13]

In seeking to locate responsibility for Bonapartist planning, then, one comes back again to the inevitable Vice-Emperor, who rose each morning at five to tackle his voluminous correspondence, so as to leave the later morning free for the horde in his anteroom and for the committee, in which self-important mediocrities ruminated vaguely about a future, the details of which they left to him. Small wonder that on the morning when he heard that Chambord's final letter had made a Monarchist restoration impossible, Rouher celebrated by calling off that day's session.[14]

If the committee had met, the practical Baron Eschasseriaux might not have attended. From the beginning he found the committee so ineffectual that he bluntly complained to the Emperor. Out of the seven meetings for which a record of attendance has survived, he was present at only one.[15] He had, after all, more important things to do:

[13] Richard, *Bonapartisme*, 45.
[14] Eugène Balleyguier (Fidus, pseud.), *Journal de Fidus* (Paris, 1889), III, 242–243.
[15] Eschasseriaux, "Mémoires," VII, 14–15. Charles Savary, ed., *Deuxième rapport fait au nom de la commission d'enquête parlementaire sur l'élection qui a eu lieu dans le département de la Nièvre; Assemblée Nationale no. 3087: Annexe au procès-verbal de la séance du 11 juin 1875* (Versailles, 1875), 107–112.

Bonapartism after Sedan

I had received from the Emperor, through M. Rouher, the mission of organizing nine departments of the Southwest for propaganda by brochures and newspapers. To this end we should choose in each canton the political chief and several influential notables. The activity of all these chiefs of cantons should be centralized in the hands of chiefs of *arrondissements*, who should be the most prominent notables who would be of use for the formation of the list of candidates at the future election. The Committee had taken measures [so the Baron believed] to ensure that a similar job was done throughout France, but the district of which the direction fell to me was obviously the best of all.[16]

The Baron had long ago organized his own electoral district in the Charente-Inférieure with a surpassing thoroughness. Though the Southwest undoubtedly was intrinsically the most promising region among the dozen allotted to the former prefects and legislators who were to serve as Napoleon's delegates or *missi dominici*,[17] Eschasseriaux threw himself into organizing it with a characteristic energy not imitated by all his colleagues. On June 4, 1872, he met with leading Bonapartists from eight of his nine departments; among them were Paul de Cassagnac for the Gers, Magne's son for the Dordogne, Murat for the Lot, and the Comte de Bouville, a former Prefect of the Gironde, where his family was almost as influential as were those of the others in their respective strongholds. The Basses-Pyrénées, on the other hand, was represented only by the youthful son of an Imperial Senator, and the Lot-et-Garonne by a mere ex-Sub-Prefect.[18] (The Landes was not represented, but the chief there was the Baron's own father-in-law.) A week later, Eschasseriaux convened this regional committee again and "pressed the mem-

---

[16] Eschasseriaux, "Mémoires," VI, 339.

[17] Paul Corticchiato, *Les Corses et le parti bonapartiste à Marseille en 1870 et pendant les premières années de la République* (Marseille, 1921), 137.

[18] Eschasseriaux, "Mémoires," VI, 339, 367.

bers . . . to gather information in their departments, to prepare reliable notes which could serve as a basis for the work of organization with which I was charged, and the execution of which the *comité de comptabilité* was urgently requesting." [19]

The Comte de Bouville won the Baron's compliments for his zeal by presenting him within the week with a notebook packed with information on the political personnel of the Gironde. Unfortunately this exemplary promptitude did not reflect the existence in the Gironde of a political machine as smoothly running as Eschasseriaux's own. Rather it represented the best foot forward of one of the several stubborn claimants to leadership in this important department. Such disputes remained among the most frustrating difficulties with which the *missi dominici* had to deal. In the Gironde, neither Eschasseriaux's emergency missions to Bordeaux nor his exhortations to "organization, propaganda and unity" in the name of the Emperor ever sufficed to settle the argument.[20]

Contested leadership was not his only stumbling block. Where there *was* a strong machine united under one family, this powerful clan might tolerate Eschasseriaux's interference only so long as it did not run athwart their own purposes. Thus when he applied to the Cassagnacs for someone to undertake the organization of the Gers, they supplied the name of a banker of Condom, adding, "Give him your instructions, *telling him you are acting in agreement with us.*" [21]

In other departments, instead of too many leaders he found none. If in the Lot-et-Garonne a better chief than a former Sub-Prefect was found in the person of its former official

[19] Eschasseriaux, "Mémoires," VI, 343.
[20] Eschasseriaux, "Mémoires," VI, 345, 371–372.
[21] Eschasseriaux, "Mémoires," VII, 57. Emphasis added.

deputy, the editor of its only important newspaper, in the Basses-Pyrénées the problem was never solved. The half-hearted response of one man whom the Baron approached for the job, a former mayor of Bayonne who had entertained the Imperial couple at his château, is revealing. He "replied that he was quite ready to aid my efforts . . . but that he thought that his department still afforded few . . . men of action and very little chance of success." Worse, "he believed that nothing serious could be attempted for the general elections," though in his own interest he was prepared to canvass those *arrondissements* which had constituted his district when he had been an official deputy. Thus Eschasseriaux in his report to the Emperor was forced to conclude that, although a survey by a former official of the Prefecture had revealed that the rural population in the Basses-Pyrénées was still devoted to the Empire, because of the absence of leadership there "the party remains in a latent state, from which it will not escape save by an impulse from outside, or by the appearance of a great current" of Bonapartism throughout France.[22]

This was, however, almost the only discouraging note about a region which he could accurately describe as "obviously the best prepared" in the country. Yet even in the Southwest he warned against complacency: "It seems to me important to maintain and revive public opinion by more constant activity. . . ." Propaganda of all kinds would produce "inestimable results." Already, "the pamphlets have been the means of reawakening the party. . . . The services they have rendered cannot easily be described."[23]

He thus confirmed the success of a campaign whose necessity Napoleon III had quickly perceived. Before Frenchmen could again openly avow themselves partisans of the Empire, the instinctive reaction to such disparaging catchwords as

[22] Eschasseriaux, "Mémoires," VII, 13–14, 54, 63.
[23] Eschasseriaux, "Mémoires," VII, 14–15.

Paris

"Mexico" and "Sedan" would have to be eliminated, or at least weakened. An enormous campaign to reinterpret current history would have to be undertaken. As many people as possible would have to be provided as cheaply as possible with an arsenal of pro-Imperial arguments. Moreover, on the principle that the best defense is to take the offensive, Bonapartists need not be content with merely resisting the Republican version of the Empire. They could themselves throw a damaging light on Gambetta's Republic. No holds were barred at a time when cheap Republican pamphlets were depicting the Emperor as living on a fortune stolen from the nation and on memories of Marguerite Bellanger, and the Empress as a priest-ridden Messalina.[24]

Characteristically, the captive Emperor himself had been the first to take up his pen in defense of the last episodes of his regime. Equally characteristically, he had done so with such insufficient venom that his little pamphlets made hardly any impact, whatever the pleasure they gave their author. Nevertheless he did set forth many of the themes that were later embellished by scribblers with fewer scruples and more talent in polemic. He admitted that he had failed in 1870 in his duty to be wiser than the nation, but stressed his constant desire for a peaceful general European settlement, and contrasted it with the verbal bellicosity of an irresponsible Opposition.[25] Although he accepted blame for France's diplomatic isolation, he insisted that more rapid mobilization and a quick thrust into South Germany would have brought Austria and Italy into the war; the War Ministry and the Opposition had thwarted his own proposals for speeding up mobilization. He defended his role in the field, underlining his unwillingness to

[24] Eugène Hennequin, *Les prétendants au trône de la France* (Paris, n.d.), *passim.*
[25] Napoleon III (Marquis de Gricourt, pseud.), *Des relations de la France avec l'Allemagne sous Napoléon III* (Brussels, n.d.), *passim.*

hamper the execution of orders from Paris and soberly depicting his own conduct at Sedan—five hours under fire—as historians have today acknowledged it. For the war as a whole he would take only his share of the blame, since in declaring it "he had only obeyed a violently excited national sentiment." The men of September 4, by contrast, had ignored the national will and continued to shed blood in an attempt to cling to power—in vain, since no government save one chosen by all the citizens would have the stability necessary to reestablish moral and material order.[26]

Although these assertions would today win at least judicious consideration if not acquiescence, in 1871 all parties concurred in quite another version of events. According to this tale, France had been half-heartedly dragged along in the "caprice of a despot" seeking to steady his tottering throne. The Emperor, culpably ignorant or even more culpably aware of Prussia's real strength, had rushed into battle, usurping the command in order to abscond with its laurels, and dragging behind him not merely his son, so that he too could be clothed in factitious glory, but an enormous and tactically embarrassing baggage-train (including a wagonload of fresh lobsters), rather than lose which he capitulated at Sedan.

The peculiar psychological climate of France in 1871 made Frenchmen inordinately receptive to this kind of fable. A half-year had seen such a stunning series of calamities that it seemed to have lasted a century. People had forgotten the actual sequence of events before this nightmare began; what

[26] Napoleon III (Un officier attaché à l'Etat-Major-Général, pseud.), *Campagne de 1870: Des causes qui ont amené la capitulation de Sedan* (Brussels, n.d.), *passim;* Napoleon III (Un ancien diplomate, pseud.), *Les principes* (Boulogne, n.d.), *passim.* This is said by the Comte de la Chapelle to be almost entirely the Emperor's work (Comte Alfred de la Chapelle, ed., *Oeuvres posthumes et autographes inédites de Napoléon III en exil* [Paris, 1873], 7.) The other two pamphlets are so identified by Richard, *Bonapartisme,* 11.

they did remember of their collective misjudgments led them to seek a scapegoat in the person of the Emperor.[27]

On the other hand, the Republicans' barrage of denigration against the Empire might boomerang, for it implied the political incompetence of the millions who had so long supported Napoleon. Thus a campaign to reassure these people that their confidence had not been misplaced, that Prussia, not the Emperor, bore the guilt of France's humiliation, might find ready listeners, once the shock of defeat had diminished.

In the early months of 1871, the Emperor lacked the means for an effective campaign of self-justification. By midsummer, however, several hundred thousand francs had been collected, and after some argument were allocated by Rouher (who first set aside a strong reserve for general expenditures) among the three essential spheres of political propaganda. An agency was set up to distribute pamphlets and other nonperiodical materials; a *correspondance* (roughly equivalent to the modern wire service) was created for those provincial papers which could be induced to support the cause; 100,000 francs were allotted for the creation of a Paris daily, significantly dubbed the *Ordre*.[28] The reader has already discovered the ineffectiveness of the party's supreme council and some of the difficulties which beset even its most hard-working provincial delegate. He will naturally be curious to see if its several propagandistic services were simliarly afflicted.

The men in the agency at 146, rue Montmartre [29] who supervised the printing and distribution of pamphlets knew their market well. Although individual Bonapartists continued to publish substantial apologia [30] for the leisured and

[27] Fernand Giraudeau, *La vérité sur la campagne de 1870* (Marseille, 1871), 10, 229, and *passim*.
[28] Richard, *Bonapartisme*, 39.
[29] Eschasseriaux, "Mémoires," VI, 367.
[30] For example, the work of Giraudeau already cited, a volume of 200 pages packed with corroborative quotations from Republican

critical purchaser, the agency concentrated on materials which did not presuppose that those for whom they were destined could think, or even, in some cases, read.

The journalist Dugué de la Fauçonnerie, for example, worked tirelessly to place the blame for the loss of Alsace-Lorraine and for the huge war indemnity where it belonged—on the Republic. His first effort at historical rectification, an example of Bonapartist propaganda at almost its crudest, was a little tract of thirty-two pages, lacking a cover and printed on the coarsest of paper. The title page read: "THE CALUMNIES against THE EMPIRE—WAGER of 25,000 FRANCS AGAINST 25,000 sous—proposed by M. DUGUE DE LA FAUÇONNERIE former deputy—to ALL THE REPUBLICANS OF FRANCE." Within, there was a similarly frequent recourse to capitals as Dugué set out to disprove the four principal calumnies: that the Emperor had wanted the war, had been responsible for unpreparedness, had betrayed the army at Sedan, and had lost the eastern provinces. He promised to do so "not with grand phrases like those with which the lawyers of the Republic deafen and abuse the poor people . . . but with FACTS which I take from official documents." If any Republican could cast doubt on their authenticity, he would collect the 25,000 francs. If none came forward, however, the Empire's case would be proved.

Dugué later depicted even more graphically the progressive worsening of Prussia's terms between September 3, 1870, when she would have asked only an indemnity of 2,000,000,000 francs, and the signing of the Treaty of Frankfurt. An enormous broadsheet titled *What September 4 Cost* revealed, in

---

speeches and newspapers which were well calculated to embarrass their authors, or Ernest Dréolle, *La journée du 4 septembre au Corps législatif* (Paris, 1871).

Paris

four colored maps, the contrast between the peace Bismarck would have granted the Emperor and the onerous demands he made after Gambetta's needless and selfish prolongation of resistance.³¹

There is no way of telling how many readers were convinced by these ingenious efforts at the rewriting of contemporary history. At least there were plenty of readers. Dugué offered *Les Calomnies* for ten centimes a copy, with a 20 per cent discount on orders for a hundred, and a 50 per cent discount for a thousand. At these rates 1,750,000 were "broadcast in all of France, even in the smallest villages." ³²

The "official documents" on which Dugué relied were drawn to a considerable extent from the volumes of the National Assembly's inquiry into the fall of the Empire and its sequel, an investigation launched on the initiative of Baron Eschasseriaux. In May of 1871, the Baron, who was sincerely convinced that the events of September 4 were the result of a conspiracy uniting the Republicans, the International, and the Prussians, had with Haentjens proposed the resolution which brought the record of the Government of National Defense under prolonged hostile scrutiny. The Republicans had hastened to publish the secret Imperial papers left behind in the Tuileries. Now they were paid back in their own coin.³³

The resulting disclosures doubtless helped the Bonapartist propagandists to take the offensive. Equally useful were the pro-Bonapartist verdicts in actions for libel brought by Generals Trochu and Wimpffen, both men who had betrayed the

---

³¹ H. J. Dugué de la Fauçonnerie, *Les calomnies contre l'Empire* (Paris, 1874); *Ce qu'a coûté le 4 septembre* (Paris, n.d.).

³² H. J. Dugué de la Fauçonnerie, *Souvenirs d'un vieil homme* (2d ed.; Paris, n.d.), 227–228.

³³ Eschasseriaux, "Mémoires," V, 118, 214; VI, 70–71. Cf. Robert Dreyfus, *La République de Monsieur Thiers* (Paris, n.d.), 35.

Bonapartism after Sedan

Empire in its hour of need.[34] Indeed, it was inevitable that public opinion would swing back, even without the stimulus of propaganda, to a less one-sided view of the Empire than had prevailed at the close of the *Année terrible*. We are accustomed today to regard the National Defense as the apogee of Gambetta's anticlimactic career, but many conservative Frenchmen of his day must have been glad to find confirmation of their belief that the seditious Bohemian lawyer had been in no way transfigured by becoming a virtual dictator.

The way in which the men of 146, rue Montmartre played upon this inclination could not better be illustrated than by the following outline of their 1875 *Guide for the Bonapartist Voter* (price, fifty centimes) which offered the thriftiest purchaser a veritable Mosaic table of Republican "lies" and Bonapartist "truths."[35]

Lie: "The Republic saved the honor of France." The *truth* was that the Government of National Defence had been worse than incapable, it had been corrupt. And this was only to be expected. The honest, hardworking peasant knew what sort of men Republicans, the "heroes of the National Decadence," were: ambitious braggarts trafficking in the stupidity of the needy and lazy idolators of the Commune.[36] Far from rescuing an abandoned and prostrate France on September 4, they had plunged their knives into her back. Yet they dared profess horror at the memory of the *coup d'état* of December 2, 1851, a deed which had been endorsed by millions of votes in a plebiscite.[37] Once in the saddle they had ridden France

---

[34] Fidus, *Journal*, III, 72–73, 330–331; cf. Dreyfus, *République*, 184–185, and Daniel, ed., *Année politique*—1875, 61–64.

[35] Ernest Dréolle, *Le guide de l'électeur bonapartiste* (Paris, 1875), *passim*.

[36] Edouard Guillemin, *A mes compatriotes: pourquoi je ne suis pas républicain* (Annecy, 1875), *passim*; *Les héros de la décadence nationale* (Besançon, 1876), *passim*.

[37] Paul Granier de Cassagnac, *Histoire de la Troisième République* (Paris, 1876), 76.

nearly to death. At Tours and Bordeaux, Gambetta, the self-appointed Minister of the Interior, "handed over armies to civil engineers," and while the *Gardes mobiles* slogged barefoot through the snow in futile campaigns, found time from his fireside to telegraph to a crony: "YOUR CIGARS ARE EXQUISITE." Fortunately he had been ousted before he was able to issue *assignats*.[38]

Lie: "The Republic can be a conservative government."

Lie: "M. Thiers saved France." The *truth* was that the so-called conservative Republic was a dangerous chimera, devised by the eternally ambitious Thiers in the vain hope of perpetuating his power. The tragi-comedy of the Republic without the Republicans could not go on forever, and the Republic of the Republicans would be anything but the government which least divided Frenchmen, for it would pit the virtuous against the vicious.[39]

Lie: "Respect is owed the Republic because it is the legal government of France." The *truth* was that the National Assembly had had no authority to revoke the plebiscites by deposing the Emperor, and that the courts had acquitted journalists indicted for publicly pointing this out.[40] Filled as it was with bickering Legitimists who rejected equality, Orleanists representing the "monarchy of 200,000 aristocrats," [41] and Republicans, the Assembly's claims to be constituent were absurd. Away with it, then! and let Frenchmen themselves decide, as they had since Clovis, who should rule.[42]

Lie: "The *appel au peuple* will not restore the Empire" (and consequently Bonapartist demands for it were insincere.) The *truth* was that a plebiscite would "found a na-

[38] Cassagnac, *Histoire*, 134, 228–229, 242.
[39] *L'Ordre*, September 29, 1872.
[40] Cassagnac, *Histoire*, 318–319.
[41] F. Perron (Un ancien républicain, pseud.), *Le salut* (Paris, 1872), *passim*.
[42] Evariste Bavoux, *Appel à la nation* (Paris, 1874), *passim*.

tional government to which the parties should submit. The Bonapartists wish nothing else. They propose the Empire, but whatever the outcome, they will obey the sovereign will of the nation." [43]

Not that there was any real doubt which regime Frenchmen would choose, especially with pamphlets to remind them of the superior attributes of the Bonapartes, who alone could forcefully defend the equality won in 1789 from the reactionaries who repudiated it and the revolutionaries who exaggerated and denatured it.[44] Whenever a Napoleon had sought confirmation of his mandate from the people they had given it unstintingly, from *Brumaire* until 1870. Never had a Napoleon been overthrown by popular revolt, but only by the invader.[45]

The most ingenious form of propaganda which the Bonapartists produced managed to compress the three chief themes of the pamphlets—defense, counterattack, and refurbishment of the whole Napoleonic Legend from *Brumaire* onward—within two paper covers, interleaved with tables of phases of the moon and calendars of feast days. Paul de Cassagnac published an edition of his *L'Aigle: Almanach illustré du suffrage universel* every year from 1875 to 1878. For his fifty centimes the purchaser was treated not only to portraits of the Imperial family and the Bonapartist deputies and journalists (with short biographies appended), but also to a schedule titled "The Benefactions of the Empire," showing the dates on which great acts of social betterment had been accomplished. Cassagnac also threw in the best of his vitriolic editorials from the *Pays*, thus placing in the hands of people

---

[43] Dréolle, *Guide*, 74.

[44] F. Perron, *Le retour de l'île d'Elbe*, (new ed.; Paris, 1876), *passim*.

[45] Edouard Guillemin, *Les titres de la dynastie impériale* (Paris, 1874), *passim*.

who never saw a Paris newspaper a succinct account of the political events of the past year.[46]

As cunningly as it was designed to appeal to the peasant, even the *Aigle* could hardly stir the one Frenchman in four who was still, in the 1870's, unable to read. For him, however, the rue Montmartre produced (after 1873) the famous photographs of the Prince Imperial:

> The most certain means of propaganda, which . . . never failed to be effective in by-elections. . . . I have seen honest voters weep with joy at receiving one of these badly-printed and clumsily-colored portraits, and place them piously in their pocket-books like precious objects.[47]

The potency of these images of the "little Prince," now grown up into a moustachioed cavalier, is revealed both by the abandon with which Bonapartists broadcast them and by the energetic measures which the Republic took to repress such activity. Politicians and journalists sometimes distributed them openly to schoolchildren or to peasants come to market, but this could lead to prosecutions and stiff fines. Sometimes, therefore, the distributors resorted to the roads—tossing portraits and pamphlets into passing vehicles or village squares—or even to the railways, dropping bundles along the line in hopes that they would find their way into safe hands.[48] At this rate, Rouher ran through a stock of some half-million portraits in less than two years. Such improvidence was to cost the party dear in the general elections of 1876; what few then

[46] Paul Granier de Cassagnac, ed., *L'Aigle: Almanach illustré du suffrage universel 1875–1878* (Paris, 1878).

[47] Richard, *Bonapartisme*, 158–159.

[48] Attorney-general, Amiens, to Keeper of the Seals, October and November, 1874, and May 20, 1875 (in AN BB^{30}1121, "Correspondance échangée entre le Ministre de Justice et les Procureurs-généraux à l'occasion d'affaires de colportage ou d'élections 1874–1879"); Minister of Public Instruction to Minister of Justice, March 31, 1875 (AN BB^{30}1122).

remained were strictly rationed, and no more could be got, since the photographers were under such vigilant surveillance that they would rather have risked printing obscene photographs than Imperial portraits.[49]

Whatever may have been the real sympathies of the police, they dogged the agents of the Bonapartist propaganda network at every level, from headquarters (where a raid on 146, rue Montmartre led to the seizure of the mailing lists and the books) [50] to the humblest provincial peddler. The case of the itinerant watchmaker Verney illustrates both how the Bonapartists sought to recruit dependable distributors and the penalties their recruits might incur. After the police had apprehended Verney for selling *L'Aigle* in the streets, they discovered a veritable warehouse of propaganda in his home. He confessed that he had answered an advertisement placed in the local Bonapartist paper by one of the party's most prolific publishing houses and had become their agent, less out of political conviction than because the terms offered made it an attractive speculative venture. Letters in his possession showed just how attractive it was both for him and for his customers. For each subscription he collected to a forthcoming "popular illustrated history" of Napoleon III (price, twenty-two francs) he could elect to receive either a free copy or three francs in cash. Subscribers were offered an opportunity to buy stock (5 per cent dividends promised twice yearly) in a new company being capitalized at 200,000 francs to centralize Bonapartist publishing and increase its efficiency by associating the party rank-and-file in the enterprise. Verney, despite his occupation, had not proved the ideal man to launch this self-perpetuating venture, being delinquent in his payments for his wares and under threat of prosecution at

[49] Richard, *Bonapartisme*, 158–159; cf. Eschasseriaux, "Mémoires," VII, 390.
[50] Renault to Thiers, July 24, 1872 (BN Naf 20659).

Paris

the time of his arrest. This did not recommend him to the mercy of Republican justice, however, and he was sentenced to two months in prison and a fine of twenty-five francs for the distribution of unauthorized materials.[51]

The limitations which such hazards imposed upon the distribution of pamphlets make a quantitative assessment of this phase of the propaganda campaign impossible. The historian may know, for instance, that Dugué de la Fauçonnerie planned to distribute 100,000 copies of his broadsheet *What September 4 Cost*, but since his source is a letter from the public prosecutor reporting that copies were to be seized if exhibited for sale,[52] he cannot begin to guess how many Frenchmen saw them, let alone how many were persuaded by them to revise their attitude toward the Imperial regime. The only generalization he can advance is that if any phase of the propaganda effort deserved special credit for sustaining or reviving Bonapartist faith, it was the pamphlets, for it can be shown quantitatively that in the provinces the party's Parisian dailies and its local papers fell far short of these goals.

Pro-government journalism in the last years of the Empire had fallen into three categories: "liberal" papers infused with Bonapartism to varying degrees, an "official" press whose leadership Rouher had futilely sought to establish, and the *Pays*.[53] Precisely the same categories apply to Bonapartist journalism under the Republic.

As early as August, 1871, the party had once more found a spokesman in the Parisian daily the *Gaulois*, which its owner, Edmond Tarbé, spontaneously put at the service of the Emperor. It was definitely not at the service of the Vice-Emperor,

[51] Attorney-general, Chambéry, to Keeper of the Seals, March 16, April 23, and May 22, 1875 (AN BB^{30}1122).
[52] Prosecutor of the Republic, Paris, to Keeper of the Seals, September 9, 1875 (AN BB^{30}1123).
[53] Irene Collins, *The Government and the Newspaper Press in France* (London, 1959), 157–161.

however, and though it could be as frantically conservative as the *Pays* in times of social peril, the *Gaulois* generally preached a temperate "progressive" Bonapartism, wary of alliances with ultra-reaction. Even more inclined toward a "liberal" Empire was the *Liberté*, which had once been the creature of Ollivier. Its editor, Léonce Détroyat, contented himself under the Republic with advocating a plebiscite and avoided a violently partisan stand. Papers like the *France, Paris-Journal* and the *Presse*, which for some years between 1870 and 1876 were fellow-travelers in the movement for a Third Empire, were even less inclined to accept compromising editorial direction from the rue de l'Elysée.[54] Nor did a more sustained Bonapartist loyalty necessarily mean dependence on the party's chief: the *Patrie* was edited from 1871 to 1892 by a determined Bonapartist, but took its orders from its owner, the banker Baron de Soubeyran, who kept his distance from the official party.[55]

Rouher was unable for some time to find means for disseminating the authentic line of Caesarean democracy in the *Ordre*, though it was meant to be the new "journal officiel." Its first editor was Clément Duvernois, a former Republican whose paper before the war had been subsidized from the Emperor's private purse and who saw no reason now to subordinate himself to an intermediary. Instead of trumpeting an unconditional Bonapartism, he adopted toward M. Thiers' regime a comparatively mild tone which astonished the Empire's enemies and fostered the rumor that the President of the Republic had arranged some sort of secret cooperation

[54] Richard, *Bonapartisme*, 23, 70, 101; *L'Ordre*, May 31, 1875. Details on the political evolution of some Paris dailies are found in Henri Avenel, *Histoire de la presse française* (Paris, 1900), and of most, though from an intolerantly Republican point of view, in the Larousse *Grand Dictionnaire* (articles on each).
[55] *L'Ordre*, October 7, 1873; Avenel, *Histoire*, 807.

Paris

with the Bonapartists.⁵⁶ The new paper seems initially to have flourished under his direction, though its claimed first-week circulation of 18–22,000 must have included many a complimentary copy.⁵⁷ A decline in sales which he seemed incapable of arresting finally permitted Rouher to oust him in favor of a man of his own, Dugué de la Fauçonnerie. The whole episode, however, was symptomatic of a lack of cooperation between politicians and journalists which never ceased to plague the party.

Jules Richard, one of the ablest of the newspapermen, complained that the "deputies and bigwigs" constantly "affected rather comical patronizing airs" toward the press. His complaint reflects not merely the perennial disdain of the craftsman of language for the mere politicians who employ him, but also resentment at such ungrateful parsimony as the withdrawal in 1874 of all stipends paid to individual journalists.⁵⁸ On the other hand, the politicians understandably begrudged the very substantial sums which had to be paid out to these mercenaries, men of lowly origins whose private lives were sometimes scandalous. Had they been able to read the reports of the Prefect of Police, much of whose information obviously came from venal and disloyal journalists and was sometimes identified as such,⁵⁹ their distaste would only have been augmented.

The only real remedies for this sort of conflict are a winning cause and overflowing coffers, neither of which the Parisian Bonapartist press possessed. The circulation of the *Ordre* fell steadily during the last half of 1872, while the party leaders,

⁵⁶ Collins, *Newspaper Press*, 159–160; Richard, *Bonapartisme*, 41; *L'Ordre*, November 6, 1872.
⁵⁷ *L'Ordre*, October 9, 1871.
⁵⁸ Richard, *Bonapartisme*, 112–113; Fidus, *Journal*, III, 359–361.
⁵⁹ Renault to Thiers, December 20, 1872 (BN Naf 20659). Police report of September 23, 1873 (APP BA864, "Jules Amigues.")

Bonapartism after Sedan

finding that it cost far too much for whatever services it was rendering, pondered whether to replace it altogether.[60] Dugué fell heir to a hand-to-mouth operation and, while borrowing heavily, resorted to raising prices, cutting staff, and withholding the wages of those who remained, in an effort to compensate for the subscription renewals which failed to come in. Circulation reached its low point of 5,000 copies a month after the Emperor's death. Dugué then managed to halt the downward spiral and to make the paper if not profitable, at least self-sustaining,[61] but a comparison between its provincial circulation in mid-1872 (when the decline had already begun) and early 1876 (at the moment of the general elections) shows that *it had lost one subscriber in four.* During the same period, the circulation of Gambetta's *République française,* founded only a month later, rose by 40 per cent.[62]

The causes for this substantial decline were several. It can be explained partly by prudent cancellations of subscriptions after the revelation of the "great Bonapartist conspiracy" in 1874, and partly by the fact that the *Ordre* was simply not a very good newspaper. (Because of the leadership's disdain for

[60] Renault to Thiers, July 13, July 18, August 27, 1872 (BN Naf 20659).

[61] Renault to Thiers, November 6, December 22, 1872; February 4, February 19, 1873 (BN Naf 20659); Richard, *Bonapartisme,* 99–101.

[62] AN F^{18} 526–531, "Presse départementale—Journaux distribués 1872–1876." These are quarterly reports by the Prefecture of each department of the number of copies of each Paris and local paper delivered through the mails. Certainly they are not infallible indices of public opinion; quite apart from the fact that some are now missing and that originally some were prepared more carefully than others, they can tell us nothing of the copies hawked on the streets of larger towns, or sold in shops. And one subscription might reach many people, particularly if it was taken out by a local Bonapartist club or *cercle.* Nevertheless, apart from voting figures, they are the only tangible clues to public opinion in this period. So the Ministry of Interior itself must have felt, since it collated and totaled them.

Paris

the press, which contrasted markedly with the attitude at the more socially homogeneous *Gambettiste* milieu, the journalistic talent Bonapartism attracted was not first-rate.) But there was more to it than that. Baron Eschasseriaux, a stalwart supporter of Rouher from an enthusiastically Bonapartist region, had noted that while the muted editorial tone of Duvernois was "very suitable in Paris," in departments like the Charente-Inférieure "something a little more lively is needed."[63] If, as the Baron was suggesting, the kind of people in the provinces who could afford to spend forty-eight to sixty-four francs a year for a Paris newspaper[64] wanted a more truculent profession of authoritarian democracy, circulation should have risen when Dugué de la Fauçonnerie succeeded Duvernois. It did not; in fact, the *Ordre's* decline was only an extreme example of a general trend which can be easily discerned in the accompanying maps.

In mid-1872, the number of subscriptions to *all* the openly or guardedly Bonapartist Paris papers, proportionate to total subscriptions to the Paris press, was surprisingly uniform across France. In most departments, from one in four to one in six of this select audience was getting a Bonapartist daily. Only in Corsica did these papers reach a majority of subscribers, but they sold especially well in parts of Normandy, of central France, and of the Southwest, and nowhere did they reach less than 10 per cent of the readers. The second map compares the circulation of the seven principal Bonapartist journals in 1876 and in mid-1872. Clearly the trend is downward, with the highest average rate of decline in the northern and eastern departments and sizeable drops not only in central France and on the Mediterranean littoral, but even in the Southwest.

[63] Eschasseriaux, "Mémoires," VI, 419.
[64] Schulz et fils, *Catalogue des journaux publiés à Paris en 1874* (Paris, 1874).

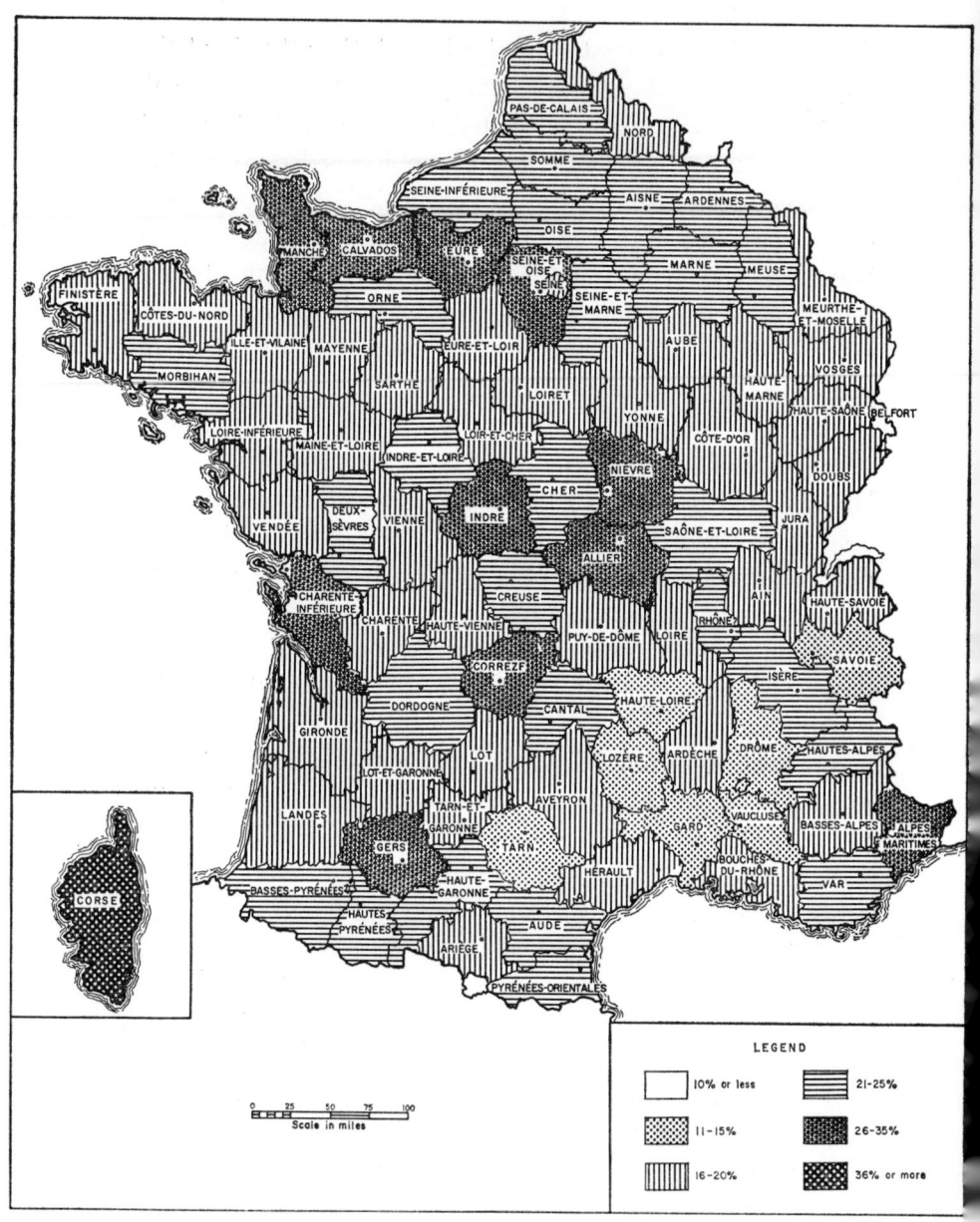

Map 1: Subscriptions to Bonapartist or sympathizing newspapers as a percentage of subscriptions to all Parisian *journaux d'opinion*, April–June 1872

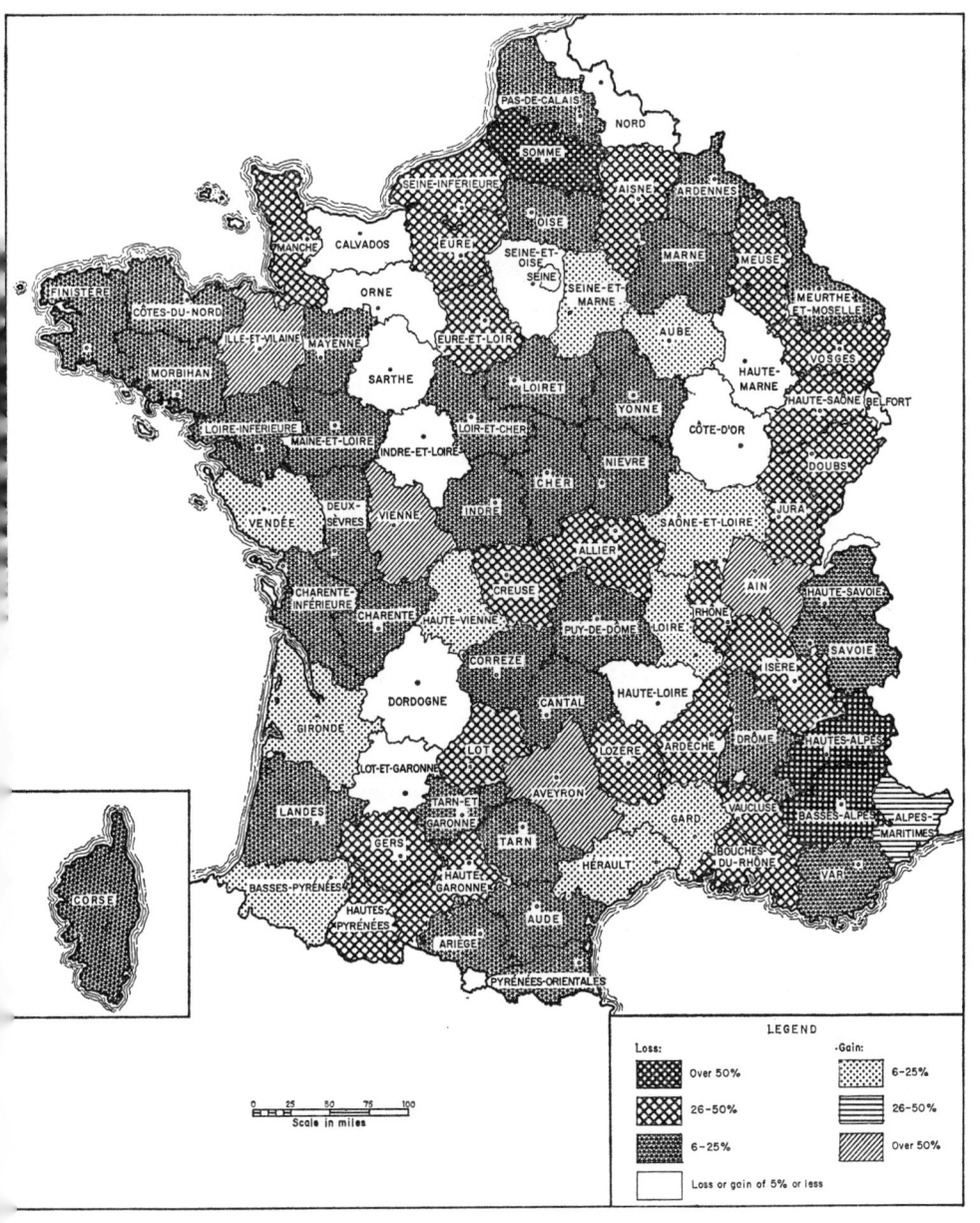

Map 2: Net change in the provincial circulation by mail of seven Bonapartist Parisian dailies, 1872–1876

Bonapartism after Sedan

It is safe to assume that when people ceased to believe in a particular political solution, they cancelled their subscriptions to the papers which espoused it. (The official mouthpiece of the Legitimist pretender lost one-third of its readers in this same period, 1872–76, most of them within less than a year after the publication of the letter in which Chambord insisted on the white flag of his ancestors.) [65] The conclusion is inescapable that Bonapartism had reached a high-water mark among the *gens aisés* of the provinces amid the uncertainties of 1872, well before the Bonapartist propaganda effort had really begun. Thereafter these people began slowly to accept the idea that their interests could be better safeguarded by the Republic than by a Napoleon not yet twenty years old.[66] Thus, even as the Bonapartists in 1874 and 1875 were exhilarated by a mounting wave of electoral successes, their chief Paris papers, discordant and ill-supported, were proving unable to win or hold the influential people to whom they were designed to appeal. The provincial bourgeois were rejecting not only the reactionary violence of the *Pays* (which consistently had the lowest circulation among the Bonapartist dailies), but also Dugué's authoritarian democracy and even the cautious liberalism of papers like the *Gaulois*.

This rejection by an audience whom the Bonapartists were disproportionately anxious to please would have been less serious had the party been advancing more rapidly on another, more vital journalistic battle ground. Newspapers from the capital had never been the first line of defense or attack for a political party in the provinces. They might keep an instructed

[65] Cf. Table of "Nombre de bandes des journaux de Paris" for 1874–5 (APP B^A1621).

[66] Most of the Republican papers registered substantial increases in circulation 1872–1876. At least one of the few large Bonapartist increases, on the other hand, was the result of a most exceptional circumstance: a six-fold growth in the circulation of the *Patrie* in the Vienne after its purchase by Soubeyran, deputy of the department.

Paris

reader abreast of doctrine, but they naturally had little space for politics on the local level, where most Frenchmen felt really involved. This was the concern of the more modest papers of the *départements*, making them much more relevant to the masses of ordinary readers. As Ernest Lavisse explained to his pupil, the Prince Imperial:

> One would win much by winning these journals, since they are the only intellectual fodder of the leisured proprietor, of the country bourgeois, on whom they have a great influence. All those [in his department of the Aisne] to whom I spoke of a necessary Imperialist restoration as inevitable and imminent were extremely astonished, because "the paper didn't say anything about it." The day on which the paper does say something, these people will open their eyes to the evidence, and by their conversations . . . they will persuade a crowd of the undecided. Then the atmosphere will be created in which an Imperialist candidacy will become possible.[67]

As late as 1867, the Imperial government had virtually commanded the field of local journalism. The liberalization of the press laws, however, had reversed this situation, and the few papers which had remained loyal until the war had not resisted the tide of condemnation sweeping over the regime they had served.[68] Thus a formidable task of reorganization had now to be faced. Mansard had either to persuade old and influential papers to commit themselves by accepting the articles distributed by his *Correspondance* or, failing this, somehow to set on foot viable new journals. The former alterna-

---

[67] Ernest Lavisse to the Prince Imperial, November 14, 1874, in C. L. d'Espinay de Briort, ed., "Une correspondance inédite: le Prince Impérial et Ernest Lavisse, 1871–1879," *Revue des Deux Mondes*, 7th period, L (1929), 562.

[68] Ernest Merson, *Confessions d'un journaliste*, (2d ed.; Paris, 1890), 230–233, 237; Roger Marlin, "La presse du Doubs pendant la guerre de 1870–1871," *Etudes de presse*, new series, VIII (1955), 179–184; Avenel, *Histoire*, 540–542.

tive, winning the "oldest paper of the *chef-lieu,* the one to which the people of the region have subscribed for years from father to son," was certainly advantageous: "The politics of the paper may change, the subscribers do not, and since they believe their paper, their opinion follows its own." [69]

Unfortunately it was often just this sort of paper which took good care not to show its politics too perceptibly, a sensible rule to ensure longevity in nineteenth-century France. One example among many was the *Mémorial* of Lille; the *Ordre* always optimistically listed it in the Bonapartist stable, but the Prefect of the Nord reported that though it sometimes let slip "memories" of the time when it had been the Imperial Prefect's official paper, it was generally "very reserved." [70]

At least the *Mémorial* cost the party nothing and gave no trouble, which was more than could be said of many of the clients of M. Mansard, who bore the responsibility not only for circulating his *Correspondance,* but also for providing the papers which printed it with cash—the initial *caution* of 3,000 to 24,000 francs which Thiers' legislation required aspiring publishers to advance, as well as restorative subsidies, given "as infrequently as possible." [71] The goal of such incentives was nothing less than a paper in every department. What was actually accomplished by mid-1874 was not inconsiderable; the Prefect of Police then reported that the *Correspondance* was inserted in seventy-one newspapers across France, including twenty-seven dailies, twenty-one tri-weeklies, seven bi-weeklies and sixteen weeklies, together publishing about a

[69] Alfred Magne, "Deux visites à Chislehurst en 1872," *Revue hebdomadaire,* VIII (August 17, 1912), 303.

[70] Jeanne Gaillard, "La presse de province et la question du régime au début de la Troisième République," *Revue d'Histoire Moderne et Contemporaine,* VI (1959), 306. Prefect of Nord to Minister of Interior, March 18, 1872 (AN F18 309, "Imprimerie et librairie: Dépêches officielles, 1870–1876").

[71] Richard, *Bonapartisme,* 42; Avenel, *Histoire,* 651.

Paris

half-million copies per week.⁷² The total, however, is less impressive if one takes the trouble to locate these papers on the map, and to weight them, insofar as data are available, according to their relative place in the journalism of their respective departments.⁷³ (See Maps 3 and 4.)

In late 1872, Bonapartist provincial journalism was strongest in the West and Center of France. This was still true three years later, at the time of the general elections; indeed, it was in these regions that Bonapartist editors could be found upholding the cause a whole generation later, on powerful papers like the *Union bretonne*, the *Journal du Lot-et-Garonne*, the *Journal du Cher*, the *Adour* of Dax, the *Courrier de l'Eure*, the *Journal de la Vienne*.⁷⁴ Not all of these were capable of existing without subsidy in the early years of the Republic; the *Adour* would have collapsed without one, and in 1874 the editor of the *Journal de Bordeaux* threatened to switch to a less controversial editorial policy unless his fidelity were better rewarded.⁷⁵

Nevertheless, the maps unmistakably suggest that the Southwest was fertile ground, and even a temptation to overplanting. After a quarrel with the owner of the *Charentais* of

---

⁷² Eschasseriaux, "Mémoires," VI, 225. Daniel, ed., *Année politique —1875*, 68. Renault to Thiers, March 13, May 2, 1872 (BN Naf 20658).

⁷³ Sources for these maps are: for circulation, the figures given in AN F¹⁸526–531; for the identity of the papers, the more or less complete lists published by the *Ordre* on November 10, 1873, and October 31, 1876, as well as a list drawn up by Mansard and later seized by the police, which appears in Savary, *Deuxième Rapport*, 120. These were compared with the political identifications given in an "Essai d'un travail d'ensemble sur la presse départementale au mois de septembre 1873" (APP B^A1621) and in *La presse des départements*, a supplement to the *Figaro* of December 7, 1874. N.B.: I have not shown a paper unless confident from these lists that it was *Bonapartist at the time*, hence a few peculiar differences between the two maps.

⁷⁴ Renault to Thiers, November 12, 1872 (BN Naf 20659); Avenel, *Histoire*, 808.

⁷⁵ Eschasseriaux, "Mémoires," VI, 337; VII, 328.

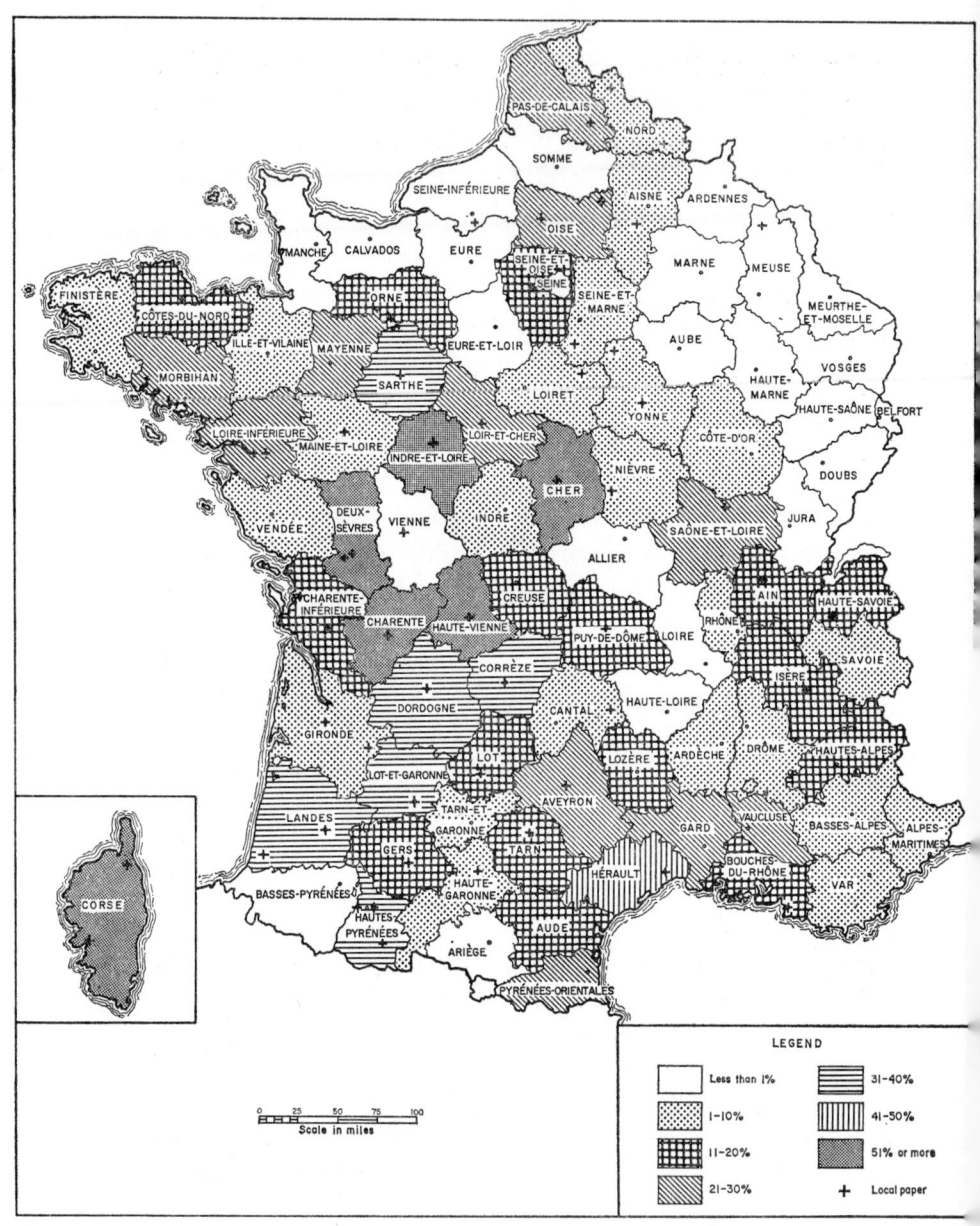

Map 3: Mid–1872 circulation by mail of local Bonapartist papers as a percentage of total subscriptions

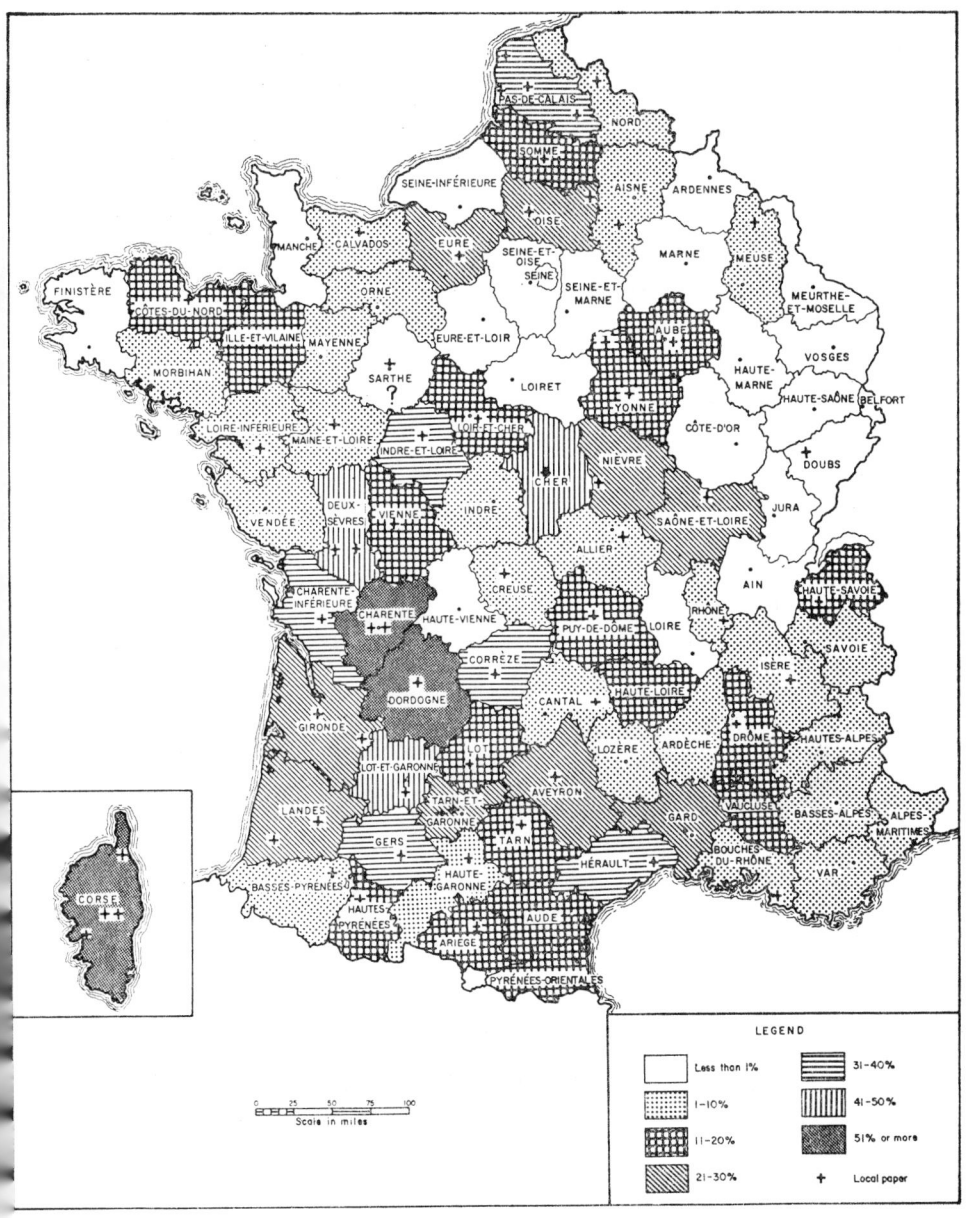

Map 4: January–March 1876 circulation by mail of local Bonapartist papers as a percentage of total subscriptions

Angoulême, its editor left to found his own *Suffrage universel des Charentes*, even more Bonapartist, and kept it going, though not without aid from Rouher and the local party chiefs.[76] It was an audacious Republican journalist who ventured here; five in succession gave up the struggle against the Bonapartist *Echo de la Dordogne*, and not until 1877 was an enduring Republican paper founded at Périgueux.[77]

By contrast the lands to the east and southeast of Paris appear remarkably sterile. Continuing martial law, under which publication of a paper might be forbidden or interrupted, certainly hampered the Bonapartists, notably in the Côte-d'Or and the Massif Central.[78] Yet this will not explain the pitiful scattering of feeble papers which the maps reveal, especially when the party's investigations reported a substantial potential audience. In Franche-Comté in 1873, for example, an agent who had traveled throughout the region insisted that half of the urban and most of the rural population was still Bonapartist. (The bourgeoisie was following Thiers without conviction, while there were but few Legitimist priests and aristocrats, Orleanist bankers, and worker or *déclassé* Republicans.) Yet "the partisans of the Empire . . . unanimously complain of lacking information, mutual contacts, direction, and the means of replying to the insults of their adversary, of being reduced, as they say, to playing dead."[79]

---

[76] Gustave Cunéo d'Ornano, *Réponse au gérant du Charentais* (Angoulême, 1875), *passim*; Eschasseriaux, "Mémoires," IX, 23, 27.

[77] Jacques Kayser, "La presse en Dordogne sous la Troisième République," in Jacques Kayser, ed., *La presse de province sous la Troisième République* (Paris, 1958), 33.

[78] Collins, *Newspaper Press*, 159; Eschasseriaux, "Mémoires," VIII, 126.

[79] Quoted in Roger Marlin, "La presse du Doubs et l'établissement définitif du régime républicain," in Kayser, ed., *Presse de province*, 120–121.

Paris

A local paper was the obvious remedy, yet there was none until 1874, when the *Franche-Comté* was induced to accept the *Correspondance Mansard*—three months exactly before it went bankrupt and ceased publication, despite urgent pleas to the *comité de comptabilité* by the regional *missus dominici* that no candidate would run in the Doubs, Jura, or Haute-Saône without it. Again there was no paper until just before the general elections, when one belatedly launched achieved only an infinitesimal circulation.[80] There were but three Bonapartist candidates for the thirteen seats of these departments, none successful.

Napoleon III had given a rueful answer to a visitor who hinted to him that progress toward the goal of a paper for every department seemed too slow: "We lack, you see, the sinews of war: money. We are doing what we can, but we are obliged to go slowly for lack of funds, although people can certainly organize."[81] He was proud "of having fallen from the throne without having put money away abroad";[82] the numerous visitors to Chislehurst were frequently struck by the simplicity, not to say austerity, of the Imperial household. At his death the Emperor left only a modest legacy,[83] certainly not enough to finance a national political party. Thus the more honorable of Napoleon's followers were reluctant even to ask the Imperial family for much.[84]

For the "sinews of war" Bonapartism was dependent on its rank and file, and especially upon the wealthiest among them. In 1873 pledges for a 100-franc subscription were circulated in

[80] Marlin, "Presse pendant la guerre," 178; Marlin in Kayser, ed., *Presse de province,* 121; Eschasseriaux, "Mémoires," VII, 352.

[81] Magne, "Deux visites," 303.

[82] Napoleon III, "Lettres à l'Impératrice Eugénie 1870–1871," *Revue des Deux Mondes,* 7th period, LIX (1930), 9.

[83] Richard, *Bonapartisme,* 37–38.

[84] Eschasseriaux, "Mémoires," VII, 61; IX, 394–395; Fidus, *Journal,* III, 159.

Bonapartism after Sedan

an obvious attempt to draw upon the humblest sympathizers —one ticket could be subscribed for by several individuals. This does not seem to have been a successful experiment, however, for it was not repeated. It would have taken many such small contributors, in any case, to equal the sums extracted from the wealthiest, men like the Marquis de Lavalette who could refill a depleted treasury by simply taking out their checkbooks.[85] To these men there came regularly with the new year requests for contributions which sometimes even stipulated the amount expected. The response at first was generous,[86] but these benefactors later limited their generosity, understandably, for while they were being called on to support the party's central treasury, they had also to bear most of the expenses of Bonapartist journalism and politics in their own regions. When the party's leaders after the 1876 elections asked for a sum sufficient to prevent the *Liberté* and *Paris-Journal* from escaping the party's control altogether, these magnates simply balked. The Duc de Mouchy replied that they must turn to those who had not had to fight three elections in a row, with all the costs they entailed. Comte Le Marois objected that for four years he alone had supported the paper of his *arrondissement*; for the same period he had made considerable sacrifices for a regional paper, and in addition had interests in the *Ordre* and several other Paris papers.[87]

Electoral costs were a particularly sore point. Despite the importance for the Bonapartists of contesting every by-

[85] Eschasseriaux, "Mémoires," VII, 61. Richard, *Bonapartisme*, 139–140.

[86] D'Hauterive, *Napoléon III et le Prince Napoléon*, 333; cf. Fidus, *Journal*, III, 173, 178.

[87] Duc de Mouchy to Raoul-Duval, May 30, 1876; Comte Le Marois to Raoul-Duval, May 24, 1876; in dossier "1876" of Raoul-Duval papers, château of Le Vaudreuil (Eure).

Paris

election, when Rouher, whose funds were tied up by the agency of the rue Montmartre, applied to Napoleon III for a special electoral fund, the Emperor was obliged to give a categoric refusal. Thus it became the general rule that there was a Bonapartist candidate only where he could himself finance his candidacy, in a contrast with the Republicans' practice which Bonapartists bitterly resented.[88]

Subsisting on what was really almost charity, the party's central treasury was caught in a vicious circle; greater contributions depended on an appearance of success and hence of imminent dividends for the contributor, but such an appearance could only be created if every district were contested, which required a bountiful treasury. Thus only four months before the general elections of 1876 Rouher was confiding: "For a battle on all fronts money is naturally lacking, subscriptions are not pouring in, and the official well is almost dry." Less than a month before the general elections of 1877 it was the same story.[89]

This state of penury accounts in large measure for the wide stretches of France left without a local newspaper to rally the faithful and convince the undecided. In departments with a flourishing capital city like Marseille, a sufficient number of wealthy men might be found to advance the necessary support; in regions like the Southwest where the party was already well organized, local notables like Baron Eschasseriaux might subsidize a journal to safeguard their own political futures.[90] Without such local initiatives, however, the loyalty of a paper might prove precarious, if the editor was refused a

[88] Eschasseriaux, "Mémoires," VI, 357, 373–375, 383; VII, 65, 104.
[89] Rouher to Madame Lepic, August 31, 1875 (dossier "Lettres de Camden," Raoul-Duval papers); Rouher to Eschasseriaux, September 15, 1877 (Eschasseriaux, "Mémoires," IX, 171).
[90] Corticchiato, *Corses*, 243; Eschasseriaux, "Mémoires," V, 63–64; IX, 419.

share, or became dissatisfied with his portion of the 10,000 francs which Mansard periodically paid out.[91] He might even express his dissatisfaction by switching his paper's politics from Bonapartist to *conservateur sans épithète* and leaving yet another region deprived of this essential propaganda.

The transition to conservative would be an easy one, since, from 1871 to 1876, no word came to Bonapartist lips or flowed from Bonapartist pens more frequently. The Emperor himself had declared that "the question is posed between Empire and Commune, between conservation and revolution," [92] and his followers of all shades of opinion seemed for the moment to have blended into one in taking up the refrain. Dugué de la Fauçonnerie, for example, who in 1869 had been too proud an authoritarian democrat to accept the Liberal Empire, in 1872 urged the formation of a great "SOCIAL League . . . against demagogy . . . [in] a common idea of resistance." [93]

This was doubtless music to the ears of many *bien-pensants* for whom Napoleon III's paramount weakness was his dabbling in socialism, which he must now abjure. Such people would rally gladly to a restored Empire, but "on condition that it will be above all *authoritarian*. If he should . . . deal again with the working classes (that is, with the *canaille* of the International). . . . he may have a return from . . . Elba, but he will not hold out a hundred days." [94]

Ironically, however, the morrow of the repression of the Commune may have been just the moment for Bonapartists to bid for the support of the working classes, and even the

[91] Savary, *Deuxième Rapport*, 120; cf. Renault to Thiers, August 8, 1872 (BN Naf 20659). Rouher's paper in the Puy-de-Dôme was allotted more than a quarter of this money.
[92] Magne, "Deux visites," 305.
[93] Dugué, *Souvenirs*, 111; *L'Ordre*, November 7, 1872.
[94] Letter to Baron de Saint-Paul in Saint-Paul papers, château of Poudelaye (Ariège).

Paris

canaille of the International. Under the Empire, of course, they had been the most recalcitrant group in the nation, and some had even ascribed their plight to the mere existence of Napoleon's regime.[95] The horrors through which they had recently passed, however, had not been at his hands, and many dogmas were now at a discount, as the former leader of the International at Lyon, Albert Richard, forcefully demonstrated when he called on his comrades to recognize realities and to abandon the Republic for the Empire. A colleague of Bakunin embraced Napoleon the Little!

And yet the evolution of Richard's ideas is comprehensible enough. Coming from a city with a long history of the bloody repression of worker discontent, he did not feel that there was any natural affinity between socialists and bourgeois of any sort, "Republican" or not, and the advent of the Republic of Thiers, the butcher of the Commune, and of Gambetta, who denied that there was a social question, merely confirmed his suspicions. Such an outcome after years of hope and days of slaughter understandably drove this youthful idealist to desperate courses.[96] Richard had become convinced of the futility of all apocalyptic systems; he was confident that the lot of the proletariat could be improved by the workers themselves, not through politics but through "economic solidarity" and individual initiative. Any government which permitted these need not fear the workers, who asked only to be allowed to compete on equal terms within the existing economic system.[97] It was not very far from this vague, moralistic, almost

[95] David J. Kulstein, "The Attitude of French Workers toward the Second Empire," *French Historical Studies*, II (1962), 356–375, especially 371.

[96] Albert Richard, "Les propagateurs de l'Internationale en France," *Revue socialiste* (1896), 652; cf. Albert Thomas, *Le Second Empire* (Paris, n.d.), 337, 366–367.

[97] Albert Richard, *L'Association internationale des travailleurs* (n.p., n.d.), *passim*; *Le socialisme* (Lyon, 1869), *passim*.

Bonapartism after Sedan

"petit-bourgeois" socialism to the ideas of the chief Bonapartist social thinker. Richard, visiting Chislehurst, encountered a kindred spirit who filled him with a new hope he did not hesitate to voice repeatedly, though his fellow Socialists excommunicated him and he bore the stigma of this apostasy for the rest of his life.[98]

Richard's conversion was less important in itself (there is no evidence that his pro-Imperial pamphlets had much influence) than as a symbol of a challenge to the Bonapartists' political skill. He cannot have been the only one of his social class who recognized that the new Republic held out no hope for him and that some alternative must be found. Would the Bonapartists' emphasis on conservatism—and the fundamental attitudes to which it gave expression—prevent the Empire from becoming that alternative? To answer this question, one need only consider the career of Jules Amigues, the only Bonapartist, such as he was, who knew the way without guidance from the rue de l'Elysée to Belleville.

Republicans portrayed Amigues as a sinister phantom, recruiting Communards immured in the remotest prisons for the Imperial cause or materializing at Chislehurst with a delegation of "workers" culled none knew where.[99] To frock-coated respectability, he *was* a singular figure, though characteristic of the intellectual demimonde to be found up the side-streets of any great European capital; he had lived long abroad, sometimes on the secret payroll of the Quai d'Orsay, had written an unsuccessful play and founded unsuccessful newspapers, and was hounded by creditors.[100] He revealingly

[98] Renault to Thiers, February 9, 1873 (BN Naf 20660). Cf. Thomas, *Second Empire*, 337.

[99] Daniel, ed., *Année politique*—1875, 74, 206–207. Letters from Communard convicts, containing shrewd advice on winning the workers to the Empire, were found in his possession by the police (APP B^A864).

[100] Police report of May 27, 1872 (APP B^A864); Félix Ribeyre, *Biographie des sénateurs et des députés*, (new ed.; Paris, n.d.), 578–

described himself as "a man of study and labor . . . perhaps something of an artist, a bit curious." [101]

The particular object of his "curiosity" was the solution of the social question. His sympathy for the humble was, in fact, so outspoken that it could only appear quixotic or venal to the many Frenchmen who did not share it. Consequently he was charged with having worn many colors; he replied that he had abandoned Emile Ollivier when he saw that the Liberal Empire was a surrender to oligarchy, and had ceased to be a Republican when he witnessed the martyrdom the Republic inflicted on those who had brought it to power.[102] In 1872, still in quest of a solution, he went to Chislehurst, where the Emperor at once recognized in him the sort of "new man" he needed; and thus it was that Rouher, one dark autumnal evening, "received the visit of a man with sunken and burning eyes, draped in a long coat, who asked point-blank, without knowing him, for 75,000 francs to buy a democratic newspaper." The Vice-Emperor never completely recovered from the "surprise and . . . distrust" [103] of this first encounter with a man who had publicly defended Communards. Nevertheless, Amigues' *L'Espérance nationale* duly appeared, and the menace of Caesarean socialism thus became another preoccupation of M. Thiers' Prefect of Police.

Léon Renault knew already that there was a potential audience for a Bonapartist *Enragé* among "the little world of the shopkeepers . . . barbers, newspaper vendors, etc.," and

---

579; A. Robert, E. Bourloton, and G. Cougny, eds., *Dictionnaire des parlementaires français 1789–1889* (Paris, 1891), I, 54; Fidus, *Journal*, I, 34–35.

[101] Jules Amigues, *Lettre à M. Imgarde de Leffemberg* (Paris, 1875), 10.

[102] Jules Amigues, *Epître au peuple: Comment l'Empire reviendra* (Clichy, 1872), *passim*. Cf. *L'Ordre*, January 14, 1872.

[103] Richard, *Bonapartisme*, 55–56. Comte de la Chapelle in *Le Spécial*, December 8, 1887, quoted in Comte d'Hérisson, *Le Prince Impérial*, (4th ed.; Paris, 1890), 183.

Bonapartism after Sedan

among the craftsmen whose livelihood depended on an opulence which a provisional Republic did not encourage. (The Empire, on the other hand, had been a "veritable horn of plenty" for them.) While the ordinary worker, with his habits of "intemperance and dissipation," was a Communard radical who expressed in vulgarity his attitude to the Emperor, this better class, with its "spirit of economy and order, is close to the *petite bourgeoisie.*" If they preferred any one regime it was the Empire, under which "saving was easier for working people."[104] This estimate is confirmed by the list of the workers whom Amigues led to Chislehurst for the Emperor's funeral; they were in the main skilled artisans—hatters and shoemakers, gas-fitters and turners, a cabinet-maker, a gilder, an engraver—from all the poorer *arrondissements* of Paris.[105]

The economic doctrines which Amigues professed were well calculated to appeal to this kind of occupational group; indeed, when he called for what was really a reconstitution of the guild system, he was repeating a lesson he had learned from the artisans themselves. He had become acquainted, during an ill-fated attempt at mediation between the Commune and Versailles, with the leaders of the *Union nationale du commerce et de l'industrie,* a federation "which unites in a single *faisceau* about twenty *chambres syndicales,* numbering altogether more than 7,000 members." He believed it to be not only a symptom of "a profound movement in French commerce and labor toward the reconstitution of corporative groups," but an actual prototype for the future economic and political organization of France:

Suppose . . . that each *corps de métier* is organized, perhaps within the city, perhaps within the state, perhaps even from one

[104] Renault to Thiers, January 6, February 10, October 18, 28, December 29, 1872 (BN Naf 20658-20659).
[105] Jules Amigues, *Réponse à MM. Savary et Léon Renault* (Paris, 1875), 49. Cf. police report of April 26, 1873 (APP B^A864).

state to another, in a vast corporative group. Any conflict between a boss and his workers would become a question of general interest for the entire corporation. . . . The difficulties . . . would thus be solved by a sort of parliament or corporative tribunal. . . . The institution of the corporative regime is the economic revolution, is the liberation of labor by permanent discussion of its relationships with capital. . . . Let us not fear to say . . . [that] the constitution of corporative groups and their . . . "federation" was foreseen rather clearly by the Commune.[106]

He thus had the wit (and the courage) to perceive that the Commune had been something more than an insensate orgy; its "municipalist" character resulted, he felt, from the fact that France was overcentralized and governed by a fictitious representative system in which the deputy had nothing in common, socially, with his electors. The remedy lay in relearning the lessons of classical and medieval history and instituting a system of local self-government based on economic units.[107] This scheme for a corporative return to the *ancien régime* later would find much more famous expositors; if it seems economically reactionary, so too was most of his audience.

Together with the creation of the corporate state Amigues called for specific social reforms which he proudly contrasted with Gambetta's evasions: an end to all restrictions on association; community (or corporate) care for the aged; free and compulsory education; an end to purchased exemptions from conscription; the suppression of episcopal sees, to restore the Church "to the democratic and elective state of its origins"; and the replacement of levies on consumption by an income tax.[108] (If the reader recalls how long it took the

[106] Jules Amigues, *Les aveux d'un conspirateur bonapartiste* (Paris, 1874), 20, 22, 50, 162–163; *Lettres au peuple* (Paris, 1872), 35–36.
[107] Jules Amigues, *La France à refaire: La Commune* (2d ed.; Paris, 1871), *passim*.
[108] Amigues, *Lettres*, 69–72.

Bonapartism after Sedan

Republic to enact some of these, he will be able to gauge to what extent Amigues had broken with conventional thinking.)

He never wearied of pointing out that nothing of this kind could be expected from the sterile politicking of a parliamentary Republic. When Rémusat and Barodet were locked in their crucial struggle for a vacant Paris seat in 1873, he declared that the outcome, whether "Rémuset" or "Barodat," would be quite the same for the lower classes of the city: they would suffer equally under "bourgeois imbecility" or "revolutionary madness." Consequently he plastered the walls of the capital with 25,000 posters of "JULES AMIGUES, A RARE CANDIDATE WHO DOES NOT WANT TO BE ELECTED," in which he suggested that if the people enjoyed their position as "beast of burden" they could vote for either one, but if not, they should refuse to "vote again for anything or anybody" until a plebiscite, "ending the reign of the blabbermouths," would enable them to directly constitute the "DICTATORIAL AND POPULAR GOVERNMENT" which would carry out their demands.[109]

It may have been the reckless panache of such language that won for Amigues the support of Paul de Cassagnac, the only prominent Bonapartist who cared or dared to join him in forays into working-class districts. Late in 1875 the fiery editor of the *Pays* addressed an audience in the heart of Belleville with a bluntness which scandalized Republicans and Bonapartists alike. He took his hat off to the Communard chief Flourens, "since he knew how to fight and to die." During this harangue Cassagnac even called for an income tax, a proposal which the *Gaulois* and the *Ordre* both promptly de-

[109] "Déclaration de Jules Amigues," April 24, 1873; cf. Jules Amigues, *Rémuset et Barodat* (Paris, 1873), *passim*. Police report of April 25, 1873 (APP B^A864).

Paris

nounced.[110] Such wild ideas, especially coming from a spokesman of the Bonapartist "Coblence," were incomprehensible to the men of the party's "Plain." To the Norman deputy Raoul-Duval, who was seeking to lead them toward a "progressive" Empire, such outbursts were "ridiculous Gasconnades" which he hastened to repudiate lest they discredit the whole party. From Raoul-Duval's home district, a friend assured him he had done well, "for our calm and cold country of Normandy does not understand these exaggerations," these "frankly socialist schemes." [111]

In fact the society and outlook of Belleville on the one hand and Normandy on the other were further apart than any map could reveal. Consequently the hopes of Albert Richard would remain unfulfilled [112] and the efforts of Jules Amigues isolated, ill-understood, and increasingly ill-supported by the Bonapartist party. The Third Republic's concern for the growing class of slum-dwellers was tardy and uncomprehending, but it is unlikely that a Third Empire would have treated them very differently.

The *comité de comptabilité* and the master of 4, rue de l'Elysée had remained skeptical of the practicality and desir-

---

[110] *L'Ordre*, November 26, 1875; Daniel, ed., *Année politique—1875*, 325–326.

[111] Correspondence in dossier "1875," Raoul-Duval papers.

[112] By 1876 Richard was forced to admit to himself that he had followed a will-o'-the wisp; though Napoleon III was "personally the best man in the world," he was unable to escape "the yoke of his party," which after his death passed under the control of men for whom the Empire "has no other social function than to maintain the police." So great was his disappointment that he turned (without great success) to the Comte de Chambord. Albert Richard, *Union française des amis de la paix sociale* (Turin, 1873), *passim*; *La révolution sociale et la guerre européenne* (Geneva, 1876), 4–5. Comte de Blacas to Richard, October 5, November 1, 1877 (AN AB XIX 776, "Papiers Albert Richard").

Bonapartism after Sedan

ability of a campaign to win the working classes, and Amigues had had his way only by going over their heads to the Emperor. The meager sales of the *Espérance nationale*, however, seemed to refute his claims, and did nothing to compensate the party for the embarrassment caused it by the paper's language—even by its existence. After the Emperor's death, the *Espérance nationale* was permitted to cease daily publication in April, 1873, Rouher having made up his mind to refuse "any sort of subsidy to a man whom he judges compromising for his party." [113] The conservative union with the Monarchists to overthrow Thiers was about to be consummated, and participation in it would attract to Bonapartism—or so many Bonapartists thought—far more important people than the collection of Parisian vintners and tinkers whose numbers the credulous Amigues was so prone to overestimate.[114]

He was henceforth allowed to pursue in the slums his peculiar notion that the Bonapartists should imitate Gambetta's Republicans and the *Carbonari* by building a comprehensive network of local committees, though the speed with which his own Parisian committees disintegrated seemed to confirm the impracticality of the idea. Bonapartist candidates whose districts included working-class quarters like Argenteuil or Saint Denis also condescended to call on his help from time to time.[115] Every initiative which would have increased his importance within the party was, however, firmly discouraged; there was no workers' delegation at Chislehurst when the Prince Imperial came of age, for in addition to the "natural repulsion inspired in an elite personnel" by the "inhabitants of Charonne and Belleville" whom Amigues had led to

[113] Renault to Thiers, August 4, October 21, October 23, 1872; February 28, March 2, March 5, April 11, 1873 (BN Naf 20658-20660). Cf. Amigues, *Réponse*, 28.

[114] Richard, *Bonapartisme*, 56.

[115] Police reports of October 27, 1872, March 23, 1873, February 4, 7, 1875 (APP B^A 864).

the Emperor's funeral, bringing them over "had cost a lot of money, said M. Rouher." [116] A mission to Corsica was invented for him at the time of the general elections of 1876, since it was felt that as a candidate in Paris he would be too democratic and would frighten the bourgeoisie.[117]

In 1877, however, when he ran as an unknown (and *not* as a candidate of the *Seize Mai*) in the second district of Cambrai against a rich Republican industrialist who was supported by his own local paper, the result should have given the Bonapartist leadership pause. Though Amigues was repeatedly refused halls in which to campaign, and, when he found one, foremen stood at the doors taking names and threatening dismissals, in this district largely populated by hand-loom weavers struggling under the putting-out system he won by a narrow margin. What seems to have tipped the balance was his poster. In it he quoted his opponent's speeches urging workers to be thrifty and temperate and pointed out that in fact workers had no clothes for their children and only water to drink.[118]

There had been reports before his victory that "his political associates themselves would not look upon his arrival in the Chamber with a very friendly eye." They need not have worried. The Republicans promptly invalidated his election; he was not given long to sit among his Bonapartist colleagues at Versailles, to try to persuade them "that a politics of universal suffrage cannot be carried on by the subtle and specious

[116] Police report of January 16, 1873 (APP B^A418); Fidus, *Journal*, III, 273.
[117] Letter of "A. Barreson, stonecutter," asking Raoul-Duval to intervene for Amigues. Barreson bitterly inquired whether the Bonapartists were still counting on the bourgeoisie to remake the Empire. (In dossier "1876," Raoul-Duval papers.) Cf. police report of January 8, 1876 (APP B^A864).
[118] Jules Amigues, *Discours prononcé . . . dans la séance de la Chambre des Députés du 9 mai 1878* (Cambrai, 1878), *passim*.

Bonapartism after Sedan

proceedings suggested by aristocratic genius or bourgeois intelligence"—like conservative union.

The difficulty was that Amigues insisted that "democracy is by its nature indivisible, . . . it includes all the classes." [119] Many a deputy of the Bonapartist "Plain" (though by no means all) would stoutly have insisted that he did believe in authoritarian democracy—on his native provincial soil, among his peasants, men whom he knew and understood as they knew and understood him. If he gave any thought to the urban working classes at all, however, he was baffled by their behavior, which he could explain at best as the folly of children, at worst as the ferocity of an incalculable species of wild beast. Recalling the mob thronging the Palais Bourbon on September 4, Baron Eschasseriaux wrote: "One can wonder in what surroundings such men live; in what depths, in what furnace of blind and brutal passions these people spend their lives? These men do not speak our language, do not understand us, and yet they live a few steps away from us." This separation the Baron took good care always to preserve; he would rent an apartment in Paris only if the building contained no "tradesmen or manufacturers or suspicious characters." [120]

If one studies the social backgrounds, education, and occupations of the Bonapartist Senators and deputies of the Republic, one finds few with first-hand knowledge of the industrial world, especially, of course, from the point of view of the employee. Only a handful were self-made men; many were descended from families which had been prominent for generations, if not centuries. An overwhelming majority had been trained in the law, and comparatively few at schools like the *Polytechnique* and the *Ecole des Mines*. Among the eighty-

---

[119] Amigues, *Réponse*, 69–71; police reports of October 17, 1877, June 22, 1878 (APP B^A864).
[120] Eschasseriaux, "Mémoires," V, 175; VI, 326.

Paris

odd for whom substantial occupational data can be established, almost half were landed proprietors while only a half-dozen were actively engaged in industry, and of these, some can be so described only because they sat on a board of directors. (Some, indeed, had *inherited* industrial fortunes, but had proceeded to invest them in land.) One can find only a single practitioner of Bonapartist socialism in the old style: Laroche-Joubert of the Charente, a paper-maker, who gave shares in the business to his employees (they still voted for his Republican rival).[121]

Even those men of the Bonapartist "Plain" who were not animated by an active hatred of the working class or disgusted by its flagrant ingratitude [122] thus were not equipped to share Jules Amigues' pity for the workers' plight and his ambition to convert them. They regarded Amigues with the mingled wonder and suspicion of laymen confronted with an expert in some occult specialty or with an explorer of nether regions. Certainly they were not prepared to allow his hopes or desires to divert Bonapartism from what they considered its proper conservative objectives.

Perhaps their indifference to the victims of industrialization was no great loss. After all, even supposing that the majority of the urban lower classes could have been won over (which is improbable), they would not have constituted a decisive weight in the French political balance. The lukewarm attitude of Rouher and his council towards Amigues and the curtailment of the newspaper specifically directed to the workers were not necessarily deadly sins of omission.

The same cannot, however, be said of the failures to de-

[121] Occupational and other data were taken largely from Ribeyre, *Biographie*, and Robert, Bourloton, and Cougny, eds., *Dictionnaire des parlementaires*. Biographical sketches supplementing those in the notes of this book will be found in the Appendix.

[122] Fidus, *Journal*, I, 370, 375; II, 478; F. Perron, *Le reveil de la France* (Paris, n.d.), 32–34.

Bonapartism after Sedan

velop an effective headquarters organization, to complete the network of local leadership throughout rural France, to strongly reinforce the pamphlets and photographs with persuasive Parisian journals and a sufficient number of local ones, and to find the money to back candidates in every district. The consequences of these failures emerge clearly from a letter which Ernest Merson—himself a provincial editor—wrote to the Prince Imperial in 1876 when the final electoral tallies were in:

> The Bonapartist party is passing through a very grave crisis. . . . The three causes of the trouble are: The lack of permanent and comprehensive leadership making itself felt everywhere. The lack of a sufficient organization. The lack of action . . . developing faith while maintaining hope.
> LEADERSHIP . . . The general-in-chief of a great army has other obligations than the commander of a troop of partisans, and, on pain of failing in his work, he must surround himself with sufficient personnel. . . . What M. Rouher needs is a staff, or . . . a ministry. . . .
> ORGANIZATION . . . Under this heading much has been attempted in five years; in reality, almost nothing has been done. While the Republican party has been organized by the secret societies, while the Legitimist party possesses very well-organized cadres formed of nobles and priests . . . the Bonapartist party is abandoned almost to itself. It is a very numerous army, without noncommissioned and commissioned officers, which scarcely rallies to the command of several generals, who are seen from time to time almost by chance. . . . We must finally finish the work imperfectly undertaken thus far. To do this twelve or fifteen devoted, prudent men of active, adroit political skills must be chosen, to each of whom would be delegated the responsibility for organizing the departments comprised in a given region. . . . We are speaking not of a platonic, superficial, and consequently sterile organization, but rather of a serious organization, practical and permanent, in the program of which compulsory residence for

several months each year will be included. Residence in the provinces, indeed, is the only way to keep up continuous relations with the population, to create a clientele among them, to develop influence and acquire political information. . . .

ACTION . . . By action is meant propaganda . . . the creation of Bonapartist papers everywhere that none exists. This is the *to be or not to be of the party*. . . . With newspapers, everything is possible, . . . without the papers, nothing is practicable. . . . The population give up when their direction is neglected. . . . [He gave examples.] What is needed is at least one paper per department. For a time, it was thought that regional sheets could be effective. This was a mistake. Just as the influence of the Parisian paper is nonexistent in the provinces except to maintain doctrine, the influence of a provincial paper is sterile outside the department in which it is published. . . .

If these deficiencies were promptly remedied, Merson believed, Bonapartism was assured of ultimate victory. But he concluded with a solemn warning: if nothing were done, then the party "will weaken little by little, crushed by the fact of the Republic . . . and the Empire, once more, will become a mere legend." [123]

[123] Ernest Merson, *Confidences d'un journaliste* (Paris, 1891), 263–269.

Chapter III

Versailles

The news of the death of Napoleon III, as it was whispered from bench to bench of the theater at Versailles during the National Assembly's session of January 9, 1873, smote the deputies of the party of the *Appel au peuple* "like a thunderbolt."[1] Might not this blow thrust Bonapartism once more into the limbo from which it had so astonishingly escaped during the past two years? Such was no doubt the hope and expectation of the government of M. Thiers, which immediately ordered all of its Prefects to report[2] how the news had been received in their respective departments. Had the Bonapartists been able to read the replies, they would have found some disappointing, others reassuring. The latter would have revealed, however, that where the Imperial ideal withstood the catastrophe, it was upheld by groups so diversified in social position and aspirations as to require the most thoughtful calculation of the role Bonapartism was to play in the parliamentary drama which was soon to unfold.

The most extreme reactions were reported from the Midi and from Bonapartism's island redoubt. In the Var, the report that the Emperor was dead was received not merely with indifference but with joy by all the parties save his own, and its

---

[1] Jules Richard, *Le Bonapartisme sous la République* (3d ed.; Paris, 1883), 1–2.
[2] AN F⁷12429: "Police générale: Agissements bonapartistes" (hereinafter cited as AN F⁷12429).

Versailles

numbers were insignificant. In Corsica, however, even Thiers' Prefect felt obliged to "show much consideration for the grief and discouragement felt." [3]

In the Southeast and in the Massif Central, no such violent emotions were detected. In the Isère, the news produced "only cold indifference," and was universally interpreted as signaling the end of Bonapartism, while in the Haute-Loire "the effect produced was . . . almost nil," there being "few people who had been directly attached" to the dynasty.[4]

The Prefects of the central, western, and northern regions of France, however, offered evaluations less thoroughly satisfying from a Republican point of view. To be sure, here the results of slothful Bonapartist management and inadequate propaganda were evident, as in the Loiret, where the attitude was one of extreme indifference since the party had "neither an organization nor avowed chiefs" although the Empire had "hitherto possessed a latent strength among a considerable proportion of our rural population." But in the neighboring, better-organized Nièvre, there had been consternation. Bonapartism had made great gains among the peasantry, who feared a Legitimist restoration under which they would fall victims to clerical domination. As for the bourgeoisie, they preferred a return of the Empire to the provisional Republic, since the inactivity of the Orléans princes had ruled out that third alternative.[5]

In the very conservative western department of the Vienne, the bourgeoisie took a different view. They also distrusted the

---

[3] Police Superintendent, Les Arcs, to Director of Sûreté générale, January 16, 1873; Prefect of Corsica to Minister of Interior, January 11, 1873 (AN $F^7$12429).

[4] Police Superintendent, Lyon, to Ministry of Interior, January 17, 1873; Prefect, Haute-Loire, to Minister of Interior, January 18, 1873 (AN $F^7$12429).

[5] Prefect, Loiret, to Minister of Interior, January 12, 1873; report of Police Superintendent, Nevers, January 12, 1873 (AN $F^7$12429).

Bonapartism after Sedan

Republic, but far from preferring the Empire to either of the monarchical dynasties, they expected that the altered circumstances would bring together the supporters of all three, "unifying and fortifying the conservative party." The Poitevin peasants did not share this sentiment of their betters; now that the prospects of an Imperial restoration had become remote, their sympathies were inclining toward the conservative Republic. Any regime which provided "guarantees of material order, security of employment and interests" would seem "excellent" to them, and if Thiers could satisfy their instinctive desire for authority as the Empire had done, the peasants would prefer his regime to the dreaded monarchical restoration.[6]

This attitude was not limited to the rural masses in the West of France. The Prefect of the Nord assured Paris that the great majority of its inhabitants had no political passions, and that any government whatever, monarchical or republican, if it firmly maintained order, would encounter no serious difficulties. (It was not the northern peasant who bewailed his loss, but the numerous miners, who were "generally unthinking and passionate partisans of Napoleon III.") Likewise in the rare northeastern department which could be described as strongly Bonapartist (the Aube), the Prefect declared that the peasant nevertheless would be prepared to accept the Republic if it assured him tranquillity.[7]

In the Saône-et-Loire also, some of the few Bonapartists declared their preference for the conservative Republic over the monarchical alternatives, both less liberal than the Empire. Others insisted, however, that "the Prince Imperial not

[6] Prefect, Vienne, to Minister of Interior, January 12, 1873 (AN F7 12429).
[7] Prefect, Nord, to Minister of Interior, January 11, 1873; Prefect, Aube, to Minister of Interior, January 13, 1873 (AN F7 12429).

Versailles

being responsible for the errors of his father, Bonapartism will become stronger." [8]

This second line of reasoning was the one adopted by the party's parliamentary leadership. In Rouher's estimation the death of Napoleon III was a personal, but not a political loss. Some of the Empire's least convinced supporters might now turn elsewhere, but universal suffrage remained just as powerful a slogan, and the prestige of the dynasty was unimpaired. In fact, led by a youthful pretender unencumbered by an equivocal record, Bonapartists could be more certain of their eventual triumph, though they might have to wait a little longer for it. Rouher's fellow deputies agreed that their bereavement did not lessen their chances. Indeed, before the Prince Imperial came of age, the rival parties, incapable of providing orderly government, would have time to discredit themselves. The Bonapartists' optimism was supported by reports from those regions where allegiance to the fallen regime was instinctive and uncalculating; a correspondent of Eschasseriaux's cited the comment of a Charentais peasant: "Well! don't we have the son? instead of twenty years of happiness the son of the Emperor will give us forty." [9]

Bonapartists had only to wait patiently, according to this view, for the ripening fruit to drop into their hands. Such a policy had the added advantage, in the eyes of men like Magne who had accepted conservative-liberal patronage in 1871, that it ruled out any demagogic displays of unseemly eagerness. "To remain faithful to their banner," the former Minister of Finance wrote to the Empress, "the Imperialists

---

[8] Police Superintendent, Chagny, to Director of Sûreté générale, January 12, 1873 (AN F⁷12429).

[9] Eugène, Baron Eschasseriaux, "Mémoires," twenty manuscript volumes at the château of Oyré (Sarthe), VII, 24–25, 34–35; Richard, *Bonapartisme*, 92–93.

Bonapartism after Sedan

in the Assembly should, I think, unite themselves more than ever to the great conservative party so as to aid public authority to defend social order against its mortal enemies." An inactivity which would amount to renunciation of their cause was impossible, he admitted. But he went so far as to advise supporting Thiers if he consented to lead a united conservative party, since his government would be the best guarantee against the success of the Bonapartists' rivals.[10]

These counsels might well satisfy the bourgeoisie of the Vienne. A conservative unity which embraced Legitimism would not appeal, however, to the miners of the Nord, or to those Nivernais peasants who saw in the Emperor a protection against the King. It could do nothing to arrest the drift, out of fear of Legitimism, of the Poitevin or Champenois peasant toward the Republic. It might make no difference to the loyal Charentais, but if in the Loiret the Bonapartists had been unable to organize when a restoration seemed imminent, they would be unlikely to do better submerged in a conservative bloc. All these disadvantages might not outweigh the desire of some influential Bonapartists for cooperation with the Monarchists, however, particularly now that even the nominal leadership of the Emperor had disappeared. Only six weeks after Napoleon's death, Paul de Cassagnac was complaining publicly that Bonapartists eager to be obedient no longer knew from whom to take their orders.[11] Coming from a man who seldom obeyed at all, this was an ominous pronouncement.

Certainly few people, whatever they said, would turn for lessons in political tactics to the seventeen-year-old who had hurried home to Chislehurst from the artillery school at

---

[10] Pierre Magne to the Empress, January 28, February 10, 1873; in Joseph Durieux, *Le ministre Pierre Magne 1806–1879* (Paris, 1929), II, 298–299, 303–304.

[11] *L'Ordre*, February 22, 1873.

Versailles

Woolwich in the vain expectation of finding his father still alive. Bonapartists invariably chanted the praises of the Prince Imperial "first because it was politic" and incidentally because he "was a really charming child," but their practical attitude toward him was in fact only the obverse of the joke current in Parisian salons that he was "not on the throne because his moustaches are not long enough to hide *ses dents*." [12]

The final tragedy in Zululand, indeed, was not the only element of pathos in the brief life of Napoleon's son. At first, conscious of his youth and inexperience, he insisted on completing his schooling before assuming the full obligations of a pretender. The criticism which his return to Woolwich provoked became especially vociferous when it appeared that, while he was learning the skills of a subaltern in the Royal Artillery, the Comte de Chambord might become King of France. Yet when, having completed his professional training, he did begin to grope for effective direction of his party, he discovered that, like the prince of some grotesque fairy tale, he had been condemned to an eternal childhood. As he remained for the peasants of France, sentimentally, the "little prince," [13] so for the politicians he remained the pupil, not the teacher. It was cold comfort that he was allowed a part of his father's role—he could be the reputed echo of other people's pet ideas and the scapegoat for their mistakes.

The various schools of Bonapartism all claimed with equal assurance that he had accepted their interpretation of the Napoleonic mission. Fidus claimed to have had a hand in his emancipation from revolutionary ideas, and printed as an appendix to his memoirs a draft constitution for the Third Em-

[12] Robert Henrey, ed., *Letters from Paris 1870–1875* (London, 1942), 220; Richard, *Bonapartisme*, 97–98.

[13] Comtesse des Garets, *L'Impératrice Eugénie en exil*, (Paris, 1929), 74–75, 82. Ernest Pinard, *Mon journal* (Paris, 1892–1893), III, 192.

Bonapartism after Sedan

pire which he asserted the Prince had sent him; it rejected universal suffrage and confided legislative power to a chamber of peers, many hereditary, from which even great industrialists and merchants were to be excluded. The Comte de la Chapelle, on the other hand, charged that though the Prince was completely devoted to his father's principles of authoritarian democracy and found it particularly galling that they might be compromised by alliance with "the retrograde parties of monarchy," his ideas were generally ignored by the great personages who abused the authority of his name. Certainly his ineffective efforts to formulate policy between 1875 and 1877 bear out the Count's version of his views, but the only conclusion that the historian need underscore is that it did not really matter what the Prince Imperial thought, even supposing that a young man whose only companions were courtiers and cadets had succeeded in working out a coherent political philosophy.[14]

He was as helpless to repair the party's organizational deficiencies as he was to define its doctrine or legislative tactics. Though he often had a clear perception of what was needed, he could do no more than urge attention to such problems as the enlargement of the local press. Even for information he was dependent on the infrequent reports of politicians who were preoccupied by their own electoral battles.[15] After 1877, he relapsed into isolation. There was no foreseeable end to his confinement in an ill-omened English country-house, where time hung very heavily for an ardent youngster eager to prove that he was more than a *fils à papa*. "Writing letters of condolence, putting up politicians overnight, slapping journalists'

---

[14] Eugène Balleyguier (Fidus, pseud.), *Journal de Fidus* (Paris, 1889), IV, 132–134, 157–158. Cf. the text, 361–370. Comte de la Chapelle in *Le Spécial*, December 22, 1887; quoted in Albert Verly, *Souvenirs du Second Empire* (Paris, 1896), II, 265.

[15] Eschasseriaux, "Mémoires," VIII, 370–371.

Versailles

backs, acting like their pal and working with them to stir up social problems," [16] such a sterile routine could not, he was convinced, advance his cause at all. A battlefield was the place for an artilleryman named Napoleon; when at last he saw a chance of reaching one in South Africa, he gladly discarded his place as gilded figure-head, and departed from the politicians and the journalists—forever.

The son of Napoleon III could exercise little control over the men at Versailles who purported to act in his name. Was it actually the Empress, then, who propelled the Bonapartists into the fateful alliance with clerical Monarchism which overthrew M. Thiers and opened a new phase in French post-war politics? This explanation was advanced at the time,[17] and has satisfied some historians. It absolved the deputies who cast the votes, and has fitted in neatly with a conventional idea of Eugénie's political views. The historian who has observed how tenuous were the lines connecting Chislehurst with Versailles, however, must regard this theory with skepticism, particularly if he recalls that Bonapartist hostility to the Empress dated as far back as possible: to the very fortunate marriage of Mlle. de Montijo.

Admittedly when she suspected that her worst enemy, Prince Napoleon, had a hand in any projected liberal policy, she was likely to denounce it violently. Yet it is difficult to label as a romantic reactionary one who could write: "The wise man should try to have on his side what you call the popular Hydra, and there is no force which can directly oppose it. . . . In this world one cannot merely regret the past; but must use the elements at hand without dreaming of others." [18]

---

[16] Des Garets, *Eugénie*, 200.   [17] Richard, *Bonapartisme*, 111.
[18] Baron de Bourgoing to Mme. Lepic, undated letter in Raoul-Duval papers, château of Le Vaudreuil (Eure). Empress to Countess de Montijo, September 26, 1876; Empress Eugénie, *Lettres familières*,

Bonapartism after Sedan

Even had the Empress been as enthusiastic a reactionary as her many enemies were eager to think her, she was unwilling, or perhaps psychologically unable, to involve herself very closely in the direction of the party. "And how do you envision the Prince returning to France?" she inquired of a visitor one day. The other replied with an apocalyptic description of Napoleon IV, acclaimed by the rural departments, confronting the barricades of Paris. "Napoleon I could do that," murmured Eugénie.[19] She said no more, but in letters to her mother she described her own anxieties openly: "The idea of taking a single step to win the crown of France, which is a real crown of thorns, leaves me cold and indifferent. . . . I am incapable of taking responsibility myself; I content myself with . . . preventing, if I can, others from risking the life of my son in their own interest." [20] It is as improbable that she was capable of devising a political strategy as that any of the exiles of Chislehurst could have enforced one at Versailles.

As a matter of fact, the curious liaison with Legitimism which marked the first strategic option of the Bonapartist delegation in the Assembly considerably antedated the death of Napoleon III. It took shape almost imperceptibly, and in the beginning was as insubstantial as the cigar-smoke in Parisian salons, where the Bonapartists of "Coblence" gossiped with Legitimists about the Pope's advice to Chambord to transmit his rights to the Prince Imperial, or speculated on the possibility that the Bourbon pretender would adopt the

---

conservées dans les archives du palais de Luria et publiées par les soins du duc d'Albe . . . (Paris, 1935), II, 60, 63–64.

[19] Famille Fournier, "Mémoires," twelve manuscript volumes numbered I–VI, VIII, X–XII, XVI–XVII (ACM 4J1509); XVII, 386–387.

[20] Empress to Countess de Montijo, March 7, 1876; Eugénie, *Lettres familières*, II, 52–53.

Versailles

boy. By early summer of 1872, a more realistic plan of an alliance was being actively canvassed in Bonapartist circles, though it encountered considerable opposition.[21] In December, things had gone so far that the Emperor summoned Rouher to England to express his displeasure at the advances made to the Monarchists, wishing it to be understood that he had no intention of becoming the satellite of Legitimism.[22]

Two days after Napoleon's death, however, Paul de Cassagnac proclaimed that the Bonapartists would renew the alliance more closely than ever, and in February Legitimist deputies began to appear at Levert's weekly soirees. It was in vain that the party's ostensible leader, Rouher, pronounced the alliance a chimera which would only involve Bonapartism in the Legitimists' unpopularity: Cassagnac was not to be diverted. At his initiative, a public meeting of the two parties was held in April to choose a joint third candidate for the crucial Paris by-election which Rémusat and Barodet were contesting. The meeting did not go entirely smoothly; hardly had Tarbé of the *Gaulois* taken the chair when someone stood up to demand that there be no union of Bonapartists and Legitimists, and the proceedings were further marred by an occasional cry of "Down with the Empire!" Silence did reign during Cassagnac's address, in which he looked forward to the general elections and foresaw the two parties marching united against the common enemy, the Republic, "which divides us least because it disgusts us most." Nine Parisian

---

[21] Fidus, *Journal*, III, 33, 38, 112, 187–189, 193; Renault to Thiers, June 23, 1872 (BN Cabinet des manuscrits: Nouvelles acquisitions françaises 20658; "Rapports journaliers du Préfet de Police" (hereinafter cited as BN Naf 20658-20660).

[22] The fact that Cassagnac denied that this rebuke had been administered makes it the more likely that it was. *L'Ordre*, December 14, 1872; cf. police report of December 13, 1872 (APP B^A 1257, dossier "Eugène Rouher").

dailies, including the three principal Legitimist ones, endorsed the candidate selected, Colonel Stoffel.[23]

Despite such backing, the Colonel won only 26,000 votes out of a total of almost 350,000. Many Parisian Bonapartists, discontented by the alliance with the Legitimists, voted for Barodet. The first fruits of joint action were thus negligible, and had been gathered at considerable cost, for in a conservative campaign "the party of the *Appel au peuple* lost much of its originality and power." [24]

Why had the Bonapartists allowed Cassagnac to consummate the Legitimist alliance with this bargain, which ended as inauspiciously as it had begun? Up to a point, of course, alliance might be looked upon as a tactical ploy to end the Bonapartists' parliamentary isolation. The less mystical Legitimists who had already perceived that their pretender's principles made his accession to the throne impossible might be willing to throw their support to the Empire and its representatives in order to frustrate the Republic and, especially, the hated house of Orléans. This prospect held out the hope of practical dividends for Bonapartism, not merely in local elections, but also in the Assembly, where a doubled bloc of votes might result.[25]

Yet was not such a liaison so unnatural that it must inevitably prove fleeting? Bonapartists, after all, were supposedly the sons of regicides, and during their periods in power they

---

[23] Richard, *Bonapartisme*, 105; *L'Ordre*, January 11, April 21, 1873; Renault to Thiers, February 18, February 26, April 16, 1873 (BN Naf 20659–20660). Cf. Robert Dreyfus, *La République de Monsieur Thiers* (Paris, 1930), 320.

[24] Richard, *Bonapartisme*, 105, 107–108.

[25] In the Oise by-election, a Bonapartist had already bid for Legitimist support by adopting a nonpartisan platform (Renault to Thiers, October 2, 1872; BN Naf 20659). It was hoped to attract a score of the Extreme Right at Versailles (Renault to Thiers, February 25, 1873; BN Naf 20660).

had, according to fervent Catholics, maltreated the Altar even more than the Throne. Now, however, Bonapartists publicly adopted an expiatory attitude toward the Church. This course was natural for the Bonapartists of "Coblence," but it was surprising to find the *Ordre*, under both Duvernois and Dugué de la Fauçonnerie, attacking laic instruction, urging the prohibition of funerals at which the clergy did not officiate, and even calling for the abolition of the University's monopoly of higher education. An editorial policy of this sort no doubt produced a favorable impression in the Vatican (and thus on the ultramontane faithful in France); how well it conformed to the Napoleonic tradition was another question. Yet these were pronouncements of the party's official voice. A contrary view, for example that the division of Republicans and Bonapartists magnified the threat to the Revolution from Legitimist clericalism, was expressed only by men like Marcus Allart and other members of the "Mountain" who had little influence in the party.[26]

Their new-found odor of sanctity had not been the only surprise of the Bonapartists' party line during the last months of M. Thiers' presidency. The logical corollary of the appeal to the people which had given their group its name and watchword was the dissolution of the Assembly which had condemned their Emperor and from which they had nearly been excluded; there were rumors that they would back Gambetta's campaign to put an end to this unrepresentative body. As the alliance with the Legitimists flowered, however, the *Ordre* declared that since the Assembly included "what remains, except for us, of the conservative forces of French society," Bonapartists would not allow it to be overthrown "by the maneuvers of demagogic barbarism." In mid-December,

[26] *L'Ordre*, November 19, 1871; October 3, 5, 1872; August 7, 1873; Marcus Allart, *Contre-fusion! Réforme! Empire et revanche!* (Paris, 1873), 10–11.

Bonapartism after Sedan

1872, when the issue had come to a head, the *Ordre* announced that the Bonapartist deputies, though confident that new elections would greatly swell their numbers, had decided for reasons of social order to vote against a dissolution.[27]

Against this background it is clear that the Stoffel candidacy was only the culmination of a trend which the Emperor himself, by summoning Rouher, had been unable to arrest, and which had become irresistible now that the pretender's youth required postponing hopes of restoration. The party was already edging toward the conservative unity recommended by Magne, already bidding for the support of the clericalist bourgeoisie before the Emperor's death. Cassagnac had merely carried this policy to its logical conclusion, at a moment when there was no one to stop him. It remained to be seen if Stoffel's fiasco had demonstrated to the Bonapartists that conservative union was a double-edged weapon, and that alliance with the Monarchists might cost them far more than it was worth.

Their judgment would soon be tested, for the victory of Barodet had made a prompt showdown between the President of the Republic and the Monarchist majority at Versailles inevitable. The Bonapartists' choice between the two might seem predetermined, even without the added incentive of conservative union. Apart from the role M. Thiers had played in the history of the Empire, there had since been the harassment of the Bonapartist press, devised with malicious ingenuity by Léon Renault, there had been Prince Napoleon's enforced departure from France under police escort, there were even rumors that Thiers had sent *agents provocateurs* to Chislehurst to tempt the Emperor into a landing straight into the arms of the *gendarmerie*. As for Thiers' own feelings, they were well summed up in his untranslatable

[27] Renault to Thiers, August 13, 1872 (BN Naf 20659); *L'Ordre*, November 29, December 15, 1872.

Versailles

remark: "*Des bonapartistes je m'en f . . . ; ce sont des gredins.*"[28]

Despite such provocations and hostility, Napoleon III had hesitated to encourage the overthrow of his onetime ally and persevering enemy. Though he regretted Thiers' apparent decision to abandon the leadership of the "great conservative party," the Emperor knew that only the President could carry out France's obligations to Prussia. To replace him with MacMahon, whose name was already circulating, would procure no advantages for Bonapartism; it would be far more likely to facilitate the restoration of the Orléans dynasty. Napoleon thus found himself in total disagreement with leading journalists of his party like Dugué and Cassagnac, who scoffed at any monarchical restoration, and insisted that the defeat of Thiers would demonstrate the possibility of the Empire's return.[29] They were already in full editorial cry after the President of the Republic, while Rouher, in line with the policy of conservative union, had pledged his votes to the Right in the first open skirmish with the President in November, saying that a new government at least "would clean house, and that is already something."[30]

The changed circumstances after the Emperor's death led some Bonapartists to think twice about continuing the attack. Their own pretender was unready, and there were disquieting

---

[28] Renault to Thiers, February 10, August 24, 1872 (BN Naf 20658-20659). *L'Ordre*, October 15, 1872. Richard, *Bonapartisme*, 29; Dreyfus, *République*, 17.

[29] Alfred Magne, "Deux visites à Chislehurst en 1872," *Revue hebdomadaire*, VIII (August 17, 1912), 293, 299; Renault to Thiers, April 5, September 22, December 20, 1872 (BN Naf 20658-20659); Comte de la Chapelle, *Déclarations des Napoléon* (Paris, 1878), 17; cf. Comte de la Chapelle, ed., *Oeuvres posthumes et autographes inédites de Napoléon III en exil* (Paris, 1873), 114–115, 269.

[30] Mme. Eschasseriaux to her father, November 28, 1872 (Eschasseriaux, "Mémoires," VI, 441); cf. Renault to Thiers, November 29, 1872 (BN Naf 20659); *L'Ordre*, November 18–19, 1872.

rumors of a fusion of the two Monarchist parties behind one claimant of the throne.

Craftily, Thiers played upon these Bonapartists' misgivings to tempt them into supporting him. Chatting with Pierre Magne early in April, he artlessly turned the conversation to the advantages of the Prince Imperial: "Certainly he would not be my choice, but we must not be blind." Innocent of his country's misfortunes, popular with the peasants, representing a strong government, "it could certainly happen that in a moment of distress, the nation would seek its salvation in him. But, admit it, there are many madmen in his party; they try to create embarrassments for me, to hamstring me." Magne admitted it, but pointed also to the "sensible, moderate, foresighted men" who realized that the Prince's only feasible means of return lay in a plebiscite and that his youth made the postponement of even this desirable for a time. "Thus I do not think that the Bonapartists have the least interest in your departure; on the contrary. They should offer up prayers for the prolongation of your powers and aid you, by merging with the conservative groups, to maintain order." When Thiers objected that the number of Bonapartists of this persuasion must be very small, Magne insisted that it was larger than he thought, and included the Empress.[31]

In mid-May, the Prefect of Police bore Magne out to the extent of reporting that the deputies of the *Appel au peuple* had adopted an attitude of reserve toward the formation of the anti-Thiers coalition. Levert responded to inquiries from the Monarchists with a declaration that he and his friends would preserve their freedom of action and would not pledge their votes except in return for a guarantee of their own interests; their independence was perfectly justifiable, since "they had not had the honor of being invited to the preparatory meetings held by the leaders of the Right." [32]

[31] Durieux, *Magne*, II, 310–311.
[32] Renault to Thiers, May 15, 1873 (BN Naf 20660).

Versailles

Relying upon such information, the President of the Republic sought a midnight meeting with Rouher. There is no telling what he would have been prepared to offer in return for the slim margin of votes which would have assured his victory—perhaps nothing more than what he had delicately hinted to Magne: "A *modus vivendi* . . . which would recognize Bonapartism's right to platonic hopes." But he was never given the opportunity to bid. Rouher, "who scented traps from afar and who especially feared ridiculous adventures," had no intention of making his way stealthily to the appointed rendezvous in the house of a minor bureaucrat. He sent back word that M. Thiers might accost him in broad daylight on the Place de la Concorde, but that he would take "no steps surrounded by mystery." This reply, naturally enough, put an end to the matter. Bonapartist votes would not keep the beleaguered President in office.[33]

Regardless of the Emperor's warnings, the possible advantages of keeping him in power, and the risks of replacing him, the most determined Bonapartists were eager, despite Levert's angling for guarantees, to finish off M. Thiers at the first opportunity. Even the Vice-Emperor, who was certainly capable of a cool balancing of alternatives, could be roused to an unwonted passion by merely thinking of his old adversary of the *Corps législatif*; he wondered aloud why God had left Thiers so long on earth and surmised that it was because the devil feared he would foment a revolution in Hell.[34] The party's rank and file took a similar view. Magne had envisioned a deal with Thiers only if the latter consented to lead a united conservative party, but the President of the Republic had chosen quite another course. As ex-Mayor Fournier saw the coming showdown, "If M. Thiers wins, we shall very soon have the legal Commune;" if he fell "universal suffrage by

[33] Richard, *Bonapartisme*, 103–104.

[34] Rouher to Raoul-Duval, October 28, 1875 (dossier "Lettres de Camden," Raoul-Duval papers).

means of the *appel au peuple* will soon . . . resolve the question of government." [35]

When Baron Eschasseriaux came to compile his memoirs a quarter of a century after the dramatic session of May 24, 1873, he was still as untroubled by doubts as to the wisdom of destroying M. Thiers as he had been at the time. The Baron did not set foot in the *hôtel* of the President after the spring of 1872 because he "understood that the policy of M. Thiers was to arrive at the Presidency of the Republic with the aid of the men of September 4 and even with that of the Communards, over whom he sought to gain influence by consideration and compromise." Although he exulted that his colleagues had been "the arbiters of events which we could turn one way or another at our discretion," their choice seemed to him inevitable. He did not recall any argument among the twenty-five Bonapartist deputies who met at Rouher's on the night of May 19; all agreed that it was the "right" of the Bonapartists to be admitted to the conservative coalition.

> Therefore I was delegated by the meeting, with my colleagues Haentjens and Levert, to come to an understanding next day with the chiefs of the Right and Right Center to obtain guarantees of security and liberty [for the Bonapartists] and of representation in the new ministry which events would produce.

This mission was promptly executed; in response to the statement of the three "that in these negotiations we wanted all the parties to have nothing in view but social order," M. Batbie, for the Orleanists, and the Duc de Bisaccia, for the Legitimists, solemnly gave assurances "that nothing would be done against our rights and our interests, and that we would be kept in touch with all incidents of the crisis." These anodyne promises were renewed on May 21; the two Monarchists "again assured us that nothing would be done without our

[35] Fournier, "Mémoires," XVI, 337.

Versailles

previously being informed, and that we would be given at least M. Magne in the next ministry."

Satisfied, the Bonapartists of Versailles kept their word. The vote which decided Thiers' fate was very close: 360–344. The two dozen Bonapartists voted as one man against him, almost the only time in the history of the National Assembly that they achieved such unanimity. Strong pressure was applied to the few who were hesitant. Eschasseriaux remembered that "it was not without difficulty that we had succeeded in detaching from M. Thiers certain colleagues who liked to work both sides of the street [*vivre entre deux eaux*], to profit from governmental favors, and did not want to quarrel with the President of the Republic, in whose fall they did not believe." Sarrette of the Lot-et-Garonne, for example, was on good terms with the Prefect of his department and would have voted to save Thiers if Eschasseriaux "had not vigorously lectured him in the name of the whole group and . . . escorted him to the vote, to make very sure he was not found and recaptured" by the President's supporters.

Hardly had the votes been safely recorded when the story went round Versailles that the Duc d'Audiffret-Pasquier, one of the bitterest Orleanist enemies of the Empire, was to be the new Minister of the Interior. Eschasseriaux, Levert, and Haentjens at once left the Assembly, now busy electing MacMahon, and hastened to the side room in which the Duc de Broglie was concocting his government. There they expressed their formal intention of obtaining guarantees of the exclusion of Pasquier and the inclusion of Magne. Broglie, who already knew very well that Pasquier had no intention of accepting office, hinted to the three what the composition of his cabinet might be, and without discussing either Pasquier or Magne, "promised us" (as Eschasseriaux's account vaguely concludes) "satisfaction." Whereupon the emissaries, without further argument, withdrew! In his last defiant speech Thiers had warned Broglie that he was doing the Bonapartists' work for them and had inadvertently become their *"protégé."* In fact, it was the Bonapartists who did Broglie's work, and the Duke told the truth when he insisted in his memoirs that this brief, impromptu, inconclusive and very belated interview "was all the protection I received from the Empire and its friends before I became minister!" Against M. Thiers, Bonapartist votes had been practically free for the asking.[36]

After the vote, the Bonapartist press burst forth in an orgy of rejoicing and self-congratulation. Under the headline "THE GOVERNMENT OF DECENT MEN," the *Ordre* proclaimed "God has taken pity on France. Her evil genius . . . has been overthrown." The Bonapartist party, "which so modestly stands back today after having given the monarchical majority the necessary arms," could look to the future with confidence, since "with a strong and resolute government, good Prefects, *parquets*, and mayors, there are always good elections." It was futile for the beaten Thiers to circulate stories that he would champion a plebiscite in order to separate the Bonapartists from their conservative allies; the party's deputies had all agreed to lend their support to the government, whose mission it was to "defend social interests, while renouncing all dynastic preoccupation."[37]

At Versailles the Bonapartist deputies were already discovering that the modest goal of good Prefects and *parquets* might be difficult to attain. On May 25, Eschasseriaux met with his party colleagues of the Charente-Inférieure to plan the changes they would require in the administrative personnel of the department, "for we supposed that the new

---

[36] Eschasseriaux, "Mémoires," VII, 105–109; cf. Duc de Broglie, *Mémoires* (Paris, 1941), II, 175–177. For the Bonapartists' records on all the crucial votes of these years, see Jules Clère, *Biographie des députés* (Paris, 1875).

[37] *L'Ordre*, May 26-29, May 31, 1873.

Versailles

ministers were going to honor faithfully their engagements of the previous day, and that we could expect . . . a rigorous expulsion of all the compromised [Republican] officials. But we soon had to recognize that our hopes would be disappointed." The first change of which they got wind, in fact, was the naming of a Republican Prefect. Confronted with such a direct, personal threat, the Baron went at once to the under-secretary responsible, his colleagues trooping after him, and declared "that it was not in order to have a Republican Prefect that we had joined the Right to overthrow M. Thiers, and that I demanded . . . that the promises made to us by M. de Broglie be kept." He wanted a Prefect "whose ideas and past could inspire confidence in men of order," and threatened "a refusal of cooperation" if his demands were not met. Overwhelmed, the under-secretary yielded, promising to name a personal friend "with whom we would be very satisfied." But Eschasseriaux derived small comfort from this concession exacted by main force: "We felt at once that we could not at all count on the good will and impartiality of men of whom we had been the faithful auxiliaries, but who would soon exclude and combat us."

And so it proved. At Jonzac the Broglie government installed as Sub-Prefect a very young, very timid Legitimist whose only desire was not to cross Eschasseriaux, but in the other half of the Baron's old district, at Saintes, the new appointee was a man with whom he "had no relations . . . since he was a Republican." The Charente-Inférieure was recognized as "a dangerous department in which the former *fonctionnaires* must be maintained to contain and combat if necessary the Bonapartist mentality." Moreover, the new ministers were eager not to antagonize the Republican Left Center, "whom the Orleanists hoped to win over, so as to get rid of us." The Minister of Justice was as reluctant as his colleague at the Interior to meet Eschasseriaux's requests for changes in personnel; in general the men appointed by Thiers remained on the bench.

On the whole, throughout France, not only were Bonapartist deputies denied their hopes for friendly Prefectures and *parquets*; in addition, Bonapartist administrators and jurists who had resigned in 1870 were not reemployed. In the shake-up after May 24, "some Bonapartist Sub-Prefects were taken, but very few; as for the Prefects, there was no thought of taking them." The same was true all the way down the hierarchy of *fonctionnaires*. Eschasseriaux was deluged by job applicants to whom he was unable to give satisfaction; these office-seekers had not understood that the overthrow of Thiers "had not been our work and that we had not entered into the affair except in the interests of social order, seeking to obtain from the members of the [anti-Thiers] coalition a complete abstention from political preoccupations." [38]

Only their concern for social order, indeed, *can* explain why the Bonapartists chose a course of action which, while it brought them no tangible advantages (Magne, himself no militant, was isolated in a government of Monarchists), ended by simply exchanging one implacable adversary for another, slamming the door momentarily on the Republic only to open it to the Monarchy.

For it soon became obvious that there was anything but a "complete abstention from political preoccupations" among the Monarchists with whom they had elected to throw in their lot. The summer of 1873 was hardly half over when the Comte de Paris went to salute the Comte de Chambord at Frohsdorf, thus apparently sealing the pact of fusion between Legitimists and Orleanists which would permit Chambord, as King, to come back into his own.

The *Ordre*, despite its talk of conservative union, had hith-

[38] Eschasseriaux, "Mémoires," VII, 109–110, 112–114, 116, 118, 126–128, 133.

erto treated the restoration of so archaic a regime as the divine-right monarchy as a ludicrous impossibility, since Hugh Capet "would not emerge from his tomb with his knights in order that his family might prevail." In August and September, however, with all Versailles buzzing with rumors of completed preparations, the paper betrayed its anxiety by increasingly shrill denunciations of the Monarchist plotters, into which there crept phrases like "the sublime movement of '89" which had not been heard from official Bonapartism for some time. There was real reason to fear that "all the *hobereaux*, all the people who have changed or lengthened their names in order not to be like their neighbours" (those, that is, whom the policy of conservative union had been designed to attract), might try to "make us submit . . . to the principles and the dynasty which reigned over feudal society." [39]

Rouher himself long remained so obdurately skeptical of the possibility of fusion that he did not interrupt his sojourn in the country, and came to Paris only two days a week. He wondered if the whole affair might not be a characteristic case of Orleanist double-dealing: suffocated by their embrace, Chambord might be forced to put them at arm's length by reiterating his principles, thereby removing himself from contention.[40] The Vice-Emperor's absence from the rue de l'Elysée spared him from having to listen to people who not merely believed in the imminent advent of the Monarchy, but railed at his inaction, which was letting slip a prospective share for Bonapartists in the spoils. One could not wait forever, after all, for readmission to the Prefectures and *parquets*; surely the disappointing sequel of May 24 would not have to be endured again? Rather than face that possibility, many prominent Bonapartists would defect.

[39] *L'Ordre*, January 22, October 9, 1873.
[40] Rouher to Eschasseriaux, September 15, October 2, 1873 (Eschasseriaux, "Mémoires," VII, 165, 174); cf. Richard, *Bonapartisme*, 128.

Bonapartism after Sedan

So many of the "bigwigs" of the party, who "regretted their positions and importance rather more than the Empire," seemed "ready to go over bag and baggage to Royalism,"[41] in fact, that Rouher decided at length to speak out. He publicly approved the calling of a meeting of the deputies of the *Appel au peuple*, which, as on May 24, could anticipate exercising a decisive influence. In May, the Bonapartists had "tried to protect, by a truce, the interests of order, threatened by radicalism." They were not abandoning those interests, and would resume their defense when necessary. Now, however, they were obliged "to take up the defense of the work of our fathers, modern society," for the Legitimist regime was "the manifest negation of democracy," and its restoration would imperil not only universal suffrage, but "civil, political, and religious equality."[42]

His statement was both an epitome of the convictions of authoritarian democrats, and an unambiguous warning to the fusionist plotters that they could not look to the Bonapartists for support or even sympathy, contrary to rumors then circulating. The necessity of publishing such a call to battle, however, revealed how shaky such convictions might be in some Bonapartist minds. On the very day the *Ordre* printed it, the *Gaulois* calculated that the Monarchy would get 340 votes, including fifteen from Bonapartists. This claim the *Ordre* indignantly rejected: the party of the *Appel au peuple* was absolutely united, and the *Gaulois* was counting "a certain number of deputies who have from time to time attended meetings . . . without ever being considered as absolutely belonging" (the very politicians, in other words, whom the party had courted for the past year with slogans of conservative union, rather forgetting in the process that democracy it was now necessary to uphold.) Even the majority of these

[41] Richard, *Bonapartisme*, 125–126.
[42] *L'Ordre*, October 12, 1873.

Versailles

fellow-travelers were absolutely opposed to fusion, the *Ordre* claimed. Brave words, but only five months before, when the Duc d'Aumale had been suggested as a possible successor to Thiers, one-third of the official party of the *Appel au peuple* would have voted for him, according to the observations of a Bonapartist journalist.[43]

As the crisis reached its height in the last week of October, Rouher, scoffing no longer, summoned his following to defeat Chambord on the floor at Versailles. The Bonapartist deputies "unanimously" adopted a firm resolution declaring that since France did not want a revolution in reverse, they would vote against all proposals for a monarchy.[44]

Nothing the fusionists tried had availed to temper this categorical *non possumus*—neither attempts to frighten the Bonapartists at being on the same side as the Reds, nor pleas for abstention, nor threats of MacMahon's resignation, which invited them to choose between fusion and chaos. By October 27, Baron Eschasseriaux, who felt that the Bonapartists' manifesto had had a great effect, found even the supporters of fusion admitting that their chances were diminishing. The danger of defections continued to haunt him; one of his colleagues of the Charente-Inférieure, an Orleano-Bonapartist conservative, was "hiding from us, which proves he has abandoned us." Still, the Bonapartists hoped to win by twenty to twenty-five votes.[45]

As it happened, the decisive vote which would have proved or disproved Eschasseriaux's calculations was destined not to take place. All the King's horses and all the King's men had been mustered in vain; in a letter which the Bonapartist press helped to force from the hands of its thunderstruck recipients

---

[43] Richard, *Bonapartisme*, 114.
[44] *L'Ordre*, October 29, 1873.
[45] Eschasseriaux to Mme. Eschasseriaux, October 27, October 29, 1873 (Eschasseriaux, "Mémoires," VII, 193, 197–198).

and make public, Henri V declared that he would uphold the white banner of his ancestors.[46]

Having contributed materially to the exposure and ruin of fusionist intrigues, the Bonapartist newspapers immediately displayed a remarkable leniency toward the intriguers. Though Bonapartist anxieties had been great and Chambord's letter a providential denouement, far from heaping recriminations on the Monarchists, the *Ordre* hastened to proffer them an olive branch. There was no question of blame for anybody: "The Legitimists find their excuse in the mysticism of their belief." Now that their dreams had been rudely shattered, "the manifest interest of all the conservative groups is to ally, and the duty of the government is to offer them a ground on which they can honorably join to maintain order." What was needed was "a new May 24 . . . with clearer views and more energetic action." [47]

Almost at the moment that the Bonapartists were publicly forgiving the Monarchists, they were privately and even casually rejecting the tentative advances of the Republicans, who understandably supposed that the fiasco of fusion might have created a new situation. On November 3, Thiers, with the backing of the entire Left Center, proposed through Tarbé of the *Gaulois* to elect Eschasseriaux as vice-president of the Assembly, and another Bonapartist as one of the secretaries, if they would support his candidate for the crucial position of president. The Baron asked for time to consider this proposal, but did not feel it urgent to consult the leader of his party. Instead, in the course of the evening he chatted about it with two of his colleagues. They agreed that he should refuse, "not being accustomed to draw personal advantage from decisions taken in the interest of the party." Moreover, "it did not seem

[46] *L'Ordre*, October 27, October 30, November 1, 1873.
[47] *L'Ordre*, November 2–3, 1873.

right to us . . . to take sides with people we had just ousted from power a few months before."

Next morning, Eschasseriaux revealed in a letter to his wife that despite the urgings of a friend of Prince Napoleon's that he accept the deal, he had himself made up his mind to refuse: "It would mean abandoning ourselves without profit to intrigues concerned with people and not principles, and we would appear to desert the banner of order which is our strength." He felt sure that both the *comité de comptabilité* and the deputies of the party would concur in his refusal, and so it proved. Having "fought the fusionists and prevented the success of their plans," they agreed that their duty was "to refuse all cooperation with other opponents, equally dangerous, with whom our self-respect prevented us with dealing after having overthrown them." [48]

The advocacy by a friend of Prince Napoleon of an arrangement with the Left doubtless reinforced the Baron's decision to reject it. The troublesome Prince had in October with characteristic impetuosity endorsed the proposals of a Radical newspaper for a joint Bonapartist-Republican attack on fusion, to arrest the march of clericalism. His intervention, as usual, had been enough to stifle reasonable debate and to relegate the course he advocated to the limbo of Jérômiste aberration. Most Bonapartists had been as quick as the Republicans to repudiate the alliance. The *Ordre* demonstrated that the principles of the two parties were divided by an impassable abyss; while the Republic was "the negation of the monarchical form," the Empire was "the affirmation of a very concentrated and authoritarian monarchy." Republicans considered legitimate "a government imposed on the country by the massed scum of a great city," while Bonapartists knew that if "a good peasant of the first village you come to" were

[48] Eschasseriaux, "Mémoires," VII, 201–203.

asked what he meant by a Republican, "he will reply that it is an incompetent or a drunkard." Tarbé of the *Gaulois*, which was now beginning to take a more "progressive" line, had not been quite so sure (no doubt the reason why Thiers later selected him as an intermediary.) He had pointed out that if cooperation with the Republicans was distasteful, "it nonetheless responds to a political necessity, the necessity of finding a base of operations from which to oppose the parliamentary *coups d'état* with which we are threatened." To checkmate the fusionists, would it be utter folly to sound out the Republicans on the possibility of their supporting a plebiscite? [49]

The instinctive reaction of Eschasseriaux and his colleagues to actual overtures from the Republicans demonstrates how far they were from following Tarbé's reasoning. Though occasionally Republicans might be led by their selfish interests to espouse the same position (as on fusion) that the Bonapartists took, apart from such accidents of circumstance nothing could unite them, not even a common enemy. The hatred of Rouher for the "mountebank" Gambetta, to whom he spoke only once during these years, and his "vile retinue," was only a shade less violent than his loathing of Thiers. The spectacle of Republican successes drove the Vice-Emperor to anguish: "To what a degree of shame this unfortunate country has fallen! Must we despair of seeing it rid itself of this ordure?" [50] As long as he alone was attempting to direct the party's strategy, there would be no alliance with Republicans.

If the little Bonapartist group at Versailles was unable to conclude an alliance with the Left, need it really fall in once more with the baffled but still formidable Right? A decision would have to be taken promptly, for the fusionists, balked of

[49] *L'Ordre*, October 2–3, 1873.
[50] Rouher to Eschasseriaux, April 30, 1875 (Eschasseriaux, "Mémoires," VIII, 99); Richard, *Bonapartisme*, 133.

Versailles

their king, had no alternative but to seat MacMahon more firmly on the vacant throne until the death of Chambord should clear the way for a more tractable pretender. The Bonapartists had proposed a plebiscite as soon as the Assembly reconvened, but without the support of at least one of the other parties, this proposal was hardly more than a gesture. The real question to be decided was the proposed extension of MacMahon's term for seven or ten years, perhaps more. On the face of it, to agree to such a proposal seemed sheer madness. If it passed it would mean that for the duration of this lengthy term the party could not propose the Prince Imperial as an alternative without appearing subversive. Worse, a providential man peeping awkwardly year after year from the wings would become ludicrous. In the meantime the Monarchists would be left sheltered behind MacMahon to pursue whatever nefarious aims they might still harbor, and the Republicans could take satisfaction in the fact that the Marshal, whatever his personal inclinations, would still be called President of the Republic.

Mindful of all this, the editors of the *Ordre* now penned editorials warning that a prolonged mandate for MacMahon was a new May 24 they were not prepared to endure. Yet there was a rub. The Bonapartists had helped replace Thiers with MacMahon as a guarantor of order; could they now refuse to confirm his powers and thus appear to put their own selfish concerns before the preservation of society, to which conservatives in general agreed he was indispensable? Cassagnac and Tarbé argued that they should accept a reasonable prolongation, and if the Monarchists insisted on more than this, should content themselves with abstaining. Thus undermined, the *Ordre* abandoned its attitude of categoric refusal. On the day the question was to be decided, however, it reiterated the limits beyond which Bonapartists must not go: "Except for a prolongation of two or three years, . . . our

friends cannot lend their hands to any combination which
... resembles a defrauding of national sovereignty." The
deputies of the *Appel au peuple* "should vote ... against
the ten years ... the five years ... the seven years of
Marshal MacMahon." [51]

The language employed, significantly, was exhortatory, for
the argument among journalists reflected the divisions of the
Bonapartists at Versailles, and the party's official paper was in
no position to declare what its deputies were about to do.
Rouher had pointed out to the Orleanists the pointlessness of
prolonging a provisional solution, but had agreed to negotiate,
to try to shorten the proposed term to three years at most,
and to obtain a pledge from MacMahon that Broglie would
not, after using their votes, turn from the Bonapartists to the
Left Center for support. The Vice-Emperor soon found, however, not only that the Government would ask for a seven or
even ten year term, but also that a good number of Bonapartists, disregarding his wishes, were ready to support this
proposal.

The meeting of the deputies to determine their stand broke
up without a decision, since men like Haentjens and Levert
shared "the rather general desire among timorous conservatives to give the Marshal ten years of power, thinking thus to
assure themselves ten years of tranquillity." Haentjens, to
conciliate the Monarchists with whom he had been elected in
the Sarthe, even announced to the press with all the authority
of a former president of the *Appel au peuple* that they would
vote for a seven-year term. Rouher gave him such a tongue-
lashing that he ended up by abstaining, but others did not
give in so easily. At a second meeting on the very eve of the
vote "the opinions were still so divided that it was agreed that
each member would vote as he chose ... in order not to
make a spectacle of our disagreement and the indiscipline

[51] *L'Ordre*, November 5–7, November 12, November 19, 1873.

reigning in our ranks." As it was, the spectacle was sorry enough: though Eschasseriaux could pride himself on being among the faithful who voted with Rouher against the Septennate, his colleague of the Charente-Inférieure, Roy de Loulay, was not alone in voting for it, while others unwilling to alienate either Rouher or the Monarchists took refuge, like Haentjens, in abstention.[52]

No doubt the Septennate, which passed by a margin twice as large as the one which had brought Thiers down, would have been enacted even had the Bonapartists voted solidly against it. Nevertheless a dozen deputies (as well as the departmental press syndicate, which had assured MacMahon of its backing) had supported a measure from which, again, it was not easy to see how the Imperial cause would benefit. The disadvantages, on the other hand, quickly became apparent. In December, for example, Eschasseriaux learned from his agent in the Charente-Inférieure that he was having little success in circulating petitions for a plebiscite, since "it was too late, now that the powers of Marshal MacMahon had been extended."[53] If this was the effect in the Southwest, what must have been the case in regions where the Imperialist flame already burned much lower?

For the remainder of the year, the *Ordre* grumbled that the Orleanists by enacting the Septennate had done Gambetta's work for him; the voters, noting the *de facto* existence of the Republic, naturally voted for candidates who endorsed it. With the coming of 1874, however, Rouher let it be known

---

[52] Eschasseriaux, "Mémoires," VII, 94, 208–211, 215–219, 226. The account of the various Bonapartists' votes given by the Baron is not in complete agreement with some contemporary tabulations. Since even the *Journal officiel* of the period has many errors, I have chosen to rely on the Baron's memory; the important thing in any case is that there was serious division in the party.

[53] Ernest Merson, *Confidences d'un journaliste* (2d ed.; Paris, 1890), 143–144; Eschasseriaux, "Mémoires," VII, 232.

that he had resolved to make the best of a bad bargain, counseling his journalists no longer to attack the Septennate. Bonapartists could at least take comfort in the fact that the hopes of both the monarchist parties had now been eliminated, and that at the expiration of the seven years only the Republic would confront the Empire. (After all, it could not reasonably be supposed that the Monarchists would now join with Thiers and Gambetta to consolidate the Republic; they would in that case have had no reason to overthrow Thiers on May 24.) This being so, every effort must be made to bring it home to France that the Prince Imperial was now the only hope of the conservative party.[54]

The pretender was soon to have his eighteenth birthday. Baron Eschasseriaux, convinced that "silence on the date of March 16 would be a sort of suicide, certainly a great cause of discouragement," proposed the public celebration at Chislehurst of his coming-of-age to "make a great impression on public opinion and accelerate the return . . . to the Empire by demonstrating its vitality." Some of his colleagues were dubious: "The timorous, those who had no entourage and no influence in the departments, feared a failure." His insistence carried the day with Rouher (who overcame the misgivings of the Empress), and the Baron proudly proceeded to lead the largest delegation (except for the one from Paris) to the rally.[55]

It was an impressive occasion. A special company had to be formed to manage the transport, lodging, and feeding of the 7,000-odd pilgrims who on March 16 arranged themselves on the lawns of Camden Place round signposts designating their departments. (There was even a delegation from Oran.)

[54] André Daniel, ed., *L'Année politique—1874* (Paris, 1875), 109–110; Richard, *Bonapartisme*, 134–135; *L'Ordre*, December 19, 1873.

[55] Richard, *Bonapartisme*, 135; Eschasseriaux, "Mémoires," VII, 237, 250–252, 285; cf. Fidus, *Journal*, III, 284.

Versailles

They heard the Prince, in a short speech, define the *Appel au peuple* as "salvation and law, restoring power to public authority and reopening a long era of security," and its advocates as "a great national party, without victors or vanquished, rising above all to reconcile them." As the day drew to a close and the faithful, after handing in letters from Frenchmen whose official positions had prevented their coming in person, took their departure, many must have agreed with Eschasseriaux that the real success of the day had been the revelation of the Prince's aplomb and intelligence.[56] Yet the anxieties of the "timorous" were widely shared. Ernest Merson, traveling down to Kent with six former Imperial Prefects, had wondered aloud if he were alone in thinking that this blatant demonstration of Bonapartist strength would frighten the Orleanists into beginning an all-out attack on the party. He was surprised to encounter general agreement.[57]

A more confident Bonapartist might have retorted that, in the spring of 1874, it was not the Bonapartists who should fear the reprisals of Broglie, but the other way round. After the passage of the Septennate, the deputies of the *Appel au peuple* should have been under no illusions that conservative union could afford them any dividends. Eschasseriaux indeed privately declared that they had "no confidence in the ministry, which seeks authoritarian laws against us for the benefit of the Monarchy or the Republic of the Duc d'Aumale." Yet the final break was, predictably, rather long in coming. Composing his New Year's letter to the Empress, the Baron had admitted that "the Septennate is . . . a wide-open field for Orleanist intrigues," but had concluded that "at the risk of more or less fortifying our opponents," he and his colleagues had "decided to support the government in all the measures of order and authority which were the basis of the Empire."

[56] Eschasseriaux, "Mémoires," VII, 275, 288; Fidus, *Journal*, III, 273, 275, 283, 288–290, 292; Daniel, ed., *Année politique—1874*, 142.
[57] Merson, *Confidences*, 242–243.

Bonapartism after Sedan

Although some of Broglie's Prefects were using their powers in Orleanist party interests, others, the Bonapartists hoped, might yet see the necessity of cooperating with the spokesmen of the Empire. It was in accordance with this reasoning that on January 12, 1874, the Bonapartist deputies had voted for a motion of confidence in Broglie. But their votes were ill-requited: the fête of March 16 "encountered the greatest hostility" from the Orleanists; the government began using its new power of appointing mayors to name Republicans in towns which Bonapartists regarded as within their domains. This was the last straw, and most, though again not all, of the deputies of the *Appel au peuple* joined in the coalition of discontents which brought Broglie down on May 16, 1874.[58]

It was less than a year since Bonapartist votes had helped to put Broglie into office. The party had accumulated a long list of grievances against the haughty Duke before it reversed its stand. He had failed properly to reward the Bonapartists for their part in overthrowing Thiers; he had so mismanaged the purification of the government that the *Ordre* frankly declared to complaining Republicans that "if we were the masters, the purge would have been quicker and more complete"; and also, in supreme bad faith, he had been a witting accomplice in the intrigues of fusion. After that had failed, he had, in forming a new government, first approached the Left Center. (The Bonapartists did not know that Broglie's own preference was to preserve conservative union, but his preference did not matter since it was not shared by his Orleanist friends. This view of the majority of the Orleanists was to be of the greatest import in the next few years.)[59]

After Broglie's fall, at a new turning point, the Bonapartists

---

[58] Eschasseriaux to Mme. Eschasseriaux, November 30, 1873; Eschasseriaux to the Empress, December 29, 1873 (Eschasseriaux, "Mémoires," VII, 228, 239, 248, 266, 274).

[59] *L'Ordre*, February 28, June 5, June 11, June 17, October 9, 1873; Broglie, *Mémoires*, II, 274–276.

again brushed off the advances of the Left. On the evening of May 16, with France once more without a government, Eschasseriaux had left the château of Versailles and was boarding the Paris train with Rouher when the latter was informed that the leaders of the three groups of the Left were asking for an interview with him to decide upon the composition of a new ministry from the new majority. The Vice-Emperor, "rightly not caring to involve himself personally in negotiations of this nature where persons rather than principles would be involved and not having much faith in a serious result from a momentary coalition," delegated the Baron to represent him. Hurrying back to the Assembly, Eschasseriaux had an interview with Duclerc, president of one of the Republican groups, but he saw at once that "the individual pretensions of the chiefs and their spirit of exclusiveness would soon make all agreement impossible." The Left really did display very little desire to accommodate their guest, offering, at the insistence of the Left Center, such fantastic lists of presumptive ministers as no Bonapartist could have accepted. So when the clock struck 8:30, the Baron left them, as he had agreed with his chief that he would.

Meanwhile the *Gaulois*, ever hopeful, was championing the plan which probably had prompted the Left's approach— formation of a ministry drawn from all the parties for the express purpose of carrying out an *appel au peuple*. If the intransigence of the Left Center had not served to burst such a bubble, the analogous attitude of the Bonapartist deputies certainly did. Meeting next day, they "agreed in advance that no member of the group . . . would enter a ministerial combination. We could not and would not associate ourselves with the policy of an Assembly which basically was hostile to the Empire and dominated by the idea of fabricating a constitution to prevent its return." [60]

If the plan for such a constitution had not yet germinated

[60] Eschasseriaux, "Mémoires," VII, 312–315.

in the minds of the Republican Left Center and Orleanist Right Center when Broglie fell, the next week brought an event which undoubtedly hastened its development. The throngs of picnickers at Chislehurst had already been a powerful warning: now came a *coup de foudre*. On May 24, 1874, a by-election in the Nièvre pitted a Republican and a Legitimist against the Baron de Bourgoing, a former Imperial equerry who had ringingly declared in his *profession de foi*: "My convictions have not changed. I have remained faithful to the Empire." Forecasts favored the Republican in a department which only six months before had sent a Radical to Versailles. The results were: Bourgoing, 37,599; M. Gudin, Republican, 32,157; the Comte de Pazzis, Legitimist, 4527. Bourgoing triumphantly took his departure for Chislehurst to receive the congratulations of Napoleon IV. He was the first of a series of new deputies who were to make that journey in the remaining months of the Assembly, but one was enough. Ministers "could not disregard this event which had a great impact on the country"; it "terrified the Orleanists and was the start of new persecutions against us." [61]

After the *coup de foudre*, the *coup de théâtre*. A fortnight after Bourgoing's triumph, the Orleanist Charles Savary mounted gravely to the tribune of the National Assembly to lay before it a document, providentially discovered on the floor of a railway carriage, which gave the shocked deputies a glimpse of the labyrinthine conspiracy which had enveloped all of France in its meshes. The letter, which bore the printed heading and seal of the *comité central de l'appel au peuple*, contained detailed and cynical advice to the Bonapartists of the Nièvre on what to promise to retired or active army officers to elicit their influence in favor of Bourgoing's candidacy. (The signature was illegible.)

[61] Eschasseriaux, "Mémoires," VII, 317–318; Daniel, ed., *Année politique—1874*, 220–221.

Versailles

From what he already has learned of the proceedings of the central committee, the reader may judge of the astonishment which the reading of this document evoked on the Bonapartist benches. There had been suspicions that the Orleanists were preparing to mount some kind of counteroffensive, but this seemed so preposterous that Eschasseriaux's impulse was to spare the Government the embarrassment of heeding it: "As I saw it was false from beginning to end, I leaned forward to the Minister of Justice sitting in front of me and told him to keep calm, that this document was false and that it was an unworthy maneuver launched by the beaten opponents of M. de Bourgoing." Eschasseriaux did not even suspect what the Bonapartists later learned, "that this document had been fabricated at the Prefecture of Police in the office of M. Léon Renault with the participation of Duc Decazes and M. Emmanuel d'Harcourt, secretary to the Marshal." [62]

Rouher confidently demanded an investigation, a safe move to make if one assumed that Savary's allegations were going to be treated according to the rules of evidence, since his "document" was literally too good to be true. It was less prudent of the Vice-Emperor to deny that he knew of any committee after the Minister of Justice had announced that he would investigate the "comité central" and its activities, and the Minister of the Interior had added that any such committee discovered would be broken up and prosecuted.[63]

His complacency reflected his assurance that the police themselves would give him ample warning of any perquisitions, and in this he was not mistaken. When the news came, toward the end of June, he speedily removed all his papers to

---

[62] Eschasseriaux, "Mémoires," VII, 323–324; Daniel, ed., Année politique—1874, 234–235. Broglie (Mémoires, II, 300), no friend of the Bonapartists, agreed that the letter was "apocryphal."

[63] Richard, Bonapartisme, 141; Daniel, ed., Année politique—1874, 235.

Bonapartism after Sedan

a place of safety, and asked Eschasseriaux, who was busy concealing his own dossiers and laying false trails to confuse his shadowers, to call on Mansard and make sure he was doing the same. (The minutes of the meetings of the *comité de comptabilité* as well as documents relating to the newspapers the party subsidized were in Mansard's possession.) The Baron found him in a room filled with papers in disorder, apparently faithfully executing Rouher's orders. Satisfied, he went on his way, after Mansard had assured him that everything would be removed that night.

When the police swooped down next morning, they were nevertheless able to carry off this treasure-trove intact, fortunately for the Orleanists and their ally, Renault, since it enabled them not only to give Rouher the lie, but to abandon Savary's initial red herring. Why Mansard allowed this to happen remained a mystery. A charitable explanation was that he had an archivist's temperament, besides being "very *paperassier*, very full of his own importance and very naive." Eschasseriaux and Rouher had darker suspicions of this man "who had a beautiful apartment, with the expenses of a mad wife and of an irregular *ménage* as well." When they learned that he had allowed the seizure of such vital papers as the "correspondence of our principal friends in the departments at whose homes searches were later made," they could not doubt "that our secretary received his principal resources from the police." [64] In either case, the fact that such an individual had been permitted to occupy a key position at the very center of the party's councils was, ironically, the best argument one could advance that the "great Bonapartist conspiracy"

---

[64] Eschasseriaux, "Mémoires," VII, 337–339; Richard, *Bonapartisme*, 141–143. A police report of March 9, 1875 in Mansard's dossier (APP B^A 1171) declared that Rouher had obtained "the most irreproachable proofs" of his treason.

Versailles

posed no very serious threat to the existing institutions, such as they were.

At the next meeting of the committee, the several former *Gardes des sceaux* who sat on it were asked their opinions of the legal position. They agreed that the committee, not having more than twenty members, was safe from the law. It was pointed out to the one member who gave vent to recriminations that the minutes of the committee had been kept at the request of the Prince Imperial, whose right and duty it had been since coming of age to receive them. From a judicial point of view, indeed, the Bonapartists were in a quite defensible position: the central committee was small enough to be legal, and had no organic connection either with similar groups in the provinces, or with the press syndicate. (It was coincidental that Mansard, secretary of the committee, was also the press syndic.) Since the Public Prosecutor himself doubted the authenticity of the Savary letter, he really had no case to prosecute, and he admitted it: "I am still persuaded that some relations must exist between M. Rouher and many of the other committees established in the provinces, who receive instructions from the chief of the party; but I do not have proof, and I do not see, at present, where I could find it." Thus in December of 1874 the judicial proceedings were closed by an *ordonnance de non-lieu*.[65]

However the judicial branch of the government was not the only one with a word to say on the matter: there was the legislative. The Assembly authorized a committee to investi-

[65] Charles Savary, ed., *Deuxième rapport fait au nom de la commission d'enquête parlementaire sur l'élection qui a eu lieu dans le département de la Nièvre; Assemblée Nationale no. 3087: Annexe au procès-verbal de la séance du 11 juin 1875* (Versailles, 1875), 69; Eschasseriaux, "Mémoires," VII, 340–341, 349; VIII, 11; Daniel, ed., *Année politique—1874*, 405–407; Daniel, ed., *Année politique—1875*, 207–209.

gate the Nièvre election, and the committee, after some difficulty, obtained the evidence on the basis of which the prosecutor had refused to prosecute, with the intention of giving it the widest possible circulation.[66]

While the public waited in suspense for these revelations of the Bonapartist plot, it could see on every hand the presumable results of the plot, as Bonapartist after Bonapartist won by-election after by-election. In fact, of the thirteen elections held between May, 1874, and February, 1875, the government won one, whereas seven Republicans and five Bonapartists divided the rest. What was equally frightening from an Orleanist point of view was that Bonapartists had compiled impressive totals in five of the seven departments where they did not win.[67] Since these elections were scheduled at almost monthly intervals, the results were a constant bludgeoning—from the victory of Le Provost de Launay in the Calvados in August to the victory of Cazeaux in the Hautes-Pyrénées in January, less than a fortnight before the National Assembly, by one vote, adopted the Wallon Amendment.

Had the public and the government known something of how organizationally negligent and ideologically rigid the Bonapartists continued to be during 1874–1875, they might have found this roll of victories less impressive. In the Maine-et-Loire election, for example, they knew that the Bonapartist, Berger, had come in on the first *tour de scrutin* virtually neck-and-neck with the Monarchist candidate of the government, and had desisted in favor of the latter for the second *tour*. They could not know that Rouher, informing a correspondent that he had written Berger "not to be dis-

[66] Daniel, ed., *Année politique*—1875, 64–67, 200.
[67] Two seats were vacant in the Alpes-Maritimes. Jacques Gouault, *Comment la France est devenue républicaine: Les élections générales et partielles à l'Assemblée nationale 1870–1875* (Paris, 1954), 176–177.

Versailles

couraged, to work from this moment to prepare for the general elections and complete his organization," had wondered "Will he do it? Inertia is our great problem; we want to win without taking any trouble." Nor could they measure the potential consequences of the Vice-Emperor's conviction that the Bonapartists must "appear to prefer" the Monarchist to the Republican in the run-off, even though the government had applied pressure against Berger, and in spite of the fact that some 5,000 Bonapartist voters ignored Berger's advice and voted for the Republican on the second *tour*.[68]

Another fact also was easily overlooked: chance had dictated that ten of these thirteen by-elections be held in the northern, central, and western regions. Bonapartism might not have come so close to matching Republican victories had the contests been more evenly distributed geographically. Nevertheless, in Eschasseriaux's summation, "The year 1874 saw a great Bonapartist current develop. . . . But our increasing successes . . . led our adversaries first to persecute us, then to come to an understanding to block our path with a constitution. . . ."

A symbolic conjunction of these two campaigns occurred at the session of the National Assembly on February 25, 1875, when, after voting the laws which were to form the longest-lived of modern French constitutions, the deputies heard M. Savary's preliminary report on his sifting of the great Bonapart conspiracy.[69] His final report, complete with a 500-page documentary annex in quarto, did not appear until the summer of 1875, when it was quickly smelted down into cheap pamphlets for mass distribution by Republican propagandists. The Orleanist and Republican deputies had not awaited these

---

[68] Eschasseriaux, "Mémoires," VII, 390–392, 398; Daniel, ed., *Année politique—1874*, 338–339.

[69] Eschasseriaux, "Mémoires," VIII, 25; Daniel, ed., *Année politique—1875*, 76–77.

details; in the opinion of the Duc de Broglie, it was while discussing their publication in the committee investigating the Nièvre election that the two groups had sealed the unholy alliance from which the Third Republic emerged.[70]

The reaction of public opinion to the Savary report was disastrous for the party of the *Appel au peuple*. Respectable people who had previously subscribed openly to the *Ordre*, *Pays* or *Gaulois* now had them sent to their servants or tenants; the *fonctionnaires* stopped subscribing altogether rather than run the risk of discharge.[71]

Thus the Bonapartists, denied further victories by the government's decision to hold no more by-elections, simultaneously saw themselves branded as conspirators and confronted with a duly legitimized Republic in whose presence "conspiracy" would be regarded by many of the *bien-pensants* to whom they had been so eager to appeal as even more reprehensible. Ironically enough, both of these enormous obstacles to their hopes ultimately could be traced to the famous *comité de comptabilité*. Futile in Paris and in the provinces for Bonapartist purposes, the committee had admirably served Orleanist purposes at Versailles.

Even this disaster was not the last of the Imperialists' misadventures in the National Assembly. There was to be one more ironic twist; they finally entered into effective negotiations with Gambetta—but only because his help was essential if they were to conceal the division in their own ranks over yet another question of principle.

The issue this time was whether to support *scrutin d'arrondissement* or *scrutin de liste* in the electoral law which

---

[70] Broglie, *Mémoires*, II, 342–344. (The Duke thought the whole investigation a hypocritical farce abetted by the ambitious Renault.) Daniel, ed., *Année politique*—1875, 200; cf. Eugène Jacquet, *Le complot bonapartiste* (Paris, 1875).

[71] Richard, *Bonapartisme*, 147.

Versailles

was to complement the new constitution. The *Ordre* had long insisted that the former method was infinitely preferable: in the *arrondissements*, the peasants with their preferences for "order and conservation" dominated the electorate. They would vote for a familiar local "agricultural, industrial, or other notable" whose candidacy was based on "family position, fortune acquired," or membership in the department's *Conseil général*. *Scrutin de liste*, on the other hand, meant a "packet of candidates," not necessarily notables, relying chiefly upon the appeal of their party to a diverse, department-wide electorate.

When the former Prefects and deputies of the Empire were asked for their opinions, *scrutin d'arrondissement* was defended by "those who had stayed at home since September 4 without involving themselves in politics," but who knew that their influence, a noncommittal platform, and perhaps some cozy arrangement with fellow conservatives could get them elected within the confines of one *arrondissement*. The majority, those who had "remained on the firing line," with whom Baron Eschasseriaux sided, favored *scrutin de liste* as "more independent of administrative pressure and especially capable of developing in the masses a great current against the present regime." Rouher had made the Baron responsible for calculating in how many departments this form of polling would return a complete Bonapartist slate. Eschasseriaux learned from the Republican *rapporteur* of the eventual government bill (which prescribed *scrutin d'arrondissement*) that the Minister of the Interior had predicted a Bonapartist sweep in thirty-six departments with *scrutin de liste*, three more than his own figure. To counter this threat, the Orleano-Republican coalition advocated voting in the *arrondissements*. Short of an ever-more-problematical *coup d'état*, indeed, lists of candidates who would generate a "great current" by campaigning for an Imperial restoration were obviously the only means now left to the Bonapartists to undo the work of which M. Wallon had laid the cornerstone.

When, in November, the party's deputies met to discuss their stand, however, Eschasseriaux found that there was a considerable sentiment in favor of *scrutin d'arrondissement* "resulting from personal preoccupations about reelection which prevailed over the interests of the party," among the least courageous, astute, and electorally well-established of his colleagues. The eloquence of Rouher and Raoul-Duval failed to sway the dissidents, men like Sarrette of the Lot-et-Garonne "who had only a local position," or like Ganivet of the Charente who "confined themselves to an *arrondissement* of which they were sure and were satisfied with an easy success." They were noisily supported by Paul de Cassagnac "who treated as dishonest all those who did not wish to vote for *scrutin d'arrondissement*." (He and his father knew they could count on being elected in the two most Bonapartist *arrondissements* of the Gers, but were not nearly so confident of leading a victorious list in a department whose politics were characterized by an embittered polarity.)

A second meeting quite failed to resolve the dispute, which divided the deputies into roughly equal camps. Since neither side would give way, it was proposed that the party abstain *en bloc*, but to the supporters of *scrutin de liste* this compromise seemed nothing less than a betrayal of Imperial interests. Finally the meeting agreed that each deputy would vote as he chose, but "in order to conceal such a regrettable decision on a question of this importance, it was decided to have an understanding with the Left . . . to settle the question by a secret vote."

Gambetta condescended thus to cover the divisions of his enemies in the hope that he could later have their votes for a project of his own. The secret vote was close—356–326 in favor of *scrutin d'arrondissement*; a united Bonapartist bloc would have been almost enough to reverse it. "Thus," lamented Eschasseriaux, "we returned by this Orleanist vote to the electorate of the *régime censitaire*. . . . This personal polemic of the Cassagnacs against *scrutin de liste* brought about its defeat . . . and had fatal consequences for the party of the Empire." The general elections soon to be held would be much more parochial in character, much less like a plebiscite, and, in battles fought on local lines, the lack of a Bonapartist newspaper in every *chef-lieu d'arrondissement* would be much more sorely felt.[72]

After this fiasco, in the very last days of the Assembly, in December 1875, the Bonapartists took the ultimate step which brought them to a position diametrically opposed to the conservative union of May 24, 1873. Many of them now thirsted for revenge on the Monarchist constitution-makers. Already in midsummer Eschasseriaux had spoken out against any further cooperation with the parties of the Right. Even to aid in the repression of Republican activities, he insisted, his party should not relinquish for an "alliance with the enemies of universal suffrage and national sovereignty" the independent position dictated by both its principles and its interest.[73] Now, having accepted Gambetta's help, the Bonapartists returned the favor by actively backing his plan for the destruction of the Orleanists.

On December 21, Raoul-Duval, who had come to exercise great influence over the strategy of the group, informed the Prince Imperial that his plan for "crushing the Orleanist center between the Lefts and the Right is . . . today realized, thanks to the cooperation of M. Rouher and to the conduct of the majority [again, not all] of the group of the *Appel au peuple*." In the elections of the 75 life-senators, only three

[72] Eschasseriaux, "Mémoires," VII, 309–310; VIII, 138–139, 185–189; *L'Ordre*, February 3, 1874.
[73] Eschasseriaux, "Mémoires," VIII, 50–51, 121.

Bonapartism after Sedan

Orleanists had been named, though life-senators had been their own idea. Once again the Bonapartists' votes were crucial, and this time, under the spurs of Raoul-Duval and Gambetta, they cast them with decision. Each morning while the balloting went on in the Assembly, the two met to agree on a list of candidates. Raoul-Duval "posed our conditions, which were to exclude . . . all the Orleanists and to replace them with Legitimists, called *chevau-légers*, who had not voted for the Constitution." The Bonapartists themselves "refused to appear on these lists and . . . insisted only on excluding those who had persecuted us the most since the fall of M. Thiers by betraying their engagements." Gambetta's contribution to the bargain was to discipline those of his friends who found it repugnant to vote for Legitimist antiques. The transactions concluded in mutual satisfaction; Gambetta maneuvered into the second "conservative" chamber a phalanx of Republicans, while Raoul-Duval pricked for proscription the names of the most troublesome enemies of the Bonapartists. (Eschasseriaux vetoed a safe senatorial berth for the Republican Prefect of September 4, as well as for M. Dufaure, another nemesis of his in the Charente-Inférieure.) Better still, the Orleanists found themselves barred from the sanctum sanctorum of the constitutional edifice they had built in fear of the Empire.[74]

Thus the end of the Assembly saw a total reversal of alliances. Having struck their first blow in 1873 for Broglie against M. Thiers, the Bonapartists now struck the party of Broglie a blow which was of indirect aid and comfort to M. Thiers. In later years, as the party's fortunes ebbed, some

---

[74] Raoul-Duval to Prince Imperial, December 21, 1875; Gambetta to Raoul-Duval, December 19, 1875 (Raoul-Duval papers); Eschasseriaux, "Mémoires," VIII, 217–219. Cf. Daniel, ed., *Année politique—1875*, 345–347.

Versailles

reflective Bonapartists blamed its downfall on these apparently inconsistent tactics. The historian who evaluates the performance of the Bonapartists at Versailles cannot overlook such a serious charge as that set forth in 1878 by Léonce Dupont in his pamphlet entitled, pointedly, *Les deux démocraties: République-Empire*.

Dupont argued that the Bonapartists, if they deigned to descend into the parliamentary cockpit at all, should have had the wisdom to elect the opposite course from the one they had initially taken. Choosing between the Monarchist Right and Thiers should have been "a matter, not of recalling our preferences, grievances or repugnances," but "of weighing carefully the advantages for democracy and for the Bonapartist cause of an alliance with one or the other." Rouher might have had no other aim than the humiliation of a man who was his personal, as well as political enemy, but others, less biased, should have recalled that in 1848, Thiers, frustrated in his desire to lead the Republic himself, had turned to Louis Napoleon. In 1873, to maintain himself in power with Bonapartist votes, the President of the Republic "appeared disposed . . . to make a formal contract" to guarantee a plebiscite when he eventually left office. The ages of the President and of the Prince Imperial would have made agreement on a date quite easy. Of course there was the risk that the wily old man would not honor such an engagement; but a provisional Republic under him offered Bonapartism a better prospect than did his overthrow, which might well have led to a monarchical restoration of indefinite duration. Failing to sign the "contract" which Thiers himself accepted had been a blunder. It would at least have guaranteed what alliances with the Right could never secure: a plebiscite, the only real way to restore the Empire. If Bonapartists took their own doctrine seriously, their best hopes had lain in the old schemer, for if there was one man capable of bringing the Republic to an end, it was the one "who, alone, had been able to procure its acceptance."

Neglecting these considerations, the party had joined in the coalition of May 24, though "in reality, it would have been very difficult . . . to specify the advantages which we hoped to derive from it in the present and for the future." After this, Rouher could not block the Septennate, for it was the natural sequel of May 24. "What he had done to shake the Republic consolidated it, and his allies . . . turning toward a political establishment which brought them the support of . . . Republicans, left the little group of the *Appel au peuple* in sad abandonment," and itself divided. The Vice-Emperor dethroned had been a hopelessly inept tactician in comparison with the Opposition under the Empire. Then, the Republicans had lined up with the Legitimists against the majority; but now "the Imperialists did everything in the world to escape alliance with the Republicans" against the Monarchist majority.

This instinctive preference, in Dupont's view, demonstrated that the Bonapartists' failure proceeded from causes more fundamental than the tactical clumsiness of the Vice-Emperor. He contrasted the tenor of the Prince Imperial's speech on coming of age with the sentiments of most of the deputies of his party: "The democratic doctrine of the appeal to the people and the Napoleonic tradition were affirmed at Chislehurst as they had never yet been affirmed in the Assembly of Versailles either by the speeches or by the votes of any Imperialist." He complained that the party took little interest in discovering the inclinations of the masses and appealing to them. Indeed, it positively opposed them. As a result, "always they preferred their enemies on the Right to their enemies on the Left." In fact, in many ways they were *indistinguishable* from their enemies on the Right: "There were very few who troubled themselves to any degree whatever to formulate the doctrine which bound them to the Empire rather than to any other portion of the conservative party." [75]

It is easier to dispose of Dupont's first criticism (that there was a profitable alternative parliamentary alliance which the Bonapartists chose to ignore), than of his second, which is not entirely compatible logically with the first (that the deputies, lacking a coherent, characteristically Bonapartist outlook, invariably inclined to conservative preferences.)

Applying hindsight from a greater distance than Dupont did, one suspects that his dissatisfaction at the admittedly substantial setbacks the Bonapartists suffered led him to postulate illusory benefits from the alternative course they had spurned. Even Ollivier had admitted that the propaganda for conservative union which began before the Emperor's death was "perhaps a tactic: while Thiers and the Radicals try to swindle each other, Rouher tries to absorb the Monarchists, who themselves hope to destroy him." The trouble with it, even as an opportunistic tactic, is implicit in that last clause: conservative union, while limiting Bonapartist freedom of action, would not pay dividends until the Monarchists gave up their own hopes, but then they would not necessarily turn to their conservative allies. The Bonapartists had genuine difficulty understanding this. They could not see why Monarchists would not recognize realities and enter a (Bonapartist) conservative union, though they were provoked to howls of rage at Legitimist impudence in suggesting that they should enter a (Monarchist) conservative union. (The only condition that Bonapartists stipulated was that the union end with a plebiscite—why should anyone object to that?) [76]

[75] Dupont, *Deux démocraties*, 7, 9, 15–21, 24, 36.
[76] Ollivier, *Lettres*, 141, *L'Ordre*, November 29, 1871, June 21, 1872.

Bonapartism after Sedan

It was certainly true that, once at Versailles, the Bonapartists had to find an alliance, on pain of remaining in impotent isolation. But it is by no means so clear that a democratic union launched by the preservation of Thiers in May, 1873, would have been any better a choice. The old man would not have returned from the grave to enforce a plebiscite secretly pledged to the Bonapartists if he had died in the Elysée in 1877. He had already shown himself quite capable of using Bonapartism as an *épouvantail*; he might well have proved a more adept scenarist than the Orleanists of the great Bonapartist conspiracy, even if he had owed the party his political life. Overthrowing him had promptly raised the danger of a monarchical restoration, but that threat in the end proved groundless, thus vindicating those, like Rouher, who had been loath all along to believe in it. Subsequent *pourparlers* with the Left added little to the attractiveness of democratic union. The Bonapartists can be blamed for casually leaving negotiations to a man like Eschasseriaux, with his quaint emphasis upon consistent "principles" rather than "personal advantage," but the offers of the Left were never particularly inviting. Surely the most to be hoped for from that quarter was the sort of temporary juxtaposition of interests which Raoul-Duval and Gambetta exploited in 1875.

The defect of Dupont's reasoning, as of the opposite reasoning of those who clung to the principle of conservative union while the Orleanists deserted it for the Republic, was that it assumed that only the Bonapartists, who spoke for the majority of the population, had liberty of action. They had only to choose *either* conservative *or* democratic union, and the other elements of the political kaleidoscope would fall obediently into place around them. The Emperor, as his hesitations suggest, knew better than this. Rouher also knew better, if not before, then certainly after the overthrow of Thiers. "Our position in the Assembly," he wrote to Eschasseriaux in

1874, "will continue to be difficult. We have only the value of a makeweight [*appoint*] there, and that makeweight does not have a great deal of cohesion; we shall be condemned to go from one tack to the other [*louvoyer*]." [77] Caught between the two extremes of French politics, Legitimism and Radicalism, while grotesquely underrepresented at Versailles because of the conditions of the election of February, 1871, the Bonapartists could not hope to control the game while the other players stood inertly by or played the hand the Bonapartists dealt them. The most they could hope for was to prevent a coup which would end the game altogether, and incidentally to avoid playing into the hands of their opponents. Rouher's defenders could argue that these modest aims had been realized by 1876; Thiers and Chambord had been stopped, the deal with Gambetta had crippled the Orleanists. True, there was now a duly enacted Republican constitution, but it provided for revision, and in any case Republics did not last in France. Thus one might reply to Dupont that what the Empire's representatives faced was not a *choice*, "either . . . or" but an *imperative*, "neither . . . nor," and that the Vice-Emperor's policy had rightly been governed by that imperative. True, in following it he had been more often on the Monarchist than on the Republican side, but this was because Dupont's analogy with the tactics of the opposition under the Empire was a false one: the Republic, not the Monarchy, was the real obstacle to the immediate advent of a Third Empire.

Yet the necessity of applying his makeweight first on one side, then on the other, had shown Rouher how lacking it was in cohesion. This raises the question implicit in Dupont's second criticism of the Bonapartists at Versailles: were they always governed, in casting their votes, by such a reasoned

[77] Rouher to Eschasseriaux, October 28, 1874 (Eschasseriaux, "Mémoires," VII, 425).

strategy, or sometimes by an instinctive preference for conservative principles?

Often, of course, they did not think in such lofty terms. Remember the indignant accents of Baron Eschasseriaux: "It was not in order to have a Republican Prefect that we had joined the Right to overthrow M. Thiers." When the echo of the last rhetorical flourish had died at Versailles, all these men had to return to the provinces to fight elections, reward their henchmen, punish their enemies, under the eye of a powerful administration. The very practical consideration of how their votes might help or hinder them in these tasks inevitably weighed heavily in their decisions. Indeed they were far more adept at this sort of calculation than at the negotiations in the corridors which were to make the parliamentary history of the Third Republic so baffling to the uninitiated. Unwilling or unable to accept that they now represented only a faction of opposition, Rouher and Eschasseriaux invariably recoiled from the hard bargaining necessary in such traffic. Never, until Raoul-Duval's stratagem of 1875, did the Bonapartists exact a full price for their frequently crucial votes.

Disdain or lack of aptitude for the parliamentary game, however, cannot explain all their gifts of votes to the ungrateful conservatives. For some of the deputies of the *Appel au peuple* Dupont's second indictment holds true. They *were* instinctively more conservative than democratic. Though, according to Napoleon III, Republic and Empire were the twin offspring of the Revolution, many Bonapartists were confident that their place was invariably in the opposite camp from Republicans. Mayor Fournier of La Rochelle, for example, wondered why the Republic so attracted the young and illeducated. He thought it must be because these groups, ignorant alike of traditions and social realities, uncritically accepted the notion of human equality, and aspired to the unattainable goal of universal freedom and happiness. People of greater experience like himself, however, knew that public security and French grandeur required "the monarchical form" of government—he did not feel it necessary to specify *which*. What the Empire meant, then, to this characteristic figure of the Bonapartist "Plain" was little more than the "monarchical form." His denial in 1871 that his fate was linked to the Bonapartes reflected the fact.

When he was elected to the Chamber of Deputies in 1876, Fournier, who had thought he would "elevate" himself "by contact with worthwhile men," actually found most of his colleagues in that heavily Republican body repugnant. The atmosphere, particularly in the bars, was like "that of the cafés of the Palais Royal around 1830." The only compensations he found for these unpleasantly democratic surroundings were in the party caucuses of the Right, where everyone he encountered had had a good education.[78]

For Fournier, a *polytechnicien* and founding member of most of the learned and artistic societies of La Rochelle, this was an indispensable qualification. Naturally he, and *grands bourgeois* like him, felt closer to men of similar education and tastes who happened to be of the various Monarchist persuasions than they did to a Bohemian parvenu like Gambetta. They barely tolerated the efforts of Jules Amigues for their own party; they had even less in common with the Republican Tribune.

In the Chamber the Bonapartists, while they had some benches to themselves, shared others with Monarchists.[79] Such proximity not surprisingly sometimes produced a similarity of views, even at the expense of cardinal tenets of Bonapartist doctrine. One of the most glaring examples occurred shortly before the fall of Thiers, when Haentjens read to the Assembly a declaration which suggested that his party, despite

---

[78] Fournier, "Mémoires," XI, 271; XVII, 198.
[79] *Guide manuel et plan colorié de la Chambre des Députés élue les 14 et 28 octobre 1877, par un employé de la Chambre* (n.p. 1878).

the contradiction with its very name, would be prepared to support the curbs on universal suffrage of which the Monarchists dreamed. The *Ordre*, in obvious embarrassment, could only explain that while this was the private opinion of some Bonapartists, the great majority believed that "the role of real conservatives consists in winning universal suffrage by trusting it, not in mutilating it." [80]

This incident reveals the two tendencies between which the Bonapartist "Plain" was torn. The more the individual deputy's beliefs inclined him to be a "Brumairean," an authoritarian democrat *à la* Rouher, the more faithfully he followed the Vice-Emperor's Bonapartist-conservative line, with the accent on "Bonapartist." On the other hand, the more affinity he felt for the Monarchists, the more he was inclined to heed the Bonapartists of "Coblence" and to be a conservative-Bonapartist, with the accent on "conservative." As long as Rouher and the *Ordre*, for tactical reasons, tolerated the conservative union Cassagnac favored, the parliamentary party remained united. Defections began when the issue clearly forced the deputy to choose between conservatism and Bonapartism; because of Chambord's letter, the supreme temptation was never offered, but on eleven issues as important as the Septennate, the overthrow of Broglie, the dissolution of the Assembly, and the election of the Senate by universal suffrage, almost 20 per cent of the Bonapartists' votes were cast, from 1871 to 1875, against the party's official position.[81] A staunch "Brumairean" like Eschasseriaux backed Rouher in opposing the prolongation of MacMahon's powers, eventually rejecting Broglie and the Assembly, and seeking to thwart their Orleanist schemes by proposing to make the Senate a duplicate of the new Chamber. By 1875 he was ready to disavow conservative union even if it meant countenancing Re-

[80] *L'Ordre*, March 2, 1873.
[81] Percentage computed on basis of votes listed in Clère, *Biographie*.

Versailles

publican victories, and to follow Raoul-Duval in a malicious reassertion of Bonapartist independence. Conservatives with the attitudes of a Fournier, however—Pierre Magne is a good example—regarded MacMahon, Broglie, the Assembly, and an oligarchic Senate as essential to the defense of "society" (which meant conservative interests) and voted accordingly.

These two tendencies were *not*, it should be repeated, mutually exclusive, but a matter of degree. Even Rouher, who had cast off the characteristic political outlook of the *grande bourgeoisie*, felt that their principles required Bonapartists to "appear to prefer" Monarchists to Republicans in elections. For some of the deputies he sought to lead, however, and for even more of the men he would soon be requiring as candidates, the primacy of conservatism over Bonapartism was more than a matter of tactical appearances—it was an instinctive reaction. Evoked in the National Assembly, it had considerably distorted the Bonapartists' appeal and limited their effectiveness:

Our party, which could not live except by authority, wallowed and crumbled in the parliamentary slime. Each deputy . . . saw only his own electoral interests, and without caring for the instructions he might have received, had but one idea: flirt with the parties of the Right. . . . There were among us some Orleanist parliamentarians who were only waiting for a chance to return to their original party and some clericals who would never have been content with the concessions made to them.[82]

The general elections of 1876 would reveal to what extent the failure of many Bonapartist politicians to control the prejudices of their class with the doctrines of their party imperilled their hopes of proving that Frenchmen of *all* classes—peasants of the Nièvre and miners of the Nord as well as bourgeois of Poitiers—wanted a Third Empire.

[82] Frédéric Masson in preface to H. J. Dugué de la Fauçonnerie, *Souvenirs d'un vieil homme* (2d ed.; Paris, n.d.), xv–xvii.

Chapter IV

"Pyrénées-Occidentales"

Not long before February 20, 1876, when Frenchmen were to elect the first Chamber of Deputies of the Third Republic, Paul de Cassagnac published a pamphlet he called "The Revenge of the Polls: A History of Nowhere and of Everywhere." Written with Cassagnac's usual caustic verve, it was not only a propagandistic tour de force but a revelation of how the Bonapartist mind envisioned the course and outcome of the imminent contest in an ideal district.

Cassagnac chose for his setting the "Department of the Pyrénées-Occidentales," which, though fictitious, was much like any in France. Its *chef-lieu* was dominated by Radicals like its mayor, an impecunious lawyer who ostentatiously smoked his pipe at atheistic funerals, but they were far outweighed by the sound rural majority. Enriched by the economic policies of the Empire, the hard-working peasants abhorred the Republic and treasured photographs of the Prince Imperial and vehement Bonapartist brochures (perhaps by Paul de Cassagnac). The voting of a Republican constitution had so alarmed them that they marched, cudgels in hand, on the *chef-lieu*, led by proud wearers of the Medal of Saint Helena and by their venerable curé, and drove the Republican townsmen to take refuge in their customary lairs, the cafés and cabarets. When civil war threatened between town and country (particularly since the Orleanist Prefect

"Pyrénées-Occidentales"

was known to be hand-in-glove with the Republicans), the local committee of the *Appel au peuple* sought a peaceful solution by calling for a great public debate among the electoral candidates. They all came: the Orleanist, "Philippe Hottard," a man of seventy-five hobbling on the enormous umbrella which symbolized his dynasty, a Voltairean usurer who hoped to force his clients to vote for the *régime censitaire*; the Legitimist "Comte Dieudonné de Chevrefeuille," an ostentatiously devout Papal Zouave, who, at the height of hopes for fusion, had all but commanded the peasants to pass their nights silencing the frogs croaking in the moat of his crumbling château; the Republican "Gracchus Latripe," the son of a *Conventionnel*, who had shared glasses of absinthe and the use of a single shirt with Gambetta in the Latin Quarter until war-profiteering had made him rich, a man still ignorant of the use of a comb or of soap and water. And finally the Bonapartist "Napoléon Vannois," son of an old soldier who had died, faithfully, the day after the Emperor had, a volunteer hero of the war whom only Rouher's pleas had persuaded to quit his simple life among his peasants for the hustings.

One by one they advanced to address the throng: Hottard denounced universal suffrage to the approbation of one man in the audience—who was stone-deaf. Chevrefeuille, eyeing the peasants through his monocle, announced that the Revolution must be reversed, and was flung out of the hall. Latripe, contemptuously dismissing the previous speakers, foully slandered the Empire but refused to defend his opinion on the field of honor. It was left to Vannois to point the moral: he alone of the conservatives could successfully challenge Latripe. His message went unheeded, and all three of his rivals finally united in a "conservative-liberal" committee against the candidate of the Empire. But (Cassagnac concluded triumphantly) their cabals were in vain. The results were: Registered, 25,000; Voting, 20,000; Vannois, Imperialist, 15,000, elected; Latripe, Republican, 5,000.[1]

Detailed investigation of the actual elections, the decisive political test for the Bonapartists after Sedan, reveals that while in one region of France events followed Cassagnac's model with considerable fidelity, in the others the story did not have such a happy ending. In these regions, even where the peasants had not learned to accept a "Latripe," there was often no "Napoléon Vannois" in the running, or at least none who could easily be distinguished from a "Philippe Hottard."

Bonapartists who shared Rouher's concept of authoritarian democracy agreed with Cassagnac that the peasantry was the essential element in any electoral victory. They were also aware, however, of the peasant's inclination to vote for whichever he took to be the winning side, and Rouher had therefore seen a fearful significance in the heavily Republican by-elections of July, 1871. "The monarchical parties are all outdistanced. The Republican passions are reaching the countryside." Baron Eschasseriaux had also feared that "the peasants, no longer having in their hearts the cult of the Napoleonic legend," would turn to the existing regime. "The idol has been broken and they know not whom to follow. Warned against Legitimism, they will let themselves be led to the Republic."[2]

The by-election of 1873 in the Charente-Inférieure had proved that this drift could be arrested, at least in some parts of France. The votes of the Charentais peasants had swept to victory a frankly Bonapartist candidate (Boffinton, the former Prefect), even after his Republican opponent, backed by Thiers' administration, had won the towns. The impact of the

[1] Paul Granier de Cassagnac, *La revanche du scrutin: Histoire de nulle part et de partout* (Paris, 1875), *passim*.
[2] Eugène, Baron Eschasseriaux, "Mémoires," twenty manuscript volumes at the château of Oyré (Sarthe); VI, 120–121.

"Pyrénées-Occidentales"

rural vote provides the dramatic element in Mayor Fournier's account in his diary of the scene in front of the Prefecture at La Rochelle on the night the votes were counted. Within the building the Republicans had gathered, but outside "also, groups form; they grow, they talk with certain precautions . . . but it is quickly recognized that . . . there are none but Boffinton voters." At 7:30 the first results were announced: Rigaud (the Republican), 1,989; Boffinton 751. "About twenty people cry 'Long live the Republic.'" An hour later there was "rejoicing in the salons. . . . Uneasiness outside," with the count Rigaud 8,232, Boffinton 2,236. At eleven o'clock came "a thunderbolt. . . . Boffinton 14,969; Rigaud 21,237." With 26,000 more votes in, the Republican's edge seemed to be widening. But "these are the corrupted centers, say the old soldiers [of Bonapartism]." Soon, "you'll see the good battalions, coming from afar." And they did; at 11:30 it was Boffinton, 25,900; Rigaud 27,300. "There is less joy upstairs. There is more laughter outside." At midnight, Boffinton was leading by 1,600 votes: "the young Republicans, whose lesson is finished, are sent to bed. . . . Outside, the old troopers, considering the battle won, are going to retire. Good night, *mes braves!*" By half-past two, with Boffinton leading by 3,000, the lights had gone out in the Prefecture, and the local Republican club had emptied, "less noisily than usual. At 3:30 all the town seems asleep. . . . The Charente-Inférieure has remained true to itself."[3]

Boffinton that night was the guest of Baron Eschasseriaux, who had chosen him as candidate and had drafted his platform. To the Baron, no election had seemed more certain, but when the first returns showed him trailing, his guest betrayed signs of alarm. Eschasseriaux reassured him by pointing out that the early results came from the towns and the *chefs-lieux*

---

[3] Famille Fournier, "Mémoires," twelve manuscript volumes numbered I–VI, VIII, X–XII, XVI–XVII (ACM 4J1509), XVI, 332–336.

of cantons equipped with the telegraph, and that "the results of the rural communes favorable to us which were brought in by the gendarme" would come later to redress the balance.[4]

To ensure such victories as Boffinton's, Bonapartist propaganda had not only to flatter the "providing fathers of the country . . . who make France rich and prosperous" and to remind them of the servants of the Emperor "who helped to embellish your villages, to create your great roads, to build your railways, to endow your churches, to change your *gros sous* into gold pieces, to give to your fields, your patrimony, a value much greater than they had before." The peasants had also to be warned against the pernicious electoral advice of "notables of your countryside, men who have always lived among you," who denounced Bonapartist candidates because "they wish to deprive you of the right to vote in order later to be able to impose the Orléans dynasty on France." Such traditionally influential persons might claim that "the administrator of your *arrondissement* wishes you to vote for this or that candidate . . . but they will be lying," since *fonctionnaires* were legally forbidden to influence elections.[5]

Though universal suffrage had been practiced in France for a generation, the necessity for such elementary but urgent admonitions reveals the degree to which the peasant electorate's judgment of the issues was still beclouded by its ignorance, parochialism, and passivity, or even its venality. In 1876, it was still possible for a Bonapartist mayor to swing his commune to the Bonapartist candidate by publicly announcing that Napoleon III was not dead, but hidden in a well-known château of the region, ready to resume the reins of government at the first opportunity. Likewise, Legitimists might swing a commune against a Bonapartist candidate by

[4] Eschasseriaux, "Mémoires," VII, 86, 89, 99.
[5] Comte Alfred de la Chapelle, *Les représentants de l'appel au peuple* (Paris, 1875), *passim*.

"Pyrénées-Occidentales"

reminding its inhabitants that he had an interest in the local railway and, if elected, was likely to force the abandonment of the coaching service on which the commune's prosperity depended. In Brittany, on the other hand, the peasants were sufficiently enlightened and unconcerned with parochial issues to give their vote freely—to the candidate whose fortune permitted his agents to open unlimited credits with the barkeepers of the town. (In one little commune of the Côtes-du-Nord casting 368 votes, no less than 128 liters of alcohol were consumed on election day.)[6]

Choosing between the representatives of the Empire and their opponents was not everywhere such a happy occasion. In the Haute-Garonne, the Comte d'Ayguesvives, a former Imperial equerry, found ways to exert strong pressure on peasants who remained unconvinced by such propaganda as a map depicting a Republican France partitioned by the great powers of Europe, with the inhabitants of the third district of Toulouse becoming Spaniards. In one commune, his auxiliary was the *garde-champêtre*, going "from house to house . . . speaking especially to women, reading them a Bonapartist brochure . . . accompanying it all with diatribes" against the Republican candidate. In another, it was the landowner, handing marked and distinguishable ballots to his *métayers* and workers and discharging those who refused them. It was the curé who passed ballots out in still another commune, recommending that the father of the family vote for

---

[6] AN C3158, "Chambre des députés-Ier législature—Procès-verbaux de la commission d'enquête sur les élections de MM. d'Ayguesvives et Tron," dossier 321, no. 3. Enclosure in letter from Attorney-general, Rennes, to Keeper of the Seals, March 3, 1876 (AN BB^{30}1124, "Correspondance échangée entre le ministre de la justice et les procureurs-généraux à l'occasion d'affaires de colportage ou d'élections"). Attorney-general, Rennes, to Keeper of the Seals, March 15, June 14, 1876 (AN BB^{30}1124). (Hereinafter cited as AN C3158, AN BB^{30}1121, etc.).

d'Ayguesvives, with the warning that his children would be expelled from the nuns' free school if he did not.[7]

Though they immensely complicate the task of the electoral analyst, he cannot entirely overlook influences of these kinds, which often made the elections of 1876 so much less than clear-cut expressions of the preference of the rural voters for the regime upheld by the victorious candidate. A Bonapartist—or even a Republican—total may reflect anything from the enthusiastic conviction depicted by Cassagnac to the dumb acquiescence of peasants voting with identifiable ballots under the eyes of their social and economic superiors.

Under the Empire the rural vote had frequently been well-controlled. In those days, however, Bonapartist candidates had been reasonably sure that the *garde-champêtre* and often the curé, when they helped the peasant to make up his mind, were acting in favor of the official nominee. In 1876 (despite their efforts in the Haute-Garonne), the Bonapartists could not necessarily count either on the support of the clergy or on the official help of the hierarchy of *fonctionnaires*.

It was in vain that the *Ordre* had gone so frequently to Canossa. Bonapartism's new-found piety, expressed at such a cost to its fundamental doctrines, had not sufficed to rally the Church to the *Appel au peuple*. The minority of prelates loyal to the Imperial dynasty could do little to increase the electoral totals of its partisans. When the Government in 1879 asked its Prefects to evaluate the political opinion and influence of the Bishops of their respective departments, only fourteen of seventy-nine prelates were adjudged capable of affecting voting totals. Of these, only three were thought to be Bonapartist, and two of these, ironically, had been given their charge after 1876. The influence of the Bishop of Ajaccio was reckoned to be considerable; for, "in Corsica, the very numerous priests are the leaders, almost always followed, of

[7] AN C3158, dossier 321, nos. 3, 11.

their flocks, especially in the countryside." The second held sway in a region almost as disinherited: the Bishop of Saint-Flour in the Cantal, a militant Bonapartist, led a clergy even more sympathetic to the Empire than he was. The aged Bishop of Digne was less dangerous, having lost part of his influence.[8]

Among the forty-nine prelates whom the Prefects reported to be politically powerless, they detected a fair number (from nine to fifteen, depending on the rigor of the definition) with Bonapartist inclinations. Some simply did not care to intervene in politics, like the Bishop of Evreux; he was the instrument of the local Bonapartist leader, but the Prefect felt sure that though he disliked the Republic he would never openly combat it. Others, like the Archbishop of Avignon and the Bishop of Saint-Brieuc, liberal Catholics and Imperialist sympathizers, were prevented by the hostility of their Legitimist and ultramontane clergy from reaching the electorate and remained neutral in the struggles of parties. (Their colleague of Vannes had wearied of similar antagonism and had turned himself, after the advent of MacMahon, from a Bonapartist into an ultra-Legitimist, a change of heart which had restored his authority among the noble families of the Morbihan.)[9] In regions characterized by religious indifference rather than the fervent belief of parts of Brittany, on the other hand, Bonapartist prelates and Legitimist clergy were equally incapable of influencing the outcome of elections; such was the

---

[8] Secretary-general, Corsica, to Minister of Interior, October 9, 1879; Sub-Prefect, Saint Flour, to Prefect of Cantal, October 3, 1879; Prefect of Basses-Alpes to Minister of Interior, September 25, 1879 (AN $F^{19}5610$, "Agissements politiques du clergé"; hereinafter cited as AN $F^{19}5610$.)

[9] Prefect of Vaucluse to Minister of Interior, September 22, 1879; Prefect of Côtes-du-Nord to Minister of Interior, September 19, 1879; Prefect of Eure to Minister of Interior, October 7, 1879; Prefect of Morbihan to Minister of Interior, September 27, 1879 (AN $F^{19}5610$).

Bonapartism after Sedan

case, for example, in the Yonne, the Eure-et-Loir, and the Marne.[10]

In some regions of France where Bonapartism held the allegiance of the rural population, even a Bonapartist bishop enjoyed little influence. An example is the Lot-et-Garonne. The Bishop of Agen was so much a Bonapartist that he sent his communications to the Bonapartists' local paper and ignored its Legitimist-clerical rival. Yet he had no great influence within the Bonapartist party, and none over any group of the population. The position of a Legitimist bishop in the Southwest was naturally even worse. Thus the political role of the Bishop of Auch was not great; "the inhabitants of the Gers are in general attached to their religion, but do not tolerate the clergy's taking part in their affairs." Anti-Republican communes there were equally anti-clerical. It was the same story in the Charente, where the fervently Legitimist bishop was little to be feared. Such prelates were as isolated among the Bonapartist masses as were their confreres in Republican regions like the Var or the Isère.[11]

This survey clearly establishes that insofar as Bonapartist clericalist propaganda had been intended to win an auxiliary for the capture of the peasant vote, it had been misconceived. Only in the most forlorn regions, like the Massif Central or Brittany, could the clergy still dominate the populations, and there their pressure, with some exceptions, was exercised in favor of Legitimism, which the ordinary curé tended to pre-

[10] Prefect of Yonne to Minister of Interior, October 18, 1879; Prefect of Eure-et-Loir to Minister of Interior, September 13, 1879; Prefect of Marne to Minister of Interior, September 16, 1879 (AN F^{19}5610).

[11] Prefect of Lot-et-Garonne to Minister of Interior, October 28, 1879; Prefect of Gers to Minister of Interior, September 12, 1879; Prefect of Charente to Minister of Interior, November 5, 1879; Prefect of Var to Minister of Interior, November 11, 1879; Prefect of Isère to Minister of Interior, September 18, 1879 (AN F^{19}5610).

"Pyrénées-Occidentales"

fer. On the other hand, the regions most devoutly Bonapartist were so in spite of the clergy, not because of them.

Thus Cassagnac's picture of the peasants of the "Pyrénées-Occidentales" led by their venerable curé in the battle for the Empire was not a realistic one. But if Bonapartists could not count, in 1876, on the functionaries of the Church, what of those of the State? Were they, as Cassagnac charged, Orleanists sympathetic to Republicans?

On the morrow of the election, the *Ordre* lamented that the Prefects had opposed the candidates of the *Appel au peuple* with all the means at their command. In flat contradiction is a contemporary Republican assertion that the prime minister, Buffet, preferred Bonapartists to men of the Left Center, and even to Liberals of the Right Center who had rallied to the Republic.[12] In reality, since in this contest, unlike the one which followed the *Seize Mai*, there was neither a confrontation between only two clearly demarcated camps nor a government determined to "make" the elections, the direction and degree in which official patronage was employed varied from one district to another, depending on the inclinations of the individual Prefect and his judgment of the political possibilities of his department. In this connection it must be recalled that the French administration had now undergone three considerable transitions in six years—from the Empire to the Government of National Defense, from the latter to the presidency of Thiers, and from Thiers to Broglie and his Orleanist successors—and might reasonably expect another if the elections proved to be overwhelmingly Republican. The effect on the mind of a careerist official of these successive upheavals can be imagined, particularly when his immediate superior or subordinate might be a man who had entered public service under a regime now officially

[12] *L'Ordre*, February 21, 1876; André Daniel, ed., *L'Année politique* —1876 (Paris, 1876), 37.

anathematized. According to a survey published by the *Liberté* in the fall of 1875, of the 452 *fonctionnaires* who commanded the Prefectures (Prefects and Secretaries-general) and Sub-Prefectures of France, 213 had begun their careers under the Empire, only twenty-five under Gambetta, 104 under Thiers, and 110 under MacMahon. Of the 213 one-time Imperial bureaucrats, only *five*, significantly, had been Imperial Prefects, and only 122 Secretaries-general or Sub-Prefects; sixty-seven had been *conseillers de préfecture*, just beginning their climb of the administrative ladder when the regime fell. (The unprofitability of the overthrow of Thiers for the Bonapartists is confirmed by the fact that of the 213, seventy had been retained by the hard-pressed Government of National Defense, ninety-eight had been reemployed by Thiers, and only forty-five by Broglie and his successors.)[13] Thus if former servants of the Empire formed the largest component of the administrative corps, most of them had been promoted, or were still hoping for promotion, under its successors, and the corps as a whole was far from homogeneous in its political origins, insofar as such uncertain times made it prudent to admit to any. The mere reading of these statistics leads one to infer that most *fonctionnaires* would be quite circumspect in their electoral role in 1876, and that those who were not would be as likely to attack the Bonapartists as to favor them.

Precisely this conclusion emerges from a survey of the administration published by the Republican *Siècle* during the first week of 1877, when sixty-two of the eighty-six Prefects who had supervised the elections were still in office. The paper regarded only forty-eight as actually hostile to Republican institutions, and of these twenty-one had not openly manifested their hostility, either because they were assigned

[13] Quoted in *L'Ordre*, September 24, 1875; cf. Fournier, "Mémoires," XVI, 100–105.

"Pyrénées-Occidentales"

to a department where it would have been fruitless, or because prudence counseled them to make enemies in no party, not even the Republican one. These twenty-one might be, privately, lukewarm Orleanists or Bonapartists, but they could be counted on to obey the orders of any government.

There thus remained twenty-seven—less than half—of these *fonctionnaires* of 1876 whom the *Siècle* judged sufficiently unreliable to require their purge from a really Republican administration. Only ten of these could be clearly identified as Bonapartists, even including the Prefect of the Hérault, whose friends claimed that he was a family man eager to remain a Prefect, who would be as good a Republican as he was a Bonapartist, and the Prefect of the Ardèche, who had been "very Bonapartist before September 4, very Republican under Thiers, very royalist and clerical under May 24, and today again . . . Bonapartist." Four of the ten had been in a position to exercise the influence of their office in favor of candidates who upheld the Empire. The Prefect of the Vienne, a "Bonapartist by birth, temperament and conviction," had been named through the influence of Baron de Soubeyran, despite the protests of the Bishop and Legitimists of Poitiers, and had elected "the whole Soubeyran clan." The Prefects of the Manche, the Sarthe, and the Landes had been of similar use to their party, but the other six administered departments where it was running but few candidates and none with hope of success.

In a half-dozen other departments the Prefect, though his personal preference would have been for one of the other "reactionary" regimes, had lent his support to the partisans of the Empire. This had not guaranteed their victory: though the Prefect of the Ain had become the "docile instrument" of the local Bonapartist chief, the Ain elected an entirely Republican delegation in 1876. On the other hand, in some cases the open enmity of a Monarchist Prefect did not harm the Bona-

Bonapartism after Sedan

partist cause, or even helped it, as in Corsica or in the Orne, where the clerical Orleanist appointed to further the interests of his party had "assured the election of three Bonapartist deputies by his mistakes." Not far away, in the Morbihan, however, a Prefect who "continued the tradition by which the Prefecture . . . is an outpost of Frohsdorf" guaranteed the victory of a Legitimist candidate by publicly attacking his Republican and Bonapartist opponents.[14]

Thus the only generalization possible on the help which a Bonapartist candidate might receive in 1876 from the chief representative of the State in his department is that, owing to the heterogeneity and hesitancy of the administrative personnel, it could by no means be counted on. For many Bonapartists this must have seemed a fatal handicap when they reflected on the role the Prefect had once played in their campaigns. (Raoul-Duval, campaigning in the Eure, felt that his prospects had been much improved when he was joined in his travels from village to village by the fabulous Janvier de la Motte, who as Prefect from 1856 to 1868 had been largely responsible for the department's economic development. His popularity even a decade later was incredible: "Men and women all came out onto the street when it was known he was there. I saw an old curé . . . kiss his hand, speaking of all the good he had done.") [15]

In some departments universal suffrage was, indeed, still managed in 1876 much as it had been under the Empire. In the Haute-Garonne, the Republican candidate also blamed the Prefecture for d'Ayguesvives' victory, charging that it had "advised" mayors to oppose his candidacy and had ordered the *gendarmerie* to arrest the distributors of his ballots. Such

---

[14] *Le Siècle*, January 4–7, 1877.

[15] Raoul-Duval to Mme. Raoul-Duval, January 23, 1876; in dossier "Lettres à sa femme," Raoul-Duval papers, château of Le Vaudreuil (Eure). Cf. Daniel, ed., *Année politique—1875*, 73.

"Pyrénées-Occidentales"

activities had given credit to "the rumors generally current in the countryside that, the Republic not being possible, the Marshal . . . remained at the head of government, awaiting the return of the Prince Imperial, which must be hastened by naming Bonapartist deputies." [16]

More typical, however, was the behavior of the Prefect of the Charente-Inférieure, an Orleanist, but so determined not to compromise his advancement, whatever the future regime might be, that he accepted the constitution of 1875. Thus, though a conservative enemy of Radicalism, he was careful to keep his distance from the Bonapartists.[17]

In many departments in 1876, then, Church and State, once so essential for Bonapartist electoral hopes, stood as spectators of the battle, if they were not actually hostile. Was it possible to fight against the Republican *fait accompli* and to win, with only the support of one's own personal organization to rally the voters? More than one former deputy asserted at Chislehurst that it was. Not all—far from it—were proved wrong, but a Bonapartist journalist who was in a position to judge knew of "only a single man in the party from 1870 to 1877 who could speak thus without fear that events would give him the lie." [18]

A full-length portrait of this uniquely successful politician will reveal, by its sharp contrast with most of his fellow Bonapartists, why they were unable to match his achievements at the polls. The difference was not that family background or social position made him an uncharacteristic figure among nineteenth-century French notables. Nor was the department he ruled radically atypical of much of the French countryside, though ecological factors and the economic consequences of

---

[16] AN C3158, dossier 321, no. 4.
[17] Fournier, "Mémoires," XVII, 135–136, 138.
[18] Jules Richard, *Le Bonapartisme sous la République* (3d ed.; Paris, 1883), 153.

Bonapartism after Sedan

its dramatic modernization under the Second Empire may have made it more propitious than the average department for the development of a broad-based Bonapartism. Rather, the crucial contrast is to be found in the political methods which the evolution of the fallen regime had obliged him to develop.

In the turmoil of 1789, two brothers of an old family of modest importance, the Eschasseriaux, rose to sudden prominence in the newly created department of the Charente-Inférieure. Joseph, the elder, became first the administrator of Saintes, then a member of the departmental directory; his brother René joined him as a substitute. As was not uncommon in the first stages of the Revolution, Joseph moved quickly from local to national government, sitting first in the Legislative Assembly, then in the Convention. At first he was little remarked. His speeches tended to be rare and terse: "I vote for Death" was all he said when the fate of Louis XVI was being decided. He spoke with equal firmness against Robespierre, and on the morrow of 9 Thermidor was named, on the suggestion of Barère, to the Committee of Public Safety, as an economic and financial specialist. When the Convention dissolved itself, the two brothers (for René had joined Joseph in Paris) headed the list of those from the Charente-Inférieure whose reelection to the Council of 500 was compulsory; in that body they sat with the democratic "Left Thermidorians." They negotiated the next twists of the path of revolution with equal aplomb. Both sat in Bonaparte's assemblies, both escaped purging in 1802, and Joseph, named minister plenipotentiary to Lucca, became Baron Eschasseriaux in 1810. He retired from politics with the first Restoration, unlike René, who sat in the Chamber of the Hundred Days, and was throughout the Restoration (after his return from exile) a leader of the liberal (and Bonapartist) opposition forces in the Charente-Inférieure.[19] Such were the great-uncle and grandfather of the Baron of the Second Empire and the Third Republic. It was a lineage with which he had a conscious identification, which helped make him a characteristic "Brumairean" Bonapartist.

His father had been only briefly a deputy under the July Monarchy, rejecting the Government's proposal in 1831 that he become its man in the Charente-Inférieure. The Baron, running as a young man of twenty-six for his first political office in 1849, displayed the same independence. Though he denounced the Republic (which had been irretrievably compromised in the department by the scenes of the June Days), and declared in his first *profession de foi* that the Revolution should have stopped in 1789, he declined to run on the list patronized by the supporters of the Prince-President. He was elected to the *Conseil général* and to the Assembly because his name was Eschasseriaux, not because he subordinated it to the name of Napoleon. He was to hold both mandates without interruption for forty-four years.

In January of 1851 he joined the parliamentary minority which supported the Elysée. He saluted the *coup d'état* as a "great act of strength accomplished with . . . the assent of the population," which assured "security for the future and the complete exercise of universal suffrage," but did not choose to serve in the Consultative Assembly while some of his parliamentary colleagues were in prison.[20]

For, despite his heritage and his own predilections, despite the fact that he was its official candidate through the election

---

[19] E. Reveillaud, *Histoire politique et parlementaire des départements de la Charente et de la Charente-Inférieure* (Saint-Jean-d'Angély, 1911), *passim*. Cf. Pierre Rainguet, *Biographie saintongeoise* (Saintes, 1851), 223.

[20] Eschasseriaux, "Mémoires," I, 136, 188–189, 197.

Bonapartism after Sedan

of 1863, the Baron did not feel himself a mere satellite of the new regime. There was much that needed to be done for the Charente-Inférieure which the Empire could do for him; on the other side of the ledger, he felt that there was much that he could do for the Empire in the Charente-Inférieure. He saw his own task as dual: initially, in cooperation with the Prefect, to weed out the elements of disorder which the revolution of 1848 had sown in the department, then to develop its prosperity by endowing it with improved education and communications. (When he was first elected in 1849, he was unable to distribute ballots, since there were no local roads; in his old age he recalled arriving in Saintes one November day in 1853 after a seven-hour walk over tracks impassable to any vehicle, and reflected scornfully that "the Sub-Prefects and Republicans of today hardly suspect the efforts made at the beginning of the Empire for the transformation of the countryside.") [21] The two tasks went hand-in-hand. The first years of the Second Empire saw the appropriation of a million-and-a-half-franc subsidy for the construction of a railway from Poitiers to La Rochelle, and the decision of the *Conseil général* to establish a telegraph system in the department (the Baron forcing it through despite the older councilors' suspicion of the newfangled thing). Though his own local eminence made him, inevitably, "the chief agent of the transformation of the department from the stage of revolution," he was careful to assign the credit for modernization to the Imperial regime. Coming from an Eschasseriaux, his support conferred far more prestige on the government than that of the four deputies originally elected as Bonapartists. He had a corresponding idea of the respect due him. Proudly conscious of his responsibility, he "would never have permitted the Prefects and Sub-Prefects to try to seize or to turn to their own

[21] Eschasseriaux, "Mémoires," I, 189, 255–256, 311.

"Pyrénées-Occidentales"

use any part whatsoever of the influence and power which I considered the essential attribute of a deputy's mandate." [22]

He had insisted even more forcefully on this definition of the correct relationship between a deputy and the central power as the Empire moved into the troubled decade of the 1860's. In March of 1861, annoyed at the delays a railway law for the Charente-Inférieure was encountering, he sent an ultimatum to the Emperor: either the bill would be presented that year, or the deputies of the department would vote against the budget, explaining publicly their reasons for doing so. In 1863, he argued against official endorsement for a new candidate in a neighboring district because the man was a stranger to the department. He preferred Roy de Loulay, a local man, fearing that the newcomer, "not living in the countryside, would be a weakness in the deputation." The Charentais peasants wanted their deputies to be independent: they would quickly have rejected an outsider sponsored by Paris.

In the Baron's judgment there were already too many weaknesses in the deputation as it was, too many men content to be the supine creatures of the Prefecture. One of his colleagues, a banker of Rochefort, totally ignored his rural electors. Another, Vast-Vimeux, "took little interest in his district, and did not occupy himself with the affairs of the rest of the department." Both, lacking "electoral strength and incapable of fighting a battle themselves without the support of the administration," were objects of contempt for Eschasseriaux, for whom the middle years of the Empire were "a period of action and almost feverish expansion." Unlike them, he found time, between throwing open his estate for great rustic balls when the grapes had been gathered in and serving as the secretary of the *Conseil général*, for "errands, tours,

[22] Eschasseriaux, "Mémoires," I, 190, 192, 259, 341–342; II, 22.

receptions, to maintain my contacts and consolidate my political position." And invariably, as the peasants gathered before him to watch one of their number receive an official prize for meritorious agricultural achievement, he spelled out simply what the regime he endorsed meant to them:

Farmers! . . . It is to encourage agriculture that the Government of the Emperor has negotiated treaties of commerce which permit you to sell your products abroad and to buy more cheaply all the things you use. To attain this end, it has subsidized your local roads, so useful for the transportation of your harvests. . . . Your profession, mark it well, is the most important of all . . . without you the nation could not live. . . . Count on the Emperor to improve your lot.[23]

It was none too soon for the Baron thus to consolidate his personal position, for the storm-clouds which were gathering over the regime boded ill for even such a staunch (though not servile) supporter. For Eschasseriaux, who did not think often or deeply about the great national or international problems which confronted Napoleon III, the Italian war (which he blamed on the Emperor's Carbonarist affiliations) was the fatal turning point. "After having carried liberty abroad, the Emperor was obliged to grant it at home. . . . Less could not be done than for Italy." The Empress, *parvenue* that she was, had compounded the error. "In 1868, preoccupied by the health of the Emperor, and by the transmission of the crown to her son, she made her influence more felt." She thought to perpetuate the regime "by eliminating M. Rouher and the founders . . . [and] finding their successors in the ranks of the Liberal party." [24]

This trend was already visible in the general elections of 1863 in the Southwest. Official patronage had been withdrawn from local Bonapartist chiefs and given to "Liberals"

[23] Eschasseriaux, "Mémoires," II, 127, 225, 349, 389–390, 421.
[24] Eschasseriaux, "Mémoires," V, 186–187.

"Pyrénées-Occidentales"

—clerical Orleanists. The affronted voters had defiantly reelected the original Bonapartists, now independents, instead. Even then, Eschasseriaux had understood the writing on the wall: "From that moment I was on my guard and sought my strength and support only among my friends and from universal suffrage." He had no intention of yielding his place to help the Empire placate the dissident bourgeoisie. He could refuse the more confidently because he knew that his position on the Roman question (voting consistently against the Pope "to affirm the principles of 1789 and the right of a country to dispose of itself") was far more congenial to the people of the Charentes than a clerical's could ever be. These were departments where a new Bishop who displayed his coat-of-arms in the parish churches saw the peasants invade more than forty of them, to rip it down and demolish the furniture, because they took the shock of wheat on his escutcheon to be a symbolic threat to resume the collection of tithes.[25] Yet the Government, not condescending to consult the Baron, had deliberately courted the rebuff it received by draping prominent clericals in the official colors. To Eschasseriaux, Ministers seemed "stricken with a kind of vertigo," and he therefore thought it only natural to take precautions against their "delusions and abuses of influence" by looking more exclusively for support "to the electoral body and to public opinion. . . . Prudence demanded that I strengthen my position for fear of a similar brain storm."

From year to year the estrangement between the Baron and a government he thought to be drifting farther and farther from its proper course continued to worsen. By 1865 he already questioned whether official endorsement would help or hinder him. In 1866, when a new Prefect imposed upon the department without warning told the mayors of the Charente-Inférieure that henceforth he, and only he, would dispense

[25] Eschasseriaux, "Mémoires," III, 89-90, 198-199; IV, 25.

governmental favors, Eschasseriaux retaliated by signing the amendment of the Forty-five calling for the development of liberties—by such an ironical route did he, an authoritarian democrat, arrive in the camp of parliamentary liberalism. When he went to England late in that year, the Ministry of the Interior received a report that he had gone to take orders from the heirs of Louis Philippe.[26]

The Baron's worst fears were confirmed when late in 1867 (at the instigation of the Empress, he believed), Magne and Pinard entered the government. It would be their function, he expected, to "carry out the conversion to Liberalism, win over the clericals and protectionists," and "destroy Rouher," (to implement, in fact, precisely that policy of conservative union even at the expense of Bonapartist fundamentals which Magne was to preach so insistently after 1870). If no mercy was to be shown to the Vice-Emperor, the Baron, who thought him the only great minister the Empire had produced, could hardly expect a better fate. By the summer of 1868 he knew that he could not even count on the Government's remaining neutral at the next election. An old, old enemy, Comte Lemercier, a covert Legitimist whose support for the temporal power of the Papacy was closer now to official policy than was the Baron's position, was accorded an audience with Napoleon and promised a neutrality which Eschasseriaux could justifiably only regard as a disguised endorsement. (If he had any doubts, they were resolved when he bluntly inquired of the Prefect what his orders were; the Prefect as bluntly replied, "I have orders to hunt you down like a mad dog.") As he watched the administration setting up a newspaper to attack him, as he watched Lemercier uniting his enemies of all breeds, the Baron was sick at heart. This was not merely politically inept, as he wrote to Rouher,

[26] Eschasseriaux, "Mémoires," III, 117–118, 206–207, 220–221, 259–260.

"Pyrénées-Occidentales"

"a clerical candidate in a region which is so unclerical." It was morally outrageous: Lemercier was the grandson of a Senator who had voted for the deposition of Napoleon I, while Eschasseriaux's grandfather had endured four years of exile for having signed the *Acte additionel* in 1815. Did the Government really think men like Lemercier could ever form a reliable new basis for the regime? (In fact all of those who now united to oppose Eschasseriaux in the name of the regime— the Prefect, the Sub-Prefect, the Bishop, Lemercier and almost everyone who voted for him—would have no word too harsh for the Empire on September 5, 1870.) [27]

Rouher, himself threatened by the cabals of the Tuileries, did what he could for his beleaguered friend. Although he could not get the hostile *fonctionnaires* transferred, he did procure the Baron a promotion in the Legion of Honor and a personal interview with Napoleon III. But the Baron did not feel much better when he left this audience. The Emperor "listened with his usual benevolence and replied that he would have a report made on the matter," but this "clarified nothing." It was obvious that Lemercier had received his promise, that the Emperor saw no way of getting out of it, and could only hope that it would not harm Eschasseriaux's position. The Baron thus "got nothing positive except some words of kindness," words that he was unable to interpret. Nothing could more clearly reveal the role to which Napoleon III had been reduced in the last years of his reign than this evasive embarrassment before the pleas of the man who led one of his most enthusiastically Bonapartist departments.

The Baron remained undaunted. Before leaving Paris for the campaign he cast another vote with the bloc—soon to be the famous 116—which demanded liberal institutions. Helping to curb the autonomy of Ministers was the only way he

[27] Eschasseriaux, "Mémoires," III, 417–418, 430–431; IV, 66–67, 71, 73, 78, 83, 116, 151.

Bonapartism after Sedan

could hit back at the remote forces which had decided on his annihilation. On his home ground he defied them to do their worst, to decree that there would be no Eschasseriaux meetings in the *mairies*, no distribution of his ballots by the *garde-champêtre*. The result of this election amply justified his self-confidence. In this battle, "unique in France, of seven opponents, among them the official candidate, leagued against one single candidate," the results were: Registered: 48,917; Voting: 41,475 (a remarkable turnout); Eschasseriaux, 23,795, elected. (Comte Lemercier, who led the pack of losers, got 6,314 votes.)

"It was," the Baron recalled with pardonable pride, "a crushing success." The peasants, "grateful for what I had done for twenty years," had remained "indifferent to the schemes and promises of my opponents." Their verdict was an "affirmation, uncontested to the end of my political career, of my preponderance." Henceforth the "element of order" would prevail in a department which was destined to be among the most loyal to the Empire after September 4, and which would have been more loyal still "but for the detestable and culpable policy conducted in 1868 and 1869 by the representatives of the Imperial government themselves." [28]

This remarkable triumph was *not* won by the buying of votes; this was not Brittany. Eschasseriaux was scandalized by the idea that legislative seats might be for sale: "In no sense did I want money and pressure to create corruption in the electorate." [29]

Rather the Baron had harnessed the force of his own popularity and that of the regime with which he unfailingly identified himself to operate a systematic and omnipresent political machine dependent only upon himself. His increasing ali-

[28] Eschasseriaux, "Mémoires," IV, 71, 82–83, 167–168, 174–175, 186, 224, 259, 261–263.
[29] Eschasseriaux, "Mémoires," II, 434.

"Pyrénées-Occidentales"

enation from liberal ministers and his dread of becoming their catspaw had driven him to employ his limitless energy "to explore my ground, to study and follow more closely the electoral personnel and my adversaries, and to create an organization which was my salvation in the succeeding battles." [30]

Thus he began keeping a set of books (carefully hidden later from the police of the Republic) which became legendary in the Bonapartist party, where none "knew his voters and concerned himself with them as he did." On the list of voters he inscribed "all the information which reached him on the life and needs of each." Every name was followed by an indication of political preference, with arbitrary signs to show whether the man was solid or shaky.[31] With such information always at his fingertips (for he continued to accumulate it even when his fortunes were at their brightest), Eschasseriaux was able to forecast the outcome of any given election with phenomenal accuracy. (In 1876, of 578 senatorial electors he reckoned 326 as "good," sixty-four more as "good, doubtful"; the three Bonapartist Senators elected from the Charente-Inférieure received 357, 341, and 330 votes respectively.) When he had to decide, in 1892, whether to abandon his political career, he calculated scientifically on the basis of the local elections of the past twenty years the possibility of his reelection to the *Conseil général*. His projection gave his Republican opponent 1,485 votes, including 730 in the town of Saintes, to his 1,409, including 250 at Saintes. When his resulting decision not to run had been overcome because he saw that he "must go on to the end when those who had followed me for forty-five years asked me to," the actual results were 1,466 for the Republican, 1,403

---

[30] Eschasseriaux, "Mémoires," IV, 176.
[31] Richard, *Bonapartisme*, 154; cf. Eschasseriaux, "Mémoires," VI, 365–366. "Baron Eschasseriaux," *Revue de la Saintonge et de l'Aunis* (*Bulletin de la Société des Archives Historiques*), XXVI (1906), 351.

Bonapartism after Sedan

for him. As carefully as ever, Eschasseriaux pored over them. Certain rural communes had not come up to his expectations. In one, for example, he had counted on seven more votes. The Republican vote there had doubled "because of the indifference or defection of Baron Oudet, who was said to be reconciled to the government." [32] In 1892, Baron Oudet would come under no pressure to mend his ways; Eschasseriaux, obedient to the universal suffrage he knew in such intimate detail, announced his retirement.

At the height of his career, however, he would not lightly have borne such an affront. For if he repudiated pressure applied by administrators foreign to the department, he did not hesitate to use it himself. His comprehensive dossiers marked his enemies well, and when an opportunity came, he struck them down. The change of regime in 1870 made little difference, as M. Thiers' Sub-Prefect tried to explain to his superiors. For long years the Baron had "loaded his creatures and adherents with favors and pitilessly broken *fonctionnaires* rebellious against this all-powerful influence." The "sentiment of gratitude among some, of terror among the majority" was still very real: "mayors, *cantonniers, gardes-champêtres*, teachers know without a shadow of a doubt that a hard punishment is reserved for the unfaithful and *even for the lukewarm* if the men of the Empire return to power." [33]

When the Republican government sought to replace such *fonctionnaires* and thus to make clear to the population who now held the whip hand, it was balked by the Baron's occult influence. The Sub-Prefect rewarded an individual who had opposed the Bonapartist ticket in one little commune in 1876

---

[32] Fournier, "Mémoires," XVII, 140, 184; Eschasseriaux, "Mémoires," XVI, 348, 422, 425, 427.

[33] Sub-Prefect, Jonzac, to Prefect of Charente-Inférieure, July 7, 1871 (ACM 2M4/20, "Elections complémentaires à l'Assemblée nationale").

"Pyrénées-Occidentales"

by naming him mayor. At once the seven members of the municipal council resigned. For them, to oppose the Bonapartists was a crime, the Sub-Prefect explained. "This feeling was exploited by the agent of M. Eschasseriaux in the commune, . . . who hoped to be named mayor." The Republic was thus faced with a disagreeable choice: it must either maintain a mayor at odds with his most prominent constituents or ignominiously withdraw the appointment and thus discourage anyone else from daring to oppose Eschasseriaux.[34]

Who can know whether the seven councilors resigned out of gratitude to the Baron or out of fear of his reprisals if they did not? A political machine operates not only by exclusion and punishment; it also operates by inclusion and rewards. This one was commanded by a man born for the paradoxical role of the absolute master of a fervently democratic movement. Physically imposing, he had the "countenance and bearing . . . of a major of *cuirassiers.*" His character matched his appearance. "Proud and energetic, he is confident of his strength and influence, he knows how to be useful, he wants people to be devoted to him," noted Mayor Fournier, a very different sort of man, with a touch of envy. "He does not know how to compromise, he is all of a piece, one is for him or against him."[35] He himself best expressed his political code: "To preserve my friends, my tactic was never to abandon them, and to show them that I always fought with them, even in difficult circumstances, having no other aim, in such a case, than to fulfill a duty."[36] This was the counterpart of the destruction which awaited traitors. Toward his loyal band he stood in a relationship curiously quasi-feudal (in the

---

[34] Sub-Prefect, Jonzac, to Prefect of Charente-Inférieure, March 25, 1876 (ACM 4M2/36, "Affaires politiques et diverses, 1872–1879").
[35] Fournier, "Mémoires," XVI, 146.
[36] Eschasseriaux, "Mémoires," V, 52.

Bonapartism after Sedan

broadest sense of that term), though he spoke as a representative of the dynasty built on the overthrow of feudalism. Reversing the practice of most candidates for office, he did not go among his voters only before elections, but constantly, *except* at election time, when he deemed it wise to be at the center of action, ready to bring his decisive influence to bear where it was most needed. Though on his tours he avoided demagogic promises, "no one . . . showed as much skill in handling the voters, with that manner, both of the good fellow and of the master, which was peculiar to him."

"There was only one M. *le Baron:* no need to add the name," [37] but even the power of his personality would not have been enough to keep his machine functioning, had it not had the additional driving force of a genuine and widespread popular Bonapartism in the Charentes. History and geography had long prepared the ground for such feeling: a region easy of access and populated with relatively prosperous peasants had accepted first the Reformation and then the Revolution with enthusiasm.[38] The achievements of the Second Empire, however, had been decisive for the evolution of political opinion. Firms still celebrated today date their foundation from that epoch of unprecedented prosperity, and Cognac still boasts probably the only rue Richard Cobden in all France.[39] After the negotiation of the commercial treaty of 1860, total French exports of brandy to England tripled, and the Charente-Inférieure increased its shipments more than eight-fold. It would have been the grossest ingratitude if its peasant population "forgot for a moment to whom it owes

---

[37] "Baron Eschasseriaux," 351; cf. Eschasseriaux, "Mémoires," VIII, 284.

[38] Reveillaud, *Histoire,* 7–9 and *passim.*

[39] I am most grateful to M. Maurice Hennessy for supplying me with this information.

"Pyrénées-Occidentales"

the opening of the English market, the principal and unique outlet for its products.[40]

Certainly the Baron himself was not, at the darkest hour, ungrateful to the Empire, despite the vicissitudes of recent years. In September, 1870, his first impulse was to quit Paris: "I decided . . . to go among my electors. . . . I intended to return not as one vanquished, but as a defender of the past." He brushed aside a warning from Gambetta's Prefect, Mestreau, that the Republican railway workers of Saintes were threatening to march on his estate. The "ramblings of drunkards" might alarm such a "ridiculous Prefect," but the idea of lying low never crossed Eschasseriaux's mind. Within a week of September 4, indeed, he was hard at work contacting possible candidates for any constituent assembly that might eventually be convened.

He soon realized, however, that the task of steering his party safely through the debacle and of once more going to represent it in the Palais Bourbon would not be simple. He would have to wage war on two fronts: not only with the Republicans, but with conservatives who would have liked to appropriate his political influence while ending his career. At first he had hoped to preserve political continuity and unite non-Republicans by acting through the *Conseil général* to draw up an electoral list which would include his own name and those of his Bonapartist colleagues, but would add some "conservative-liberals." But the Monarchy and the Republic quickly dealt this plan irreparable blows: the Royalist committee of La Rochelle sent him word that it would endorse no list which bore the name of a former deputy. In Eschasseriaux's eyes, this refusal, which really amounted to collusion with Gambetta, was characteristic of the "proud, jealous, and unthinking bourgeoisie of La Rochelle, eager to court all the

[40] Eschasseriaux, "Mémoires," VI, 244–245.

Prefects to gain some advantage, whom Orleanism well suited, and who successively served Mestreau, Thiers, MacMahon, and so on." Then Gambetta decreed that the Imperial *Conseils généraux* should be dissolved and replaced by new departmental commissions, eliminating one of the Baron's prime strongholds. (It was some consolation that the Prefect Mestreau was never able to form a departmental commission, because the Baron and his followers so "stirred up people's minds, and revealed the moral and pecuniary responsibilities of usurpers of elective functions, that no one dared assume that role before public opinion.") [41]

In addition to this opposition on two flanks, the Baron was still faced, only a week before the elections, with the hesitancy of his former colleagues. He was himself determined to run regardless of Gambetta's decree of proscription, feeling that he "owed it to those who had formerly elected me, and who all advised me to run, to defend the past and watch over their interests in the future." But he could not overcome the reluctance of Roy de Loulay and Vast-Vimeux, who had good reason to be less confident of victory. There seemed to be no solution but to publish a list omitting all the former Bonapartist deputies and backing instead a motley group headed by the name of Thiers. This at least would give the voters an alternative to the Republican list and to the Royalist-clerical list, which bore such fetid names (for a Bonapartist) as that of General Trochu, as well as that of M. Mestreau himself. At the very last moment came word that Jules Simon had abrogated Gambetta's decree, encouraging Eschasseriaux's doubting colleagues finally to join him. Though only twenty-four hours were left to inform the voters of the new list which bore their names, so well did the Baron's machine function that he was still able to send bundles of ballots to the polls. Under

[41] Eschasseriaux, "Mémoires," V, 193, 195, 202, 210, 216, 229, 231, 260, 310–311.

these conditions he could justifiably claim of their victory that "never had a demonstration of the countryside been more spontaneous." [42]

The by-elections of July, 1871, however, proved that Bonapartist campaigns could be defeated even in the Charente-Inférieure if they were improperly managed and combatted with sufficient administrative energy. Prince Murat and Rouher were beaten by a Republican ticket headed by Mestreau. Analyzing this failure, Eschasseriaux blamed it above all on his own absence from the scene, at a time when the Prefect and Sub-Prefects were threatening dire consequences for any hostile mayor who meddled in the polling. "There were close to 65,000 abstentions, which were those of our friends, intimidated in our absence to the point that they did not dare act or demonstrate." Moreover, the candidates themselves were ill-chosen: the name of Rouher, leading free-trader though he was, evoked no response from the peasants even in the Baron's own *arrondissement*, without the Baron there to sanction it. The voters had preferred a local name, even Mestreau's, since "the campaign was carried on for M. Rouher and Prince Murat by compromising agents, who appeared to be acting only as outsiders for outsider candidates, and who, not knowing the countryside, spent clumsily the money placed at their disposal." The lesson of this, the only substantial defeat the party suffered in the first years of the Republic, was that even in a region Bonapartist by conviction, success could not be assured without the efforts of a comprehensive locally-based organization.

Although the Vice-Emperor had to look elsewhere for his seat in the Assembly, Eschasseriaux did not feel that the July returns were a threat to his own personal position, since his electoral books showed him that neither the Legitimist

[42] Eschasseriaux, "Mémoires," V, 349–350, 352–353, 356–357, 365–366.

Bonapartism after Sedan

Lemercier nor Mestreau had much increased his totals since the last elections. He proved it in October, when elections for new *Conseils généraux* were held. The inevitable Mestreau was his opponent, backed by the Bishop's newspaper and the Bishop in person. This was one of the Baron's hardest-won victories, achieved by a narrow margin despite "the bewilderment of the countryside, which had not had time clearly to judge men and affairs." His reelection to this decisive vantage-point for command of the local scene confirmed his belief that Bonapartists should boldly reenter political life, instead of remaining in the shadows and encouraging nonpartisan conservative candidacies, as fainter hearts in his party urged him to do. He was sure that he could have elected Rouher and Murat if they had all three gone before the electorate together, unshrouded by prudent phraseology. He dated the resurgence of his party from his own uncompromising October triumph.

Once more upon the high-road to victory, Bonapartism drove forward irresistibly, spurred by Thiers' return to protectionism, which "coincided with an absolute cessation of business, causing consternation to everyone." Not since 1848 had the Baron seen such a violent reaction of public opinion as became evident early in 1872, sweeping all before it and driving momentary converts to the Republic back into the Imperial fold.[43] Not content to ride a crest of public opinion, he spent the summer extending and improving his organization, particularly in those *arrondissements* which lay outside his own Imperial electoral district. At the year's end, as he drafted his report to Napoleon III, he could take complete satisfaction in his department's situation. It had remained Bonapartist; the tendency toward Orleanism which had appeared after September 4 had disappeared. Public opinion

[43] Eschasseriaux, "Mémoires," VI, 97, 103, 112, 198–199, 208–209, 296–297.

"Pyrénées-Occidentales"

was sustained by the Baron's local paper, the *Progrès de la Charente-Inférieure*, which reached the whole department and circulated all the Bonapartist pamphlets, as well as the Imperial portraits "which are very eagerly sought after." Nine out of ten of the mayors were favorable. Thus, the Baron was not afraid to express his hope of a complete success for an exclusively Bonapartist list at a general election. The by-election of 1873 amply confirmed his hopes; significantly the Bishop had now abandoned his pretensions and threw whatever weight he could bring to bear behind Boffinton.

Unfortunately the behavior of the latter, who was reluctant to inconvenience himself by becoming an essential part of the electoral machine, rather clouded this triumph for Eschasseriaux. Boffinton preferred "the easy position of a deputy" in Paris to the ennui inseparable from the parochial concerns of the *Conseil général* and evaded the Baron's pointed requests that he run for this local office. The Baron finally appealed to Rouher to force his hand, pointing out that as a *conseiller général*, Boffinton would "become the candidate designated in advance, so to speak, in case of *scrutin d'arrondissement*," but that if he disdained the office, it would cause great disappointment in the party and "risk the loss of the *arrondissement* . . . which would be left without a chief." Eschasseriaux himself could not "be constantly on the firing line, nor act at all points without real help from anyone." A letter from the Vice-Emperor would be an order which Boffinton could only accept. Rouher, however, was in no position to give, and still less to enforce, orders, and Boffinton continued his evasions. The Baron characteristically then put his name in nomination without his consent, but it is a rare unwitting candidate who wins, and the defeat undermined the ex-Prefect's standing as a deputy.[44]

[44] Eschasseriaux, "Mémoires," VII, 5–7, 73, 80, 100, 382–385, 393, 408.

Bonapartism after Sedan

The ultimate fate of the Bonapartist party depended on the relative incidence in its higher ranks of men like Boffinton and men like Eschasseriaux. For the Baron, however, who seldom thought in such general terms, the ex-Prefect's shirking of the obligations of democratic politics was an annoying incident, not a portent. At the end of 1875 Eschasseriaux exulted in leading a united and confident department, and looked forward to victory in the general elections of 1876.

In November, 1875, he and his colleagues met to concert their plans. The Baron's original idea had been to run for the Senate, bequeathing the first district of Saintes to his son René, aged twenty-five. He found, however, that his colleagues Boffinton, Roy de Loulay, and Vast-Vimeux also laid claims to one of the three Senate seats available. All, the Baron scornfully judged, were "seeking an election which would flatter their vanity without involving extensive expenses or great demands from the electorate," since a Senator, elected for nine years by a college of notables, could stand aloof from democracy. The Baron gave way to their insistence, and it was decided that he would himself run for the Chamber in the first district of Saintes, the center and *chef-lieu* of the department, "in order to remain more in contact with universal suffrage, which was the real basis and force" of his power. His friend Jolibois, one of the brilliant forensic personalities of the party, would be patronized by him in the second district, while René would run in the *arrondissement* of Jonzac. Mayor Fournier, who had also hoped for a place in the Senate and was "a little disturbed . . . at the thought of facing a battle of universal suffrage," would be the candidate at La Rochelle, while Roy de Loulay's son, aged thirty, would seek his father's old seat at St.-Jean-d'Angély. No one in particular wanted the almost hopeless task of running in the *arrondissement* of Marennes. It "was a pocket borough for M. Dufaure, since he had for him, apart from the numerous

"Pyrénées-Occidentales"

voters controlled by the government, the Republican Protestants and the Catholics, who thought him a clerical." Believing that it was important to contest every district even in the face of certain defeat, and having found no one so altruistic on the spot, Eschasseriaux turned as a last resort to Rouher. The outsiders the Vice-Emperor suggested all begged off when they learned how slight were their chances, and Dufaure was eventually elected without opposition.

Marennes lay beyond the range of the Baron's machine, but almost everywhere else in the department it worked perfectly. On January 29, 1876, Eschasseriaux and his son boarded the Bonapartist special train for Saintes at the head of many of the men who would elect the Senators of the Charente-Inférieure the next day. That evening Jolibois at a meeting attended by many of the senatorial electors pronounced the three Bonapartists elected in advance, while at the same hour Dufaure addressed a thin attendance elsewhere. For two days the Prefect had tried to round up some electors to introduce to Dufaure, who was a minister as well as a candidate, but "he had not had great success, and the Republican meeting was pitiful and sad." Next day, on his way to learn the results, Eschasseriaux encountered the lethargic Vast-Vimeux and congratulated him on his victory. The other told him "naively, with an overflowing heart, 'I owe it to you.' Indeed we knew," the Baron acidly reflected, "that he would not get the vote of the Republican elector of his own commune." Having learned the official results, the Baron simply added the figures to the victory telegrams he had already prepared for the rue de l'Elysée and Chislehurst, and sent them off.[45]

Three weeks later, the elections for the Chamber of Deputies proceeded almost as smoothly, though in the hurly-burly of an appeal to universal suffrage there was room for Eschas-

[45] Eschasseriaux, "Mémoires," VIII, 196–197, 236, 241, 265–268, 271, 284, 287.

seriaux's enemies to employ the only sort of tactic which might have brought his machine to a standstill. René's opponent was Comte Duchâtel, an old enemy of the Baron's who had now undergone a conversion to the Republic. When René came into Duchâtel's commune to campaign, the Comte, fearing a Bonapartist demonstration in his own town, sought to prevent it by sending a swarm of men armed with cudgels to take over the cafés, where they shouted drunken praise of him and abuse of his young opponent. The band then invaded the house in which René was meeting his future constituents, but its owner "compelled the hired assassins of M. Duchâtel . . . to leave his premises. Just in time, for a criminal action was about to be committed." Eschasseriaux was convinced that murder was a predictable Republican campaign tactic, and that the criminal would have been allowed to escape with the collusion of the authorities.

Though this election was almost literally a struggle to the death, the Baron did not direct it with any less precision. First the districts were blanketed with thousands of photographs of the Imperial family. Next, on February 11, nine days before the polls opened, "we sent out all our electoral papers . . . with a covering letter for each commune, which indicated their number, prescribed the posting of placards on February 12 and the distribution of ballots on February 17, 18, and 19." The *Progrès* stood ready to deal with last-minute maneuvers of the enemy, such as Duchâtel's attempt to mislead credulous voters by declaring that he, too, was a Napoleonic candidate.

Duchâtel's wiles were in vain. On February 20 the Baron calmly retired to his estate, as was his habit, to await the returns. The first were reported from neighboring communes in the afternoon by his own supporters, who remained to watch the totals mount. Through the evening they waited, the master of the house within, the peasants on the lawn

"Pyrénées-Occidentales"

outside. By midnight, the Baron and his son knew they had been elected; by 2 A.M. Jolibois also was sure of his seat. Thereupon the doors and windows of the dining room were thrown open, and all who could pressed their way in, while even those still outside could hear Jolibois' victory speech. It was a sort of *tableau vivant* of authoritarian democracy.

Roy de Loulay *fils* and Fournier had also been elected, while at Rochefort the Bonapartist candidate had been defeated by a margin of only 400 votes among 13,000. Five seats out of seven—it was almost a sweep. While retaining control of his department's political capital in a ferocious battle against "a man who neglected no means, no outrage, spent much money, had powerful means of action, and was backed by the municipal government of Saintes and by the railway personnel," Eschasseriaux had also elected a youth and an outsider on the strength of his name or his endorsement alone.[46]

It should be clear from this feat that Cassagnac's "Napoléon Vannois," even in a department as like the "Pyrénées-Occidentales" as reality is ever like dreams, had to possess more substantial attributes than the simplicity of his manners and the eloquence of his doctrine if he were to defeat his several enemies. He had to be a tenacious and systematic organizer, a generous friend and an unforgiving foe. Above all he had to be possessed of a certain obstinate conviction of his own inevitable necessity. But as Rouher was all too bitterly aware, such men were hard to come by. In the middle of a letter to Eschasseriaux, the Vice-Emperor suddenly exclaimed: "How essential it is to have a man, an organizer!" Not only did such a leader arrange and discipline the forces of his party, he increased them ten-fold. "But alas! He is a *rara avis*, we unfortunately almost never find him in most of the other departments." Thus while he hardly worried about

[46] Eschasseriaux, "Mémoires," VIII, 285–286, 290, 293–294, 299–303.

the Charente-Inférieure—"you are there"—he confided to Eschasseriaux that "what profoundly disturbs me is the Charente," though it was a department so like its neighbor in economic foundations and political inclinations as to be almost its twin. "There all is confusion and disorder," he wrote on January 3, 1876. "Those who should be directing are shirking, or confining themselves to their personal objectives, and thus we are exposed to the most unexpected results." The various leaders were continuing to wrangle even at this late date over the allotment of the places. "I shall write to them," he concluded resignedly, "but frequent interviews have shown me to be powerless." More than a month later he had received no response to his supplications for agreement, and when the polls opened, as he had feared, in two districts there were Bonapartists opposing each other (thus forcing a *scrutin de ballotage*) while in another there was no Bonapartist candidate at all.[47] This sort of unwillingness to subordinate one's own interests to the party's, which might compromise its prospects even in so auspicious a department, stood in stark contrast with the orderly discipline in the Republican ranks which even Bonapartist propagandists ruefully admired.[48]

The rarity of dynamic leaders who, like Eschasseriaux, were willing and able to organize a whole department and thus effectively to mobilize the peasants for the Empire was not the only crippling disability Rouher foresaw his party would face in the general elections. He knew also that many of his followers, precisely because they had not built up this kind of organization, would be inclined to mute their Bonapartism in a search for votes anywhere they could find them. Personally he was as convinced as ever that in a democratic election the wise candidate would run on an uncompromisingly Bona-

[47] Rouher to Eschasseriaux, April 25, 1875, January 3, 1876 (Eschasseriaux, "Mémoires," VIII, 94, 239, 243, 281).
[48] F. Perron, *Le reveil de la France* (Paris, n.d.), 47–48.

partist program, which would attract far more votes than any alliance with the other parties of the Right. "Candidacies whose significance is precise and uncontested," he wrote, "alone can create currents in the rural populations; only they prepare and assure the future of the Empire." A mixed conservative ticket, on the other hand, was "only a factitious hodgepodge painfully put together during the electoral period, which comes undone at the convening of the Assembly." But he was forced to confess that his ideas were not widely shared among the Bonapartist notables of the departments. "Our friends are separated from the masses by the curtain of the bourgeoisie, which closes their horizon. They concentrate all their politics in their personal relations, and are always ready to come to an agreement with their neighbor, whatever he is." This was why he was so anxious for an election by *scrutin de liste*, which would require the adoption of the same unambiguous *profession de foi* by a complete slate of candidates in a department. *Scrutin d'arrondissement*, leaving each candidate free to concentrate on his own district and to abandon the others to his conservative neighbors, "would be the signal for a real rout." [49]

Because of the financial embarrassment of the rue de l'Elysée, however, Rouher was in no position to prevent this rout. He had at first hoped to present a strongly Bonapartist candidate in every *arrondissement*, but since he could not pay for them, the *comité de comptabilité* was obliged to settle for much less. According to the report of a police spy, "instead of supporting energetic candidacies, they will support those of rich men," upon whom they could not hope to enforce outspoken fidelity to Bonapartism. They had, however, "no choice but to take what they can find, that is, what will cost little or nothing." As a result the choice of candidates and the

[49] Rouher to Mme. Lepic, August 31, 1875 (dossier "Correspondance avec M. Rouher," Raoul-Duval papers).

Bonapartism after Sedan

effective direction of the campaign escaped from the Vice-Emperor's hands, and the central organization constituted for the elections called itself *not* a National Imperialist Committee, or even a National Committee for the Appeal to the People, but rather the *Comité national conservateur*, an alias which even caused it to be confused with the Monarchists' *Comité central de l'Union conservatrice*. The propaganda which it distributed limited itself to a discreet reference to the "rights of universal suffrage" on the "day when the Constitution can be legally revised." Apart from this obscure concession to plebiscitary principles, the language of its manifestoes was suitably banal: its candidates stood for "obedience to the law; support for Marshal MacMahon; . . . affirmation of the ideas of peace, order, progress." [50]

Baron Eschasseriaux received his share of placards in this vein, but took good care not to have them distributed, since "they were a sort of catch-all [*selle à tous chevaux*] which said nothing in particular, which I did not need, and the text of which might not have pleased some of my voters." Boffinton and Roy de Loulay did not use them either.[51]

Outside the Charente-Inférieure, however, many candidates were glad to employ the placards, whose evasive language accorded so well with the guarded tone of their own platforms. This coyness was not a new problem in 1876: two years earlier Eschasseriaux had vainly urged a colleague running in the Vienne to adopt a boldly Bonapartist platform. The other had replied that his *profession de foi* had been drawn up in agreement with conservatives of all parties, as his circumstances required, an answer which the Baron had correctly interpreted to mean that it was "colorless, uninteresting

---

[50] Police reports of December 10, December 20, December 27, 1875; January 27, 1876 (dossiers "Eugène Rouher," APP B^{A}1257). *L'Ordre*, January 26, January 30, 1876.
[51] Eschasseriaux, "Mémoires," VIII, 295–296.

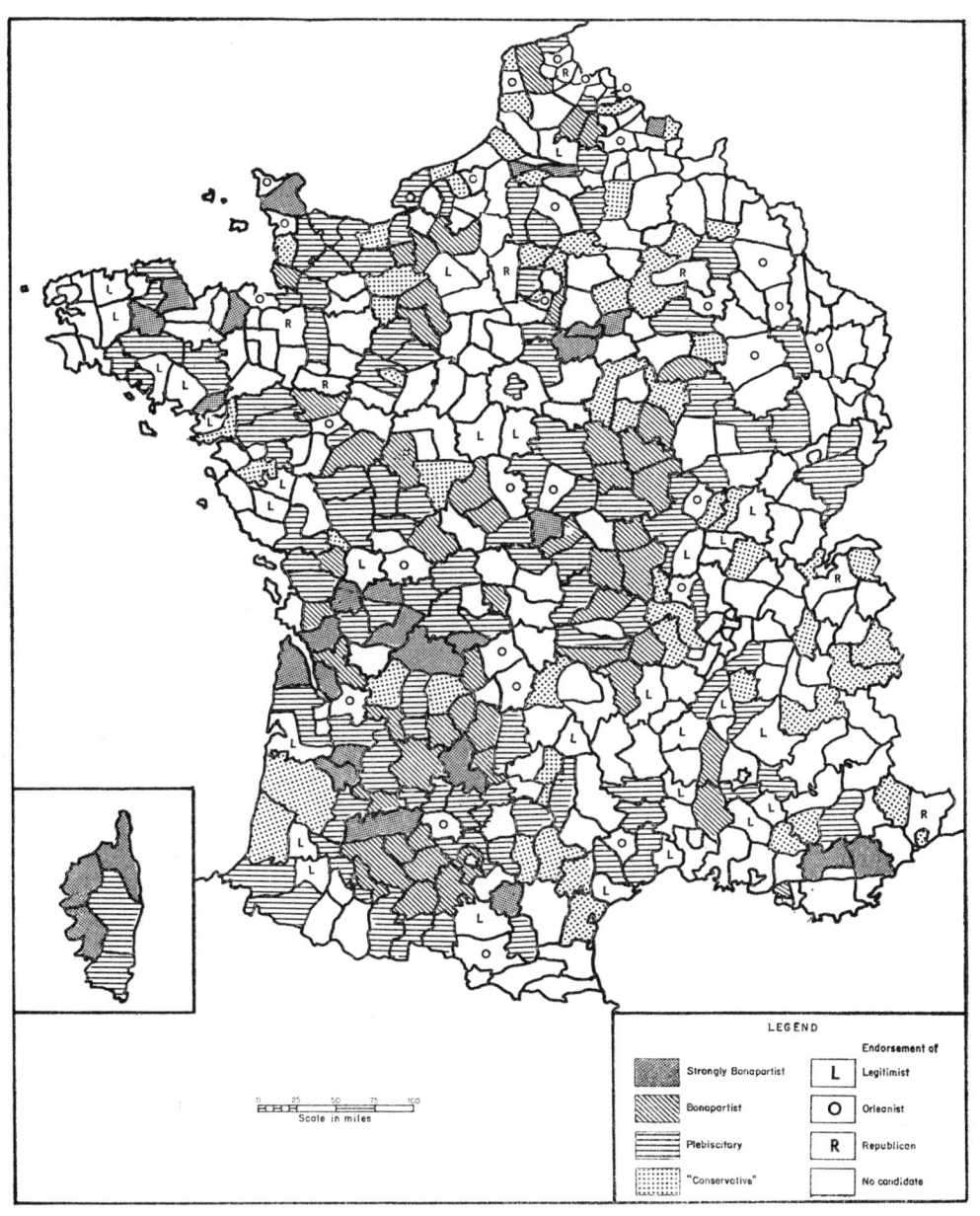

Map 5: Platforms of candidates endorsed by the *Comité national conservateur* for the general elections of February 20, 1876

to the voters, and that he would be beaten." In the town of Poitiers, where the bourgeoisie favored conservative union, he had lost few votes, but he had been "abandoned by the countryside, which went over to the red banner out of hatred for the white" (since the Republicans naturally insinuated that the nondescript platform concealed a Legitimist.) This disaster had led Rouher to insist that all candidates wishing his support must run on unambiguous platforms.[52]

How far he was able to enforce this principle in 1876 the reader may observe by consulting the first of the maps which illustrate this chapter. It portrays the extent to which Bonapartist themes outweighed conservative ones in the platform of each of the candidates endorsed by the *Comité national conservateur*. To the first category, the strongly Bonapartist, belong the words of Paul de Cassagnac: "If you have faithfully cherished the memory of the two Emperors . . . who both died for you, martyrs of the people, victims of feudal Europe . . . elect me; since, after the Marshal . . . I see only the popular candidate, . . . who will be called, by law and by the national will, Napoleon IV."

The platform of Baron Dufour, candidate in the Lot, less declamatory, is still clearly Bonpartist. He counted himself "among those who have not forgotten the Empire and its benefits," did not conceal his "regret at its fall," or his conviction "that the immense majority of the country is grateful to the popular government which gave it twenty years of order and prosperity." But he would "energetically support the powers and the conservative government of Marshal MacMahon," until the moment of legal revision, when "I shall ask that France be freely and directly consulted." [53]

[52] Eschasseriaux, "Mémoires," VII, 271–272, 276; *L'Ordre*, March 22, 1874.

[53] Félix Ribeyre, *Biographie des sénateurs et des députés* (new ed.; Paris, n.d.), 387, 433. In addition to Ribeyre, the map is based on

"Pyrénées-Occidentales"

Running in the Southeast, not the Southwest, Ernest Pinard drew up a platform which was merely plebiscitary. Declaring that he might have dispensed with a platform since "as you have known me, so I have remained" (clearly an effort to recall his past to Bonapartists and conceal it from others), he reiterated his desire "to support the ideas of order and social conservation." He sincerely accepted "without mental reservations" the existing constitution, and would "resolutely support" MacMahon. In case of revision, though "respectful of all convictions, as of all hopes, wishing to leave the last word to experience and opinion," he would ask that "before any discussion of the form of government, the entire country be previously consulted." Only by the last phrase did his platform really qualify as plebiscitary, yet, in a department where the conservatives had apportioned the districts to prevent dividing the anti-Republican vote, he was bitterly criticized even for that most subdued reference to an appeal to the people.[54] If he had omitted it, his *profession de foi* would have fallen into the fourth category, the conservative, bidding as it did for the support of all the groups of the Right with its respect for "all convictions."

Certainly the events of the past year had provided good reasons in 1876 for candidates to temper their language, lest their own propagandistic weapons be turned against them. A poster in the Gironde on the eve of the elections warned the voters that they must "defend the ideas of order, conservation, and peace against the doctrines and claims of a party whose program can be summed up in two words: War and Revolution!" This was published by a *Republican* against a

---

the texts of, or excerpts from, *professions de foi* given in the *Ordre*, the *Temps*, or the *Figaro* of the month preceding the election, or in A. Robert, E. Bourloton, and G. Cougny, eds., *Dictionnaire des parlementaires français 1789–1889* (Paris, 1891).

[54] Pinard, *Journal*, II, 278–279.

Bonapartism after Sedan

Bonapartist.[55] After five years of uncertainty, many voters would not gladly see jeopardized the comparative stability promised by the constitution of 1875.[56]

This general consideration, however, cannot explain the *distribution* of these several sorts of *professions de foi*; they were likely to be more Bonapartist to the west and southwest of Paris, more conservative to the east and southeast. The most compelling reason for the writing of a noncommittal platform was that the candidate, lacking an organized Bonapartist following in his district, had come to an understanding with the other conservative parties, preferably to avoid two anti-Republican candidates in any one *arrondissement*, or at least to avoid an Orleanist or Legitimist candidacy in his own, or even at worst to ensure that the conservative with the lowest total on the first *tour* desisted in favor of the other for the *scrutin de ballotage*. (Cases of Bonapartists coming to such agreements with Republicans against Monarchists were very rare.) Even Eschasseriaux, at the farthest ebb of his fortunes in 1871, had thought of a rapprochement in the "interests of order" with the Legitimists, but the resurgence of Bonapartism had led him quickly to repudiate a conservative union with men in whom he had so little trust.[57]

These electoral marriages of convenience celebrated with rivals on the Right, if consummated at all, were not, indeed, necessarily destined for tranquillity, as Pinard, a former minister of the Emperor who had made no mention of the Emperor's heir in his platform, soon discovered. The Legitimist paper of his department, alarmed at his prospects of success, advised its readers to abstain, since Pinard represented only

---

[55] AN BB^{30}1121, dossier Bordeaux.
[56] Prefect of Seine-Inférieure to Raoul-Duval, December 2, 1875 (dossier "1875," Raoul-Duval papers).
[57] Eschasseriaux, "Mémoires," VI, 120, 430–431.

"Pyrénées-Occidentales"

"temporary order," and "immediate disorder" following the election of his Radical opponent was preferable, since "evil, worsening, evokes immediate reactions"—that is, a Monarchist restoration.[58]

The Monarchists of Pinard's department had broken an initial agreement in adopting this *politique du pire*. In many departments, however, they practiced it from the first: throughout France, about half the Bonapartist candidates in 1876 faced a three-cornered struggle, battling a Republican on the Left and a Monarchist of some sort, sometimes disguised as a "constitutionalist," on the Right. (Of course the third and weakest candidate was not always the Monarchist.) This statistic alone serves to throw grave doubts on the *general* desirability and efficacy of the conservative union which the Bonapartists had so long pursued at Versailles and which they again emphasized by dubbing their campaign headquarters the "conservative" National Committee. Such tactical expedients might sometimes be helpful or even indispensable on the local level. On the national level, however, they ran quite counter to what might seem the natural policy of the Bonapartist party: to "convert the . . . elections into a plebiscite" by having "all the Imperialist candidates sign the same single declaration, in which they pledge themselves *to ask revision of the constitution in favor of an appeal to the people*." Either France wanted the Empire or not. The only way to find out was to ask her. If the candidates who signed such a declaration had a majority in both chambers, the answer would be irrefutable.[59]

If the *Comité national conservateur* had elected almost all of the 320-odd candidates it endorsed (for 525 electoral districts in metropolitan France), a plebiscite still would not have been voted at the convening of the new Chamber of

[58] Pinard, *Journal*, II, 279–280.   [59] Perron, *Reveil*, 57–58.

Deputies, for, as the student of the map has already noted, many of the committee's candidates *were not Bonapartists*, not even the kind who avoided mentioning the Empire in their *professions de foi*; they were Orleanists or Legitimists. A half-dozen of those men endorsed were actually running on frankly Republican platforms. The Bonapartist party, which had boasted so ostentatiously (as did Cassagnac's "Napoleon Vannois") that it alone was capable of facing universal suffrage, was in fact able to muster only about 225 candidates of its own in 1876 (while the other conservatives from the extreme Right to the constitutionalist Center produced almost 400, and the Republicans of all nuances close to 600.) In some of the many districts where it could find no one to run, it could only endorse the most palatable of its opponents in the hope that this kindness would be reciprocated where its candidate was the Republican's sole challenger.

Given the inadequacy of the party's central treasury, only a rich man could face the exorbitant expenses of an election, a fact which must have deterred many potential candidates. There were thousands of ballots and handbills to be printed, and sometimes placards to deny last-minute calumnies; the printer's bill might come to over 500 francs in a small and lightly-populated district.[60] Paying electoral agents to distribute these materials and to gather information in the communes came higher: one candidate paid 5,000 francs for such services, including copying out the electoral lists (2,000 francs) and correcting them (850).[61] And these were merely the ordinary expenses; bidding against a well-backed opponent might go far higher. The Bonapartist running in the second district of Le Havre dropped out on the second *tour* because the prodigality of his constitutionalist rival had con-

[60] Bill in Saint-Paul papers, château of Poudelaye (Ariège).

[61] A. Tardiveau to Raoul-Duval, March 16, 1876 (dossier "1876," Raoul-Duval papers).

"Pyrénées-Occidentales"

verted the contest from an election into an auction. His opponent spent on the two *tours* no less than 200,000 francs, much of it in direct payment for votes.[62]

Some potential candidates for the Chamber who remained undismayed by the prospect of such financial sacrifices may well have been discouraged by the results of the senatorial elections of January 30, 1876. These were a virtually unmitigated disaster: the Bonapartists, who had no life-Senators, managed to elect fewer than thirty of their candidates for limited terms. Nor did all the rare victories reflect the same methodical preparation which had brought a sweep in the Charente-Inférieure; often they were the result of a deal concluded with the Prefect or with the government. On the other hand, even good organization had not availed in the Pas-de-Calais, thanks to the Monarchists' indifference to conservative union; the Bonapartist list was beaten there by a compromise ticket including three Legitimists—and a Republican. The *Ordre*, however, had written off in advance these Orleanist-inspired consultations of a few hundred great electors under the eye of officialdom. Confidently it looked to the elections of February 20, when "the work of universal suffrage will begin."[63]

Before embarking on a *tour de France* to test this assertion that a democratic contest would tell another story, it will be well to recall to what extent Republicans and Monarchists had made inroads on Bonapartist strength before the Empire fell. The second map illustrating this chapter will permit a judgment of the degree to which Bonapartism was losing,

[62] A. Corneille to Raoul-Duval, March 8, 1876 (dossier "1876," Raoul-Duval papers).

[63] Richard, *Bonapartisme*, 153–154; *L'Ordre*, January 31, 1876; Daniel, ed., *Année politique*—1876, 19, 21, 86. For a list of Bonapartist Senators, see 25, but compare the biographies of these men in Robert, Bourloton, and Cougny, eds., *Dictionnaire* (hereafter cited as RBC).

Bonapartism after Sedan

holding, or regaining ground in 1876. (The results of the Emperor's last plebiscite should also be borne in mind.) [64]

In 1870 the southwestern region of France had been, from the point of view of the Ministry of the Interior, the most satisfactory of all. In only three departments of fourteen had independent or opposition deputies been elected; in only one, the Gironde, had there been less than 60 per cent *oui*, reflecting the subversive disposition of Bordeaux. Toulouse also had given a majority of noes, but, taking the countryside into account, the Southwest was thoroughly Bonapartist. The West, from Poitou to Normandy, presented a rather less satisfactory picture. Its showing in the plebiscite had been quite good, with only two departments registering less than 65 per cent *oui* (one of these being the Seine-Inférieure, where the opposition of the industrial proletariat was reinforced by a general attitude toward free trade very different from that prevailing in the Charente-Inférieure). But the incidence of independent or opposition deputies suggested the strength of Orleanism and particularly of Legitimism in some of these regions, though public opinion there might acquiesce in a reformed Empire. Judging by their failure to elect the Opposition and by their enthusiastic response in 1870, the Vendée, the Deux-Sèvres, and the Vienne were fully as Bonapartist as the neighboring Charente; the same could not be said of the Breton and some of the Norman departments.

In the region of Paris and the Center, opposition decreased in proportion to the distance one traveled from the capital (the department of the Seine was one of two in France to cast a majority of negative votes in 1870). Departments like the Indre and the Allier, on the fringes of the Massif Central, gave

[64] Sources for this map are Félix Ribeyre, *Biographie des députés* . . . (Paris, 1864), checked with *Liste de Messieurs les députés* (Paris, 1869), and *Liste de Messieurs les députés* (Paris, 1870). For the plebiscite, see Jacques Gouault, *Comment la France est devenue républicaine: Les elections générales et partielles à l'Assemblée nationale 1870–1875* (Paris, 1954), 27.

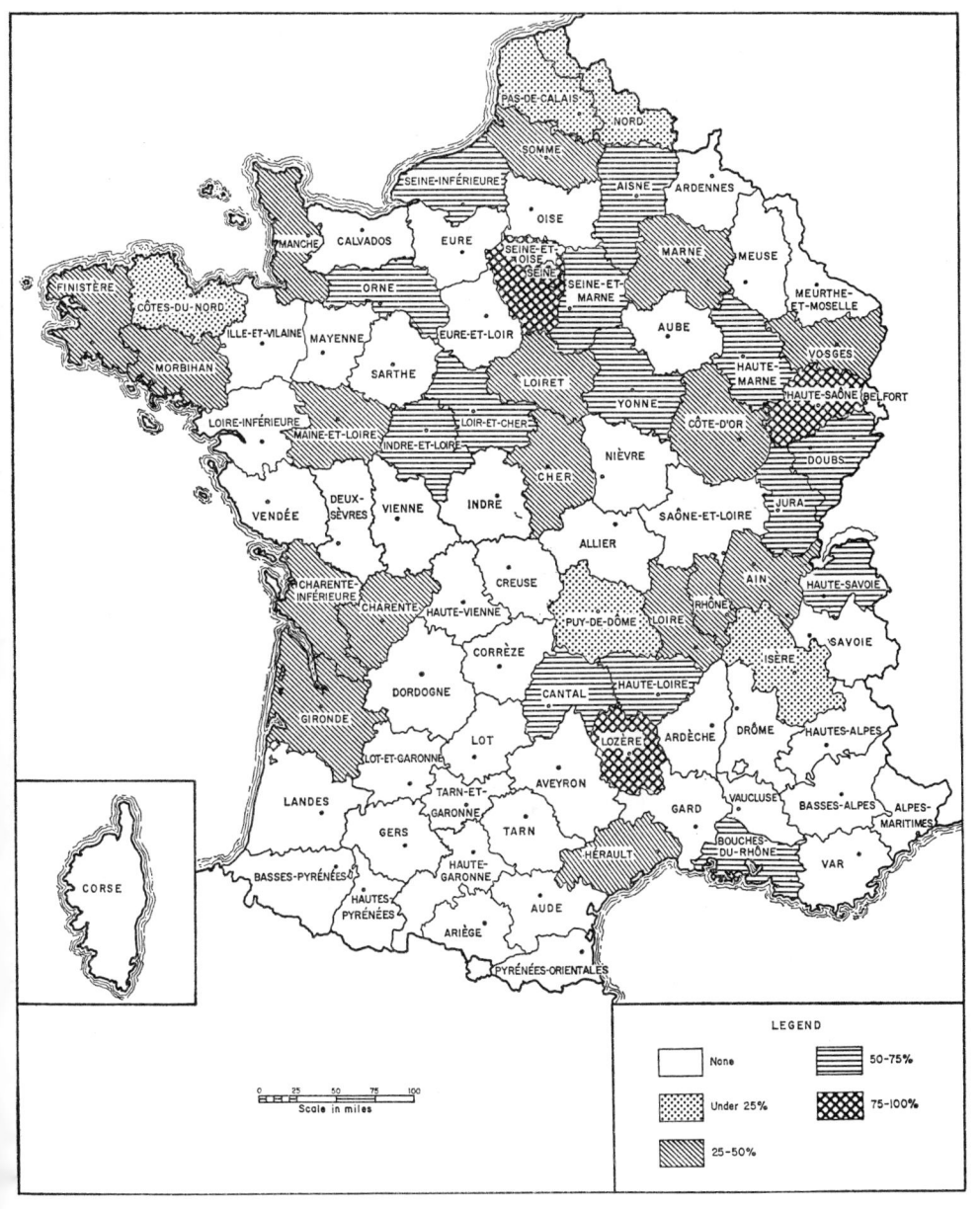

Map 6: Percentage by *département* of independent and opposition deputies in the *Corps législatif* in 1870

no encouragement to the Opposition either by electing its candidates or by voting *non*, whereas the Seine-et-Oise did both. The North was similarly divided: despite the hostility of industrial towns, it offered such figures to gladden a Bonapartist heart as the Pas-de-Calais' 171,000 *oui* to 9,600 *non*. Yet in the Aisne, the total was not so impressive, and half the deputation were not official deputies.

It was in the regions of the East, of Lyon, Savoy, and Dauphiné, and along the Mediterranean littoral that opposition had been most strongly displayed in 1869–1870. Although the Ardennes and the Meuse had manifested in both consultations a strong preference for the Empire, the East counted four departments with less than 60 per cent *oui*, and the Rhône, the Isère and the Drôme had bare majorities, reflecting in some cases again the workers' hostility to the regime, in others the anticlerical Republicanism of the Burgundian low-landers. Dauphiné remained a Republican stronghold, though a backward department like the Hautes-Alpes could be won over by special efforts of charity on the part of the government before the polls opened. Along the coast, in Languedoc and Provence, the prognosis for Bonapartism was gloomiest of all; out of nine departments, only one had produced more than 70 per cent *oui*, five others gave the Empire only a bare majority, and one, the Bouches-du-Rhône, shared with the Seine the lonely grandeur or ignominy of a *non* majority. Marius tended to be either Red or White, uninterested in the somber Imperial blue. The Legitimist Whites, by electing clericals rallied to the Empire, concealed the real extent of opposition, but the Republican Reds, not only of the towns but also of the countryside, made their weight felt in 1870.[65]

[65] Charles Seignobos, *Le déclin de l'Empire et l'établissement de la Troisième République* (Paris, 1921), 97–101. Cf. Gordon Wright, "The Distribution of French Parties in 1865; An Official Survey," *Journal of Modern History*, XV (December, 1943), 295–302.

"Pyrénées-Occidentales"

Against this background we must now analyze, region by region, the results in 1876, to see to what degree the departments of each conformed to the fanciful socio-political model of Cassagnac's "Pyrénées-Occidentales" or the real one of Eschasseriaux's Charente-Inférieure. (See Maps 7 and 8.)

Obviously the Southwest remained the Bonapartists' bastion, with half of its departments approaching and two achieving an absolute majority of votes cast. These fourteen departments together sent well over one-third of the Bonapartists elected to the Chamber. Everywhere political machines similar to the Baron's assured victory by fostering the kind of peasant enthusiasm Cassagnac's pamphlet depicted.

In his letter to the Emperor at the end of 1872, Eschasseriaux had reported even better prospects in the Charente than in his own department, since it had fewer Protestant Republicans and a higher proportion of rural voters. Under the guidance of a powerful local paper which penetrated into every commune, the population would give the Empire a majority of over 80 per cent as they had done in 1870.[66] Leadership in 1876, as Rouher's laments attest, had not been concentrated as it was in the Charente-Inférieure, but a dominant popular personality, whose energy the Baron praised, was at last emerging.

When the Republicans, having been unable to prevent the repeated elections of the young editor Gustave Cunéo d'Ornano,[67] resorted in despair to the invalidating him, the testimony of their witnesses before the investigating committee of the Chamber was an involuntary tribute to his knowledge of the Charentais peasant. He worked hard, re-

[66] Eschasseriaux, "Mémoires," VII, 7–8.
[67] Gustave Cunéo d'Ornano, born 1845, employed in the Prefecture of the Seine under the Empire, journalist in Paris 1871–1873 and thereafter in the Charente; grandson of a companion-in-arms of Napoleon I. (Ribeyre, *Biographie*, 528; RBC, II, 230–231.) Eschasseriaux, "Mémoires," VIII, 182.

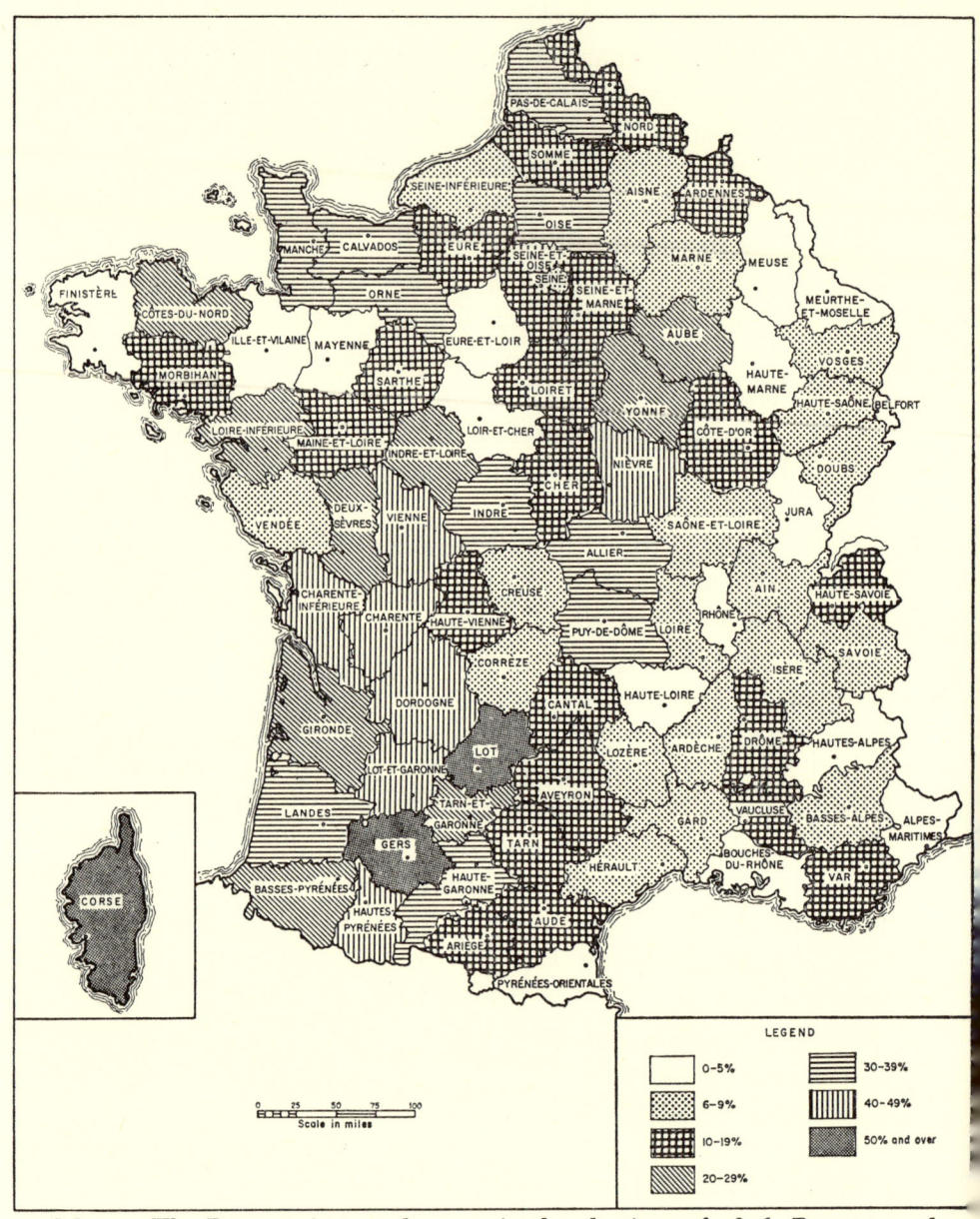

Map 7: The Bonapartist popular vote in the elections of 1876: Percentage, by *départements*, of votes cast February 20

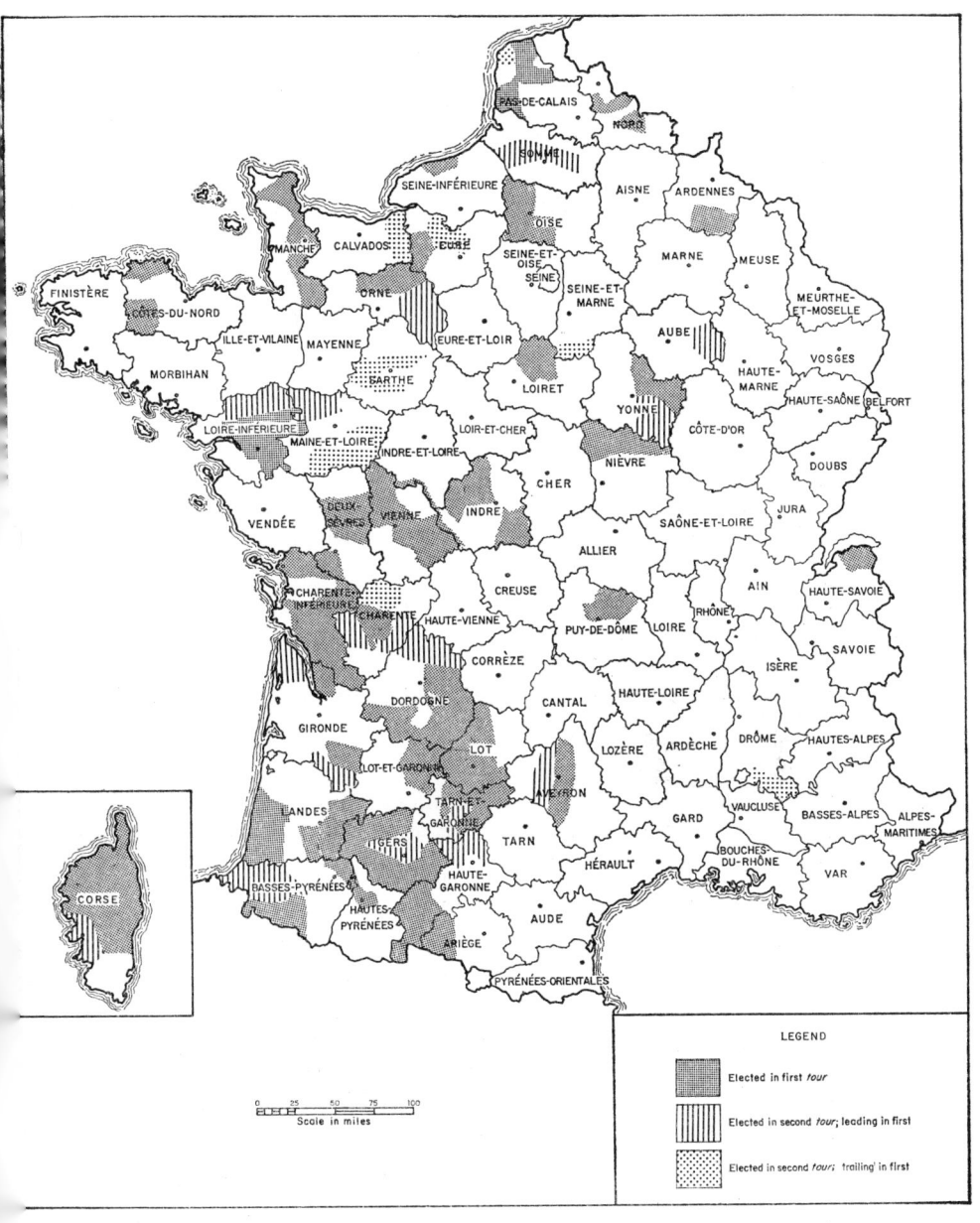

Map 8: *Arrondissements* electing Bonapartist candidates on February 20 and March 5, 1876

ported one, at "provoking and maintaining . . . hatred between the city and the countryside," where the voters had an "absolutely unthinking" attachment to the Empire. Like Eschasseriaux, he recalled how the Empire's commercial treaties, its railways and roads, had benefited the peasant. This theme was echoed, explained the Mayor of Angoulême, by the most authoritative personages, the "lower *fonctionnaires*, who are almost all hostile." It was only natural that the voters were skeptical of a new government attacked by its own representatives, and voted against it. As a Republican, however, the Mayor felt that the domination of Bonapartism would not prove unending. He bluntly declared: "The number of illiterates is 35 per cent. It is among them that the adherents of the Bonapartist party are recruited." Already its membership was stationary, while the Republicans were constantly growing. With a purge of the bureaucracy, the extension of primary education, and the advent of a new generation to the privilege of suffrage, the Bonapartists would soon be outpaced.[68]

As *missus dominici*, Eschasseriaux had also been optimistic about the department of the Gironde, which was "bad only in Bordeaux and the *chefs-lieux* of the *arrondissements*." The rivalries and selfish preoccupations of the several leaders had prevented the development of the department-wide electoral organization, commune by commune, which the Baron recommended. Rouher indeed thought that the Monarchists of the Gironde were not only more practical and richer, but better organized than his own party.[69] Within their individual districts, however, the Bonapartists skillfully employed their personal influence to secure their power by means of

[68] AN C3230, "Chambre des députés—2e législature—Enquête parlementaire sur les élections générales des 14 et 28 Octobre 1877," dossier 1217 (hereafter cited as AN C3229, etc.).

[69] Rouher to Eschasseriaux, July 31, 1873; Eschasseriaux, "Mémoires," VII, 8–9, 141–142.

"Pyrénées-Occidentales"

"the services they continually render to their voters," according to the testimony of a hostile witness. Like their friends in the Charente, Girondin Republicans took comfort in what they expected would be the inevitable effect of spreading civilization. In communes along the new railways it would soon be impossible to convince the peasants that the advent of the Prince Imperial was only a few weeks off.[70]

The Dordogne in 1876 largely confirmed Eschasseriaux's prognostications. The work of "actively and tenaciously assembling the elements of an electoral organization by *arrondissement*, canton, and commune" had been carried out by Pierre Magne's son. The local press was favorable, and "except for a few points, the countryside is in general very conservative."[71] The peasants remembered the prosperity they had owed to the Empire and proved it with their votes, electing five Bonapartists, including Magne's brother-in-law. The future Minister of the Interior of the *Seize Mai*, Fourtou, though not a member of the *Appel au peuple*, also was elected with Bonapartist support, accorded in the spirit of conservative union preached by Magne.

The Lot, the Lot-et-Garonne, and the Landes, all under the active leadership of powerful individuals or families, also lived up to the expectations of their *missus dominici*. The political complexion of the Lot—Republicans opposing Bonapartists, with nothing in between—derived less from convictions than from the influence of two powerful rival families: Murat and Calmon.[72] The clan of the cavalryman who became a King still held the upper hand here in their ancestral home, as they had in 1871.

In the Lot-et-Garonne the leader was Noubel, the owner

---

[70] AN C3234, dossier 1225, no. 1.
[71] Eschasseriaux, "Mémoires," VII, 9–10.
[72] Attorney-general, Agen, to Keeper of the Seals, October 19, 1874 (AN BB30 1121); cf. Eschasseriaux, "Mémoires," VII, 12–13.

Bonapartism after Sedan

and editor of the only important local paper, who had been an official deputy throughout the Empire. The party had acquired as a convert a deputy of the department, Sarrette, who had been elected in 1871 largely in recognition of his patriotism in enlisting, at an advanced age, as a private in the *Garde mobile,* but though Eschasseriaux admitted he was "very devoted," he also thought him "too new in politics and too far from the center of the department to have an effective and preponderant influence on the direction of business." Here as elsewhere in France the Bonapartism of the Republic was the almost exclusive affair of the old Bonapartists of the Empire. It was under Noubel's orders that free trade committees were established in every canton by the end of 1872. Such direction produced encouraging results—"the young men of the richest and most influential families . . . are almost all Bonapartist and prepare good cadres for the future"—and Eschasseriaux could report that Noubel hoped, "as does my father-in-law, . . . a former deputy, very involved in politics in this department," for a Bonapartist victory in the general elections. Their popular vote did prove impressive, although, owing to the *scrutin d'arrondissement* which some Bonapartist deputies had helped enact, the Lot-et-Garonne sent only one to Versailles. (A more proportional system of representation would have given them at least one more seat.)

In the Landes, it was Eschasseriaux's *brother*-in-law who led the Bonapartist party, through the *Adour* of Dax. Their total was less impressive in this department only because he thought it wise to allow a Legitimist a place on his conservative ticket.[73]

There could be no question of such toleration in the Gers, where perhaps the most formidable family machine of all, a veritable car of Juggernaut, was ready to be wheeled into action in 1876. There was both admiration and fellow-feeling

[73] Eschasseriaux, "Mémoires," VII, 10–12.

"*Pyrénées-Occidentales*"

in Baron Eschasseriaux's tone when he wrote that "the Gers is rightly thought the most Bonapartist department of . . . the Midi. The honor of having kept it on the straight and narrow path belongs to MM. de Cassagnac." The power of father and son had seemed on the wane at the end of the Empire; then M. Thiers had sent a Legitimist Prefect to this "basically democratic and revolutionary" department, populated, like the Charentes, largely by winegrowing smallholders. This blunder they were quick to exploit, for while Paul de Cassagnac in Paris was the most outspoken champion of the Bonapartist "Coblence," at home in the Gers he was an ardent authoritarian democrat, as the language of his *profession de foi* suggests. Rapidly they reasserted their ascendancy, employing not only a bureaucratic personnel under their sway, but also their powerful newspaper, which indulged, according to an official report, in "unheard-of violence and . . . wild exaggerations of polemic," to which its Republican rival replied in kind. The Legitimists were not to be left out: ironically, this home department of one of the chief artisans of conservative union was one of only two in France in which there were three-way struggles among Bonapartists, Republicans, and Monarchists in every district. That it was also one of three in France which gave absolute majorities to the Bonapartists says a good deal about the organizational abilities of the Cassagnacs, however their conservative mentality injured the larger interests of their party.[74]

There were the makings of a similar dynasty in the Tarn-et-Garonne, though unfortunately for the Bonapartists its influence did not encompass the whole department. After Prax-

[74] Eschasseriaux, "Mémoires," VII, 13; AN C3233, dossier 1224, nos. 2, 14; Attorney-general, Agen, to Keeper of the Seals, November 20, 1876 (AN BB^{30}490$_1$, "Elections législatifs de 1876: fraudes et délits électoraux"; hereafter cited as AN BB^{30}490$_1$ etc.). Cf. G. Palmade, "Le Gers," in Louis Girard, ed., *Les élections de 1869* (Paris, 1960), 185–214.

Bonapartism after Sedan

Paris had been reelected by both districts of Montauban, he opted for the first, leaving the other to a certain M. de Loqueyssie, who claimed as his chief qualification for election the fact that Prax-Paris was his uncle.[75]

Even in the Southwest, Bonapartist candidates were not always able to organize their entire departments, to appeal with complete frankness to memories of the Empire, and to scorn the aid of the other conservative parties. In the Ariège, though Baron de Saint-Paul was well aware of the need for complete organization by means of local committees, he concentrated on his own *arrondissement*, leaving the others to an Orleanist and a Legitimist, whose cooperation was essential to his success. To seal the bargain it was necessary to write a "very well thought out platform, Bonapartist enough to electrify our friends, but nonetheless reserved enough not to alienate our friends of the moment."[76] (It fell, in fact, into the category of plebiscitary *professions de foi*, and the *Comité national conservateur* endorsed Saint Paul's two Monarchist neighbors.) Nevertheless, it can be said that Bonapartism had held its ground well in the Southwest in the first five years of the Republic—and particularly by comparison with other regions.

One need go, for purposes of contrast, no farther than the region of the West, no farther even than the department which borders the Charente-Inférieure on the north: the Vendée. Leadership here should have been exercised by the banker Alfred Le Roux, who had been the Empire's official deputy for eighteen years and briefly its minister. But, lacking a machine like Eschasseriaux's, he was not to be lured from the retirement into which he had withdrawn after September 4 until he could again have official support (after *Seize Mai*) and by default the responsibility for leadership fell to a lesser

[75] AN BB^{30}490$_1$, dossier Rennes-Toulouse.
[76] Saint-Paul papers.

"Pyrénées-Occidentales"

man, Pugliesi-Conti, Prefect of the Vendée in 1869. How unsatisfactory a substitute he was, Rouher was well aware. It was true, he admitted to Eschasseriaux, that the "culpable inertia" of Le Roux was an "immeasurable obstacle" for Pugliesi, but in addition the former Prefect "does not have much of a way with people and does not know how to manage when faced with difficulties and personal conflicts." In the Vendée as in other departments, he ruefully concluded, "we suffer from the inferiority of our instruments without being able to do too much about it." All his efforts to goad Pugliesi into action had been without effect. Only five weeks before the senatorial elections the Vice-Emperor was still urgently pressing him to leave Paris, "to get organized, to make up his senatorial list, and to get candidates accepted in each district." Despite Pugliesi's promises, he wondered "Will he act? God grant that he does." Two weeks later he was able to report that Pugliesi had at last reached the Vendée, but it made little difference: "The defection of Le Roux has broken our back in this department. Pugliesi has not the strength to carry on a campaign." And so it proved; far from getting candidates accepted for each district, Pugliesi could not get his own accepted by the voters of the second district of Fontenay-le-Comte, a district of which the social structure bore considerable resemblance to that of the Charente-Inférieure. The Empire in 1876 thus received only a derisory sprinkling of votes in a department honeycombed, according to Republicans, with Bonapartist *fonctionnaires* and other influential personages.[77]

Under abler and more energetic leadership the Vienne and the Deux-Sèvres did comparatively well by the Bonapartists.

[77] Rouher to Eschasseriaux, December 26, 1875, January 12, 1876 (Eschasseriaux, "Mémoires," VIII, 231, 246); AN C3242, dossier Vendée. Cf. M. Faucheux, "La Vendée," in Girard, ed., *Elections*, 127-162.

Bonapartism after Sedan

Farther north, with isolated exceptions, the Republicans and Legitimists divided Brittany, Maine, and Anjou, the former winning the towns, the latter the countryside. Only in parts of Normandy did Bonapartism really manage to hold its own in the West, sometimes aided by official pressure.

In the region of Paris and the Center also, the prewar pattern held true. Bonapartist candidacies were concentrated on the edge of the Massif Central (together with the Nièvre) and immediately around the capital. Some of the former were successful (though *scrutin de liste* would have given the party more victories); none of the latter was.

In the five departments of the North, Bonapartism, where it had been weakest before 1870, went into an accelerated decline; even in the areas where it was still thought after the advent of the Republic to be predominant, the results of 1876 did not really show it to be holding firm.

Less than six months after the Prince Imperial had come of age, his tutor, Ernest Lavisse, was imploring him to take action to restore his party in Lavisse's native Aisne. Though the Opposition had made extensive gains there before 1870, Lavisse was convinced that the election of an exclusively Republican deputation in 1871 had been an accident of circumstances. None of the peasants or bourgeois, and few of the workers were enthusiastic Republicans; they had voted Republican simply because no one had told them that the Empire was still a respectable alternative. Now they had simply lapsed into passivity, tolerating Republican activities but skeptical of the Republic, "the ideal of little men, deserving the amusement of serious people."

Lavisse could envisage two ways by which the Aisne might be shaken out of its apathy and restored to faith in a regime toward which it harbored no fundamental antipathy. The advance of Radicalism might become so menacing as to provoke a panic reaction in favor of the Empire among the population.

"Pyrénées-Occidentales"

If this did not happen, Bonapartism's only salvation would be "the intervention of a directing hand," which Lavisse was convinced could "work miracles." Again and again he returned to this point: the Aisne, socially and economically similar to the Oise, would support the Empire as enthusiastically "if the party were organized among us as it is among them," if it had "a man at its head." But he had also to confess to his Prince that while he could name "several soldiers, among whom I rank myself," he could think of no general. Even in so important a matter as winning over a local conservative newspaper, he had to turn to Levert of the Pas-de-Calais, the *missus dominici* of the North.[78]

Even the most conscientious of *missi* could not be expected, however, to take on the additional burden of organizing a department whose inhabitants themselves were incapable of it. As a result, among the eight districts of the Aisne in 1876, there was but one candidate endorsed by the *Comité national conservateur,* and he, though he had been an official deputy for eighteen years, issued a *profession de foi* in which only a diviner could have detected a tinge of Bonapartism. He was soundly beaten by his Republican opponent. The difference the absence of the vital organizer made (since even the closest connections with Chislehurst could not provide one) is suggested by comparing this result with that of the Oise, led by the Chevreau brothers.

Elsewhere in the North the Bonapartist percentages looked more impressive than in fact they were. For the North was the peculiarly congenial habitat of conservative Bonapartists who were more conservative than Bonapartist. (Clercq, a deputy who in the last months of the National Assembly

---

[78] Ernest Lavisse to the Prince Imperial, November 14, 1874, in C. L. d'Espinay de Briort, ed., "Une correspondance inédite: le Prince Impérial et Ernest Lavisse, 1871–1879," *Revue des Deux Mondes,* 7th period, L (1929), 561–564.

actually tried to organize a new group midway between the Orleanist Right Center and the *Appel au peuple*, came from the Pas-de-Calais.) [79] The last thing these Orleano-Bonapartists wanted was too candid an evocation of Bonapartism, and when, in 1874, they had been confronted with that possibility, they had quickly blocked it. Baron de Saint-Paul had been a Prefect *à poing* in the Nord and the right-hand-man of Rouher. Therefore, a letter to Saint-Paul bitterly informed him, the faint-hearted leaders of the Bonapartist party found him too embarrassing a by-election candidate, and promised their support instead to a conservative, on the sole condition that he include in his platform a vague reference to an eventual plebiscite. It was to be feared that if Saint-Paul insisted on running anyhow, he would be defeated by this rival whose noncommittal position was better suited to the cautious politics of the Nord, especially since Bonapartism had no organization and just one local paper, read only at Lille.[80]

The same attitudes and conduct prevailed in 1876. The Orleano-Bonapartists were above all economic protectionists devoted to the parliamentarism which could guarantee their indispensable tariffs. Thus they had many reservations about the regime of Napoleon III, yet were still anxious to retain the votes of the pro-Imperial countryside. Balancing between the special interests of their class and the democratic electorate, they were political tightrope-walkers, as their uncompromising *professions de foi* revealed. One such candidate of the *Comité national conservateur*, Hamille of the Pas-de-Calais, owed his unopposed reelection, according to an official report, to his moderate voting record (he had parted from the Bonapartists by voting, for example, for Broglie in 1874) and to "the great cleverness of his platform."[81] The care with

[79] See his biography in RBC, II, 134–135.
[80] Saint-Paul papers.
[81] Attorney-general, Douai, to Keeper of the Seals, February 17, 1876 (AN BB^{30}490$_3$).

"Pyrénées-Occidentales"

which some deputies of the North hid their real preferences of regime, in fact, sometimes makes it difficult to tell whether they (and therefore the votes cast for them) were "Bonapartist" or not. In any case their percentages cannot be interpreted in any plebiscitary sense. Conservative union here was all too real in many *arrondissements*.

From the eastern and southeastern regions the party could not derive even the small comfort afforded by the election of the Orleano-Bonapartists in the North. There had already been a crucial test of the survival of the Imperial idea in the Aube in 1873, and the result had been anything but encouraging. Rouher and Eschasseriaux had closely watched their candidate, Argence, in this by-election, and both had approved his decision to refuse any concession to the idea of conservative union by openly advocating a plebiscite. But the Baron had soon begun to receive warnings "that the mentality of the inhabitants of the Aube was not the same as that of the Charente-Inférieure, that the theory of the *Appel au peuple* found many contradictors, and that the election of Argence, combatted by six papers of the department, was very problematical." A grim analysis of Argence's defeat, given Eschasseriaux by a correspondent, suggests that in the East even a well-organized Bonapartist party had been unable to reverse the inclinations of the voters. Though Argence had benefited from the support or at least the neutrality of the Monarchists and from the help of the former Prefect and Sub-Prefect, though he was "regarded by all as the expression of Bonapartism," his Republican opponent had outdistanced him by a margin which no one had foreseen. Clearly the peasants of the Aube had forgotten "their former cult of Bonaparte" and in any plebiscite would vote as "red" as the population of the towns.[82]

After a disappointment of this magnitude, it is not surprising that in 1876 there were few Bonapartist candidacies and even

[82] Eschasseriaux, "Mémoires," VII, 164, 171, 201, 213, 217.

Bonapartism after Sedan

fewer victories in these regions. Rouher himself wrote them off, admitting in 1875 that they were not organized. He had sent his *missus* on three successive trips to Franche-Comté, but there were virtually no candidates to be found, and those who did consent to run were, he thought, defying common sense. (In fact, one of the two victors in the East said nothing of the Empire in his platform, while the other, who had been an official deputy, categorically denied that he was still a Bonapartist, though he had no compunctions, once elected, about joining the *Appel au peuple*.) [83] The party's position was as weak in Dauphiné as in Franche-Comté. In 1874, an official report had declared that though there might still be latent Imperial sympathies in the Isère, "for lack of organizers, Bonapartism does not exist in this department as a political party." [84] The results of 1876 make clear that in two years nothing had been done to repair the deficiency.

That it was essential for victory to have a candidate of local eminence to lead the campaign, the results in the Massif Central clearly demonstrated. In this region a complete Bonapartist slate was presented only in Rouher's own Puy-de-Dôme; elsewhere even the most outspoken platforms did not help weak and isolated candidacies. In the Haute-Vienne, a Bonapartist general, a stranger to the department but a relative of a former Sub-Prefect, campaigned actively at fairs and markets, but since he had no personal connections to match the influential family and friends of his Republican rival, he went down to defeat. In the Creuse, an obscure associate of Jules Amigues ran at Bourganeuf. Though he ended his platform with a pledge to support MacMahon "until we may

---

[83] Rouher to Mme. Lepic, August 31, 1875 (dossier "Correspondance avec M. Rouher," Raoul-Duval papers). RBC, III, 509; IV, 638.

[84] Attorney-general, Grenoble, to Keeper of the Seals, October 21, 1874 (AN BB^{30}1122).

"Pyrénées-Occidentales"

legally cry 'Vive Napoléon IV,' " the peasants turned a deaf ear on this impecunious lawyer back from radical Paris. He got 493 votes. With candidates of this caliber, the complete failure of the Bonapartists in the Haute-Vienne, the Creuse, and the Corrèze might have been anticipated, though a Republican official found it "remarkable" since "formerly . . . the rural populations seemed to have preserved great sympathies for the Empire." [85]

As for the Mediterranean littoral, which before Sedan had been the most refractory region of all, few Bonapartists entertained any illusions that the Republican tide could be rolled back there. Even in 1873 there had been a consensus that in the Rhône valley and in the Midi there was nothing to be done.[86] In 1876 there were few candidates here. Emile Ollivier, running in two districts of his native Var, alone openly invoked the memory of the Emperor, and he had little to lose by frankness. Lieutenant-Colonel Bourcart, running in the first district of Marseille, was virtually the *only* Bonapartist in all of France to present himself to the voters of a large city. His candidacy had been launched in the expectation that the Corsican seafarers of the port would march as one man behind him. The Bonapartist chiefs belatedly discovered, however, that hardly any of these islanders were registered voters in Marseille. Deprived of their ballots, the Colonel came in dead last, with less than a thousand votes, trailing even the Legitimist.[87]

Corsica itself, however—to conclude this survey by a brief visit to that forgotten department—conformed to the universal expectation by remaining almost entirely the pocket

---

[85] AN BB30 4904, dossier Limoges.

[86] Mme. Eschasseriaux to her father, March 21, 1873 (Eschasseriaux, "Mémoires," VII, 61).

[87] Paul Corticchiato, *Les Corses et le parti bonapartiste à Marseille en 1870 et pendant les premières années de la République* (Marseille, 1921), 175–179.

Bonapartism after Sedan

borough of Bonapartism. Was this, as Bonapartists liked to think, because every Corsican's bosom swelled with pride at the memory of the island's most famous son? Not entirely, as Republican deputies discovered when they voyaged out to enquire why the island persisted in its electoral perversity. They found a land as unlike the Charente-Inférieure as could be imagined; even so, it is not too far-fetched to suggest that popular Bonapartism continued to flourish there partly for the same reasons that it survived in the southwestern mainland.

The Corsican commune, one of their witnesses told the deputies, was still almost a primitive village, divided between parties who turned elections into occasions for armed conflict. Under such circumstances, the results of universal suffrage could only be deplorable, especially when "to all these disorders and evils are added great ignorance, rare communications, not only with continental France but with the civilized parts of the island, and poverty." Among these folk, another witness declared, the *fonctionnaires* had great power. Land in Corsica had been divided almost infinitely, though not one family in ten possessed valid title to its holdings. Thus the justices of the peace wielded an authority which they did not hesitate to exploit at election-time, spreading the word that "those who are not with us are against us." The voters well understood the menace of these words and voted accordingly. With a few rare exceptions, all of these magistrates had been named by the Imperial government. Since the Empire apparently continued to rule, it was hardly astonishing that the Corsicans had not become Republicans. Yet even Republican witnesses, whose lives under such conditions certainly would not dispose them to indulgence for Corsican Bonapartism, admitted that it had other causes besides backwardness and bureaucratic intimidation. Said one: "Corsica is a country which believes in government. . . . The Corsican is very authoritarian and wants a government which asserts itself."

"Pyrénées-Occidentales"

Reinforcing this temperamental inclination were the personal relationships developed by the men of the island who had joined their fortunes to the Imperial regime; the repeated candidacies of Denis Gavini won "the sympathies of the voters less even because of his political opinions than because of his personal friendships and the public and private services which the Gavini family has always generously rendered." [88] Even in this wild and remote country, then, it was possible to construct a machine, as in the Charente-Inférieure.

In most of metropolitan France, however, the Bonapartists had failed to build or rebuild one, as the final tallies in 1876 revealed. The *Ordre* claimed the election of 110 deputies; the *Liberté*, more modestly and more accurately, reckoned them at 94.[89] Against the obstacles which have been described, even the lesser number did represent a relative success: "Never had a defeated party, under the Restoration, the government of July, or the Empire, returned to the Assembly in such a compact battalion," Jules Richard claimed. But magnificent though the results were, they were also, Richard admitted, insufficient.[90] The only reason for the existence of a Bonapartist party was to recall the Empire; it could not hope to win a mandate to do this by contesting only half the con-

[88] AN C3231, depositions at Bastia, Calvi, and Corte.

[89] *L'Ordre*, March 8, 1876. In the first years of the Third Republic, ascertaining the affiliation of a candidate was sometimes difficult, at least before his election and subsequent inscription with a *réunion* of the Chamber. For example, Baron Reille of the Tarn was listed by some contemporary sources as a Bonapartist (his candidacy was endorsed by the *Comité national conservateur*, though he ran on a very vague platform; cf. RBC, V, 110). Having written to his grandson to inquire if any materials on his Bonapartist career had survived, I received the reply that he had been much more an Orleanist than a Bonapartist. (Letter of M. le Duc Reille-Soult de Dalmatie.) Omitting Reille has doubtless minimized the Bonapartist vote total in the Tarn; yet it hardly seems that his votes can in good conscience be included, nor can he be shown as an elected candidate.

[90] Richard, *Bonapartisme*, 162.

stituencies and winning less than half of those it contested.

All the party's sins of commission and omission in the years since September 4 were punished by the voters in a day. Léonce Dupont, himself a Bonapartist, catalogued its failings with merciless rigor. "Where," he inquired, "were its arms of combat? Where were its committees, which the parliamentary investigations gave it credit for having? Where were its agents, where was its propaganda?" In an election year, the flow of pamphlets had diminished, either because the authors were not sufficiently encouraged, or because their ingenuity had run out. In the vital matter of organization, "the Imperialist party was very far from possessing the electoral apparatus with which the Republicans had taken care to provide themselves." Money was so short that for the elections "on which the imminent realization of the dynastic hopes of the Imperial family might depend, care was taken to give candidacies only to men capable of bearing the costs." As at Versailles the Bonapartist deputies had increasingly diverged from a truly Bonapartist toward a merely conservative policy, so too in the platforms of the candidates of 1876 "one would have sought in vain the pure and real Napoleonic doctrine." The most that could be said was that despite the inadequacy of their efforts, the reticence of their *professions de foi*, they had won enough seats to demonstrate that in many departments, the Napoleonic cause was not lost.[91]

Particularly was this true in the Southwest, the only whole region in which the Empire still received widespread mass suppport. Paul de Cassagnac's decision to locate his electoral drama in the "Pyrénées-Occidentales" was thus geographically appropriate, though his tract made no reference to the arduous labors by which the "Napoleon Vannois" of this region assured his triumphs.

[91] Léonce Dupont, *Les deux démocraties: République—Empire* (Paris, 1878), 31–34.

"Pyrénées-Occidentales"

Not the least irony of the whole Bonapartist saga after 1870 was that some of the party's most resounding successes were scored by a man whom the Empire had finally tried to discard as a liability. The same interference with what he regarded as his legitimate authority which had driven Baron Eschasseriaux, though an admirer of Rouher, into the ranks of the 116 "because of the abuse of personal power committed against me and of the position in which I had been placed . . . by the Government," [92] also had forced him to improvise the set of political techniques (including the collection of funds) for the unaided management of universal suffrage which stood him in good stead long after 1869. Imperial legislation had given much of the Southwest special economic reasons for attachment to the Empire. Eschasseriaux and others like him there had learned how to exploit it to run their machines (as their elections even in 1871 had demonstrated.) But as Rouher declared, men of these abilities were rare in his party. Eschasseriaux's vast knowledge of his constituents—though really only what a latter-day professional democratic politician would regard as indispensable—was a source of wonder to his colleagues precisely because it was so uncommon. Even in the Charente-Inférieure, men like Boffinton, Fournier and Vast-Vimeux hung back from a daunting race in 1871, or disdained the wearisome necessity of cultivating the roots of democracy in the *Conseil général*, or sought to escape universal suffrage in the sanctuary of an Orleanist Senate. They were still content, as they had been under the Empire, to leave the hard work of democratic politics to someone else, and to ride the Baron's coat-tails.

Eschasseriaux held their selfish indolence in the same contempt he reserved, confident as he was of his peasants, for the proud bourgeoisie of La Rochelle. Like Rouher, he was convinced that the way to win was to run on an uncompro-

[92] Eschasseriaux, "Mémoires," IV, 300.

Bonapartism after Sedan

misingly Bonapartist platform, appealing to the masses and disregarding the prudent conservative phraseology which would conciliate the classes. The historian must therefore ask: outside the Southwest, would there have been more Bonapartist victories in 1876 if there had been more Bonapartist—*declaredly* Bonapartist candidacies? Or were those who created the *Comité national conservateur* correct in believing that a conservative candidacy was to be preferred, if there was to be a candidacy at all?

There are arguments for the latter case which cannot be neglected. Almost one-third of the Bonapartists elected had received their mandate only in the *scrutin de ballotage* (March 5); that is, their winning margin had ultimately been provided by voters of whom they had not been the preferred candidate. An elliptical platform might be the means to ensure that those voters did not simply abstain in disgust on the second *tour*.

Furthermore, the by-election in the Aube in 1873 had shown that Rouher's and Eschasseriaux's formula did not always work. The few men who accepted the onerous task of running in regions like the Mediterranean coast, the Southeast, or the East, where the masses had abandoned the Empire for the Republic before or after Sedan, could certainly argue that they knew best where their hopes of a precarious victory lay. If they lay in such veiled language and such concessions to their neighbors, the Orleanist "Hottards" and Legitimist "Chevrefeuilles" that their election did not represent a plebiscite for the Empire, there was nothing that could be done about it. In such regions, to build an organization which would carry a frankly Bonapartist slate to victory would just not have been possible.

The same excuse cannot be offered, however, for the failure to organize or even to run in regions like the North and parts of the Center, the West and the Massif Central, departments

"Pyrénées-Occidentales"

not so good, admittedly, as the Charente-Inférieure, but not so bad as the Bouches-du-Rhône, either. The prefectoral survey taken at the Emperor's death suggests that here there *were* reservoirs of popular Bonapartism which were left untapped in 1876. The behavior of men like Boffinton and Fournier in the Charente-Inférieure suggests why. There simply were more Bonapartists like them than there were like Eschasseriaux; indeed, it was because the Emperor had not found enough men like Eschasseriaux to practice authoritarian democracy in local politics that he had been compelled to turn away from them—even to repudiate them—and to seek his support from the "conservative-liberals," some of whom became the Orleano-Bonapartists of the Republic.

Just as many such men had proved, in the Assembly, to be more conservative than Bonapartist, so in 1876 many, incapable of organizing the democratic masses, either gave up the battle altogether or directed their appeal to the group they knew best. With their vision obscured by what Rouher called the "curtain" of the bourgeoisie, they spoke a language—clericalist, anti-Revolutionary—calculated to please it, leaving progressive egalitarianism to the Republicans.

Nor, in a party constituted as theirs was, was there any means of inducing or compelling them to behave otherwise. The formation of the *Comité national conservateur* made it clear who called the tune. Perennially short of funds and dependent on the generosity of these very conservatives for those he got, Rouher could only entreat, not command. The careers of Gambetta's Republicans lay ahead of them, a powerful incentive to obedience; most of the Bonapartists of the Republic had substantial careers behind them, and considered it their right to vote, launch or refuse their candidacies, negotiate with Monarchists, and write their platforms as they judged best to ensure, above all, the preservation of their positions in their own *arrondissements*. Each deputy, each poten-

Bonapartism after Sedan

tial candidate, was as independent of the Vice-Emperor—not to mention the Prince Imperial—as Eschasseriaux himself. Effort was therefore not only voluntary but unrewarded, and indiscipline or inactivity could only be deplored, not punished. A Le Roux refused to organize the Vendée, and let potential Bonapartist votes go uncast; an Orleano-Bonapartist like Hamille preferred an unopposed election as a conservative in the Pas-de-Calais to a harder-fought one which would have redounded to the advantage of the Imperial dynasty. Such were the privileges of their estate.

Some of Baron Eschasseriaux's most unrelenting enemies were the employees of Saintes' new railway. To defeat them, he relied on the belated arrival of the votes of the communes most remote from the impact of innovation. These were both ill omens for the future of Bonapartism. Gradually, but inexorably, the extension of communications, of education, would undermine the curious relationship of guided democracy which he, a notable, had established with the rural masses of universal suffrage. He at least, however, offered those masses a democratic alternative to the Republic; his fellow notables who ran on platforms which said much of religion, family, and property but nothing of the Empire did not. They were merely offering another kind of Orleanism to an elite which was already learning to accept [93] the Republic as the safeguard of their interests.

Bonapartists could not with justice complain that the election of 1876 had not been a plebiscite; it was the fault of many of them who refused to run, or to run as partisans of Napoleon IV, that it had not become one. Universal suffrage was never really asked if it wanted the Empire back, but perhaps the failure to ask anticipated the answer, and the proper answer for France after twenty years of Imperial rule. Univer-

[93] See above, 80.

"Pyrénées-Occidentales"

sal suffrage ultimately requires democratic parties—or totalitarian ones. The Bonapartist party of 1876 was neither.[94]

[94] Figures used to prepare the map depicting voting percentages are those recorded in the register of the Chamber itself (AN C²*726: "Elections générales des 20 février et 5 mars 1876"). For a contemporary attempt to compute the percentages, see Edouard d'Ans, "La France parlementaire" (Paris, 1876). For another graphic portrayal of the results, see Glücq, "Deux pages d'histoire" (Paris, n.d.).

Chapter V

Prangins and Brussels

After the electoral defeat of 1876, Bonapartism fell into a decline that was never really arrested. Two events appeared superficially and momentarily to herald an improvement of its fortunes: the first was the emergence of a brilliant young leader who hoped, together with the youthful pretender, to make of Bonapartism a new kind of movement with an altered policy and a widened appeal; the second was the coup of the *Seize Mai*, in which the party of the *Appel au peuple* in reality played a rather different role than has sometimes been attributed to it. The hopes which these two events, for opposite reasons, aroused among Bonapartists proved to be illusory, and after the debacle of 1877 the party's *malaise* deepened; now there was not merely dissension in its ranks, but self-doubt and even desertion. The process of collapse was immensely accelerated when the javelins of Zulu warriors ended the Prince Imperial's search for military glory in South Africa. The new pretender—if a man who repudiated the Empire and most of its adherents could be called that—was literally little more than a bad joke to Bonapartists and their opponents alike. The year 1879 really marked the end of Bonapartism as a serious rival of the Third Republic. The state of the party after that date was similar to that of a disorderly militia routed by a superior, disciplined force; before the manifest incapacity of the ostensible commander,

Prangins and Brussels

the lesser chiefs acted more than ever at their own discretion, some passing over quietly to the enemy, others resigning themselves apathetically to their fate, still others retiring to fight another day under another banner, while a few stubbornly continued to defend their embattled pockets, more from habit than from conviction, as their resources and reserves dwindled inexorably away. On this darkening and confused scene the same doctrinal and organizational problems which had condemned the Bonapartists to disappointment since 1870 continued to harass them, and they proved as incapable as ever of finding solutions. At last even the strongholds of the Barons of the Southwest were overrun, completing the *fin des notables*, and Bonapartism became again what it had been before 1848: not a national political party, but the temperamental inclination of an unknowable number of Frenchmen.

One month after the second *tour* had confirmed the Bonapartists' failure in 1876, Edgar Raoul-Duval wrote the Prince Imperial that the results, because of "the lack of preparation and organization, the insufficiency of our journalistic means, and the isolation in which *scrutin d'arrondissement* placed our candidates," had confirmed his pessimistic predictions. Yet he added that all his efforts were "concentrated on the indispensable creation of new organs of publicity." [1]

Discouraged by their defeat, the Bonapartists were reducing still more a propaganda apparatus which the elections had proved was already inadequate. Since even for the most hopeful the imminent advent of the Empire now seemed very hypothetical, the people who had provided what funds there had been ceased to offer them. With Rouher's approval, it was therefore decided to reduce the subsidies to the provincial newspapers, to "simplify" the operations of the *Correspon-*

[1] Raoul-Duval to Prince Imperial, April 2, 1876; in dossier "Lettres de Camden," Raoul-Duval papers, château of Le Vaudreuil (Eure).

dance Mansard, and to reorganize the *Ordre.*² It was at such an hour that Raoul-Duval announced to the Prince Imperial a policy not of retrenchment, but of expansion. Who was this optimist, and what vision had he of the future of the party of the Empire to fill him not with resignation, but energy?

Edgar Raoul-Duval had been born in 1832 of a Protestant family which, after having fled France at the revocation of the Edict of Nantes, had returned to serve for several generations in the magistracy. Raoul-Duval himself wore the robes of an Imperial judge in 1870, but found his role a confining one. He had sought escape in a variety of ways which startled his colleagues on the bench, notably by volunteering as a teacher for the *Ligue de l'Enseignement,* which had been created to widen the horizons of the working class. For this unorthodox *robin,* though a conservative, was also a democrat, with a basic trust in universal suffrage which was often badly shaken but never completely undermined. Thus he respected the Empire of the plebiscites, though he abhorred its restraints upon individual liberties. Freedom of private conscience was for him so fundamental that he found political coteries distasteful, and had refused to run with the backing of one of them as an independent dynastic candidate in the elections of 1869.³

After Sedan, then, he was a man of unfulfilled ambitions and unexploited talents, still searching for the political cause which best conformed to his own guiding principles. The defeat led him to declare his satisfaction at seeing "France finally purged of that race of Corsicans which twice in a half-century has covered our country with ruins," and to affirm that he did not "share the terrors provoked by the word Re-

² Jules Richard, *Le Bonapartisme sous la République* (3d ed.; Paris, 1883), 163–165.

³ Georges Normandy, ed., *Gustave Flaubert—Lettres inédites à Raoul-Duval,* Preface by Edgar Raoul-Duval (Paris, 1950), *passim.* Cf. Eugène, Baron Eschasseriaux, "Mémoires," twenty manuscript volumes in the château of Oyré (Sarthe), XIII, 250.

public." A look at Gambetta and his friends at Bordeaux, where "the destinies of France are decided over beer-mugs, pipes and cigars, in the evening at the café," soon showed him, however, that his quest for a political party could not end with the Republicans. Never could he subject himself to the direction of such "blackguards, mountebanks, and fools"; when he was elected a deputy in the by-elections of July, 1871, he took his place among the Right Center. Shocked by the Commune, he deeply distrusted Thiers, and, disregarding his overtures, took a prominent part in overthrowing the first President of the Republic, whom he thought too lenient toward demagogy.[4]

Yet he took no comfort from the victory of Broglie, among whose followers he sat. He wanted a government which would "cleanse the social body" of its Radical infestation, but had to admit, after several interviews with the Comte de Paris, that the Orléans dynasty lacked the energy to be entrusted with the task. If Orleanism was an impossibility, the Legitimism of "these believers who expect each morning the return of the *Roy*" was an absurdity. As it became apparent that the Orleanists were lending a hand to the realization of such expectations, his amusement turned to alarm. It was positively dangerous, he felt, to associate the cause of social conservatism with the avatar of the *ancien régime*.[5] With characteristically impetuous candor he published a letter, at the very moment of highest fusionist hopes, in which he broke with the Orleanists, reminding them of the unpopularity of Legitimism in the countryside as in the cities, and of the distrust which the ideas of Chambord inspired.

Thus after only two years in the Assembly, Raoul-Duval

[4] Normandy, ed., *Lettres*, 26–28, 38, 40–41, 46–47.
[5] Raoul-Duval to Lapierre, February 14, 1872, February 4, October 27, 1873 (dossier "Lettres à Lapierre," Raoul-Duval papers); cf. Normandy, ed., *Lettres*, 53–54.

Bonapartism after Sedan

found himself politically isolated, "the scapegoat of . . . MM. the Dukes" who placed part of the blame for the collapse of fusion on his shoulders. When he continued his indiscipline by opposing the Septennate, which he thought a vain and meretricious expedient, he knew he could not hope for a reconciliation. Having parted from the Right and continuing to reject the Left, he thought it likely that he would remain isolated for as long as the Assembly lasted.

Yet there remained one alternative—the little group which had (officially, at least) successively opposed Thiers, fusion, and the Septennate as he had, and which professed as its central doctrine an idea to which Raoul-Duval wholeheartedly subscribed: that under modern conditions France could not have a definitive government without a direct consultation of the country.[6] He had many misgivings about them; though he was curious to know what impression the Prince Imperial made, he still felt that "the name he bears is a heavy burden." If practical politics now meant a choice between Radicalism and a violent Bonapartism, he told a Bonapartist friend, he would choose the latter without hesitation, but also without enthusiasm. As a newcomer in politics, he wished, without really counting on it, "that the Empire brought a little modesty to its triumph," and that "the Imperialist radicals would not compromise the cause they think they are serving by exaggerations" such as the Legitimists had displayed. "At least," he begged, "while restoring dictatorial power to us . . . in the person of a young man of eighteen, let them not utter cries of triumph as if the philosopher's stone had been found." A mere reactionary dictatorship would not cure France's political malady; a restored Empire would be a short-

---

[6] Raoul-Duval to Lapierre, October 27, November 10, 1873, and to his wife, November 20, 1873 (dossiers "Lettres à Lapierre" and "Lettres à sa femme," Raoul-Duval papers). Normandy, ed., *Lettres*, 54–55.

Prangins and Brussels

lived failure if the Prince Imperial, while restoring authority, "does not set as his goal making himself the educator of his country, by progressively accustoming it to that liberty which future generations will again ask of him." [7]

He could only discover whether such a progressive Bonapartism was possible, he finally decided, in direct conversation with the heir to the throne. In midsummer of 1875, his friend Bourgoing arranged an interview, not at Chislehurst, where the Prince would be "surrounded by a kind of court which perhaps would not suit me at all," but at Southsea. Raoul-Duval went to this rendezvous still uncommitted, with the firm intention of deliberately testing his interlocutor. The prospect of general elections required him to choose a party, and he was thus anxious "to know if the young Prince can be the most useful instrument for the application of the ideas of government which I believe the best" (though he was prepared to accept as final the decision of the sovereign nation.) After two *tête-à-têtes*, one lasting three hours, he returned to France fully satisfied. He had expected to meet a weedy adolescent, but instead found "a very vigorous young man, a good countenance, a good handshake, very simple manners, not at all affected, not a bit too assured." Though the Prince was still seeking to complete his political education, Raoul-Duval thought him already *"very very* liberal." In fact, though his ideas were "allied with a sentiment of authority, they would certainly be judged much too liberal by three-quarters of Frenchmen today." [8] For his part, the Prince Imperial was equally delighted with the spontaneous support of this new friend. He wrote Raoul-Duval that he had found in him the man he had been looking for, and that he trusted the deputy

---

[7] Letter of Raoul-Duval to a Bonapartist correspondent, June 11, 1874 (dossier "Lettres de Camden," Raoul-Duval papers).

[8] Raoul-Duval to his wife, August 1, August 5, 1875 (dossier "Lettres à sa femme," Raoul-Duval papers).

of the Eure would place the same confidence in him, closing with an assurance of his affectionate sentiments.⁹

It must have seemed to both men after this first cordial interview that together they could at last extricate the Bonapartist party from the parliamentary snares in which its doctrinal confusion had entrapped it, and set it upon a new path. The rallying of Raoul-Duval represented a substantial gain for the *Appel au peuple,* for he had long been regarded, despite— or because of—his independence, as a man to be reckoned with at Versailles. He had just added fresh laurels to his reputation as a master orator by his stubborn and sometimes singlehanded battle against the adoption, without a popular consultation, of the constitution of 1875. To a party which, with the exception of Rouher, seemed better equipped for listening than speaking, he brought powerful forensic talents, heard with the greater respect not only because of the personal magnetism of this upright and uncomplicated Norman, but also because, unlike the Vice-Emperor, he could speak without appearing always to be defending his own personal record.¹⁰

More than one Bonapartist deputy, weary of the ineffectiveness of Rouher, the savage but sterile polemics of Paul de Cassagnac, turned with relief to this new chief. Tarbé of the *Gaulois,* who had decided early in 1875 publicly to oppose the ultra-reactionary ideas attributed to the party's official leadership, so as not to "leave to Prince Napoleon the privilege of claiming for himself the really democratic principle of the Imperial regime," hailed him with enthusiasm. He declared that his campaign for a progressive Empire which would "ad-

⁹ Prince Imperial to Raoul-Duval, undated (dossier "Lettres de Camden," Raoul-Duval papers); cf. Normandy, ed., *Lettres,* 76.

¹⁰ Jules Delafosse, *Hommes et choses* (Paris, 1888), 262, 266; Léonce Dupont, *Les deux démocraties: République–Empire* (Paris, 1878), 28–29.

Prangins and Brussels

vance unceasingly along the road of progress, appealing to men of good will of all opinions" had Raoul-Duval's full support.[11] Indeed, though the latter took care, in his correspondence with Chislehurst, to indicate that he was acting in concert with Rouher,[12] he was quite convinced that Bonapartism must alter the visage it presented to France if it was to win a wider audience. As his friend and frequent adviser, Jules Delafosse,[13] explained, if Frenchmen were to understand that it was a new Empire which was appearing, in no way sharing the faults of the old, it was essential to remove well into the background the tired and unappealing old faces who were the Second Empire's chief legacy.[14]

If the shackles of the past were thrown off, the party of the *Appel au peuple* would have a freedom of action, a power of attraction, that might take it far. Raoul-Duval hoped for nothing less, for a start, than a shift of the majority from Left to Right in the new Assembly of 1876. This he would achieve by attracting moderate Republicans away from their perilous alliance with Gambetta's Radicals. To win over these moderates, he pointed out to the Prince Imperial, it was desirable "that the next elections give us a rather large number of new men, so that the old political personnel of the Empire cannot appear to furnish almost all of the general staff of the coming Empire." He urged the Prince, if he concurred, to take ac-

[11] Quoted in *L'Ordre*, May 31, 1875.
[12] Raoul-Duval to Prince Imperial, October 22, 1875 (dossier "Lettres de Camden," Raoul-Duval papers).
[13] Jules Delafosse, Paris journalist, founder of the *Nation*, then of the *Ami de l'ordre* of Caen; deputy of the Calvados after 1877 and a leader of the Right through the 1880's. (A. Robert, E. Bourloton, and G. Cougny, eds., *Dictionnaire des parlementaires français 1789–1889* [Paris, 1891], II, 302–303; cited hereafter as RBC.)
[14] Jules Delafosse to Raoul-Duval, September 23, 1875 (dossier "Jules Delafosse," Raoul-Duval papers).

Bonapartism after Sedan

count of this consideration in his "instructions relative to the choice of candidates." [15] Napoleon III, who had also sought new men, would doubtless have approved this scheme, though he would have had fewer illusions than Raoul-Duval on the efficacy of instructions from Chislehurst.

Lacking funds, his son could do little to bring such men into a party which already regarded new Bonapartists with suspicion. The elections of 1876 brought hardly any to Versailles; they merely brought more of the old men, committed to the Empire as they had known it. This offered a discouraging prospect, for Raoul-Duval had already been so infuriated by the old men's refusal to vote for *scrutin de liste* that he had resigned from the parliamentary group of the *Appel au peuple* on November 9, 1875, after only one day of membership. Furious that his arguments in support of Rouher had been unavailing "against the blindness and personal calculations of some of the members," he did not conceal his painful impressions of the meeting from the Prince Imperial. The argument had revealed "the irremediable weakness of a parliamentary group which completely lacks the spirit of understanding and the sentiment of discipline." [16]

This initiation might well have convinced Raoul-Duval that he had not found the means for the realization of his cherished principles after all. Still, he was sustained by the enormous potential he saw in the Prince Imperial, and even his party sometimes could be successfully maneuvered, as the pact with Gambetta to exclude the Orleanists from the Senate proved. It was obvious, in any event, that if the Bonapartists were profitably to exploit their greatly expanded numbers in the new Chamber, let alone to develop success-

[15] Raoul-Duval to Prince Imperial, December 21, 1875 (dossier "Lettres de Camden," Raoul-Duval papers).

[16] Eschasseriaux, "Mémoires," VIII, 187; Raoul-Duval to Prince Imperial, November 10, 1875 (dossier "Lettres de Camden," Raoul-Duval papers).

Prangins and Brussels

fully the idea of a new Empire, authority within the party must be more clearly assigned. There would have to be an executive committee.

On May 1, 1876, Rouher informed Raoul-Duval that the Prince Imperial had approved the formation of such a body. The two of them and the Duc de Padoue were to represent the Bonapartists of the Chamber on it, and Béhic [17] the Bonapartist Senators. The four were to meet periodically to plan a party strategy and try to get it accepted by the members. In order not to provoke jealous resentment, the Vice-Emperor added, it had been decided to keep the existence of this new group a secret.[18] So secret was it kept, in fact, that when Baron Eschasseriaux, who was also well aware of the need for more coherent direction for his party, arrived at Chislehurst a few weeks later to plead for it, he was not informed of the existence of the new committee. Instead, when he urged the Prince Imperial once more to reaffirm the supremacy of Rouher, the Prince readily declared he would do so. When the Baron went on to suggest that Rouher needed some sort of committee of direction to share his onerous responsibilities, the Prince did not explain that this need had already been met; instead he allowed the conversation to drift into a desultory and inconclusive argument over how such a body was to be appointed. If Rouher chose its members, his choices might make him new enemies among those passed over; having mulled over a few names, among them Raoul-Duval's, the Prince finally suggested that it should be elected by the members of the parliamentary *réunion*. No doubt in order to ensure that none of the latter felt left out, he also

[17] Louis-Henri-Armand Béhic, *Inspecteur des finances*, shipping magnate; Senator and minister of the Empire; vice-president of the *Comité national conservateur* in 1876; Senator of the Gironde 1876–1879. (RBC, I, 238).

[18] Rouher to Raoul-Duval, May 1, 1876 (dossier "Lettres de Camden," Raoul-Duval papers).

suggested that specialized committees to deal with specific questions be organized; the appointments to these he left to the Vice-Emperor.[19]

The limitations upon effective leadership of the Bonapartist party imposed by the independent status of its Senators and deputies were clearly felt in this conversation at Chislehurst, in which a ludicrous proliferation of committees was the only remedy discussed for the generally-acknowledged incapacity of the original *comité de comptabilité*. The Prince's one hope of centralizing authority lay in the creation of a secret committee which, being kept secret even from such a figure as Eschasseriaux, could hardly exert much authority. But the inevitable concomitant to conferring real authority in secret was to diffuse it in appearance so widely among the members that, had all these committees in fact been created to counterbalance the reaffirmation of Rouher's primacy, the original problem of indiscipline would hardly have been solved. In fact, of course, they were not created, but the result was the same: disorganization.

Meanwhile in Paris Raoul-Duval was becoming increasingly impatient that the one committee he knew about (since he had suggested it and had been told he was on it), take definite action to halt the projection of the reactionary image of the Empire by a man who was on no one's list for any committee, Paul de Cassagnac. The fiery Gascon was going about Paris putting into the mouth of the Prince Imperial "a language of the most impertinent intransigence" which could not fail to alienate nine out of ten Frenchmen. Under the present circumstances the Bonapartists' best hopes for a change in public opinion lay in the mistakes the Republicans might make. Their own mistakes, "the intemperance of their language, and their inclination toward a policy stamped with reaction and clericalism" were "so many aces in the hand of the Repub-

[19] Eschasseriaux, "Mémoires," VIII, 366–367.

Prangins and Brussels

lic." If the Prince Imperial were really thinking and speaking in the fashion Cassagnac was quoting him in the *Pays* and in Parliament, he would be doomed "to doing it, like the Comte de Chambord, outside France forever." Raoul-Duval found it hard to believe that the Prince had abandoned the progressive Empire they had conceived together only a year before, though he confessed that he was no longer certain in which direction the Prince intended to move. To clear the air, he asked that the executive committee be convened at Chislehurst, so that the Prince might "choose between two policies that are impossible to reconcile." [20]

Thus on June 4, 1876, Rouher and Raoul-Duval, Padoue and Béhic gathered at Camden Place. Their deliberations were not entirely private; General Fleury, for some reason, took part, and two members of the Chislehurst court also wandered in, though they at least kept quiet. The minutes kept by Raoul-Duval [21] afford an intimate glimpse at just how questions were threshed out and decisions taken by the supreme "committee" of this party of a hundred deputies and a million voters.

The Prince Imperial, in the chair, began by asking for their evaluations of the general situation, which would determine their decisions in "precise questions of parliamentary tactics." The Duc de Padoue immediately explained in a "very short and very vague" statement that since the Bonapartists were impotent in Parliament, forming only a part of the weak conservative majority in the Senate and a disproportionate minority in the Chamber, they must be "conservative and vote for all the conservative measures." Having heard out this characteristic instinctive response, Raoul-Duval suggested that they come down to specifics. Even in their weakness the

[20] Raoul-Duval to M. Bachon, May 22, 1876 (dossier "Lettres de Camden," Raoul-Duval papers).
[21] In dossier "Lettres de Camden," Raoul-Duval papers.

Bonapartism after Sedan

Bonapartists could further their interests by well-conceived parliamentary tactics.

In the Senate, they held the balance of power. By refusing their votes, they could balk the schemes of the Monarchists. At that very moment the nomination of Buffet as a Senator-for-life was pending before the upper house. Let the Bonapartist Senators withhold their support and thus continue the policy (successfully begun by the deal with Gambetta) of eliminating the Orleanists in order to "preserve the . . . dilemma between the Republic and the Empire."

In the Chamber, the party could demonstrate that dilemma to the nation. Its deputies could "propose and act for the country—remain men of Order but take from the program of Republican democracy all which we could apply if we returned to power." Thus the Empire could show that it, too, was progressive, while its constructive restraint could not but contrast favorably with Republican demagogy, since "we must abstain from appearing to violate the wishes of the electorate by hampering, through partisanship, the functioning of a system of government" for which a majority had just voted. They must "permit the Republic to bear all its fruits, resigning ourselves, if they are good, to seeing it take root, resting assured of succeeding it if they are bad."

Meanwhile they should repair the damage done to their Parisian and provincial press by the recent austerities, and try to ensure that strategy planned at the top was effectively communicated to the rank and file. Above all, Raoul-Duval warned, they must beware of any attempt to reverse the results of the election by a *coup de force*. The Orleanists, he knew, were already thinking of persuading MacMahon to dissolve the new Chamber and call new elections, but this "would not profit the party of the Empire unless it were voted under the pressure of a social danger, with the cooperation of moderate Republicans."

The comprehensive plan thus outlined was "highly ap-

Prangins and Brussels

proved by the Prince, lengthily paraphrased by M. Rouher, briefly accepted by M. Béhic." General Fleury also gave it his blessing, not without irrelevant anecdotes. "With the discussion threatening to return to idle generalities," Raoul-Duval called for a definite decision. The Prince having accepted his plan, it was unanimously adopted, which for Raoul-Duval naturally implied that "the individual acts of the party should be aimed at facilitating and realizing this policy." The first of these acts would be the vote on Buffet, and, before the meeting came to a close, Raoul-Duval, pointing out that to support him would be to return to the fatal policy of May 24, asked for a specific commitment that he would get no Bonapartist votes. Rouher said nothing; Béhic, representing the Senators, agreed with Raoul-Duval but mumbled that negotiations with the Monarchists had already begun. Raoul-Duval retorted that this was all the more reason to stop them. With that the meeting broke up, and Raoul-Duval set off again for France, happy in the knowledge that, far from forsaking his plan for projecting the image of a progressive Empire, the Prince Imperial had specifically endorsed it.

Disillusionment came within ten days. On June 13, Raoul-Duval, in shock and fury, wrote to Rouher that Béhic had just confirmed that the Bonapartist Senators would vote unanimously for Buffet, "in flagrant contradiction with the decision we took with the Prince." He was unable to understand how "a decision taken in common on such a serious matter could be abandoned without a new deliberation, if not without general agreement." Nor did he spare the Prince Imperial: the vote for Buffet, he wrote him, permitted him to "judge the fashion in which the decisions you have made . . . are executed." If the Prince had "ratified this change of front . . . behind my back," Raoul-Duval could only submit, though he could no longer remain firmly committed to the Imperial interests, but "if Your Highness has not been more informed than I, you can do only one thing: raise your voice and find out if there is still an Imperialist party in the Senate to hear it." [22]

That the Prince knew better than to try; he did all he could, and apologized to Raoul-Duval, confessing that he had not been informed of the plans of the Senators, and had sent no counterorder. He was obliged to leave some discretion to men like Béhic, but he regretted that their decisions should be taken without reference to the people he had consulted. Béhic no doubt had found that his fellow Senators had already committed themselves to Buffet through weakness or indifference, but it was very unfortunate that Raoul-Duval had not been consulted. The Prince fully realized his resentment, but asked him to forget it. [23]

As for the Vice-Emperor, his eventual reply reflected the pessimistic appraisal of the possibilities of leading the Bonapartists which had caused some to charge him with a cynical indifference. He remained convinced, he wrote, that Raoul-Duval's policy was the correct one for the party to follow, and did not think that it was really compromised by such minor incidents. He had no hope of preventing a few annoying disagreements within the party. If he were to threaten punishment for any deviation, he would incur the responsibility for diminishing the strength of the party when such sanctions were applied. A formal disavowal would have to be made in the name of the Prince, whom he did not wish to involve in personal differences, and in any case a disavowal did not always have the desired effect. [24]

Rouher thus admitted that he at least was resigned to the idea of most of the Bonapartists, that their party should be a

[22] Raoul-Duval to Rouher and to the Prince Imperial, June 13, 1876 (dossier "Lettres de Camden," Raoul-Duval papers).

[23] Prince Imperial to Raoul-Duval, June 16, 1876 (dossier "Lettres de Camden," Raoul-Duval papers).

[24] Rouher to Raoul-Duval, September 30, 1876 (dossier "Lettres de Camden," Raoul-Duval papers).

Prangins and Brussels

large, loose grouping of members free to act in their own short-run interests rather than a smaller group bound to a long-range policy by iron discipline. Even Baron Eschasseriaux, for example, felt that Raoul-Duval's exasperation was unjustified.[25]

For Raoul-Duval, the election of Buffet was not, even in itself, unimportant. Buffet had skilfully presided over the National Assembly as it had enacted the constitution of 1875 to prevent the return of the Empire; why should Bonapartists now help his fellow Orleanists reward him and afford him opportunities for further mischief? What alarmed Raoul-Duval even more, however, was the general acquiescence in the Senators' action. "I doubt very much," he wrote to the pretender, "that the policy deliberated before Your Highness and approved . . . will be resolutely and fruitfully pursued." He was filled with forebodings when he wondered "if the weakness of our Senators may not lead them to a series of new errors." He was still convinced that "a group of eighty to 100 deputies, compact, obedient to a clear political idea pursued with determination, would surely exercise a preponderant influence upon events." But he now knew how chimerical it was to expect this of the Bonapartists. The disparate elements of which their membership in the two chambers was composed did not lend themselves to that sort of continuously united action.[26]

The ensuing months more than confirmed his pessimism. Some of the Bonapartist "Plain" were, indeed, won over to the idea of a progressive Empire. Baron Eschasseriaux, for one, could follow Raoul-Duval's idea that they must allow a trial of the Republic to demonstrate to France its unworkability, and his own principles led him to agree that in the

[25] Eschasseriaux, "Mémoires," VIII, 367.
[26] Raoul-Duval to Prince Imperial, June 21, July 1, 1876 (dossier "Lettres de Camden," Raoul-Duval papers).

meantime the Bonapartists should not alienate themselves from the masses but should rather serve their democratic and egalitarian interests. Sporadic attempts were made to steal the Republicans' thunder: Rouher endorsed an income tax, and declared that a proposal to abolish the *budget des cultes* was merely premature; the old Saint-Simonian Laroche-Joubert interpellated the government on what steps it was taking to achieve "the moral and material amelioration of the lot of the majority," provoking a reply which Guizot might have made. All this was in marked contrast with the clerical conservatism so prevalent before 1876. But even to Eschasseriaux, with his combative instincts, this indirect method of attack on the Republic seemed tame. He wanted "to harass the ministers, . . . to strike them down one after another, to wreck the reputations of men and institutions before the disgusted country"—the very bellicose *politique du pire* Raoul-Duval dreaded. In general the deputies of the *Appel au peuple* adopted the latter's plan with hesitant uncertainty.[27] Part of the "Plain" clearly found the side show of parliamentary hooliganism simultaneously being carried on by Paul de Cassagnac much more to their taste. While Rouher was hinting at the possibility of religious disestablishment, the leader of the Bonapartist "Coblence" was denouncing the "materialistic and atheistic" university; when Gambetta referred to the Bonapartists as *pourriture*, Cassagnac instantly replied in kind. "There is a man," wrote Raoul-Duval, "who deserves to be called the gravedigger of his party." To the Prince Imperial he lamented: "If the first Napoleon, . . . if the Emperor your father could see the spectacle which the Imperialist party has given to France, certainly they would not recognize their own."[28]

[27] André Daniel, ed., *L'Année politique—1876* (Paris, 1876), 127–128, 206–207; Eschasseriaux, "Mémoires," VIII, 368, 374.

[28] Daniel, ed., *Année politique—1876*, 189; Raoul-Duval to his wife,

Prangins and Brussels

Naturally, the spokesmen for the reasoned program of a progressive Empire had little chance of being heard over such tumult. The first months of 1877 also saw the silencing of its principal voice among the newspapers of Paris. Raoul-Duval had long been aware that without his own journal it would be difficult to get his message accepted. It had not been easy to found one. The richest Bonapartists closed their purses to him, and he was positively unwilling to borrow capital from the existing Bonapartist papers, or from Rouher, for this would make the new paper only another edition of the *Ordre*. At last even the opposition of the Vice-Emperor, who had become very resentful of Raoul-Duval's influence at Chislehurst, was overcome, and on October 25, 1876, the *Nation*, edited by Albert Duruy, brought out its first edition.[29] Ernest Lavisse, a close friend of Duruy's, who knew that the Prince Imperial was searching for a paper he could personally inspire, warmly commended it to his former pupil. "Instead of preaching to the converted," the *Nation* would be "addressed to the unbelievers." Edited by "young men of good will, new and independent," it would try to be "neither banal nor violent."[30]

This noble enterprise was not destined for survival. The *Nation* never won more than a thousand subscribers; the unbelievers and the faithful alike already had their favorite

---

July 4, July 23, 1876, and to the Prince Imperial July 23, 1876 (dossiers "Lettres à sa femme," and "Lettres de Camden," Raoul-Duval papers).

[29] Jules Delafosse to Raoul-Duval, September 9, 1875, June 15, 1876; Raoul-Duval to Prince Imperial June 11, June 21, July 1, 1876 (dossiers "Jules Delafosse" and "Lettres de Camden," Raoul-Duval papers). Police report of November 8, 1876 (dossier "Eugène Rouher," APP B^A1257). *L'Ordre*, October 18, October 26, 1876.

[30] Ernest Lavisse to Prince Imperial, December 12, 1876; in C. L. d'Espinay de Briort, ed., "Une correspondance inédite—le Prince Impérial et Ernest Lavisse 1871–1879," *Revue des Deux Mondes*, 7th period, L (1929), 568.

Bonapartism after Sedan

newspapers. Losing a thousand francs a day, it had within six months exhausted three-quarters of its capital, and the Prince Imperial declined to come to its rescue. Rouher had the last word: the *Nation* merged with the *Ordre*. On May 13, 1877, Raoul-Duval gave notice of its impending disappearance to the Prince, bitterly reviewing its brief history. It had been founded in the first place because they had agreed that the *Ordre* could not "bring adherents to the Imperial cause by making the Empire appear more open." Yet it had come under attack from influential people in the party, who insinuated that "the Imperialism of the *Nation*, because it sought not to be exclusive or insulting, was of baser metal." When such difficulties forced its surrender, Raoul-Duval withdrew: "We had half-opened the Empire, it was being closed, there was nothing else for me to do." He ended on a note of solemn warning:

> Your Highness knows better than anyone what the *Ordre* has cost without attaining a circulation of any effectiveness. It will be the same in the future. . . . Without direction and discipline in Parliament, without a respected spokesman in the press, the party of the Empire will soon appear merely as a small, violent, and reactionary group.[31]

Three days later, on May 16, the Republican Prime Minister, Jules Simon, found on his desk a letter from the President of the Republic, Marshal MacMahon, virtually inviting him to resign. The chain of events which followed swiftly upon the opening of that letter was to seal the fate of the already moribund progressive Empire and to drive the despairing Raoul-Duval from public life.

Despite the rumors which had been circulating ever since

---

[31] Raoul-Duval to Prince Imperial, May 13, 1877; Prince Imperial to Raoul-Duval, May 24, 1877 (dossier "Lettres de Camden," Raoul-Duval papers).

Prangins and Brussels

the elections, the Marshal's impulse caught the Bonapartists by surprise, for though they knew how discouraged he was by his position as the Monarchist President of a Republic, they were also aware that his conscientious irresolution was likely to prevent him from doing anything about it. Through Baron de Saint-Paul, an old and intimate friend, they were kept constantly informed of his thinking, but the hopes raised by the initial reports had long since given way to disappointment. In June of 1873 the Empress had sent him a message of congratulations on his election through Saint-Paul. MacMahon, much moved, had admitted that he was not a lasting solution, and had hinted that when order had been reestablished, he would extricate himself by calling for a plebiscite. Nothing would have suited the Bonapartists better, but four years later they were still waiting, a good deal less hopefully. Surrounded as he was by an odious entourage of Orleanists,[32] the old cavalryman was more likely, Rouher feared, to be inveigled into one of the "combinations of Broglie, Fourtou, and other so-called conservative schemes, which will only prove miserably abortive." The Vice-Emperor hoped that MacMahon would not accept such bad advice, for dissolving the Chamber would work only if it were "imperiously demanded by an aroused country." [33]

Since France was far from aroused on May 16, the highest Bonapartist leaders all greeted the news of the *coup de tête* of the Elysée with mortification and skepticism. The Prince Imperial felt that MacMahon would have been better advised not to interrupt France's painful but salutary experiment in Republicanism by a premature reaction which would astonish

---

[32] Baron de Saint-Paul to the Empress, June 25, 1873, and Rouher to Saint-Paul, February 23, 1876; in Saint-Paul papers, château of Poudelaye (Ariège). Cf. Richard, *Bonapartisme*, 171, and Ernest Pinard, *Mon journal* (Paris, 1892–1893), II, 261–262.

[33] Rouher to Eschasseriaux, January 17, January 25, 1877 (Eschasseriaux, "Mémoires," IX, 34, 36).

public opinion. If, as seemed likely, the Marshal chose to base his next moves on the kind of coalition which had overthrown Thiers, the divisions within it would preclude success, and Bonapartists could accomplish nothing by associating themselves with the venture. There was some slight prospect that MacMahon could be made to see that his only hope of salvation now lay in turning for support directly to the Imperial party; if he did, they would of course back him with determination. But from long experience the Prince guessed that such an option would be too clear-cut for MacMahon to take it. Therefore, the Bonapartists must play their cards carefully. To dissolve the Chamber required the approval of the Senate, in which Bonapartist votes would be crucial; a high price for those votes must be exacted from the Orleanists. The pretender was resolved to use all his influence to prevent his party in the upper house from throwing itself recklessly into the Monarchists' murderous embrace.

To Raoul-Duval even this dubious assessment seemed far too sanguine. He pointed out to the Prince that, if the Chamber were dissolved, the Bonapartists would be the losers no matter who won the subsequent elections. If the Left won, the Republic would be consolidated, for the Bonapartists could no longer claim after two consecutive verdicts of universal suffrage that France really preferred the Empire. If the Right won, the Bonapartists might well get the lion's share of the majority, but the Monarchists would again ally with the Republicans to prevent an Imperial restoration. "It will be the situation after May 24, but reversed, and we shall end as the Royalists have done in the unpopularity born of impotence." Thus it was absolutely vital to prevent a dissolution: "All will depend on the votes of our friends in the Senate, and only the Prince possesses enough authority to impose on them an attitude . . . conforming to his interests. Let him not hesitate to use it." Rouher, he emphasized, agreed completely with his views; the *Ordre* maintained an attitude of cool detachment in the early days of the crisis.[34]

Such an attitude was certainly called for by the composition and activities of the new Government. The ministry, according to Eschasseriaux, was composed of Orleanists and intransigent Legitimists, save for one Bonapartist, "M. Brunet, who had gone in without consulting us as a conservative and not as a Bonapartist, and who was not a representative of the group." As spectators the Bonapartists soon saw that Broglie and his friends were mere bungling amateurs at the technique of the bloodless *coup d'état:* "Nothing . . . had been planned or decided." Three days were wasted before the crucial reassignment of Prefects was undertaken, and when it was, Bonapartist deputies and Bonapartist *fonctionnaires* hoping for employment were as disappointed as they had been after May 24, 1873. Baron de Saint-Paul, who had been the director of personnel at the Ministry of the Interior under the Empire, was called in to advise on appointments, but his recommendations were by no means universally followed. Baron Eschasseriaux, for example, naturally applied for a Bonapartist Prefect for the Charente-Inférieure; he got an "Orleano-Legitimist" who tried to have Legitimists endorsed as official candidates in place of Eschasseriaux's colleagues. (A single Bonapartist administrator, in fact, was named to the department, and he only because those supporting his appointment concealed his real opinions.) Out of sixty-odd prefectoral changes, Saint-Paul succeeded in turning a mere dozen to the advantage of his party, and even this "brought anguished cries in the Orleanist camp and . . . talk of treason." Saint-Paul thus was obliged "to withdraw his cooperation, for he very soon saw, as we all did, that the *coup*

---

[34] Prince Imperial to Raoul-Duval, May 24, and Raoul-Duval to Prince Imperial, May 30, 1877 (dossier "Lettres de Camden," Raoul-Duval papers). *L'Ordre*, May 18–19, 1877.

d'autorité of May 16 was the work of the Orleanists and that the tactic was going to be to send Legitimist or Orleano-Republican administrators into Bonapartist country" to prevent the voters from interpreting the Marshal's action as the prelude to a restoration of the Empire.[35]

Once again, then, the Bonapartists were confronted with the issue of conservative union, but this time not only did their leaders agree it would be disastrous, but there had also been enough time for individual Bonapartists to see for themselves that the Orleanists who required their support intended to give as little as possible in return. And once again Raoul-Duval, who had dreaded that the Prince Imperial's instructions would not be "expressed with enough authority,"[36] saw his worst nightmare become real. On June 16, the Senate voted, by a margin of nineteen votes, to dissolve the Chamber; the twenty-odd Bonapartist Senators were among the majority.

The Buffet election, superficially so inconsequential, had been a warning. Baron Eschasseriaux felt that the Senators had never had any understanding of the plan for a progressive Empire. Béhic and his colleagues had always "counted much more on the Marshal and on dissolution than on the effect of their personal efforts." The Baron thought this a natural result of "a mandate which they did not hold directly from universal suffrage." It was precisely because they were unwilling or unable to face a democratic electorate that men like his own colleague Vast-Vimeux had "retired into the Senate like a rat into a cheese."[37] It would be optimistic to suppose them any more capable now of resisting the conservative poli-

---

[35] Eschasseriaux, "Mémoires," IX, 82–86, 90–91.

[36] Raoul-Duval to his wife, June 13, 1877 (dossier "Lettres à sa femme," Raoul-Duval papers).

[37] Eschasseriaux, "Mémoires," VIII, 390; XII, 215–216.

cies of the government of the day than they had ever been.

Even Eschasseriaux himself, however, saw in their vote for dissolution no cause for surprise or lamentation. All the Orleanists' treachery of the past seven years, and even of the past few weeks, had not undeceived him of the notion that Bonapartists would ultimately have to be given their rightful place at the head of the party of Order. On the eve of the vote he wrote:

> Dissolution will be voted so that M. de Fourtou [Minister of the Interior] can immediately plan his policy. *After the dissolution we shall make our conditions,* as we have said to an envoy of M. d'Harcourt [the Marshal's secretary] and we shall not tolerate being excluded from the ministry any longer, we who represent the majority of the Right.[38]

Far from refusing their cooperation, or even, as the Prince Imperial desired, selling it dearly, the Bonapartists of Versailles—not only the Senators—threw themselves blindly upon the Republicans as they had in 1873, once again without exacting any real guarantees from their conservative allies. For one who, like Raoul-Duval, foresaw where it would lead, the scene in the Chamber that day was "completely disgusting; the Imperialists conducted themselves like a collection of hoodlums," acting not out of "convictions," but only "vanity and appetite." All their violent denunciations of the Republicans, he wrote the Prince Imperial, were designed merely to curry favor with a ministry which was already preparing Orleanist candidacies against them. Three-quarters of the Bonapartists had joined in, making the regime they represented look "hateful and terrible." The effect on public opinion would be catastrophic: "It is not possible that anyone of

---

[38] Eschasseriaux to Mme. Eschasseriaux, June 15, 1877 (Eschasseriaux, "Mémoires," IX, 98–99); emphasis added.

sound mind could . . . wish to see such a party of opposition ever again became a party of government." [39]

As usual, the chief followed his followers. Finding that "almost all of the deputies and Senators of the group were . . . more conservative than Bonapartist," and that an alliance with the Republicans seemed to them monstrous, Rouher cast off his own well-founded misgivings and publicly declared that he preferred being beaten defending MacMahon to winning with Gambetta.[40]

Having accepted the adventure, the most he could hope for was to elect as many openly Bonapartist candidates as possible to the new Chamber. However, even that modest objective was to prove impossible to attain, because of the inclinations both of the government and of his own supporters. At the very least he must try to win official endorsement for Bonapartists in the districts they had won in 1876 and in those where they had outpaced a Monarchist. His first conversations with Fourtou showed that this would be difficult. The Minister of the Interior not only made an unacceptable demand that all candidates run on nonpartisan platforms but even confessed that he could not make any commitment to the Bonapartists without the approval of the Legitimist and Orleanist leaders. Rouher agreed to meet with them, but felt that the conference would produce no agreement. In mid-July, therefore, he still thought it unlikely that any electoral *entente* would be achieved, particularly since the government seemed "not at all interested in the success of our friends" and persisted in regarding the Bonapartists as subordinates constrained to obedience. Ministers could not be made to see that it was their own survival which was at stake, and that to

---

[39] Raoul-Duval to his wife and to the Prince Imperial, June 17, 1877 (dossier "Lettres à sa femme" and "Lettres de Camden," Raoul-Duval papers).

[40] Richard, *Bonapartisme*, 170–171.

Prangins and Brussels

insist on assigning a district to a Bonapartist who could win rather than to a Monarchist who had no chance was to do them a great service. The explanation for this shortsightedness was that the Cabinet was "deeply divided. While M. de Broglie works for the predominance of Orleano-Legitimist candidates, M. Decazes pays court to the Left Center and again dreams of the famous conjunction [of the two Centers]. De Fourtou is overwhelmed . . . Brunet supports him but it is not enough, they cannot between themselves constitute a majority." Meanwhile, the Elysée remained hostile to the party of the Empire, and Mme. MacMahon even made the grotesque demand that it be allowed no candidates in the Indre-et-Loire.[41]

It was at this moment, while the Vice-Emperor was battling single-handedly to preserve the ground his party had already won, that some of his fellow Bonapartists plunged the daggers of public denunciation and private disobedience into his back. First the inevitable Paul de Cassagnac attacked him for resisting the government's choice of Monarchist candidates in certain districts, warning that his obstinacy might provoke a refusal of official patronage to all Bonapartists. The Vice-Emperor contained his anger and contented himself with publishing a reproof; Cassagnac, not in the least abashed, proceeded to bring suit to force the *Ordre* to print his reply. At long last Rouher's patience snapped. As Raoul-Duval had often vainly urged him to do, he had the Prince Imperial publish a letter disavowing Cassagnac. He had been driven to this step, he explained, because Cassagnac's attack had been prompted not only by his "overweening vanity" but by the Orleanists of the Elysée, who were trying to create dissension in the Bonapartists' ranks. Their aim had been to bring pressure on Rouher to give in to the government's de-

[41] Rouher to Eschasseriaux, July 13, July 25, August 4, 1877 (Eschasseriaux, "Mémoires," IX, 107, 121–123, 132, 139).

Bonapartism after Sedan

mands by frightening the many Bonapartist candidates who thought official support was indispensable and who would refuse to run without it.

The Vice-Emperor had hardly parried this insidious thrust when he received another resounding blow. Baron de Mackau [42] quit the party committee which had been named to support Rouher in his negotiations because he, too, held that the Bonapartists were compromising conservative union by insisting on too many candidacies. This was a defection of the kind the party had endured over and over since 1873: Mackau, in Eschasseriaux's opinion, had too many Orleanist ties to resist the temptations of the Marshal's entourage. "The moderate tendencies of his mind led him to remain on the fringes of all the parties, without taking a very clear position." [43]

Such disloyalty would have meant little could Rouher have been confident that the Bonapartist chiefs of the departments would stand firmly behind him in resisting the government. His running battle with Prax-Paris of the Tarn-et-Garonne made it clear that he could have no such confidence. In that southwestern department the government had conceded three of the *arrondissements* to the Bonapartists; it wished to award the official candidacy in the fourth, Moissac, to an Orleanist. This was perfectly acceptable to Prax-Paris, but not to Rouher, who saw no reason why his party should not elect a full slate in a Bonapartist region. Despite the local chief's

---

[42] Armand, Baron de Mackau, son of a minister and Senator of the Empire; official deputy 1866–1870; elected deputy of the Orne in 1876 on an evasive platform; during the 1880's, as president of the *Union des Droites*, a prime mover for conservative union. (RBC, IV, 213–214.)

[43] Rouher to Raoul-Duval, August 9, 1877 (dossier "Correspondance Rouher," Raoul-Duval papers); Eschasseriaux, "Mémoires," IX, 107–108, 136, 139–140, 143–144, 157–158, 166.

Prangins and Brussels

repeated pleas, he refused to accept the proposed allocation. In order to secure his own position, he felt, Prax-Paris was sacrificing the larger interests of his party. Enraged at this obstruction, Prax-Paris announced that he would settle the matter on the spot without reference to Paris, and even threatened that "if greater account is not taken of his opinions, he would *quite simply withdraw* from the group. . . . Really," Rouher exclaimed, "the egotism which *scrutin d'arrondissement* produces among our friends is deplorable." Ignoring the "very strong language" of Rouher's reply, Prax-Paris joined with the government to induce the Vice-Emperor's candidate at Moissac to abandon the race. Confronted with a *fait accompli*, Rouher could only give way: "Thus we lose Moissac and cannot claim compensation for this concession." There was no hope of persuading potential Bonapartist candidates to maintain their claims to a district like Moissac: "They become discouraged, have no confidence in the general result, and take the refusal of official candidacy as a pretext for their withdrawal." It made no difference that the government's choices were "made without the slightest conformity to the rules originally indicated, which are violated or invoked according to the caprices or emotions of the moment." Under these conditions the Bonapartists would lose many candidacies which really should have been theirs, but this only made the government's defeat more certain.

Fourtou was able to play upon the local Bonapartists' inclination to look first to him and only secondly to Rouher because he had at his disposal lures which the Vice-Emperor could not possibly match. Candidates who for years had been turned away empty-handed from the rue de l'Elysée now would have their expenses borne by the state. Significantly, these funds were not paid over in a lump sum to the hard-pressed Bonapartist treasury, but doled out by the Prefects to the individual candidates, who thus incurred a very compelling obligation to obedience.[44]

Pecuniary advantages were not the only ones individual Bonapartists might derive from the government's supervision of the campaign. The Minister of the Interior helped them by bringing pressure to bear on the Monarchists to prevent their presenting rival candidacies, abstaining in choices between Republicans and Bonapartists, or voting for Republicans in Bonapartist country. Yet even if the government's objective was only to unite all conservative voters behind one candidate (though Rouher suspected that they were refusing more Bonapartist candidates than that objective required), such a policy was bound, on balance, to injure the interests of the Empire as much as it helped them. The Tarn-et-Garonne was not the only place where Bonapartists were blackmailed into abandoning candidacies to Monarchists. And although Fourtou gave up his initial demand that candidates make no mention of the Empire in their *professions de foi*, he instructed his Prefects that platforms were to be modelled "as exactly as possible" on MacMahon's own conservative manifesto. A Bonapartist candidate who ingeniously tried to evade this restriction with a circular bearing the Marshal's portrait on one side and the Prince Imperial's on the other was refused authorization to publish it. If he disregarded this prohibition, the circular was to be seized and the candidate prosecuted.

For many Bonapartists, the old familiar *affiche blanche* of official candidacy doubtless seemed more valuable than the kind of circumlocutory placard they had devised themselves in 1876. At least one of them, however, made the strongest efforts not to attach himself publicly to the *Seize Mai*. Baron Eschasseriaux thought that the patronage of such an Orleanist government, "unused to handling universal suffrage"

[44] Rouher to Eschasseriaux July 25, August 4, September 15, 1877 (Eschasseriaux, "Mémoires," IX, 131–132, 138–139, 170).

Prangins and Brussels

would be "more dangerous than useful in a region as independent as ours." As he had thought the posters of the *Comité national conservateur* worthless in 1876, so now he was absolutely convinced that the *affiche blanche* would not add ten votes to his total. As might have been expected, he found that such colleagues as Mayor Fournier "were far from repudiating this patronage." Since they were adamant, the Baron compromised to the extent of allowing his name to be placed on a collective *affiche blanche* for the whole department, though he carefully preserved all his correspondence on the question so as to be able to prove his personal reluctance when the victorious Republicans began invalidating elections.[45]

For the *Seize Mai* was a fiasco, as Rouher and Raoul-Duval had perceived it must be. The Right was beaten again, and in the process the Bonapartists actually lost ground. After the first *tour de scrutin*, Rouher concluded that "the balance sheet of the enterprise . . . can be summed up in the useless winning of fifteen seats." The second *tour* provided little more reason for rejoicing, and the sequel, when the Chamber had reassembled, put an end to what reason there was. A comparison of the two general elections shows that if the Bonapartists benefited from M. de Fourtou's management in one sense (this time only one in ten of them found himself in a three-way battle), they had, as Rouher had feared, suffered in another: there were only thirty more Bonapartist candidates in 1877 than there had been in the pinched circumstances of 1876. An extra score of Bonapartists came to Versailles, but many did not stay long, for the Republicans ruthlessly invalidated no fewer than thirty of their elections. Thus

---

[45] Undated cipher telegrams from the Ministry of the Interior to the Prefects of Sarthe, Vaucluse, Pas-de-Calais, Gironde, Basses-Alpes, and Dordogne (AN F^{7}12681–12682, "Police générale-Dépêches relatives au Seize Mai 1877"); cf. Eschasseriaux, "Mémoires," IX, 133–134, 174–176.

the consequence for the party of the *Appel au peuple* of their complicity in the Marshal's venture was a net deficit in representation, at least until by-elections should return some of those invalidated.[46]

Faced with this disaster, the *Ordre* became frantic. It was unthinkable that, having magnanimously come to the aid of the Marshal and his entourage, the party of the Empire should now have to bear the heaviest burden of a defeat caused by their ineptitude! Bonapartists had not been afraid "to follow the fortunes of the Marshal *to the end*; they may certainly ask the Marshal in return not to deliver them defenseless to their worst enemies." MacMahon must take "the most energetic measures. Enough of words, speeches, declarations. Acts!"[47] But instead of proclaiming a dictatorship or calling for a plebiscite, MacMahon asked Dufaure to form a ministry. Baron de Saint-Paul, the first to see him after he had made his decision, found him "weeping with shame and rage," but unwilling, whatever Saint-Paul said, to change his mind. Though a brave soldier, the Marshal was a timid politician, obsessed by the constitutional limitations upon his office. Nothing could be expected from him. "If I had wanted to carry out a *coup de force*," he told his old friend, "I would have asked for your cooperation, but I shall never do it."[48]

For the Bonapartists, the anti-Republican spree was followed by a grim reawakening. It was all very well for them to blame their misfortunes on the Orleanists of the cabinet who had feared that any electoral reaction would be in favor of the Empire and had therefore not dared "make" the elections with sufficient vigor.[49] It was too late now to back out. When

[46] Sources used in calculating these totals the same as those listed above, 198–199, n.53; 229, n.94. AN C²*727.

[47] *L'Ordre*, November 6, November 14, 1877.

[48] Baron de Saint-Paul to his wife, December 15, 1877 (Saint-Paul papers).

[49] Eschasseriaux, "Mémoires," IX, 241.

Prangins and Brussels

there *had* been a chance for them to do so, before the dissolving of the old Chamber, they had not, despite the misgivings of their chiefs, separated themselves from the men of the *Seize Mai*. During the campaign they had appeared on the hustings as conservatives, sometimes sharing that sobriquet with Monarchists they had combatted in 1876, and in most cases sharing with them an official candidacy that the Republican triumph turned into a badge of shame.

Why had they thus committed themselves so fully to a course of action from which their party could not possibly profit? Having been burned once on May 24, 1873, should they not have learned to avoid the fire? If it was too much to expect them to back Gambetta's 363, could they not have simply held aloof from this showdown? In a series of letters to Raoul-Duval which were as much confessions as explanations, Rouher insisted that the answer was No. If they had refused to rally to the standard of Order upheld by the Marshal, they would have admitted the truth of their enemies' allegations that they valued their dynasty more than Society. Such treachery toward MacMahon would have had particularly serious repercussions in the army. But even if their leaders had thought this a risk worth taking, a policy of neutrality had become impossible, since so many Bonapartists—a majority of them, in fact—had submitted to ministerial seduction. To continue to insist upon an independent line would have been to precipitate the disintegration of a party which felt itself intended for government, not for opposition, and succumbed eagerly to governmental advances.

Although he had not, at the critical moment, been willing to take the chance of total disintegration by resisting the conservative instincts of his followers, Rouher now admitted that a party structure which tolerated such chronic infidelity was useless for practical purposes. Foreseeing that there would probably be continued reluctance to accept an autonomous

Bonapartist strategy, he swore to Raoul-Duval that he was determined to insist upon better discipline even at the risk of a loss of members.[50]

Raoul-Duval would not be on hand at Versailles to see if anything would really be done to mold the disciplined party of which he had dreamed. In spite of a *profession de foi* which made clear his skepticism of the Marshal's brain storm, the deputy of the Eure had lost his seat to a Republican opponent. Beaten, his progressive Empire buried in the ruins of the *Seize Mai*, he was a shaken and discouraged man. He found it hard to accept that the harmony he had discovered between the Prince Imperial's ideas and his own could have proved so barren. For a while he continued to exhort the pretender:

Only Your Highness can turn your party from the passion for reaction which is driving it to ruin and bring it back to the paths of democratic opposition which it should never have abandoned, for it will never find in parliamentary alliances and expedients the strength which the profound masses of democracy, disabused of their Republican hopes and illusions, can give it.

The Bonapartists' behavior had, however, demonstrated again how ill-equipped they were to fulfill the role he had proposed to give them. With the ministry of the *Seize Mai* hardly installed, they had thronged its antechambers and committed their party to the adventure; now that it had ended in disaster, they had subsided again into vapid mediocrity. Calling one day at number 4, rue de l'Elysée, Raoul-Duval found in the salon "a few perfectly insignificant deputies with no idea of what they should do, letting themselves be

---

[50] Rouher to Raoul-Duval, July 23, October 5, December 1, 1877; April 28, 1878; Rouher to Mme. Lepic, October 23, 1877 (dossiers "Lettres de Camden" and "Correspondance Rouher," Raoul-Duval papers).

Prangins and Brussels

pushed and led without knowing where they are going." [51]

Meanwhile old friends of his, unrepentant converts to the Republic who had long bemoaned his association with Bonapartism and warned him of the disillusionment to come, insistently urged him to break off once and for all. These men to whom he, an independent, had spontaneously and generously lent his talents had shown after *Seize Mai* what they really were. Would he remain with such a gang even now? His answer came in the spring of 1878, with the publication of a "Letter to an American." His ideal solution for France was still "the alliance of the Empire and democracy," but there was no prospect of that now, and universal suffrage had clearly spoken in favor of the Republic. A consistent democrat could only, however reluctantly, accept this decision, and treat the question of governmental form as closed for the time being.[52]

For this bit of candor he was at once made the target of a full-scale campaign of vilification from all quarters of the Bonapartist press. He was bitterly disappointed that the Prince Imperial did not intervene to silence their accusations of treachery and criminality. This, he wrote to Baron de Bourgoing, "made the measure overflow. . . . Weary and disgusted, I am quitting politics for a time." His association with the Bonapartists had accomplished nothing save to end his parliamentary career prematurely. "What do I owe the party of the Empire? Nothing, since I never received support from it of any kind. . . . What I did for it alienated the electoral majority from me." He was reproached with inconstancy, though, since he had never been an unconditional

---

[51] Raoul-Duval to Prince Imperial, May 30, November 1, 1877, and to his wife, November 27, 1877 (dossiers "Lettres de Camden" and "Lettres à sa femme," Raoul-Duval papers).

[52] J. Hetzel to Raoul-Duval, September 11, 1877, May 2, 1878 (dossier "Lettres de J. Hetzel," Raoul-Duval papers).

partisan of the Empire, his provisional acceptance of the Republic was perfectly consistent with his record. He was proud to admit he had "never praised 1852. . . . I would never sacrifice to any government the liberty of belief and thought for which my fathers lived for over a century outside France." By the same token, his platforms had contained no declaration of war on the Republic. "On the contrary I said that I did not seek to overthrow it but to keep it wise and moderate." He had designed for the Bonapartists a policy in keeping with that aim, but "the fatal influence of M. Béhic and the inertia of M. Rouher" had brought his plans to nothing, with the apparent acquiescence of the Prince Imperial.[53] Thus he really had no choice but to abandon his hopes in their party.

Raoul-Duval was not the only Imperialist in the early months of 1878 to declare publicly that the game was up for Bonapartism after the *Seize Mai* and that it was high time to admit it. It was at this point that Léonce Dupont's reasoned critiques of the party's course since Sedan appeared, admirably summing up the dilemma of the Bonapartists' future *raison d'être* in one sentence: "Against the Republic we have neither a majority, nor a *coup d'état*; we could have only the mistakes of the Republic itself, and that resource escapes us, since so far it is we who have made the mistakes." Dupont invited the Prince, who was "a Republican by birth, at least through his paternal ancestors," to make a fresh start by asking his followers "to bow to the government which the nation appeared resolved" to have. Republicans had long attacked the Second Empire despite the evidence of the plebiscites that Frenchmen had accepted it; could Bonapartists, with the roles reversed, pursue the same ignoble tactic? The preservation of a democratic society was the essential goal. If this were guaranteed by the Third Republic, Bonapartists had no

[53] Raoul-Duval to Baron de Bourgoing, May 24, 1878 (dossier "Lettres de Camden," Raoul-Duval papers).

right to continue their opposition. Patriotism decreed that the question of the form of government at last be closed. A first conciliatory step could be taken by withdrawing the group of the *Appel au peuple* from the conservative bloc and pledging its support to Dufaure's ministry, which would thus be relieved of its dependence on Gambetta's Radicals.[54]

With all his authority as the confidant and literary executor of Napoleon III, the Comte de la Chapelle backed Raoul-Duval and Dupont, strongly implying that he wrote with the Prince Imperial's approval. He reviewed the party's history since the Emperor's death as scathingly as Dupont had done, and reached the same conclusion: Bonapartists, "to be in full accord with their own doctrine, . . . should accept the existing government without hesitation." They had before them an indispensable role as a constructive opposition *within* the limits of the Republican constitution, reminding Republicans that "democracy is not their exclusive appanage." Any other role the Emperor, were he still guiding the party's destinies, would repudiate.[55]

No doubt it would not be as easy as these men appeared to think to put the policy they recommended into practice. Neither Gambetta nor the Bonapartist rank and file themselves would find it easy to understand a party which retained an identity predicated on dynastic loyalty yet professed a sincere constitutionalism. As Rouher objected to Raoul-Duval, cooperation between the representatives of opposed parties could only mean the surrender of one to the other.[56] And even Cassagnac had some measure of reason on his side when, in

[54] Léonce Dupont, *Les deux démocraties: République—Empire* (Paris, 1878), 42, 44, 53, 55, 58–59, 62; *La soumission: Réponse à mes contradicteurs* (Paris, 1878), 36.
[55] Comte de la Chapelle, *Déclarations des Napoléon* (Paris, 1878), 34–36 and *passim*.
[56] Rouher to Raoul-Duval, April 28, 1878 (dossier "Correspondance Rouher," Raoul-Duval papers).

comparing Dupont to Judas, he inquired, "Do you wish to serve the Republic only to deceive and betray it? Then why rally to it? . . . If you wish to serve it, turn your coat! . . . if you wish to fight it, remain in line." [57]

These attempts to find some way out of the impasse in which they found themselves were, however, symptomatic of the profound *malaise* which in 1878 spread throughout the Bonapartist party. Eight years of illusory victories and damaging defeats had conditioned its members to expect failure. The savage Republican vengeance visited upon their deputies had sharpened the instinct of self-preservation: "Above all, let's not provoke proscriptions" had become the watchword of all who still had something to lose. No longer was Rouher's salon thronged with optimists. "One wished to live peacefully. Save for a few fanatics, . . . one kept silent; one even accepted the present regime and made arrangements to live without being inconvenienced by it." [58]

The Prince Imperial continued for some time his efforts to take direct control of his party and impress his own personality upon it, despite the unsparing reports he received of general discouragement. Though he did not have so much as a reliable confidential secretary at Chislehurst, he had a questionnaire distributed to all the former Bonapartist candidates, asking particulars on the electoral sociology of their districts—probably the first time this was systematically undertaken. He busied himself with plans to launch an Imperialist review to rival the Orleanist *Revue des Deux Mondes*. Realizing that his party was "poor in men" and that the survivors of the Second Empire were aging, he continued to invite "young and enlightened men capable of making my cause triumph" to visit him in England.

[57] Quoted in Dupont, *Soumission*, 19.
[58] Richard, *Bonapartisme*, 198–199.

Prangins and Brussels

He would have been extremely fortunate to find another clear-sighted young innovator as promising as Raoul-Duval had been, or as propitious a time to take direct control as the month which had elapsed between the *Seize Mai* and the vote for dissolution. The opportunities offered by both had been lost through no fault of his, but as morale continued to decline during 1878 his partisans increasingly eased their sense of frustration by casting the burden of all their reverses upon him. Even Ernest Lavisse complained that "the party does not act, and no longer seems capable of ever acting." The "flood of recriminations against you," he informed the Prince, "mounts unceasingly. I know they ask the impossible of Your Highness; but I also know that Your Highness does not do everything possible." [59] It was taken especially amiss that he declined to recoup the party's fortunes by contracting a royal marriage. Even Baron Eschasseriaux blamed such recalcitrance on the Prince's "absence of political flair or instinct" which was "of a nature to make the whole party despair." He had to pay the penalty for his decreased usefulness to the politicians: 7000 Frenchmen had crowded Chislehurst to witness his coming-of-age in 1874, but hardly anyone except the comrades of his schooldays visited him in 1878.[60]

This estrangement from his party, which he now admitted he was unable to control,[61] was certainly one of the factors that sent him on his final journey. The *Ordre* had categorically foresworn conservative union in March, 1878, and even Paul de Cassagnac had enthusiastically applauded the deci-

---

[59] Ernest Lavisse to Prince Imperial, December 12, 1876, February 18, 1877, April 30, 1878; Prince Imperial to Lavisse, December 15, 1877, January 28, 1878; in d'Espinay de Briort, ed., "Correspondance," 571, 576–581, 586.

[60] Eschasseriaux, "Mémoires," IX, 410; Richard, *Bonapartisme*, 200.

[61] Eugène Balleyguier (Fidus, pseud.), *Journal de Fidus* (Paris, 1889), IV, 176.

Bonapartism after Sedan

sion,[62] but there was no knowing how long this mood would last. The Bonapartist "Plain," as the *Seize Mai* had shown once again, would straggle along behind a champion of a progressive Empire only so long as no more tempting possibility offered itself. If one did, they would rush, behind the Bonapartist "Coblence," into the conservative camp, heedless of the Prince's directives. A genuine Bonapartism would have to be formed with new men, as Raoul-Duval had first suggested, by a real Bonaparte. The Prince, weary of seeing himself described as the indispensable man while still treated as a boy by his doting mother, accepted this challenge with satisfaction. He was more relieved than disheartened that it was now highly improbable that he would be restored to the throne by Parliament or by the army. Such a restoration "in the Spanish manner" would have made him, like Alfonso XII, "the slave of a few men and a whole party," a position to which he did not think he could accommodate himself. After the elections of 1877, his weakened party could not accomplish anything; all hopes rested exclusively on his own future achievements.[63]

The leaders of the party greeted as a new sign of his irresponsibility his decision to set off for Africa to make his own name. It is significant that when his body was brought back to Chislehurst, the police of Calais counted less than half the number of Bonapartists passing through the port on their way to follow him to the graveside as had gone to pay similar homage to his father six years earlier.[64]

---

[62] Wilfrid Audibert, *La Troisième République et les Napoléon* (Langres, 1890), 37–39.

[63] Letter to a friend, quoted in Comtesse des Garets, *L'Impératrice Eugénie en exil* (Paris, 1929), 199–200.

[64] Richard, *Bonapartisme*, 204; Police Superintendent, Calais, to Director of *Sûreté générale*, July 13, 1879 (AN F^{7}12429, "Police générale—Agissements bonapartistes"; hereafter cited as AN F^{7}12428, etc.).

Prangins and Brussels

Bonapartism as a political force to be reckoned with had been moribund when he embarked. The despatches from Capetown which arrived in Paris on June 20, 1879 dealt it the *coup de grâce*. Once more the Ministry of the Interior demanded reports from its agents throughout France on what impression an Imperial death had made upon the population. This time the replies were much more unanimous in their evaluations. In the Gard, some of the rare partisans of the Empire declared their intention of frankly rallying to the Republic. In the Drôme, the few who had still hoped for an Imperial restoration had had their hopes totally crushed, since "Prince Jérôme had the sympathies and esteem of no one. . . . The Bonapartist party is considered extinguished."

These were departments of the Mediterranean coast or the Southeast where Bonapartism had long been feeble, but the news from the department which had elected Bourgoing in 1874 was quite similar. According to the Republic's agent at Nevers, "Prince Jérôme Napoleon has no prestige, does not inspire confidence and will hardly rally the serious men of the Bonapartist party," which public opinion considered to be "annihilated once and for all." Its moderates would rally to the Republic, others to the Legitimists, while some might turn to the Orléans family. In the Pas-de-Calais, though "the news was received by the most fervent with an explosion of grief," the less impassioned Bonapartists openly admitted that their party would disappear with the Prince Imperial. "Some of them already were ready to raise the banner of Prince Jérôme or his son Victor, but the unpopularity of the father produced from all exclamations not only of disgust, but of repulsion, which the clever men of the party would have trouble overcoming." Best of all, from the Republican point of view, the death of Napoleon IV had profound repercussions among the forces of order. At Lyon, where only among the cavalry had there been much loyalty to the fallen regime, the officers who had remained Imperialists had now for the most part decided to rally to the Republic. The same was true of the *gendarmerie*.[65]

The frequency with which the Republic's agents reported expressions of the deepest hostility to Prince Napoleon revealed the hideous prospect with which faithful Bonapartists were confronted. They had now not merely to make peace with the chief of the Bonapartist "Mountain," a man who had managed since 1870 actually to worsen the unsavory reputation he had acquired under the Empire, but to admit that he was their leader. Plon-plon had quarreled first with the Imperial family, then with the Imperialist leaders, finally with the whole Imperialist party. Only two months after Sedan he had broken publicly with the Empress, writing to Napoleon III that after her insults he would never again have any dealings with her. They clashed again, almost at the Emperor's graveside, over her refusal to allow him any role in managing her son's affairs.[66] Excluded from what he felt to be his rightful place in the party's highest councils, he had become convinced that he would have to break his way in, by popular election, but Rouher, the man whose policies he felt were leading the dynasty to ruin, had done nothing to find him a seat.[67] Worse, when in 1874 he had sought election to the Corsican *Conseil général*, he had found himself opposed by Prince Charles Bonaparte, candidate of the party of the *Appel au peuple*. When the Republican papers had seized on this incident to proclaim a schism between Imperialists and Jérômistes, the *Ordre* had explained, almost accurately but not at all charitably: "There is no Jérômiste faction; the

[65] Reports of Police Superintendents at Nîmes, Valence, Nevers, Boulogne, and Lyon, June 21–June 29, 1879 (AN F^{7}12429).

[66] Prince Napoleon to Napoleon III, November 1, 1870; in Ernest d'Hauterive, ed., *Napoléon III et le Prince Napoléon: Correspondance inédite* (Paris, 1925), 315–316. Richard, *Bonapartisme*, 96.

[67] Eschasseriaux, "Mémoires," VII, 85, 119–120.

Prangins and Brussels

Jérômistes can be counted on the fingers without using up one hand." There was only Prince Napoleon, whose Radical platform was "only an episode in the long odyssey of his political misbehavior." [68]

From the moment of his defeat at Ajaccio, Plon-plon had burned his bridges to the Imperialist party. Rouher told Eschasseriaux he was glad to be rid of him: "the Prince is destined to descend all the degrees of demagogy without finding the cooperation he hopes for." No doubt this public family dispute was an unseemly spectacle, but it was better to "finish off properly this vulgarly ambitious man, instead of dragging along in miserable equivocations. . . . The Prince will still cause us trouble, but his rebellious character will become known even to the masses." [69]

His subsequent career had been much as the Vice-Emperor had foretold. Openly competing with his young cousin, he had continued to poach upon the best Bonapartist departments, launching or acquiring newspapers in the Charente-Inférieure and in Corsica to advertise his candidacy, not for the Imperial succession, but for the Presidency of a "democratic, liberal, and above all anti-clerical" Republic. Preparing to contest the district of Ajaccio in the general elections of 1876, he went so far as to admit his affinity for Jacobinism.[70] Lest he succeed in winning control of such a stronghold, Rouher himself had been obliged to oppose him; after the victorious Vice-Emperor had decided to sit for his native Puy-de-Dôme, the Bonapartists had even persuaded a Republican to run against Plon-plon in the ensuing by-election, in a last

---

[68] *L'Ordre*, October 11, 1874; Daniel, ed., *Année politique*—1874, 341–343.

[69] Rouher to Eschasseriaux, October 28, 1874 (Eschasseriaux, "Mémoires," VII, 424).

[70] *La Volonté nationale* (St.-Jean-d'Angély), January 1, 1875; Prefect of Corsica to Prefect of Police, Paris, July 22, 1875 (AN $F^7$12428).

desperate attempt to keep him away from the rostrum of the Chamber.[71] He had lost no time in demonstrating that their apprehensions justified such an extreme measure. Not content with sitting quietly in the ranks of the Republicans, he had chosen to speak, typically, in the debate on the *budget des cultes,* "to report the abuses of the clerical party, which I consider a great danger for my country." He had revealed that the Jesuits were "today all-powerful" and disclosed the "historic fact" that but for clerical machinations, Alsace and Lorraine would not have been lost. Keller, a fervent Catholic Legitimist and the living symbol of Alsace, had arisen to retort that the Prince bore "a name carved in letters of blood in the trembling flesh" of the lost provinces, and the Chamber had then fallen into indescribable chaos, with the voice of Gambetta denouncing "the Spanish woman they made an Empress" hardly audible above the exchanges of insults and challenges.[72]

This incident conformed in every respect to the pattern of Prince Napoleon's whole life, in which a rash tactlessness time after time rendered ineffective an often discerning judgment of great issues. The *Seize Mai* had been only the most recent revelation of how far Bonapartism had drifted from its popular foundations; the Prince had clearly understood this. But such a speech by one who had never renounced his Imperial title, defying the Imperialists by recalling the worst blot upon Napoleon III's memory and pandering to the Republicans (who equally scorned him) by an exaggerated attack on

[71] Attorney-general, Bastia, to Keeper of the Seals, February 29, May 8, May 17, 1876 (AN BB^{30}490$_1$, "Justice—Elections législatives de 1876; fraudes et délits électoraux"); cf. Richard, *Bonapartisme,* 159–160.

[72] Daniel, ed., *Année politique—1876,* 340–341; Prince Napoleon, *Discours prononcé . . . à la Chambre des Députés le 24 novembre 1876* (Paris, 1876), *passim.*

Prangins and Brussels

the clergy, was quite the worst way to make the point.[73] In fact, it accomplished nothing at all. Nevertheless, undeterred by the reaction to his oratorical effort, he had voted with the 363 and in the elections of 1877 had opposed an official candidate, running on a platform which declared that only a Republican government could satisfy democracy.[74]

In his eyes, the Second Empire had been a "great lie," and he did not regret his place "on the steps of an ill-occupied throne." Its fall, he confessed to George Sand in 1870, had been a personal deliverance, since "the Prince enchained the citizen, and this was painful to me." It was as a citizen, simple Citizen Napoleon, that he still hoped to serve his country.[75] Bemused by the symbolism of the Consulate, he dreamed of the day when a third Bonaparte would be called on to defend the sacred Republic.[76] (As for many doctrinaire Republicans of the day, that word had for him more resonance than substance; paying little attention to ideas of social reform, he simply took over Gambetta's program and remained satisfied with it.) He could never understand that ever since 1804, not to mention 1851, a Republican named Bonaparte had been a contradiction in terms, or that the abuse he flung at the Imperial idea could only rebound upon him.

The petulant obstinacy with which he refused to recognize these realities seemed to many who knew him well to reflect a

---

[73] Famille Fournier, "Mémoires," twelve manuscript volumes numbered I–VI, VIII, X–XII, XVI–XVII (ACM 4J1509), XVII, 204.

[74] *Le Patriote* (Ajaccio), September 15, 1877.

[75] Prince Napoleon to George Sand, November 28, 1870 and "1871," in Frédéric Masson, ed., "Lettres inédites de George Sand et du Prince Napoléon," *Revue des Deux Mondes*, 7th period, XVI–XVII (1923), 326, 329.

[76] Gustave Cunéo d'Ornano, *La République des Napoléon* (Paris, 1894), 617.

peculiar fundamental flaw in his character. Everyone admitted that he had numerous talents, yet despite his ambition he accomplished nothing, because he did not know how to put his abilities to effective use. The missing element was "political sense. . . . One could confidently state that everything he has said or done was exactly the contrary of what he should have said or done." This "morbid predisposition to untimely brain storms," reinforced as it was by a scornful contempt for other men's ideas, drove him from blunder to misadventure and eventually into political isolation. No wonder that Napoleon III, (as Bonapartists liked to tell the story), asked one day by his son to explain the difference between an accident and a misfortune, had told the boy that it would be an accident if Prince Napoleon fell down a well, and a misfortune if someone pulled him out again.[77]

Now this black sheep had become, according to the Imperial law of succession and the plebiscite of 1870, the pretender to a throne he repudiated. When the deputies of the *Appel au peuple* gathered to discuss the situation, Paul de Cassagnac swiftly moved to avert the calamity. Though the contents of the Prince Imperial's will were not yet known, Cassagnac asserted that the young pretender had decided to disinherit Prince Napoleon in favor of his eldest son, Prince Victor, and pressed his colleagues immediately to proclaim Victor. Perhaps this would have been the best way out of their predicament, for nothing could have been worse than what eventually happened. But for most of the party, propriety outweighed expediency. Though they had no love for Plon-plon, there was no getting around the law. Some even suggested that he might now mend his ways, that the responsibility for directing a large party might make a new man out of him. Rouher stated that he personally intended to rally to Prince

[77] Pinard, *Journal*, II, 221–224, 227–228; Delafosse, *Hommes et choses*, 139–140.

Prangins and Brussels

Napoleon, and advised his followers to do the same. Thus the initiative of Cassagnac, who well knew he could have no place in a party controlled by Plon-plon, was set aside, and the legal succession ratified.

For the moment a dramatic rupture was averted. People hoped for the best; a correspondent assured Eschasseriaux that the Charente-Inférieure would accept this new representative of the dynasty it favored in spite of his record, which would be pardoned if he abjured his errors. Such optimism, however, ignored the natures both of the Prince and of his new followers. The Bonapartist party had ignored the mild instructions of the Prince Imperial; could it really be expected to take orders from a man whose ideas were even farther removed from theirs, and whose character was so curiously compounded of impetuosity and inflexibility? Eschasseriaux thought this so unlikely that he declined the honor the Prince offered him of becoming the president of the parliamentary *réunion*. Knowing how divided and disorganized the group had become since the Prince Imperial's death, he "felt it would be difficult to overcome the repugnance of a great number of the members . . . to following Prince Napoleon, who had not publicly disavowed his former quasi-Republican and anti-religious ideas." The Baron had "neither the time nor the strength" to enforce compliance upon his fellow deputies.[78] Bonapartists found Plon-plon's reluctance to use the word Empire as peculiar as he thought their continual harping on it ridiculous. No real understanding was possible, and Rouher, though he had avoided an open schism, was not above saying so privately.[79]

The end of this uneasy interlude of mutual sufferance came quickly. The struggle between the Republic, now fully in the

[78] Eschasseriaux, "Mémoires," X, 97–99, 106, 165.
[79] Ernest Merson, *Confidences d'un journaliste* (Paris, 1891), 290; cf. Paul Lenglé, *Le neveu de Bonaparte* (2d ed.; Paris, 1893), 43.

Bonapartism after Sedan

hands of the Republicans, and the Church was beginning. On April 5, 1880, Prince Napoleon published a letter endorsing the decrees which disbanded the Jesuits and threatened the same fate for other unauthorized congregations. Men of the Bonapartist "Coblence" were of course scandalized, but even people who did not share their religious views could only conclude that this characteristically gratuitous intervention revealed how little Plon-plon had changed. "Until then," according to Eschasseriaux, "he had not been a subject of argument, since he had not made a demonstration, but the letter . . . was the beginning of a rather perceptible disaffection with him." [80]

Many Bonapartists who had been hesitating, poised between hope and despair, now took their decision. Some abandoned Bonapartism altogether, passing to the Republic or to one of the Monarchist dynasties; others grouped themselves into a sort of anti-party to await the worsening of Prince Napoleon's diabetes. When the dust had settled, it was seen that only a bare dozen deputies, most of them his old friends, had remained in his camp. Within a year after the Prince Imperial's death, most of the Bonapartists' provincial press had repudiated Prince Napoleon.[81] Not without a trace of satisfaction, Rouher concluded: "He is a sower of discord by nature, his acrimonious conduct has cut him off from a group which had almost entirely rallied;" he would achieve nothing. Bonapartists could only repose their hopes in Prince Victor.[82]

Henceforth there would be *two* Bonapartist parties, the little band of "republican Bonapartists" loyal to Plon-plon and the much-diminished majority, the "Imperialist Bonapartists," who in 1884 formed a syndicate to provide Victor

---

[80] Merson, *Confidences*, 291–292; Eschasseriaux, "Mémoires," X, 233.

[81] Richard, *Bonapartisme*, 212; Lenglé, *Neveu*, 47–49; *Le Petit Caporal*, June 30, 1880.

[82] Rouher to Eschasseriaux, August 30, 1880 (Eschasseriaux, "Mémoires," X, 345).

Prangins and Brussels

with an annual income enabling him to leave his father's house and become their pretender. Victor consented thus to be kept like a woman (as his father put it) by men like Béhic, Levert, and Padoue, though even he came to realize eventually that he was being maintained more as an electoral convenience or even as a business proposition (to sustain the reactionary clienteles of the *Pays* and the *Patrie*) than as a serious pretender.[83]

Paul de Cassagnac of course had a part in launching this unfilial rebellion, though he admitted that Victor was "not very promising"; within two years he had become impatient at Victor's placid inactivity and had abandoned Bonapartism for what he called "Solutionism." Its program, phrased with coarse cynicism as "Who cares who reigns, so long as he knocks off The Bitch? [the Republic]" was the last resort of the conservative union Cassagnac had so frequently and so fatally recommended.[84]

Jules Amigues, who had won no sympathy from Prince Napoleon for his corporative theories of social improvement, and found abhorrent his acceptance of a Republic so indifferent to the distress of the humblest classes, was also a proponent of "Victorism," though he did not live to see it launched. No more than any of the conventional Bonapartists he so despised did Prince Napoleon wish to involve himself with the sinister "Enragé" and his disciples of the Parisian slums.[85]

---

[83] Lenglé, *Neveu*, 113–115; police reports of May 5, May 27, May 30, September 10, 1884, September 11, 1886 (APP B^A69: "Prince Victor Napoléon").

[84] Police report of April 28, 1886 (APP B^A69); report of June 17, 1887 (APP B^A62, "Comités bonapartistes"). Adrien Dansette, *Le Boulangisme* (Paris, 1946), 174: "Peu importe qui règne, pourvu que la Gueuse en crève."

[85] Lenglé, *Neveu*, 317; Jules Amigues, *Discours prononcé le Ier février 1881 à la réunion de l'hôtel des chambres syndicales* (Paris, n.d.), *passim*. Police reports of June 30, July 4, July 5, July 17, August 27, 1879, June 6, September 28, 1880, April 30, 1883 (APP B^A865).

Bonapartism after Sedan

The curious spectacle of a peevish father and an indolent son carrying on from their respective Paris *hôtels* an intermittent struggle over the remnants of a once imposing political movement continued until 1886, when the Republic expelled them both, along with the representatives of the other families who had reigned in France. Victor went to Brussels; his father retired to his Swiss estate of Prangins. Just before the train which took him from France for the last time began to roll, Prince Napoleon cried "Long live the Republic anyhow." [86] It might have been his epitaph.

It was at this moment of disintegration that Raoul-Duval made his great speech appealing for an end to dynastic politics and the formation, from the debris, of a genuine conservative party *within* the Republic, to endow France with the two-party system from which England had so long benefited.[87] The plan was but an extension of the design he had vainly tried to impose upon the Bonapartists a decade earlier; the aim now as then was to split the Republican bloc by giving its moderates an alternative to partnership with the Radicals. Former supporters of his progressive Empire pledged their cooperation. The Comte de la Chapelle, for example, who had taken no part in politics since the death of the Prince Imperial, wrote Raoul-Duval that at last he had found a leader of whom he approved.[88] Yet the passing of ten years and the eclipse of Bonapartism as a party had not made the transition Raoul-Duval proposed to them any easier for the ragged remanants of the Imperial battalions. A cruel critic might have said that his "republican Right" was a fitting signature to his life, inspired but impossible. His sudden death on February 10, 1887, probably spared the idealistic, mercurial deputy of the Eure one more disappointment, and one

---

[86] Lenglé, *Neveu*, 157.   [87] Normandy, ed., *Lettres*, 82–83.
[88] Comte de la Chapelle to Raoul-Duval, November 11, 1886 (dossier "Discours du 6 novembre 1886," Raoul-Duval papers).

Prangins and Brussels

more of those impatient declarations of independence which had reduced his effectiveness as a political leader.[89]

Certainly his "radical conservative" ideas [90] well equipped Raoul-Duval to inspire a French version of Tory democracy. But the formation of such a party, which might have profoundly altered the subsequent history of the Third Republic, would have required the cooperation of men as skilled as Baron Eschasseriaux in rallying the masses to the government of their betters. It seems unlikely that if Raoul-Duval had sought such men among the surviving Bonapartists, he would have found very many who would have stayed the course with him. It would never have occurred to Eschasseriaux that he could rally to a party which accepted the Republican constitution; that constitution to him represented the work of faithless enemies to whom he refused to capitulate, though his refusal condemned him to the political wilderness. The Orleano-Bonapartist conservatives, of course, would not be deterred by such a point of conscience, but they had never been the kind of adepts in the organization of universal suffrage which Tory democracy would have required.

The eyes of both authoritarian democrats and "conservatives" were turning, in 1887, in quite another direction. Closing his history of Bonapartism under the Republic in 1883, Jules Richard had predicted that the "millions of Frenchmen who believe only in the power of Authority," who had so long relied on the Napoleons to provide it, now "would accept it from the first fortunate soldier, the first great man whom events bring to the fore." [91] Now they thought they had him, in the person of General Boulanger.

As the Bonapartists had abandoned the promise of the

[89] Richard, *Bonapartisme*, 148–149.
[90] Henri Des Houx, "Edgar Raoul-Duval: Origine et avenir de la Droite républicaine," *Nouvelle Revue*, XLVII (July 1, 1887), 47.
[91] Richard, *Bonapartisme*, 212–213.

progressive Empire when they heard the appeal of Mac-Mahon, so now they disregarded the "Republican Right" and followed the new man on horseback. Not that they were thereby reunited; the little group of Republican Bonapartists made desperate efforts to keep Boulangism from continuing to drift from its original Leftist orientation, while the Imperialist Bonapartists joined an electoral coalition of Monarchists and Boulangists managed by Baron de Mackau, now president of the parliamentary *Union des Droites,* and financed by the Monarchist Duchess d'Uzès. As had been the case with the *Seize Mai,* reactionary fever was swiftly followed by the chill of reality. Even men of the Bonapartist "Coblence" had to admit, after Boulanger's ignominious flight from France, that they had now descended to the last indignity. As short of money as ever, the party had agreed to "subordinate, almost to debase itself," by selling off its Imperial name to an adventurer in return for electoral cash.[92]

Boulangism was really the Bonapartists' last fling. Their support of a rival providential man had been a tacit avowal that fidelity to one or the other of their pretenders no longer made any sense. The way in which their poverty had driven them into Boulanger's arms showed once more that Bonapartism had failed to adapt itself to a new political epoch. Significantly, it was after the debacle of 1889 that Bonapartists first contemplated the issuance of membership cards in return for payment of dues as a means of solving both the disciplinary and financial problems. Such expedients in the 1870's might have enabled the Empire to face the Republic on far more equal terms; now they merely served for the enrollment of young bloods and toughs of the capital who might as easily have joined one of the other street-fighting leagues, of anti-Semites, Nationalists, or (eventually) *Came-*

---

[92] Merson, *Confidences,* 296–298. Cf. Lenglé, *Neveu,* 213, 226–227, 240, 247; Dansette, *Boulangisme,* 172, 189, 232.

lots du Roi. Ironically, the friends of Jules Amigues had the last laugh; it was above all as an urban movement, of the Latin Quarter and the slums, that Bonapartism, a pallid shadow of what it once had been, lingered on into the twentieth century.[93]

Long before then the party's peasant-based provincial bastions had begun falling to the enemy. In the Charente-Inférieure, the strongest of all, its defenses had begun to weaken immediately after the failure of the *Seize Mai*. The first warning was a progressive diminution in subsidies and subscriptions to the *Progrès*. Though the paper had helped their candidacies as much as it had Baron Eschasseriaux's, Roy de Loulay and his son now indicated that they would not continue to support it. They had already made their intentions clear in 1876, when they invited the new Prefect to their estate although he was mounting a savage attack on the *Progrès* in an effort to destroy it. This had not surprised the Baron; it was another example of their eagerness to ingratiate themselves with authority, no matter what the regime.

While they were thus leaving the gates ajar to the Republic at St.-Jean-d'Angély, the weaker outposts of Bonapartism in the department were one by one being overrun. From Rochefort, a correspondent warned the Baron early in 1878 that he feared "the disintegration of our party. It lacks leaders, active chiefs constantly concerned with keeping their troops on the alert." The Republicans, on the other hand, lacked "neither audacity nor ardor," and since they would now have the help of new *fonctionnaires*, "everything is to be feared. I see about me many discouraged people."

At La Rochelle, Mayor Fournier failed in 1878 to persuade the voters to reelect him after his invalidation, though he had

[93] Police reports of March 10, August 23, August 30, 1887; October 11, December 12, 1889; September 20, 1892; January 12, 1900 (APP B^A69–70).

rejected the endorsement of the *Progrès*, fearing that it would compromise his effort to unite all the conservatives behind his candidacy. This was a vain concession to the bourgeoisie of the city; handicapped already by the determined opposition of the Republican administration, Fournier received no help from the Monarchists and the clergy, who stood aside from the battle in the hope that his defeat would extinguish Bonapartism in the *arrondissement*.[94] Exhausted and embittered, Fournier withdrew from public life altogether. The very cultural and learned societies he had helped to found in the heyday of the Empire were now coming to be dominated by an inferior class of people hostile to all that he stood for, and he took a masochistic pleasure, in 1878 and 1879, in listing in his diary his resignations from everything from the Literary to the Racing Society, and the dates on which he ceased to subscribe to the local newspapers.[95]

Eschasseriaux had never had any faith in the Rochelaise bourgeoisie. Now, however, circumstances were combining to undermine Bonapartism even among the peasants. Phylloxera was ravaging the vineyards, and with the collapse of exports, faith in the Imperial legacy of free trade collapsed as well. By 1879, protective tariffs were being sought for grain and livestock, the inadequate resources which remained to the agricultural population.

Against the malevolence of nature the Baron would have been willing to fight on, but after the death of the Prince Imperial there befell him something very like the death of his own son: René declared to his father his intention of giving up political life. The Baron had spared himself no expense to launch the young man's career, and had paid 36,000 francs for a house at Jonzac in which he might properly receive his cli-

[94] Eschasseriaux, "Mémoires," VIII, 67–68; IX, 283, 351, 355, 358, 421–422.
[95] Fournier, "Mémoires," XVII, 329.

Prangins and Brussels

entele. It had been in vain; despite all his father could say, René remained unshakeable. The Baron could not begin to understand the reasons for his son's repudiation of his political heritage; to Eschasseriaux's dying day the cause for which he had fought all his life never became anachronistic in his eyes.[96]

Yet he could find no consolation, no matter where he looked, for this heavy blow. From Paris, Rouher informed him that his pessimistic reports on the Charente-Inférieure, though very disturbing, were not the worst of the news. Corsica could no longer be counted on. "Gavini's letters are heartbroken, the majority in the *Conseil général*, once so numerous, has become uncertain, and the symptoms of disorganization are appearing in each canton." By lavish promises to the needy Corsicans, the Republican administrators were beginning to dismantle the Bonapartist machine there, to the point that Gavini was no longer sure that the island would again elect Bonapartist deputies.

The position in the Puy-de-Dôme was no more reassuring. During the long years of preoccupation in Paris, the Vice-Emperor had failed to build a satisfactory organization for himself in the Auvergne. He dreaded facing the elections of 1881, which he was not at all sure he could win. Besides, "a goal, an objective, are lacking. Ambition was extinguished in me, but devotion remained; death has broken it, I remain disoriented and heartsick. I shall end up, I think, by withdrawing." His faith in the historical inevitability of a return to the Empire—that faith which had often permitted him to yield in good conscience to the tactical blunders of his followers—remained as strong as ever. However dismal the present outlook, a careful observer could detect occasional signs of a coming transformation: "I do not even despair of living long enough to see the first rays of a consoling dawn."

[96] Eschasseriaux, "Mémoires," IX, 31–32; X, 9, 167.

Bonapartism after Sedan

But he would await them in peace; rather than give the Republic an opportunity for gloating over his humiliation, he did not run for reelection.[97]

Insofar as he had accepted direction from anyone, Eschasseriaux had accepted it from Rouher. The disappearance from the scene of the Vice-Emperor undoubtedly influenced the decision the Baron himself made in 1881, particularly since he had no confidence in the plans of Prince Napoleon. (He thought it absurd to expect to arrive at the Empire by way of the Consulate, and told Plon-plon so.) Yet neither then nor later, until the latter's death, did he feel he could give his allegiance to Prince Victor. He confined himself to leaving his card at Victor's *hôtel* and did not enter, for he was too scrupulous to admit the legality of his party's deposition of Prince Napoleon.[98]

Though his Bonapartism had now become a memory rather than an aspiration, the Baron did not yet follow Rouher into retirement. He decided to beat a strategic retreat. He who in 1875 had upheld *scrutin de liste* as the Bonapartist road to resurrection had been terrified by the Republican proposal to try it in 1881, although, unwilling publicly to admit his party's decline, he had abstained on the question. The retention of *scrutin d'arrondissement* provided a good excuse for shortening his lines. The public need not know that his decision had been dictated by his son's defection and by the increasing losses of the *Progrès*, resulting from "the continual decline in subscriptions and the successive disappearance of old friends, dead or discouraged by events." The death of the Prince Imperial "had, indeed, dealt the party a terrible blow from which it was not recovering. Therefore I decided to re-

[97] Rouher to Eschasseriaux, August 30, 1880, June 15, December 29, 1881; Eschasseriaux, "Mémoires," X, 344–345; XI, 39, 59–60, 83, 186.

[98] Eschasseriaux, "Mémoires," XIII, 142–144.

Prangins and Brussels

nounce militant politics, and to retreat to the *arrondissement* of Jonzac," where, in the absence of an urban electorate, victory would not come so hard. No more would Eschasseriaux maintain his department-wide organization: "Jolibois and I were going to continue to fight only to preserve our position, without thinking of carrying our propaganda into other, neighboring regions where we no longer found the enthusiastic auxiliaries of earlier days."

The general elections of 1881 "marked a great weakening of the party," as might have been expected after this retrenchment. Eschasseriaux and two of his colleagues were reelected by narrow majorities. But the man to whom he had handed the candidacy at Saintes, not having imitated the Baron's methods and style, went down to defeat. Though he had the great disadvantage of a name beginning with a particle, which led the peasants to suspect him of Monarchist leanings, this neophyte "had not even taken the time to visit his forty-five communes." Unwilling, because of his overconfidence, to undertake the *démarches* by which Eschasseriaux had secured the loyalty of the peasantry, he could only blame himself for his failure.[99]

In absolute contrast to the triumphant elections of 1876, all the Bonapartists' candidates for the Senate were beaten in the Charente-Inférieure in 1885. Their candidates for the Chamber did somewhat better than in 1881 (though for the first time in his life Eschasseriaux did not confidently retire to his estate to await the result.) After the elections, however, they were compelled to take a step which the Baron would have contemptuously rejected in the 1870's: the negotiation of a complete contract of cooperation with the Monarchists. Candidates for the Senate were to be designated at alternate elections by the Bonapartists and by the Monarchists; the latter would have a right to two of the Chamber candidacies,

[99] Eschasseriaux, "Mémoires," X, 419–420; XI, 37–38, 104–105.

or three if Eschasseriaux or one of his colleagues retired. A joint treasury would be maintained, with one-third to be returned to the Monarchists and the rest to the Bonapartists if the partnership were dissolved. The Baron himself conveyed to the Monarchists, in language he would once have scorned, the Bonapartists' approval of this "union of all the nuances of the conservative party, in view of a common action for the defense of the great social principles, conservative propaganda, and the creation of an electoral treasury." [100]

Though reduced circumstances had forced him into conservative union at home, Eschasseriaux quit Mackau's parliamentary *Union des Droites* in disgust in 1885. The Orleanists had been up to their old tricks in electing Grévy's successor; while the Bonapartists voted for their own candidate, Monarchist votes had gone to Saussier, a Republican. The Baron, with a few of his colleagues, thereupon informed Mackau that conservative union was a snare and a delusion, that henceforth they would uphold the pure principle of the *Appel au peuple*. Never again did he set foot in the salons of the *Union des Droites*.

Time after time since 1870 the Bonapartists had taken this same pledge, only to relapse into a conservative debauch at the first opportunity. The emergence of Boulangism tempted Eschasseriaux out of his semi-retirement and gave him a last occasion to dominate the politics of the Charente-Inférieure. The death of one of his fellow deputies in July, 1888, provided a chance to crush the Republican Opportunists by electing Boulanger to the vacant seat. Confident that he was not compromising Bonapartist independence, the Baron convinced his followers that "although General Boulanger necessarily called himself a Republican, it was good politics to enter the movement he had launched and to de-

---

[100] Eschasseriaux, "Mémoires," XII, 207–208, 377–378, 413–414; XIII, 45–47, 81–82, 449–451.

velop it against those who oppressed us." It was not as if they were entering into an alliance with the Left; Jolibois' secret interview with Boulanger had made it clear that he was not a proponent of disorder. Yet they would have to practice some dissimulation: Eschasseriaux undertook to manage the General's campaign in the *arrondissements* of Saintes, Jonzac, and Marennes, but at La Rochelle and at Rochefort he would be presented by Republican backers as a Republican. As a result of this combination, Boulanger beat his Opportunist opponent by more than 15,000 votes. "The government was flattened. . . . We had regained possession of the countryside in a striking manner."

The next step would be to elect another Boulangist to the General's seat, which he had immediately resigned in accordance with his plan of multiple candidacies. But here Bonapartist headquarters in Paris dared to interfere; the party's official paper proclaimed to the world that the new Boulangist victory would really be a victory for Bonapartism. Eschasseriaux was enraged. Such a statement must "clumsily compromise the outcome of the delicate campaign we were conducting amid great difficulties," since the Opportunist papers would naturally seize on such an assertion to detach Republicans from the Boulangist. In his anger the Baron dashed off a letter to the chairman of the party's central committee (there was still a central committee.) He could not permit the leaders of his party thus to "embarrass our activities and meddle in our affairs without having been asked." Since he desired "to preserve a free and independent position," he begged the chairman to accept his resignation from the committee.[101]

It was the same sort of letter Rouher, struggling to safeguard the interests of the Prince Imperial in 1877, had re-

[101] Eschasseriaux, "Mémoires," XIV, 101, 103–104, 108, 137–138, 253–254.

ceived from Eschasseriaux's neighbor Prax-Paris. To the last, the individual Bonapartist deputy persisted in gauging political opportunities from his own local point of view, not from the perspective of his party's larger interests as seen in Paris. Once again, the consequences of such indiscipline proved fatal, when Boulangism was revealed to be a *coup d'épée dans l'eau*. The General, "instead of going to the Elysée as his role demanded, . . . went very peacefully home, turning his back on the good fortune which had come to tempt him." Locked in conservative union, Boulangism and Bonapartism went down together in the elections of 1889. Eschasseriaux himself was once more reelected, but when he arrived at the Palais Bourbon he found that the party in which he had in 1876 been one of a hundred had virtually ceased to exist.

In the *arrondissement* battles, the Royalist element, supported by the clergy in many districts, had taken the place of our candidates whose clear-cut opinions became a source of weakness in the struggle. Others of our friends, of a less accentuated *nuance* or having Royalist tendencies or family traditions, had one by one passed to this party or had been elected as conservatives. They had signed up . . . with the *réunion des droites*, so that the group of partisans of the *Appel au peuple* under the Imperialist banner now counted barely thirty members, and we even hesitated to invite several of these, who had not responded to invitations and whom it was difficult to classify. During the course of this legislature the group, feeling its weakness and the hesitations of its members, confined itself to a few rare attempts at meeting.[102]

It was to be the Baron's last term. Though there was little which he could still accomplish in Parliament, his unparalleled political experience was still consulted. After the death of Prince Napoleon in 1891, he at last felt he could go to Brussels to see Prince Victor. He declared to the pretender that the party was very badly weakened, but insisted that

[102] Eschasseriaux, "Mémoires," XIV, 289–290; XV, 231–232.

Prangins and Brussels

there was still Bonapartist sentiment among the masses, which must be aroused and encouraged until some combination of unforeseen events created a favorable moment for a restoration. He had no doubt that all hopes for galvanizing and sustaining this latent sentiment lay in

> the transformation of the *Patrie* into a one-sou paper, in the creation of regional papers in the large cities with a common editorial staff in Paris [linked to them] by special wire, in the sending of materials and modest subsidies to local papers, in the maintenance of the superior committee . . . in Paris and in the nomination of chiefs, delegated by department and *arrondissement*, responsible for corresponding with the Prince and for stimulating zeal.

All this, he estimated, would cost four or five hundred thousand francs a year, which must be sought "from some very rich, vain men, who would make large loans." (When Victor later wrote to ask the Baron to join in a subscription, he explained in reply that since he had always borne most of his own campaign costs himself, it was his practice not to help pay any of the expenses for the headquarters of the party. Charitably, he enclosed a 100-franc bill in the letter.) [103]

The Baron's advice was virtually the same, item for item, as Ernest Merson (and Eschasseriaux himself) had offered the Prince Imperial in 1876. The elections of that year had revealed how damaging failure to take the steps they recommended could be. The passage of fifteen years had not made those steps any less indispensable, or any more likely to be carried out, though neglecting them had now brought Bonapartism to the verge of extinction.

The defeat in the elections of 1892 for the *Conseil général* which enabled him to give a principled reason for his complete retirement was almost a relief for Eschasseriaux. The

[103] Eschasseriaux, "Mémoires," XVI, 16, 34–35.

Bonapartism after Sedan

dynasty with which he had bound up his life had now sunk so low that Prince Victor was reduced to asking him to try to get a few thousand votes cast in the Imperial name at Jonzac, "to make people believe . . . in the secret aspirations of the inhabitants of the countryside for the return . . . of the Napoleons." (The Baron, still as minutely informed as ever on the inclinations of universal suffrage, refused, for he feared a defeat.) The party to which he belonged had so declined that it was heartbreaking, visiting its little office, to find "a very primitive installation which singularly contrasted with the crowding, the excitement, the numerous personnel once to be seen" at number 4, rue de l'Elysée. In the legislative bodies, the *Ralliement*, at last realizing Raoul-Duval's vision of a "Republican Right," had gained considerable ground. Not that Eschasseriaux had any sympathy for it: "I . . . found it painful to be associated with a Right . . . of such weak convictions, so quick to compromise, so preoccupied by its reelection, so blind to the result of its concessions." Without the slightest misgivings, he contrasted this Right's performance with "the role, preponderant on May 24, 1873, and always important, played in the Versailles assembly by the little group of the *Appel au peuple*, so well endowed with political sense." That little band, enlarged fourfold in 1876, had fallen again to a bare two dozen, and was still falling. "The most deep-rooted loyalties of earlier days were vacillating. . . . My best neighbors and colleagues, those of the Charente, by rallying to the Republic, shook and ruined Bonapartism in the Charente-Inférieure. The battle was becoming useless."

He had kept the Republic from taking possession of his district for twenty-three years; he felt he could still do so, though at St.-Jean-d'Angély Roy de Loulay was now planning to seek his next mandate as a Republican. But to continue the fight would have required "great financial resources . . . to bring new adherents to our camp and fill the gaps." Above all,

Prangins and Brussels

he was nearing his seventieth year, and beginning at last to feel the need of an occasional substitute on his endless political errands. Since his son had refused to replace him at the center of the complex network of personal relationships on which the authoritarian democracy of the Charente-Inférieure rested, he could only dismantle it.

I unbound and restored to liberty a great many friends who had followed me for the sake of honor and fidelity, but whom the continuing battle troubled, wearied, and whose interests it sometimes embarrassed. . . . I resolutely decided then, with the consciousness of having done my duty during a forty-five year elective mandate, to enter the final retirement which precedes eternal rest.

Thus it was that on election day in August, 1893, "the services of five generations of deputies which the family had numbered in 104 years came to an end." Their successor was a Radical who wore a dirty hat and traveled up to Paris in a third-class compartment full of workingmen.[104]

[104] Eschasseriaux, "Mémoires," XVII, 148, 183, 255–256, 278, 282, 310, 430–431.

Conclusion

The Limits of Authoritarian Democracy

"Authoritarian democracy" is not a political formula that evokes much sympathy or even understanding from persons reared in the Anglo-Saxon political tradition. At best, it appears to be the illogical combination of two incompatible terms, at worst cynical verbal camouflage for a regime of unscrupulous exploitation. And yet considered in its proper context of French political and social history, a formula of this kind may be recognized as a virtual necessity with which France is periodically obliged to experiment. For authoritarian democracy claims to be able to satisfy all the divergent aspirations inherent in the life of the nation which gave the world first the model of the centralizing absolute state and then the model of violent egalitarian revolution and has continued to live with the consequences of both. In particular, it is a formula intended to attract not only those Frenchmen for whom the preservation of a well-ordered society by a strong government represents the supreme good, but also those ready to sacrifice even order to safeguard the principle of juridical equality established in 1789.

Both groups, his supporters would argue, can accept the rule of the Imperial—or imperious—figure who incarnates authoritarian democracy. The men of order may be reassured

Conclusion

by the control his government imposes upon society, the men of democracy by the fact that he is not the creature of traditionally privileged groups but of the society as a whole, consulted in elections in which every vote is of equal value. Under his rule, it is argued, the conquests of former revolutions are preserved while the danger of future revolutions is eliminated.

For a society rent, at least until very recently, by conflict between an egalitarian ideology and a reality still much molded by traditions of hierarchical privilege, authoritarian democracy, then, is not necessarily an irrational idea. Indeed, in theory it represents a very predictable compromise, claiming as it does to put an end to the cycle of revolution and reaction in France by establishing a government above, and thus *between*, Left and Right. As a government of the *center*, relying upon mass support, it should defend Frenchmen equally from the enterprises of the oligarchical or even counterrevolutionary Right and from those of the socially demagogic or even revolutionary Left.

In its nineteenth-century form of Bonapartism, authoritarian democracy in France was called upon, both by its own doctrine and by the logic of its origins, to play the role which Lipset has ascribed to Fascism in the twentieth century. It was called upon to be what Lipset refers to as an "extremism" (but "authoritarianism" better describes Bonapartism) *of the center*. Fascism, Lipset argues, is distinguished from the extremisms of the traditional Right both by its ideology and by its clientele. Ideologically, Fascism is the authoritarian counterpart, differing only in its emphasis upon the strength and activity of the state, of radical or populist democracy. Hostile alike to the traditionalism of the aristocracies of birth or wealth and to the collectivism of the urban working class, Fascism appeals above all to the independent little man, the vast class of small property-holders at the center of the political spectrum.[1]

No group was more numerous and politically decisive in nineteenth-century France, with its relatively slow industrial development, than the one which frequently carried the twentieth-century extremisms of the center to victory. The distasteful features of a regime of this kind should not, therefore, blind the observer to the immense potential force of a nineteenth-century authoritarianism of the center, if its political formula were properly applied. Indeed, though the Second Empire in practice diverged widely from the formula, it was probably the most widely-accepted of the nineteenth-century French regimes. Its most determined opponents were obliged to confess only a few months before war brought it to an end that it appeared stronger than ever. In this long perspective, the surprise of the 1870's was not so much that Bonapartism reappeared on the French political scene, but that its resurgence was so limited after Sedan. After all, in the period 1848–1851, having experienced the June Days and the fusionist intrigues of the unpopular Republic's Monarchist Assembly, France had turned with relief to the Empire. After the Commune, and amid the impotent and reactionary wrangling of the National Assembly, it was not unreasonable to expect that history might repeat itself. Both Orleanists and Republicans were certainly fearful enough of that possibility to sink their differences in the constitution of 1875.

In fact, however, this study has shown that the fears of both were exaggerated. The Third Republic was actually brought into being to ward off a threat which momentarily

[1] Seymour M. Lipset, *Political Man: the Social Bases of Politics* (Garden City, 1963), 127–137. The modified adoption of Lipset's term is not intended to equate Bonapartism and other forms of authoritarian democracy with Fascism, but rather to emphasize the possibility of a centrist authoritarianism.

Conclusion

appeared more menacing than in reality it could have become, at least without a new social cataclysm. Of its own strength, the Bonapartist party of the 1870's could not persuade Frenchmen to restore the Empire.

An analysis of this incapacity, so oddly at variance with the potential strength of the idea of authoritarian democracy which the party professed to uphold, not only helps to explain why the Third Republic, unlike the First, Second, and Fourth, succeeded in outliving its youth. For analysis reveals that Bonapartist weakness can be traced to two fundamental failures: a failure *before* 1870 to develop Bonapartism as a living and deeply-rooted reality in accordance with its theoretical professions, and a related failure *after* 1870 to anticipate the political techniques which carried twentieth century extremisms of the center to victory. To understand the Bonapartists' failure after Sedan thus is to gain considerable insight into the nature of the Second Empire, the political instincts of the nineteenth-century French notable, and the development of authoritarianism from the nineteenth to the twentieth century. Finally, the story of Bonapartism after Sedan suggests some troubling questions which those who predict the durability of more contemporary versions of authoritarian democracy in France might do well at least to ponder.

The Second Empire had failed to produce a distinctive substitute for the forms of political leaderhip the earlier nineteenth century had known. As a result, the men who represented the Imperial cause after 1870 failed, as the Empire itself had failed, to maintain Bonapartism on its historically ordained and self-avowed course as an authoritarianism of the center. Their inability above all to come to terms with the revolution in French politics represented by the advent of universal suffrage in 1848 doomed them to ineffectiveness and finally to extinction. Although time and again the most clairvoyant among them prescribed the use of the political tech-

Bonapartism after Sedan

niques proper to democracy, with equal frequency their party proved itself incapable of executing these prescriptions. The immediate result was immensely to facilitate the task of Gambetta and his Republicans. Earlier Republics had been brief and either frightening or inglorious; now a country largely populated by conservative but egalitarian peasants accepted the regime of Robespierre and Louis Blanc. The real heirs of Napoleon III were not the Prince Imperial and Prince Napoleon but, paradoxically, the Radical deputies of the Third Republic, to whom the Bonapartists abandoned their party's natural position as defenders of the center—of that majority of Frenchmen who were socially conservative but politically democratic.

This neglect of the center was all the more serious because the events of the 1870's repeatedly revealed that despite two decades in power the Second Empire had not won over those elements in French society which would have provided a solid foundation for an authoritarianism of the right. Though it is just possible that if Napoleon III had landed in France in the summer of 1873 he would have swept all before him, after his death the prospects of a *coup de force* became ever more dubious. The Bonapartists' own negligence was partly at fault: unlike the successful authoritarian movements of the twentieth century, they did not carefully lay the groundwork for a coup by ensuring the complicity, or at least the indulgence, of key elements of the existing government. An ordinary general could point out to Rouher the necessity for a systematic cultivation of contacts in the Army, for a start, but nothing practical came of his suggestion. It is fair to say, however, that even more thorough efforts might have been unavailing. The evidence available suggests that the Bonapartists found that France's functional elites, not only the Army but the Church and the administration as well, were neither attached enough to the Empire nor fearful enough of the Republic to enter

Conclusion

into subversive activities. The *attentisme* of all three groups revealed their optimism that they could weather the change of regime in 1870 as they had weathered others, without having to fear substantial incursions upon what they regarded as their legitimate prerogatives. The *hauts fonctionnaires* discovered that they had miscalculated as early as 1879 when Gambetta began purging the bureaucracy, the Church and Army only in 1905 in the aftermath of the Dreyfus affair. But it was too late. Now that Bonapartism was declining or defunct, all three faced the Republican challenge alone, and went down to defeat.

Since a "return from Elba" facilitated by treacherous servants of the state (which more cautious and practical Bonapartists like Rouher deprecated anyhow) was impossible, Bonapartism's fate would be determined by universal suffrage. In addressing itself to the electorate, however, Bonapartism found itself in a very different situation after 1870 from the one which had prevailed in 1848. The difference resulted from what may be an inevitable internal contradiction in the rule of a providential man who pretends to govern above and beyond parties, relying only upon plebiscitary support. In 1848, Prince Louis Napoleon had been elected by universal suffrage in a period of social crisis as a result of the appeal of his name to widespread and diverse sectors of the electorate. He had been supported by no substantial nationwide party of his own, which was entirely in keeping with the essential theoretical concept of Bonapartism: an unimpeded dialogue between one man wielding a strong and beneficent authority and the democratic masses. Once the Prince-President had become the Emperor, however, the practical problem of sustaining this dialogue became apparent. Dialogue between the Emperor and the masses could not really be sustained by the infrequent plebiscites. Though the moral impact of a plebiscite may be great, its effectiveness for the practical business of everyday politics is nil. Yet dialogue, and thus involvement of the electorate in its own fate, had to be maintained if authoritarian democracy were not to become mere authority. To escape this dilemma the Imperial constitution included a democratically-elected legislative body, and the regime which claimed to abolish the need for parties thus provided a forum in which parties could hardly fail to appear.

Under these circumstances it was obviously necessary to create a Bonapartist party. Theoretically, the regime need not have resorted to the traditional social elite to find the members for that party. It could, like similar twentieth century regimes, have chosen as its candidates enthusiasts from among the people, thus driving its roots deep while at the same time creating a parliament of members who owed everything to the regime. In fact, however, this was probably not a realistic alternative in the mid-nineteenth century: the number of people at all equipped by education and experience to play an effective parliamentary role was too small. Napoleon III had recognized this by extending the endorsement of his government to men who were already notables, thus in fact conferring recognition upon a social status which the doctrine of authoritarian democracy should logically have ignored.[2]

It could not have reasonably been expected that these Bonapartist notables, since they did not owe their entire position to the regime, would forever remain its passive instruments. Thus the Emperor had been obliged to share his political power, to an ever-increasing degree, with those who had traditionally held or recently acquired social power. (By the late 1860's, as Eschasseriaux's experience demonstrates, this process had been carried so far that authoritarian democrats like Rouher and himself were actually sacrificed in an attempt to propitiate the "clericals and protectionists.") Thus the

[2] René Rémond, *La Droite en France de la Première Restauration à la Cinquième République* (New ed., Paris, 1963), 104.

Conclusion

Second Empire had become something like the political equivalent of the joint-stock companies which flourished under its aegis, with notables investing in it the "capital" of their social prestige and expecting in return not only the "dividend" of a seat in Parliament, but a share in the management.

After Sedan, the "company" was in reorganization, and its Imperial "chairman of the board," relegated with diminished reputation to a distant retirement, found himself obliged to listen to much unsolicited conservative advice from his "shareholders" on how to recoup. Napoleon III, ignoring it, remained as convinced as ever that he must avoid choosing a side in class conflict if he were to have any hope of achieving the reconciliation of order and democracy, baffled though he still was by that fundamental dilemma: to govern dictatorially with only the sanction of plebiscites was actually to govern in a vacuum, but to share power by increasing the role of Parliament was to eliminate the distinctive theoretical merit of his regime. Nevertheless it is no accident that both he and his son constantly sought "new men"—like Amigues and Raoul-Duval—to refloat the Empire. Recognizing that though the appeal of Bonapartism is broad, it must above all avoid becoming detached from that essential center of the political spectrum, they were seeking to recreate the situation of 1848 by subordinating or replacing their encumbering "shareholders."

While they languished in exile, however, it was these very "shareholder" notables, often prisoners of their past and of their class, who now represented Bonapartism before the democratic electorate. It is conceivable that universal suffrage, asked directly to choose between the Emperor and the uncertainties of the early Republic, might have repeated its verdict of 1870, but a plebiscite (again, barring some unforeseeable catastrophe) could only be demanded if the party of the "appeal to the people" won a parliamentary majority. Though the wisest Bonapartists clearly understood the necessary political techniques that, by restoring Bonapartism to its proper role as an authoritarianism of the center, would have made the election of such a majority possible, the "shareholders" of the Empire who now made party policy were not often equipped to understand or practice those techniques. The portents of their behavior in 1871—their hesitancy, their overriding concern for cooperation with other men of order—were all confirmed in the ensuing decade.

What modern, successful extremism of the center, for example, has failed to include some "socialistic" elements in its program in an effort to win over at least the "better elements" of the urban working class? Napoleon III had played this card in 1848, and after 1870 played it again with his encouragement of Jules Amigues. When the Emperor died, however, the "shareholders," for whom even an income tax was a heretical proposition, promptly discarded it. Amigues was backed only by Paul de Cassagnac, in whose ferocious language one can sense a presage of the nihilistic contempt for bourgeois convention of some twentieth-century authoritarian movements. Even Cassagnac, however, was a sportsmanlike duelist, not a *déclassé* street-brawler, while most of his fellow Bonapartist politicians were thoroughly respectable middle-class gentlemen, often country gentlemen with an instinctive horror of Amigues' turbulent urban milieu. They were uninterested in any prospects Bonapartism might have there, and presented almost no candidates in the cities of France.

Similarly, though these Bonapartist "shareholders" were not the devout Catholics many Legitimists were, they usually had a conventional respect for the Church. The advent of a militant anticlerical to the leadership of their party divided it and completed its ruin, while the heterogeneous Republican bloc was held together for a generation by Gambetta's cry

Conclusion

"Clericalism, that is the enemy." The Bonapartists abandoned Prince Napoleon when he took up that cry, though in doing so he showed some awareness of the demands of a real authoritarianism of the center, hostile to the power of the Church though not to religion itself. (It is only just to add that his bizarre career, culminating in his aspiration to become president of an authoritarian Republic, provoked in them an understandable mistrust.)

These conventional responses of the "shareholders" to socialism and anticlericalism were symptomatic. Intellectual interpretations of the meaning of Bonapartism were still as richly variegated in the 1870's as the visitors to Rouher's salons, ranging from the reactionary clericalism of Fidus to the corporatist socialism of Jules Amigues. But among those who now wielded the power of the party, the politicians of its parliamentary "Plain," neither Amigues the *Enragé* nor the small "Mountain" grouped around Prince Napoleon enjoyed any credit. No individual, in fact, succeeded in establishing a doctrinal ascendancy over them. Instead, they wavered, individually and collectively, between the ideas of violent reaction championed by Cassagnac and the authentic authoritarian democracy upheld by Rouher, while lingering in occasional dalliance with the vague "conservative liberalism" which Ollivier's Liberal Empire had so well represented. Thus it is not surprising that when the Bonapartists, in their unsystematic way, considered the question of which classes within French society their party should cultivate, their horizons were confined, at worst to their fellow bourgeois *bienpensants*, at best to the masses of the peasantry.

This narrow-mindedness would not have mattered had they managed effectively to mobilize these two substantial groups within the electorate. Have not both usually been essential props of modern extremisms of the center? But again, though the most perceptive Bonapartists repeatedly pointed out what

Bonapartism after Sedan

had to be done to win them, their party showed itself consistently incapable of making the necessary efforts.

Subsequent history suggests that an extremism of the center, to be effective, must be guided by a strong-willed if not omnipotent leader, aided by a small and efficient circle of devoted or even fanatical auxiliaries. The house on the rue de l'Elysée, however, and the committee which met there were more like a gentleman's club, where it was the idle who were most often to be seen, than a modern party headquarters. Whatever cautious steps the realistic Rouher took to enforce discipline were regarded as an unsporting use of the blackball, though he was also blamed for the shortcomings which discipline alone could have corrected.

Similarly, the reiterated futile proposals for a systematic nationwide organization of local committees demonstrate that some Bonapartists perceived that a successful party in an age of democratic politics must forge a continuous chain of loyalties stretching from Paris to the remotest commune. (In Paris, Amigues tried to create something like a network of "cells.") Even as energetic a politician as Eschasseriaux, however, did not successfully complete the forging of such a chain in the southwestern departments, despite his initial burst of activity in 1872. It was an unrewarding task, for the representative of party headquarters found himself constantly faced with the inertia, the rivalries, or the defiant independence of the local Bonapartist notables. In any case, Eschasseriaux had all he could do, given the political indolence of his fellow Bonapartists there, to organize his own department. When the organizational chain lacked so many links even in the Southwest, there is little reason for astonishment that not much was done in other regions, though their populations were reputedly almost as sympathetic to the Empire. As a result, in much of France Bonapartism did not recruit the essential "noncommissioned officers" to keep the electoral

Conclusion

"troops" in line. It was thus at a marked disadvantage in a struggle with Republicanism, which found its auxiliaries in the lodges, and even with Legitimism, backed as it was by many curés.

No modern extremism of the center has triumphed without a massive and well-calculated propaganda effort. Even their opponents admitted that in this respect the Bonapartists had achieved something. They did succeed in at least partially cleansing the Empire of the shame of Sedan and making it once more a political alternative for serious people to consider. Some of the party's propagandists possessed a discerning knowledge of the popular mind, heart, and pocketbook, though their efforts were only grudgingly rewarded by the party's leaders. The scurrility of their pamphlets, the elementary symbolism of the Imperial photographs were well calculated to inflame the prejudices and reinforce the instinctive loyalties of the humble people to whom they were directed. (The Bonapartists were *not* so apt at explaining how the distinctive democratic principles of their faith would enable them to deal satisfactorily with France's current problems.) The secret of successful propaganda, however, lies not merely in simplicity but in massive repetitive doses. The reader will have observed that where the Bonapartists had a strong local paper to administer that dosage, their candidate was frequently elected. Yet in far too many departments such a paper was simply not provided.

The chronic depletion of the party's treasury was an important reason for the inadequacy of its press. The Bonapartists are perhaps less culpable on this count: funds are frequently short when a party is out of power, and during the decade after Sedan millionaire industrialists still sat with Gambetta at the extreme left of the Chamber. Still it must be said that in the 1890's, when they had become an unimportant band of Parisian sectaries, Bonapartists learned the usefulness of membership cards and dues. In the 1870's, when the regime they defended still enjoyed far more widespread sympathy, their methods of fund raising were as revelatory of the nature of their party as were their indifference to democratic ideas and their inability to organize effectively both at headquarters and in the provinces. Funds were raised catch-as-catch-can, with those caught being most often the same wealthy "shareholders" who also represented the Empire in Parliament. In fund-raising too, a party professedly democratic in doctrine was actually oligarchic in structure and, correspondingly, in outlook and behavior.

The oligarchic character of the Bonapartism of the "shareholders" was manifest also in the party's performances in parliament and in electoral campaigning. Modern parties representing an extremism of the center have sometimes managed to turn a parliamentary system they did not control to good advantage, though antiparliamentarism has frequently been a cardinal point of their doctrine. They have used their bloc of votes to obtain, by alliance or intimidation, extra-parliamentary advantages; they have used both the rostrum and the hustings effectively for propagandistic purposes, to create an impression of their irresistible momentum; or they have even deliberately sought, by tactics of obstruction or opportunism, to bring the whole institution into discredit by contrast with their own authoritarian dynamism.

The Bonapartists of the 1870's did none of these things consistently. All of them on some occasions, and some of them on all occasions, freely gave their votes from 1873 to 1877 to conservatives who were as much their enemies as were the Republicans, without exacting due recompense for the dynasty they professed to represent. Not only did these continual ventures into conservative union achieve nothing for the prospects of the Empire; they actually reduced those prospects. Bonapartist votes alone made possible Broglie's

Conclusion

government of Moral Order and MacMahon's *Seize Mai.* Thus they were directly responsible for raising before the eyes of the peasantry—the indispensable element of support for an authoritarianism of the center in an overwhelmingly rural country—the spectre of a return to the rule of nobleman and priest under a Bourbon restoration.

In their campaigns as well, many Bonapartists tended to forget that the peasants were as fearful of reaction as of revolution. Instead of running on platforms which reminded this largest group of the electorate of the authoritarian democratic alternative to the Republic, many Bonapartists allowed themselves to be confused with conservative Orleanists or even Legitimists. They persisted in counseling their followers to throw their weight behind Monarchists in run-off elections, even when the Bonapartist voters rejected their advice and opted instead for the Republican candidate. They did not turn every by-election into a miniature plebiscite with clear-cut professions of their faith in the unique political formula of the regime they had served. In the general eletions of 1876 they would not take the risk of offering the nationwide electorate a choice between regimes. Instead, under the aegis of a conservative committee, many of them contented themselves with the stale slogans of "religion, family, property" with which the party of Order had run in 1849, sometimes *against* Bonapartist candidates. Though a comparison of platforms with victories in that crucial year suggests that in most cases a frank dynastic appeal was the key to success, many Bonpartists were clearly less concerned with winning the votes of the democratic electorate than with securing the approval of their fellow right-thinking notables. Unfortunately, the results suggest that their subordination of the democratic to the conservative idea, while it failed to win over the skeptical and volatile bourgeoisie, often succeeded in alienating the peasantry.

Bonapartism after Sedan

Far from rejecting parliamentarism as a deformation of democracy, the Fourniers and Boffintons eagerly sought places in the new Orleanist-designed Senate, which, with its lengthy terms and indirect election, was a blatant challenge to democratic principles. The "shareholders" of the Bonapartist party sought to win parliamentary seats, now as under the Empire, not in order to represent a distinctive political formula but in order to confirm a social preeminence in their communities that they were not all willing to justify by the hard work of local government. Thus *"Réunion"*—an assemblage of persons—was precisely the word to describe their group at Versailles, which was not an indivisible bloc strategically teleguided from Chislehurst according to Bonapartist ideology, but a loose aggregation of parochial-minded notables, responsive above all to considerations of personal advantage.

Paul de Cassagnac, in listing the rival candidates of the "Pyrénées-Occidentales," described Orleanists, Legitimists, and Bonapartists as distinct social types, distinguishable even physically, and historians have often tended to follow this example. In reality, the notables who constituted the three groups were not so readily differentiated, as became obvious when in 1873 a Bourbon restoration seemed in the offing. On that occasion as on others, more than one Bonapartist found it easy to forget the Empire in a conviction that his affiliation was with the "great conservative party" of which the Bonapartists were but one wing. Such men were naturally more inclined to sympathize with Broglie, that embodiment of elitist parliamentary "conservative liberalism," than with Rouher, and they showed it in their votes and campaign platforms.

Even devoted "Brumairean" followers of Rouher, like the Vice-Emperor himself, acquiesced, though less readily than the Orleano-Bonapartists, in the conservative venture of May

Conclusion

16, 1877. No doubt many of them were blinded by overconfidence: it seemed inconceivable that the peasant masses on whom they relied would ever abandon the Empire, whether or not its representatives aligned themselves with Monarchist reaction. But there is also a more profound explanation for their behavior. It must be remembered that whatever their remote origins in a newly-democratic society, the Murats of the Lot, for example, were now counts and princes. Their batons were no longer in their knapsacks. Securely established within the social elite, such men did not easily adjust to the stance of opposition. As for loyal and constructive opposition under the Republic, the regime of men whom Eschasseriaux considered to be traitors and assassins, it was unimaginable. Instinctively they sided with any elitist government of "men of order," though their reason told them, correctly, that they could expect from it only treachery toward their party.

This instinctive inclination explains their lukewarm response to the temperate tactics planned for them by Raoul-Duval. The deputy of the Eure was actually trying to pour new wine into old bottles. A latecomer to the party, attracted far more by the Bonapartist formula than by its personnel, he envisioned the Empire as Napoleon III had, as a unique, conservative but democratic solution to France's permanent political crisis. When he wanted these "shareholders" of the Empire, for many of whom Bonapartism was a convenient label, not a system of ideas, to preserve that solution intact by shunning the *Seize Mai*, he was asking too much. For them, the Marshal represented the defense of order by "decent men," while Gambetta stood for the disorder of democracy. Lacking any convictions that would have enabled them to steer a course between the two, they unhesitatingly chose the Marshal as they had chosen Broglie over Thiers four years earlier. Thus despite the oscillations of opinion within the parliamentary party, Magne in the end had his way, and conservative union was again realized in 1877, with fatal consequences for Bonapartism.

This disaster should have come as no surprise to Raoul-Duval. The very first issue over which he had clashed with the Imperial "shareholders," on the eve of the general elections, had revealed the consequences of the failure of the Second Empire—the first lengthy regime in French history to accept universal suffrage—to develop a political system which exploited its possibilities. The Bonapartists' divisions over the electoral law reflected Napoleon's III's reluctance to channel popular Bonapartism into an organized political party. They also indicated his failure to nurture among the social elite a sufficiently numerous new political class imbued with a credo and equipped with political techniques which set them apart from the notables of earlier regimes. Such a party, led by such men, relying upon years of persistent implantation of the ideology of authoritarian democracy among the masses, would not have been dubious of its prospects under *scrutin de liste*. Voters who were responsive to the Bonapartist idea, rather than to the identity of the candidates, could have been depended upon to elect an entire Bonapartist list. This indeed was what Eschasseriaux and his Republican counterpart agreed would happen in more than a third of the departments. Too few of Eschasseriaux's colleagues shared his optimism, however, to permit the party to take this bold, but potentially highly rewarding risk. Many of them preferred the more parochial battle of *scrutin d'arrondissement*.

The reason was that the Imperial regime, unwilling or unable to apply democratic methods under a democratic franchise, had tried instead to recruit notables and pressure universal suffrage into electing them. Unfortunately this proceeding was not calculated to make meaningful, either to the candidate or to the voters, the authoritarian democratic formula

Conclusion

in which Napoleon III believed. Thus after 1870, with official pressure removed, peasants and bourgeois, especially in regions east of a line drawn north and south through Paris, reverted to other loyalties. In the rest of France, many former official candidates, now lacking the support of the administration or of organizations of their own, either followed their colleagues in the East into retirement, or tried to eke out victories in their own *arrondissements* on the strength of their personal relations with their fellow notables of other conservative persuasions. Thus there were many districts uncontested and many equivocal *professions de foi* in 1876, at a moment when the dynasty's hopes depended on boldly challenging the Republic everywhere.

A well-organized, democratically-based, relatively disciplined Bonapartist party would have replaced these timid notables, just as it would have provided the innovations in political technique—local committees, local papers—without which they were so helpless. The success of the Republicans demonstrates that it was quite possible, in the 1870's, to build this kind of party. But the dispersion of authority and want of energy of the Bonapartists accurately reflected their situation now that the Empire had ceased to exist: reduced to living on the capital of their own local prestige, these "shareholders" concerned themselves only secondarily with the fate of the Imperial dynasty, which had apparently proved, after Sedan, to be a bad investment. The national party was an emanation of the local notables who chose to run under its colors; its message and tactics could be no more than what they were willing to allow.

Moreover, the comparatively few Bonapartists who had been more than the passive recipients of official favor before 1870 were neither able nor willing to alter this situation. Baron Eschasseriaux of the Charente-Inférieure came very close to representing in reality Cassagnac's ideal Bonapartist.

Bonapartism after Sedan

Unwilling merely to ride the crest of the extraordinary popularity the Empire enjoyed in his region, he worked strenuously to consolidate his position by means of a department-wide organization and a powerful local newspaper. Though born of a family locally prominent since the Revolution, he did not rely upon the errant, conservative bourgeoisie and instead systematically cultivated the loyalty of the Charentais peasants. He was unquestionably their "master," but at the same time his manner, unlike that of so many of his fellow notables, was that of a "good fellow"—not only authoritarian but democratic. A patrician "boss," he led his electors, but was nonetheless attentive to their views—as on the religious question. In his personality and career the difficult concept of authoritarian democracy actually became real. As a notable who enthusiastically accepted the implications of universal suffrage, he not only weathered the catastrophe of 1870 but kept his district out of Republican hands for decades thereafter.

Yet this local triumph was virtually the only contribution of Eschasseriaux—that "rare bird" among Bonapartists—to the hopes of the Imperial dynasty after 1870. Indeed the Baron had less reason than others to devote himself to its interests, for it had attempted to penalize him for his initiative, and for the independent position to which he believed that initiative entitled him. Here again the contradiction at the heart of Bonapartism revealed its baneful force. When after 1860 the declining Empire, stricken with "vertigo" at the prospect of the defection of the bourgeoisie, sought to reinforce its grip by recruiting new "shareholders" among them, it was obliged, whatever the feelings of Napoleon III, to try to jettison Eschasseriaux. Truckling to the notables, it attempted to sacrifice him because, firmly backed by his democratic electors, he refused to bow to all the decisions of authority in Paris. Retaliating in the only way he could, the

Conclusion

Baron had helped to create the Liberal Empire, which undermined authoritarian democracy still more. After Sedan, he continued his independent ways. There was much he could have taught his party about democratic politics, but he was no more eager to teach than they were to learn. He remained preoccupied above all by the affairs of the Charente-Inférieure; the national policies of his party were a secondary concern. Though always ready with advice, the Baron never felt obliged to give all of his obedience or any of his money to Bonapartist party headquarters. He, and the others like him in the Southwest who had made popular Bonapartism a force to be reckoned with, remained exceptions, not examples.

No doubt it is easy for the historian to be wise after the event, yet it is not unfair to judge a political system by its capacity for survival in adversity. The internal contradictions and failures recapitulated in the foregoing pages had already put Bonapartism on the defensive by 1869. The election of 1876 revealed that it was continuing to lose ground for the same reasons. Napoleon III had fallen between two stools: the Second Empire had neither eliminated the political power of the notables nor made of them useful auxiliaries and reliable defenders of authoritarian democracy. Bonapartism after 1870 remained only what it had been before 1848: the legend of a dynasty and the inchoate inclinations of part of the democratic electorate. To unite these two elements there were only the notables who had invested in the regime as an expedient, many of them indifferent to the necessities of democratic politics, while those who were not indifferent had learned how to win and hold the electorate not at the behest of the Imperial regime, but in defiance of it.

La France juive appeared in 1886, the same year in which Prince Napoleon and Prince Victor were obliged to continue their quarrel over the remnants of Bonapartism from exile. The appearance of Drumont's anti-Semitic volume may be regarded as the first faint, premonitory sign of the emergence in France of those political currents which were to carry twentieth-century extremisms of the center so far. It may be to the moral credit of the Bonapartists, but again it says little for their political astuteness, that they made as little use of hysterical hatred of scapegoats as of all the other innovations in political technique which democratic politics in an age of urbanization have produced. Nineteenth-century Bonapartism was not, as its failures after Sedan made clear, an embryonic Fascism. The men who controlled its destinies, far from anticipating the twentieth century, had not understood the novelty of the formula of authoritarian democracy in the nineteenth. Bonapartism in their hands became an authoritarianism—or an oligarchic parliamentarism—*of the Right*, of a minority of France's traditional rural elite.

In this guise Bonapartism made a substantial involuntary contribution to the foundation of the Republic. It is a contribution which has been little remarked, perhaps because "history is, by and large, a record of what people did, not of what they failed to do." Yet it must be remembered that "sometimes those who are defeated have made as great a contribution to the ultimate result as the victors." [3] Without in any way undervaluing the energy and shrewdness of Republican leaders like Gambetta, one may suggest that their victory would not have been nearly so easy if the parliamentarism of the center they upheld had been confronted throughout France by a real authoritarianism of the center. To demonstrate this point, one need only consider the political preference that southwestern France displayed after the men like Eschasseriaux who had kept it strongly Bonapartist for so long finally abandoned the struggle. To a large extent the Southwest turned from Bonapartism to Republican Radicalism.[4]

[3] E. H. Carr, *What is History?* (New York, 1963), 167–168.
[4] André Siegfried, *Tableau politique de la France de l'ouest sous la Troisième République* (Paris, 1913), *passim*.

Conclusion

At first glance this may appear a bewildering reversal. But it is not if one disregards the different emphasis these two political systems placed on the power of the executive. Apart from this difference, the Radicalism which had captured much of France by the turn of the century represented what Bonapartism in the Southwest had represented: a politically democratic, socially conservative movement supported by the independent peasantry—the center of the political spectrum—*against* the traditional ruling classes, aristocracy, church, and urban bourgeoisie. Like southwestern Bonapartism, Radicalism was woven into the fabric of rural society by a network of committees which extended into every commune. Like Eschasseriaux, the Radical deputy regarded the defense of the interests of his constituents, as defined by his organization, as his chief responsibility.

The triumph of Radicalism was delayed in the Southwest for decades precisely because Bonapartism there already conformed to this pattern of democratic politics. Outside the Southwest, the Republic triumphed much more rapidly not only because of Gambetta's skillful combination of determination and moderation, but also because Bonapartism was not there to challenge the Republicans with a competitive appeal to the essential center of the political spectrum.

Of course it would be too audacious to claim that had Bonapartism everywhere truly been democratic, it could have captured and held France as firmly after 1852 as Radicalism did after the turn of the century. Vast regions of the West under the sway of great clerical proprietors long rejected Empire and Republic alike. Parts of the Midi, where the extreme Left has always possessed a singular attraction, no doubt would have been incorrigible. For the cautious and noncommittal temperament of parts of the North, authoritarian democracy was probably a dubious formula. Yet when all this has been acknowledged, one may nonetheless suggest that Eschasseriaux's electors, the peasants of the Charente-Inférieure, were not unrepresentative of the majority of the French electorate, which was still more than half rural after the First World War. If he managed to retain the loyalty of such an electorate, might not others have done so as well?

Indeed, in the light of his experience, one must wonder if Bonapartism was not the last great missed opportunity of the French notables to perpetuate the essential role in political life they had enjoyed before the coming of democracy. The history of other western countries in the age of democratization suggests that where the predemocratic elite did continue to make its weight felt directly in politics, it did so by enlarging its views and embracing, more or less sincerely, the vocabulary and methods of the new politics.

Of the three political faiths among which the elite of predemocratic notables in France divided their allegiance only the Bonapartist formula could conceivably have developed into a French "Tory Radicalism." Orleanism was essentially a rationalization of the exclusive rule of an elite; it could arouse no popular enthusiasm. The same could not be said so flatly of Legitimism, for while Chambord claimed the crown of Louis XVIII and Charles X, it was also the crown of Saint Louis, the dispenser of justice to the poor under the oak at Vincennes. During its long history the French monarchy had not always been commanded by the powerful of the day, as Chambord, in defending the white flag as a symbol of the unfettered royal prerogative, no doubt recalled. Although a popular Legitimism did survive in some parts of France, however, historical memories isolated the monarchy from the center of the political spectrum. It was too easy for Republicans to declare, however unfairly, that a restoration would herald a return to the Old Regime. Legitimism could not have become the basis for a nationwide popular party led by the notables, even had Chambord, and still more the Legitimist notables themselves, thought of casting it in that mold.

Conclusion

Bonapartism, with its revolutionary origins, labored under no such disadvantages. It was a formula intended to unite the classes and the masses. Yet the notables failed after Sedan as before to exploit the link with the *nouvelles couches sociales* which it might have afforded. The development of a French "Tory Radicalism"—an intelligent, democratically-based parliamentary conservatism—from the ruins of Imperial hopes, challenging the Republicans with the strength of a hundred-vote bloc in the Chamber, would have made an enormous difference to the political history of the Third Republic. Conceivably, by becoming a powerful "loyal Opposition," it could have fostered the development of a two-party system. At the very least it might have preserved the notables from the political extinction which threatened them after 1875. A party of this sort was what Raoul-Duval was envisioning when he called for a "progressive Empire," and later for a "Republican Right." The design was not ill-conceived: the victories first of Opportunism and then of Radicalism suggest that the secret of political success in France, at least until well into the twentieth century, was to temper socially conservative policy with democratic rhetoric.

The first step toward the launching of such a party, however, was to accept the Republic, consecrated by democracy, at least for the time being. This would not have been impossible for men who admitted with Napoleon III that Republic and Empire sprang from a common revolutionary root. But this was not the idea of the notables of the *Appel au peuple*, who possessed all the anachronistic obstinacy of the Legitimists though they lacked their mystic faith, and all the oligarchic elitism of the Orleanists without their opportunistic flexibility. Though in their hands the Empire had been divested of its unique idea, they insisted upon the Imperial name. If they could not have this or some other "monarchical form," they supported whoever threatened the Republic and democracy, from MacMahon to Boulanger, and joined in wholeheartedly in the last desperate casts of the dice of the more inflexible proponents of the *régime censitaire*.

After eliminating their dynasty from effective political contention by their mistakes, they thus proceeded to eliminate themselves. Bonapartism, reduced to the undemocratic dimensions of Legitimism and Orleanism, shared their fate, and the Bonapartist notables, who at the most charitable estimate had proved no wiser than their Monarchist rivals, passed with them from the political scene. Clearly they had not lost their will to rule. To the last many of them felt, as Mayor Fournier of La Rochelle had in September of 1870, that their natural place was in the seat of government. It was the convictions—and consequently the political skills—for retaining that place that they so obviously lacked. That twenty years of supposed authoritarian democracy under Napoleon III had not served to teach them those skills suggests how ephemeral may be the political legacy of a providential man.

In fact, the conclusion one is tempted to draw from the debacle described in these pages is that authoritarian democracy, such a plausible formula on paper, cannot actually be realized, or at least cannot long survive the man who claims to rule according to its dictates. One might even venture so far as to condense the history of Bonapartism into a series of axioms, from which the historical course of any analogous regime, such as the Fifth Republic, could be plotted, as follows.

Since the peculiar form of direct democracy which the providential man claims legitimates him is in fact illusory, he is faced very early in his rule with a perplexing choice. He must follow either authoritarianism or democracy to its logical conclusion. That is, either he must govern tyrannically by the sheer power of his police (a method which authoritarian democrats, unlike the more extreme Fascists, have generally

Conclusion

eschewed) or he must create a party to bolster his antipartisan regime. If he creates a party but tramples upon the wishes of the men who compose it he has not escaped his original dilemma, but if he accedes to its inclinations it becomes difficult for him to remain the entirely impartial arbiter of social and political conflict which authoritarian democracy demands. Because the democracy of such a regime is less repugnant to authoritarians than its authoritarianism is to democrats, the effect of sharing power with the newly-created party must inevitably be to shift the regime from the center of the political spectrum to the right. The democratic dictator thus becomes by degrees or even unconsciously no more than the central figure—however imposing—of a regime of the classic Right. As a result the social and political conflicts he was invested with power to master break out with a renewed virulence, the more unrestrained because the emergency which made his original investiture necessary has long been forgotten.

When the providential man quits the political scene, he cannot expect to see his system continued. His party, improvisation that it is, will be too weak to constitute an effective opposition. If it is composed chiefly of passive personalities who have been entirely dependent on the magic of his name or the pressure applied by his government for political success, they will either follow him into retirement or transfer their allegiance elsewhere as opportunistically as they once gave it to him. If on the other hand it is composed of active and independent men enjoying the full confidence of their electors on their own merits, these men will feel no pressing need to work for the revival of the system they once defended. In either case the surviving party will appear to the electorate, unlike the man who for so long led it, to belong unquestionably to the Right, and will share the inevitable fate of such parties in France. Authoritarian democracy will therefore be forgotten until some new emergency makes it once more appealing.

If one keeps in mind the infrequency with which history "repeats itself," he will of course be chary of applying such an axiomatic projection as the one sketched above to contemporary French politics. There have been substantial changes in the French social structure since the 1870's, obviously; it is possible that Bonapartist authoritarian democracy foundered on social realities which do not exist today. Moreover, providential men are usually determined to be social innovators. Though their innovations in the past have often proved abortive, this does not prove that they will never succeed in significantly altering the social realities with which they have to contend. In the second half of the twentieth century, with ideological parliamentarism everywhere in retreat before the advance of administrative expertise, authoritarian democracy may become more permanently attractive to an increasingly homogeneous society than it has hitherto been.

After he has acknowledged the justice of such *caveats* as these, however, the student of contemporary France can still extract from the history of Bonapartism after Sedan if not predictions, then at least some useful *questions* to ask himself about the present regime. For example, has its leading figure succeeded in imparting his distinctive, sometimes highly unconventional ideas to his followers? Have they understood that his rule must be in the interests of the society as a whole, and not of a particular group? The answer to this question is probably contingent upon the answer to another: what is the nature of the party which supports the regime? Is it so democratically diversified in thought and action that it will be able to hold the center and even to tempt left and right? Or does it merely represent the ascendancy of a traditional social elite who have given it their momentary loyalty while expecting the regime to defend their particular interests? Have its repre-

Conclusion

sentatives entrenched themselves in their constituencies by constant attention to local organization, or are many of them notables indifferent to this task and content to be elected as the anointed of the regime? Is the regime, therefore, supported by a mass movement or merely by periodic expressions of mass sentiment? Upon the answers to these questions, if the Bonapartist case represents any precedent, the durability of the authoritarian democratic idea depends.

Appendix

List by Departments of Bonapartist Deputies Elected to the Chamber of Deputies on February 20 and March 5, 1876 (The candidate's name is followed by that of his *arrondissement*.)

Ardennes
Ladoucette; Vouziers. (Landed proprietor; official deputy 1852–70; ran as "constitutional" candidate.)

Ariège
Saint-Paul; St.-Girons.

Aube
Piot; Bar-sur-Aube. (Lawyer.)

Aveyron
Azémar; Rodez. (Lawyer, *fonctionnaire*.)
Roques; Rodez. (Lawyer, *fonctionnaire*, landed proprietor.)

Calvados
Comte de Colbert-Laplace; Lisieux. (Diplomat under the Empire.)
Flandin; Pont-l'Evêque. (*Fonctionnaire*, landed proprietor.)

Charente
Laroche-Joubert; Angoulême. (Cooperative paper-mill; deputy 1868–70; proponent of income tax.)
Ganivet; Angoulême. (Lawyer, *fonctionnaire*.)

Appendix

Cunéo d'Ornano; Cognac. (Minor *fonctionnaire*, journalist.)
Gautier; Ruffec. (Brandy-merchant; family connections with André, deputy 1852–76 who was elected Senator in 1876.)

Charente-Inférieure
René Eschasseriaux; Jonzac.
Fournier; La Rochelle.
Baron Eschasseriaux; Saintes.
Jolibois; Saintes. (Barrister, magistrate, Prefect and Councilor of State under the Empire.)
Roy de Loulay, *fils*; St.-Jean-d'Angély.

Corse
Rouher; Ajaccio.
Rouher; Bastia.
Duc de Padoue; Calvi. (Son of a peer of the Hundred Days who became a Senator of the Second Empire; related to Bonapartes; Prefect, Senator, Minister.)
Gavini; Corte.

Côtes-du-Nord
Duc de Feltre; Guingamp. (Son of a general and Imperial Senator; diplomat.)
Le Provost de Launay; Lannion. (Son of an Imperial Prefect; lawyer and landed proprietor.)

Dordogne
Thirion-Montauban; Bergerac. (Magne's son-in-law; diplomatic career.)
Sarlande; Nontron. (Minor Imperial *fonctionnaire*; landed proprietor.)
Raynaud; Périgueux.
De Bosredon; Sarlat. (Old family, majority deputy 1868–70, landed proprietor.)
Taillefer; Sarlat. (Grandson of a *Conventionnel*; son of the Imperial deputy 1852–68; naval career.)

Appendix

Drôme
Comte d'Aulan; Nyons. (St. Cyr; Imperial equerry 1868–70.)

Eure
Janvier de la Motte; Bernay. (Son of the official deputy of Tarn-et-Garonne; Prefect of Eure 1856–68.)
Raoul-Duval; Louviers.

Haute-Garonne
Lenglé; St.-Gaudens. (Son of an Imperial Prefect; Sub-Prefect of St.-Gaudens, 1870.)
Tron; St.-Gaudens. (Lawyer; mayor of Luchon, official deputy 1869–70.)
Comte d'Ayguesvives; Toulouse, 3. (Old robe family, Imperial equerry, majority deputy 1863–70.)

Gers
Peyrusse; Auch. (Family of the deputy of 1864–70; landed proprietor.)
Paul de Cassagnac; Condom.
Faure; Lombez. (Lawyer, Imperial magistrate; intimate friend of the Cassagnacs.)
Granier de Cassagnac; Mirande.

Gironde
Baron David; Bazas.
Dréolle; Blaye. (Journalist, agent of Rouher; deputy 1869–70.)
Mitchell; La Réole. (Journalist, ardent supporter of Ollivier.)
Clauzet; Lesparre. (Proprietor of extensive vineyards.)

Indre
Paul-Guillaume Dufour; Châteauroux. (Landed proprietor.)
Saint-Martin-Valogne; La Châtre. (Landed proprietor.)

Landes
Boulart; Dax. (Industrialist, *maître de forges*.)

Appendix

Marquis de Guilloutet; Mont-de-Marsan.
Laborde; Saint-Sever. (Lawyer, landed proprietor.)

Loire-Inférieure
Thoinnet de la Turmelière; Ancenis. (Lawyer, *fonctionnaire*, official deputy 1857–70; great landed proprietor.)
Comte Ginoux de Fermon; Châteaubriant. (Old family, *fonctionnaire*, deputy from 1871.)
Gaudin; Nantes, 2. (Lawyer, Councilor of State, diplomat; majority deputy 1869–70.)

Loiret
Brierre; Pithviers. (Wool merchant; mayor of Pithviers under the Empire.)

Lot
Comte Murat; Cahors.
De Valon; Cahors. (Old family; minor Imperial *fonctionnaire*.)
Baron Dufour; Gourdon. (Son of a general of the First Empire who was elected deputy in 1830; military career; landed proprietor.)

Lot-et-Garonne
Sarrette; Villeneuve. (Great landed proprietor.)

Maine-et-Loire
Berger; Saumur. (Lawyer, *haut fonctionnaire*, official deputy 1866–70.)
Janvier de la Motte, *fils*; Segré. (Eldest son of the ex-Prefect; landed proprietor.)

Manche
Legrand; Mortain. (Son of a deputy of Manche 1832–48; Councilor of State; deputy from 1871.)
Rauline; St.-Lô. (Rich landed proprietor; mayor of St. Lô.)

Appendix

Comte Le Marois; Valognes. (Grandson of a peer of the Hundred Days; son of a deputy and Senator of the Second Empire; military career; great landed proprietor.)

Nièvre

Comte de Le Peletier d'Aunay; Clamecy. (Son of a deputy 1830–37; Councilor of State; official deputy 1852–70; great landed proprietor.)

Baron de Bourgoing; Cosne. (Son of an Imperial Prefect, nephew of an Imperial Senator.)

Nord

Des Rotours; Lille, 4. (Succeeded his father as official deputy, 1868; sat with the Monarchists in the National Assembly.)

Brame; Lille, 5. (Son of a protectionist deputy 1857–70 who was elected Senator in 1876; Councilor of State.)

Renard; Valenciennes. (Levert's brother-in-law; son of an industrialist; chemical engineer; steelworks director and mine shareholder.)

Oise

Duc de Mouchy; Beauvais. (Ancient family; son of an Imperial deputy and Senator; married Princess Murat; deputy 1869–70; rich landed proprietor.)

Léon Chevreau; Beauvais. (Administration; Prefect of Oise 1860–70.)

Orne

Baron de Mackau; Argentan. (Son of an Imperial Senator; Councilor of State; majority deputy 1866–70.)

Dugué de la Fauçonnerie; Mortagne. (Administration; official deputy 1869–70.)

Bianchi; Mortagne. (Stockbroker; brother-in-law of Dugué; related also to Poriquet, Bonapartist Senator of Orne; bought an estate in the department just before his election.)

Appendix

Pas-de-Calais
Dussaussoy; Boulogne. (Great industrialist; first elected 1871, enrolled both with Monarchists and Bonapartists.)
Hamille; Montreuil. (Lawyer, Imperial *directeur des cultes*.)
Levert; St. Omer.

Puy-de-Dôme
Rouher; Riom.

Basses-Pyrénées
Labat; Bayonne. (Mayor of Bayonne 1853–70, official deputy 1869–70.)
Harispe; Mauléon. (Nephew of an Imperial Senator; made his fortune in Havana.)
D'Ariste; Pau. (Son of an Imperial deputy and Senator; lawyer and railway director; rich landed proprietor.)

Hautes-Pyrénées
Cazeaux; Tarbes. (Lawyer and Imperial magistrate.)

Sarthe
Haentjens; Le Mans.

Haute-Savoie
Comte de Boigne; Thonon. (Above all a clerical; election invalidated because of clerical pressure.)

Seine-Inférieure
Savoye; Yvetot. (Lawyer, Imperial Councilor of State; first elected 1871; voted often with Bonapartists though not enrolled with them.)

Seine-et-Marne
Baron Lambert; Fontainebleau.

Deux-Sèvres
Pétiet; Niort. (Grandson of the deputy 1852–58; Councilor of State; landed proprietor.)

Appendix

General Allard; Parthenay. (*Polytechnicien*, served in the Engineers; deputy 1837–1848, sitting with Left Center; General of division 1857.)

Somme

Baron de Septenville; Amiens. (Old noble family; grandson of a deputy of the First Empire; rich landed proprietor.)

Tarn-et-Garonne

Prax-Paris; elected in both districts of Montauban.

Vienne

Baron de Soubeyran; Loudun. (Imperial *fonctionnaire*; *Crédit foncier*; official deputy 1863–70.)

De Beauchamp; Montmorillon. (Brother-in-law of Soubeyran; *maître de forges*; official deputy 1864–70.)

Cesbron; Poitiers, 2. (Notary, landed proprietor.)

Yonne

Garnier; Avallon. (Son of an industrialist deputy of the July Monarchy; *Polytechnicien*; Imperial Prefect; landed proprietor.)

Martenot; Tonnerre. (Metallurgical engineer; his brother, also an engineer, was a deputy 1871–76 and a Bonapartist Senator.)

The following, though not shown on the election maps, were Bonapartist sympathizers: Bordet, Côte-d'Or; Fourcade, Hérault; Dalmas, Ille-et-Vilaine; Baron de Ladoucette, Meurthe-et-Moselle; Rendu, Seine-et-Oise.

Bibliography

I. PRIMARY SOURCES

A. UNPUBLISHED MATERIALS IN PRIVATE HANDS

Eschasseriaux, Baron Eugène. "Mémoires." Twenty manuscript volumes preserved in the library of the château of Oyré (Sarthe).

This is a source of unique value, hardly exploited before the writing of the present work, for the history of Bonapartism on both the national and the local levels. The memoirs were composed in the 1890's after the Baron's political retirement, from his collected correspondence and memorabilia, most of which are also preserved in the library at Oyré. They take the form of a retrospective diary, detailing the Baron's political career and the ordinary life of his family on a day-to-day basis throughout his life. The text of many of the letters he received is given in full.

Heavy reliance by the historian upon the memoirs of one of his principal protagonists is, of course, not without danger. These memoirs, however, have several characteristics which reduce that danger. (1) They were never intended to be published, but were written to inform his grandchildren "of what their grandfather had done with his life," and probably also to occupy the time of a compulsively energetic man. Thus there was no particular need to retouch events. The Baron was never a man to waste time on self-justification in any case. (2) In form they are much more a chronicle than memoirs; the Baron contented himself usually with recording everything and eschewed comment. A man who passes blandly from an account of a hemorrhoidectomy on one page to the text of an editorial from his newspaper on the next inspires a certain confidence in his guilelessness. (3) His bluff prejudices are easily disregarded.

Bibliography

Raoul-Duval, Edgar. Papers preserved at the château of Le Vaudreuil (Eure). The historian's use of this vast collection has been greatly facilitated by the classification undertaken by M. Edgar Raoul-Duval when writing his grandfather's biography. Of prime importance to this study were the dossiers "Lettres de Camden, Rouher, Dugué" (sixty letters, both originals and copies, including eleven from the Prince Imperial to Raoul-Duval and twenty from the latter to the Prince) and "Correspondance avec M. Rouher—Série complète" (thirty-eight letters, 1875–1878). The dossier "Lettres de M. Edgar Raoul-Duval à sa femme" (eleven booklets digested from twenty-one packets of letters, 1867–1886, by Mme. Raoul-Duval), also contains much useful material, as does that labeled "Jules Delafosse" (thirty-nine letters 1875–1886). The dossiers "Discours du 6 novembre 1886" and "E. Drumont" suggest the alternative paths which lay before this neglected figure when his life was cut short.

Saint-Paul, Gaston Paul de Verbigier, Baron de. Papers preserved at the château of Poudelaye (Ariège). Since I had only a brief opportunity to examine these totally unclassified materials, I cannot pretend to evaluate them. But since less than a day's work turned up a packet of letters from Saint-Paul to his wife throwing light on the collapse of the *Seize Mai*, a thorough sifting might reveal them to be an unexploited source of considerable significance.

B. UNPUBLISHED MATERIALS IN PUBLIC DEPOSITORIES

1. In the Archives Nationales

Lacking the Prefects' reports for the period (they were destroyed by the Ministry of the Interior), one is compelled to seek information on the political life of the departments by more circuitous paths. Series C ("Procès-verbaux des Assemblées nationales") provides the evidence on the basis of which elections were invalidated, as in C3158 and particularly C3229–3242, "Enquête parlementaire sur les élections générales des 14 et 28 octobre 1877." The witnesses were rarely encouraged, however, to speak in general terms on the balance of forces in their communities. (The two registers

Bibliography

$C^{2*}726$ and $C^{2*}727$ in which the officials of the Palais Bourbon recorded election results were used to compile the Bonapartists' percentages in the general elections of 1876 and 1877; even these, however, are marred by self-evident errors.) In series F^7 ("Police générale") the three boxes $F^7 12428$–12430 ("Agissements bonapartistes") contain the returns of surveys taken on the orders of the Ministry of the Interior to ascertain the impact of the deaths of Napoleon III and his son upon public opinion. Many of the documents, however, are concerned with the escapades of Prince Napoleon and thus have only secondary interest. In the same series, $F^7 12681$–12684 ("Dépêches relatives au Seize Mai 1877") contain the full correspondence between the Ministry and the Prefects on that abortive coup and thus provide indications of what it meant to the Bonapartists, though the terse language of many of the dispatches makes them difficult to interpret.

Some indications of a negative sort on the effectiveness of Bonapartist propaganda are to be found in $F^{18} 309$ ("Imprimerie et librairie—Dépêches officielles 1870–1876"). But the essential boxes are $F^{18} 526$–531 ("Presse départementale—Journaux distribués 1872–1876") which despite their name contain the statistics of Parisian, as well as local, journals reaching each department through the mails.

A single box in the "Cultes" series—$F^{19} 5610$—contains an almost complete file of reports on the political activity of the French episcopate in 1879. Some additional evidence on the conflict of parties in some departments, especially in the shape of candidates' *affiches*, can be gleaned from the papers of the Ministry of Justice: $BB^{30} 4901$–4904 ("Elections législatives de 1876; fraudes et délits électoraux") and $BB^{30} 1121$–1124 ("Correspondance échangée entre le ministre de la Justice et les procureurs-généraux à l'occasion d'affaires de colportage ou d'élections").

2. In the Cabinet des manuscrits of the Bibliothèque Nationale

Summarizing for the eye of the President of the Republic the information available to the police on the activities and intentions of the Bonapartists (as well as of the surviving Communards), Nouvelles acquisitions françaises 20658–20660, "Rapports jour-

Bibliography

naliers du préfet de police," are a source not to be disregarded. Though Léon Renault doubtless was eager to show himself omniscient, evidence from Bonapartist sources suggests that often he was quite successful in circumventing their negligent precautions.

3. In the Archives de la Préfecture de Police

The user of the reports of spies and informers (which form the bulk of these materials) must bear in mind the economics of those professions. If they reported that there was nothing to report, they ran the risk of unemployment. To avoid this risk, the tactic was sometimes to embroider speculatively on some rumor; the next report could then be devoted to judiciously demonstrating its untruth. The Prefecture allowed for this tendency, and the historian must likewise be wary of placing too much credence in such sources unless they are substantiated elsewhere. Nevertheless I have consulted with profit the following *cartons*, all in the series B^A:

62. "Comités bonapartistes" [1874–1889].
68. "Anniversaires de la mort de Napoléon III" [1874–1961].
69. "Prince Victor Napoléon" [1879–1887].
70. "Prince Victor Napoléon" [1888–1900].
417. One dossier: "Famille Impériale–Affaires bonapartistes 1865 à 1872."
419. "Famille Impériale-Affaires bonapartistes." [1874–1891]
864–865. "Jules Amigues" [1871–1883].
1078. "Général Fleury" [1870–1884].
1171. Dossier on Charles-Eugène Mansard.
1213. Dossier on General Pajol.
1242. Dossier on Jules Richard.
1257–1258. "Eugène Rouher" [1870–1885].
1263. Dossier on Baron de Saint-Paul.
1621. "Essai d'un travail d'ensemble sur la presse départementale au mois de Septembre 1873." Though it omits weeklies, a useful compendium, the result of over a year's research by an official of the Prefecture.
1634. Dossier of Joachim Piétri.

Bibliography

4. In the Archives départementales of the Charente-Maritime, La Rochelle

Famille Fournier, "Mémoires," twelve manuscript volumes, numbered I–VI, VIII, X–XII, XVI–XVII; 4J1509.

The contrast between these and the Eschasseriaux memoirs is the contrast between the two men; while the Baron pushed to completion his awesome project of recapitulating his whole life, Fournier left volumes which sometimes, with their blank pages interspersed with random jottings, more resemble commonplace books than memoirs. Volume XI, covering five months of 1871, represents an attempt to keep a daily dairy which soon petered out; volumes XI–XII and XVI–XVII are continuous despite their numbering, and the last ends in 1883. Despite—or by virtue of—their rather scrappy character, however, they clearly evoke the *fin des notables*. I also consulted with profit at La Rochelle the files 2M4/20 ("Elections complémentaires à l'Assemblée nationale") and 4M2/36 ("Affaires politiques et diverses 1872–1879").

C. PUBLISHED CORRESPONDENCE

Espinay de Briort, C. L. d'. "Une correspondance inédite—le Prince Impérial et Ernest Lavisse 1871–1879." *Revue des Deux Mondes*, 7th period, L (1929), 555–591. The pathos of the Prince's life is evident in these letters, in which the professor reproves not only his pupil's party, but his lessons and even his handwriting.

Eugénie, Empress. *Lettres familières, conservées dans les archives du palais de Luria et publiées par les soins du duc d'Albe* .... 2 vols. Paris: Le Divan, 1935. Vol. II.

Hauterive, Ernest d', ed. *Napoléon III et le Prince Napoléon: Correspondance inédite*. Paris: Calmann-Lévy, 1925.

Henrey, Robert, ed. *Letters from Paris 1870–1875*. London: Dent, 1942.

Masson, Frédéric, ed. "Lettres inédites de George Sand et du Prince Napoléon." *Revue des Deux Mondes*, 7th period, XVI and XVII (1923), 844–875; 303–340.

Bibliography

Napoleon III. "Lettres à l'Impératrice Eugénie 1870–1871." *Revue des Deux Mondes,* 7th period, LIX (1930), 5–30.

Ollivier, Emile. *Lettres de l'exil 1870–1874.* N.p., n.d.

Savary, Charles, ed. *Deuxième rapport fait au nom de la commission d'enquête parlementaire sur l'élection qui a eu lieu dans le département de la Nièvre; Assemblée nationale no. 3087-Annexe au procès-verbal de la séance du 11 juin 1875.* Versailles, 1875.

D. BOOKS

Amigues, Jules. *Les aveux d'un conspirateur bonapartiste.* Paris, 1874. The most substantial of Amigues' works, a detailed apologia.

Balleyguier, Eugène (Fidus, pseud.). *Journal de Fidus.* 4 vols. Paris, 1889. (The third and fourth volumes, covering the period from the defeat of the Commune until the death of the Prince Imperial, were separately published in 1886 under the title *Journal de dix ans: Souvenirs d'un Impérialiste.*)

Broglie, Jacques Victor Albert, Duc de. *Mémoires.* 2 vols. Paris: Calmann-Lévy, 1941. Vol. II.

Corticchiato, Paul. *Les Corses et le parti bonapartiste à Marseille en 1870 et pendant les premières années de la République.* Marseille, 1921.

Cunéo d'Ornano, Gustave. *La République des Napoléon.* Paris, 1894.

David, Baron Jérôme. *Actualités et souvenirs politiques.* Paris, 1874.

Delafosse, Jules. *Hommes et choses.* Paris, 1888.

Des Garets, Comtesse. *L'Impératrice Eugénie en exil.* Paris: Calmann-Lévy, 1929.

Dréolle, Ernest. *La journée du 4 septembre au Corps législatif.* Paris, 1871.

Dugué de la Fauçonnerie, H. J. *Souvenirs d'un vieil homme.* 2d ed., Paris, n.d.

Girard, Georges, ed. *La vie et les souvenirs du Général Castelnau.* Paris: Calmann-Lévy, 1930. Unfortunately (since the General remained in the army until 1879), the *souvenirs* do not continue beyond Wilhelmshöhe.

Bibliography

Giraudeau, Fernand. *La vérité sur la campagne de 1870.* Marseille, 1871.

—. *Vingt ans de despotisme et quatre ans de liberté.* Paris, 1874.

Granier de Cassagnac, Adolphe. *Histoire des causes de la Révolution française.* 2 vols. Brussels, 1851.

Granier de Cassagnac, Paul. *Histoire de la Troisième République.* Paris, 1876.

Haentjens, A. *Discours et lettres politiques.* 2 vols. Le Mans, 1886.

Lenglé, Paul. *Le neveu de Bonaparte: Souvenirs de nos campagnes politiques avec le Prince Napoléon . . . 1879–1891.* 2d ed., Paris, 1893. Indispensable for the later period, though its point of view is naturally Jérômiste.

Mels, A. *Wilhelmshöhe—Souvenirs de la captivité de Napoléon III.* Paris, 1880. Untrustworthy.

Merson, Ernest. *Confessions d'un journaliste.* 2d ed., Paris, 1890. Interesting for its account of how a Breton "Legitimist by birth" came to rally to the Empire after Sedan.

—. *Confidences d'un journaliste.* Paris, 1891. Though it contains a well-reasoned critique of the Bonapartist party, these memoirs, like so many of the *genre*, are fragmentary and anecdotal.

Napoleon III. *Oeuvres posthumes et autographes inédites de Napoléon III en exil.* (Comte de la Chapelle, ed.) Paris, 1873. Not surprisingly, these contain only a few passing remarks on the current political situation.

Pinard, Ernest. *Mon journal.* 3d ed., 3 vols. Paris, 1892–1893.

Quentin-Bauchart, Maurice. *Fils d'Empereur: Le petit Prince.* Paris, n.d. Interesting only for its numerous reproductions of Bonapartist pictorial propaganda.

Richard, Jules. *Le Bonapartisme sous la République.* 3d ed., Paris, 1883. Essential, as the only consecutive narrative by a participant. The reader should bear in mind, however, that Richard (whose real name was Thomas Maillot), seeks both to exculpate Rouher and to minimize hopes which time had proved illusory.

Savary, Etienne. *M. Rouher à Cerçay après la guerre.* Paris, 1893. An English title might be "What the Gardener Saw." The author purportedly was an under-gardener at Rouher's country home.

Bibliography

Verly, Albert. *Souvenirs du Second Empire*. 2 vols. Paris, 1896. Vol. II.

E. PAMPHLETS

The literature of this sort is immense, and it would be pointless to cite a multiplicity of titles whose progagandistic content is the same. Occasionally, however, information on the national or local history of the Bonapartists not readily available elsewhere is to be found between paper covers. Some examples are:

Audibert, Wilfrid. *La Troisième République et les Napoléon*. Langres, 1890.
Cambacérès, Duc. de. *Funérailles de Napoléon III*. Paris, 1873. With an appended alphabetical list of about 850 mourners.
Cunéo d'Ornano, Gustave. *Réponse au gérant du Charentais*. Angoulême, 1875.
Dugué de la Fauçonnerie, H. J. *Lettre . . . à Messieurs les maires du canton de Noce: A propos de distributions de portraits et brochures*. Paris, 1875.
Duruy, Albert. *Comment les Empires reviennent*. Paris, 1875.
Les complots d'Arenenberg. Paris, 1875.
Ribeyre, Félix. *Le 16 mars d'Angers à Chislehurst*. Angers, 1874.

The pamphlets in which two topics in particular have been investigated deserve a place apart.

1. Socialist Bonapartism and Bonapartist Socialism

Amigues, Jules. *La politique d'un honnête homme*. Paris, 1869.
—. *La France à refaire: La Commune*. Paris, 1871.
—. *Epître au peuple: Comment l'Empire reviendra*. Clichy, 1872. Contains an explanation of his conversion.
—. *L'Homme de Sedan et les hommes de Septembre*. Paris, 1872.
—. *Lettres au peuple*. Paris, 1872.
—. *Rémuset et Barodat: Etude sur les grands du jour*. Paris, 1873.
—. *Discours au Roy*. Paris, n.d.
—. *A ceux qui se disent conservateurs: on demande un dictateur*. Paris and London, 1873.

Bibliography

—. *Lettre à M. Imgarde de Leffemberg.* Paris, 1875.
—. *Lettre aux journaux* . . . . N.p., n.d.
—. *Réponse à MM. Savary et Léon Renault.* Paris, 1875. Amigues made repeated efforts during these years to convince the public that he was not the enemy of society depicted by Savary and Renault.
—. *Epître au peuple: L'Empire et les ouvriers.* Paris, 1877.
—. *La mort de Napoléon III.* Paris, n.d.
—. *Discours prononcé . . . dans la séance de la Chambre des Députés du 9 mai 1878.* Cambrai, 1878.
—. *La question de la capitale.* Paris, 1879.
—. *Discours prononcé le Ier février 1881 à la réunion de l'hôtel des chambres syndicales.* Paris, n.d.
—. *L'Hérédité impériale: Discours prononcé le 15 août 1882* . . . . Paris, 1882.
Bradier, A. *Les bienfaits de l'Empire.* Paris, n.d.
Richard, Albert. *Le socialisme: A propos des élections législatives de 1869.* Lyon, 1869.
—. *L'Association internationale des travailleurs.* N.p., n.d.
—. and Gaspard Blanc, *L'Empire et la France nouvelle.* Brussels, 1872.
—. *Union française des amis de la paix sociale.* Turin, 1873.
—. *La révolution sociale et la guerre européene.* Geneva, 1876.
—. *La science de la répression et celle de la révolte.* Geneva, 1877.
—. *La politique socialiste et le devoir actuel de la République.* N.p., n.d.

2. The "Revisionist" Crisis of Bonapartism, 1878

Dugué de la Fauçonnerie, H. J. *Soyons donc logiques.* Paris, 1878.
—. *Ma trahison: Lettre à mes électeurs.* N.p., n.d.
—. *La conciliation: Lettre . . . à M. de Freycinet* . . . . Paris, 1878.
Dupont, Léonce. *Les deux démocraties: République—Empire.* Paris, 1878.
—. *La soumission: Réponse à mes contradicteurs.* Paris, 1878.
—. *Le Prince Victor Napoléon.* Angers and Paris, n.d.

Bibliography

La Chapelle, Comte Alfred de. *Déclarations des Napoléon.* Paris, 1878.

Lachaud, Georges. *Que vont devenir les Bonapartistes?* Paris, 1879.

3. Bonapartist Propaganda

Allart, Marcus. *Nos frontières morales et politiques.* Paris, 1872.

—. *Un électeur à son retour de Chislehurst.* Paris, 1873.

—. *Contre-fusion! Réforme! Empire et revanche!* Paris, 1873.

—. *Appel au peuple: Gouvernement et église nationals.* Paris, 1874.

—. *Appel aux électeurs de France.* Paris, 1874.

—. *Simple requête d'un électeur à l'illustre Maréchal.* Paris, 1875.

—. *A propos de la lettre du Prince Impérial à M. Raoul-Duval.* Paris, 1875.

—. *Le Concordat: Napoléon et le Catholicisme.* Paris, 1876.

—. *La première aux Républicains.* Paris, n.d.

—. *Un discours rentré à la salle Ragache.* Paris, 1880.

Almbert, Alfred d'. *Le Bonapartisme: Son passé, son avenir.* Paris, 1873.

Bavoux, Evariste. *Les causes de la guerre: Solution à la crise actuelle.* Paris, 1871.

—. *Chislehurst—Tuileries: Souvenirs intimes sur l'Empereur.* Paris, 1873.

—. *Appel à la nation.* Paris, 1874.

—. *Les vacances du quatrième Napoléon à Arenenberg.* Paris, 1874.

—. *Il a dix-neuf ans.* Paris, 1875.

—. *Orléanisme et République.* Paris, 1878.

Blachier, Charles. *Le Prince Impérial.* Paris, n.d.

Boinvilliers, Edouard. *Lettre aux électeurs.* Paris, n.d.

—. *Princes et principes.* Paris, 1871.

—. *Causeries politiques.* Paris, 1872.

—. *Catéchisme impérial.* Paris, 1873.

—. *Le septennat.* Paris, 1874.

—. *L'Esprit des lois constitutionelles de M. le duc de Broglie.* Paris, 1874.

—. *Les droits et les devoirs de l'Impérialiste.* Paris, 1875.

—. *Le manuel de l'électeur indépendant.* Paris, 1875.

Bibliography

—. *L'Electeur et le candidat, ou Conservateur et Républicain.* Paris, 1876. Boinvilliers is an articulate spokesman for the kind of Bonapartists who would have been Legitimists if they had thought it practical, and who were fond of pointing out that universal suffrage was actually "a protection for the châteaux which disdain it."

Caillé, Adolphe. *L'Empereur et ses détracteurs.* Niort, 1872.

—. *Impérialistes et Royalistes.* Saint-Maixent, 1873.

Cazeneuve, Albert. *L'Empire et les partis.* Paris, 1875.

Cunéo d'Ornano, Gustave. *Le peuple et l'Empereur.* Paris, 1875.

—. *Le Prince Napoléon et ses doctrines.* Paris, n.d.

—. *L'Appel au peuple.* Paris, 1883.

Dréolle, Ernest. *Napoléon IV 1856–1873: Souvenir de Chislehurst.* Paris, 1873.

—. *Le guide de l'électeur bonapartiste.* Paris, 1875.

Dugué de la Fauçonnerie, H. J. *Où nous en sommes: Lettre à un maire . . . .* Paris, 1873.

—. *Les calomnies contre l'Empire.* Paris, 1874.

—. *Ce qu'a coûté le 4 septembre.* Paris, n.d.

—. *Si l'Empire revenait.* Paris, 1875.

Dupont, Léonce. *Le quatrième Napoléon.* Paris, n.d.

—. *La majorité du quatrième Napoléon.* Paris, 1874.

Granier de Cassagnac, Paul. *Empire et royauté.* Paris, 1873.

—. *La revanche du scrutin: Histoire de nulle part et de partout.* Paris, 1875.

—. *L'Aigle: Almanach illustré du suffrage universel, 1875–1878.* Paris, 1875–1878.

Guillemin, Edouard. *Les titres de la dynastie impériale.* Paris, 1874.

—. *A mes compatriotes: Pourquoi je ne suis pas républicain.* Annecy, 1875.

—. *Les héros de la décadence nationale.* Besançon, 1876.

—. *La vérité sur le 16 mai: Ruraux, on vous trompe!* Paris, 1877.

—. *Questions religieuses.* Paris, 1880.

La Chapelle, Comte Alfred de. *Les représentants de l'appel au peuple.* Paris, 1875.

Bibliography

Lenglé, Paul. *Lettres à un député*. Paris, 1871.
Napoleon III (Gricourt, Marquis de, pseud.). *Des relations de la France avec l'Allemagne sous Napoléon III*. Brussels, n.d.
— (Un officier attaché à l'Etat-Major-Général, pseud.). *Campagne de 1870: Des causes qui ont amené la capitulation de Sedan*. Brussels, n.d.
— (Un ancien diplomate, pseud.). *Les principes*. Boulogne, n.d.
Napoléon-Jérôme, Prince. *Discours prononcé . . . à la Chambre des Députés le 24 novembre 1876*. Paris, 1876.
—. *Les alliances de l'Empire en 1869 et 1870*. Paris, 1878.
Perrin, Constant. *Pourquoi Napoléon III*. Paris, 1873.
Perron, F. (Un rural, pseud.). *Ils en ont menti*. New ed., Paris, 1871.
— (Un ancien républicain, pseud.). *Le salut*. Paris, 1872.
— (L'Auteur de la brochure *Ils en ont menti*, pseud.). *Finissons-en!* Paris, 1874.
—. *Le reveil de la France*. Paris, n.d.
—. *Le retour de l'île d'Elbe*. Paris, 1876.
—. *La République et l'Empire*. Paris, 1879.
Petit manuel du Républicain-bourgeois: La conspiration bonapartiste dévoilée. Paris, 1872.

4. Anti-Bonapartist Republican Propaganda

Bourdeley, Paul. *Petite histoire du parti bonapartiste*. Paris, 1875.
Hennequin, Eugène. *Les prétendants au trône de la France*. Paris, n.d.
Jacquet, Eugène. *Le complot bonapartiste*. Paris, 1875.
Sorr, Angelo de. *Manuel du parfait Bonapartiste*. Paris, 1875. An amusing satiric portrait of the Bonapartist personality.

F. ARTICLES

"Baron Eschasseriaux." *Revue de la Saintonge et de l'Aunis* (*Bulletin de la Société des Archives historiques*), XXVI (1906), 351.
Des Houx, Henri. "Edgar Raoul-Duval: Origine et avenir de la Droite républicaine." *Nouvelle Revue*, XLVII (July 1, 1887), 37–72.

Bibliography

Gautier, Théophile. "Herr Rouher." *Deutsche Revue* (September, 1886), 272–292.

Magne, Alfred. "Deux visites à Chislehurst en 1872." *Revue hebdomadaire*, VIII (August 17, 1912), 289–314.

Moreau, Henry. "La propagande bonapartiste dans les écoles primaires." *Correspondant*, C (1875), 1275–1279.

Richard, Albert. "Les propagateurs de l'Internationale en France." *Revue socialiste*, XXIV (June, 1896), 641–667.

G. POLITICAL GUIDES AND MAPS

Ans, Edouard d'. "La France parlementaire." Paris, 1876. A map showing the political affiliation of the deputy elected by each *arrondissement*, with tables listing the votes won by each party. Not entirely reliable.

Clère, Jules. *Biographie des députés.* Paris, 1875. Republican.

Daniel, André, ed. *L'Année politique, 1874–1879.* Paris, 1875–1880.

Glucq. "Deux pages d'histoire." Paris, n.d. Two maps comparing the results of the general elections of 1876 and 1877.

Guide manuel et plan colorié de la Chambre des Députés élue les 14 et 28 octobre 1877 par un employé de la Chambre. N.p., 1878.

Liste de Messieurs les députés. Paris, 1869.

Liste de Messieurs les députés. Paris, 1870.

Ribeyre, Félix. *Biographie des députés.* . . . Paris, 1864.

—. *Biographie des sénateurs et des députés.* New ed., Paris, n.d. Bonapartist.

Sagnier, André. *Liste complète des membres du Sénat et de la Chambre des Députés.* Paris, 1878.

Villard, P. *Carte du Sénat.* Lyon, 1876.

H. NEWSPAPERS

L'Ordre. 1871–1879.
Le Temps. 1876–1877.

II. SECONDARY SOURCES

(N.B. It has not been thought necessary to include such standard accounts of the Third Republic as those of Baumont, Brogan, or

Bibliography

Chastenet, with which any reader of this study is likely to be familiar.)

A. BOOKS

Avenel, Henri. *Histoire de la presse française.* Paris: Flammarion, 1900.

Byrnes, Robert F. *Antisemitism in Modern France.* New Brunswick: Rutgers University Press, 1950.

Chalmin, Pierre. *L'Officier français de 1815 à 1870.* Paris: Rivière, 1957.

Chevallier, J. J. *Histoire des institutions politiques de la France moderne.* 2d ed., Paris: Dalloz, 1958.

Collins, Irene. *The Government and the Newspaper Press in France.* London: Oxford University Press, 1959.

Dansette, Adrien. *Le Boulangisme.* Paris: Fayard, 1946.

Dreyfus, Robert. *La République de Monsieur Thiers 1871-1873.* Paris: Gallimard, n.d.

Durieux, Joseph. *Le ministre Pierre Magne 1806-1879.* 2 vols. Paris: Champion, 1929.

Girard, Louis, ed. *Les élections de 1869.* Paris: Rivière, 1960.

Goguel, François. *Géographie des élections françaises de 1870 à 1951.* (Cahiers de la Fondation Nationale des Sciences Politiques, 27.) Paris: Colin, 1951.

Gouault, Jacques. *Comment la France est devenue républicaine: les élections générales et partielles à l'Assemblée nationale 1870-1875.* (Cahiers de la Fondation Nationale des Sciences Politiques, 62.) Paris: Colin, 1954.

Halévy, Daniel. *La fin des notables.* Paris: Grasset, 1930.

—. *La République des Ducs.* Paris: Grasset, 1937.

Hanotaux, Gabriel. *Histoire de la fondation de la Troisième République.* 4 vols. New ed., Paris: Plon-Nourrit, 1925-1926.

Hérisson, Comte d'. *Le Prince Impérial.* 4th ed., Paris, 1890.

Jerrold, Blanchard. *The Life of Napoleon III.* 4 vols. London, 1882.

Kayser, Jacques, ed. *La presse de province sous la Troisième République.* (Cahiers de la Fondation Nationale des Sciences Politiques, 92.) Paris: Colin, 1958.

Bibliography

Kurtz, Harold. *The Empress Eugénie.* London: Hamish Hamilton, 1964.

Lhomme, Jean. *La grande bourgeoisie au pouvoir.* Paris: Presses universitaires de France, 1960.

Normandy, Georges, ed. *Gustave Flaubert: Lettres inédites à Raoul-Duval.* Paris: Albin Michel, 1950. The letters are of very slight interest to the political historian, but the Preface is an excellent concise biography of Raoul-Duval by his grandson.

Rémond, René. *La Droite en France de la Première Restauration à la Cinquième République.* New ed., Paris: Aubier, 1963.

Reveillaud, E. *Histoire politique et parlementaire des départements de la Charente et de la Charente-Inférieure.* Saint-Jean-d'Angély, 1911.

Robert, A. Bourloton, E., and Cougny, G., eds. *Dictionnaire des parlementaires français 1789–1889.* 5 vols. Paris: Bourloton, 1891.

Schnerb, Robert. *Rouher et le Second Empire.* Paris: Colin, 1949.

Seignobos, Charles. *Le déclin de l'Empire et l'établissement de la Troisième République.* (Ernest Lavisse, ed., Histoire de France contemporaine, VII.) Paris: Hachette, 1921.

Siegfried, André. *Tableau politique de la France de l'ouest sous la Troisième République.* Paris: Colin, 1913.

Thomas, Albert. *Le Second Empire.* Paris, n.d.

Zeldin, Theodore. *The Political System of Napoleon III.* London: MacMillan, 1958.

—. *Emile Ollivier and the Liberal Empire of Napoleon III.* Oxford: Clarendon Press, 1963.

B. ARTICLES

Gaillard, Jeanne. "La presse de province et la question du régime République." *Revue d'Histoire Moderne et Contemporaine,* VI (1959), 295–310.

Hermant, E. "La régence de l'Impératrice Eugénie." *Revue des Questions Historiques,* CIV (1926), no. 2, 295–358; no. 3, 51–103.

Bibliography

Kulstein, David J. "The Attitude of French Workers toward the Second Empire." *French Historical Studies*, II, no. 3 (1962), 356–375.

Lajusan, A. "Les origines de la Troisième République; Quelques éclaircissements (1871–1876)." *Revue d'Histoire Moderne*, V, no. 30 (1930), 419–438.

Marlin, Roger. "La presse du Doubs pendant la guerre de 1870–1871." *Etudes de presse*, new series, VIII (1955), 177–188.

Weber, Eugen. "France." In Hans Rogger and Eugen Weber, eds., *The European Right: A Historical Profile*, Berkeley and Los Angeles: University of California Press, 1965. Pp. 71–127.

Wright, Gordon. "Distribution of French Parties in 1865: An Official Survey." *Journal of Modern History*, XV (December, 1943), 295–302.

Index

Adour, L', of Dax, newspaper, 83, 212
Affiche blanche, used in 1877, 258-259
Agen, Bishop of, 166
Aigle, L': Almanach illustré du suffrage universel, 70-72
Ain, department of, 169
Aisne, department of, 81, 205, 216-217
Ajaccio, 164, 270-271
Allart, Marcus, 32-33, 115
Allier, department of, 204-205
Alsace-Lorraine, 66, 272
Amigues, Jules, 22, 92-101, 277, 281, 299, 300, 302
Angoulême, 210
Anti-Semitism, 280, 311-312
Appel au peuple, party of the, 12, 35, 288; see also Bonapartists
Arcade, group of rue de l', 21-22
Ardèche, department of, 169
Ardennes, department of, 206
Argence, Bonapartist candidate in Aube, 219
Argenteuil, 98
Ariège, department of, 214
Aristocracy, Napoleon III on, 18
Armée, L', newspaper, 45-46
Army, French, 45-51, 138, 261, 269-270, 296-297
Artisans, 94
Association, freedom of, 95
Aube, department of, 51, 106, 108, 219
Auch, Bishop of, 166
Audiffret-Pasquier, Duc d', 121
Aumale, Duc d', 127, 135
Austria, 63
Avignon, Archbishop of, 165
Ayguesvives, Comte d', Bonapartist deputy, 163-164, 170

Bakunin, 91
Barings' Bank, 40
Barodet, Republican deputy, 96, 113, 116
Basses-Pyrénées, department of, 60-62
Batbie, Orleanist deputy, 120
Béhic, Louis-Henri-Armand, Bonapartist Senator, 239, 239n., 241-244, 264, 277
Bellanger, Marguerite, 63
Belleville, 92, 96-98
Berger, Bonapartist candidate in Maine-et-Loire, 142-143
Bisaccia, Duc de, Legitimist deputy, 120
Bishops, political views and influence of, 164-167
Bismarck, 66-67
Boffinton, Bonapartist deputy, 160-162, 189-190, 196, 225, 227
Bonaparte, Prince Charles, 270
Bonapartism: as endemic fever, 6; protean political concept, 6-7; and Fascism, 7-8, 312; in 1870–1871, 9, 12; Napoleon III's interpretation of, 19-20; schools of, 21-35; revival, 1872, 41; sympathy for, of "forces of order," 42-44; in Ministry of War, 47; in Charente-Inférieure, 184, 290; ground lost before 1870, 203-206; decline after 1876, 230-231; and death of Prince Imperial, 269-270; in twentieth century, 280-281; decline in Charente-Inférieure, 281-283; and elections of 1889, 288; and authoritarianism of the center, 293-294; two fundamental failures of, 295; and notables, 298-316; in cities, 300; and anti-Semitism, 311-312; and survival of Third Republic, 312-313; and Rad-

345

Index

Bonapartism (*cont.*)
   icalism, 312-313; and Fifth Republic, 316-319
Bonapartist party: problems of, 3-4; ideological diversity, 9; organization not needed, 53; unofficial general staff, 56; weaknesses analyzed by Ernest Merson, 102-103; claimed united on fusion, 127; see also *Appel au peuple*, party of the
Bonapartists: in general elections of February, 1871, 12-15; in by-elections of July, 1871, 15; equivocations of, 15-17; and Napoleon III, 33-34; return to political life, 1872, 35; in 1872 by-elections, 36; and Army, 45-51; new challenges after Napoleon III's death, 51-52; "truths" of, opposed to Republican "lies," 68-70; demands for plebiscite, 69-70; and working class, 90-101; social and occupational backgrounds of, 100-101; and death of Napoleon III, 104-108; and Empress Eugénie, 111-112; alliance with Legitimists, 112-114; and Catholic Church, 114-115, 300-301; and dissolution of National Assembly, 115-116; role in fall of Thiers, 116-122; disappointment in May 24, 1873, 122-124; many tempted by fusion, 125-127; announce they will oppose Chambord, 127; reject Republican advances (1873–1874), 128-130, 136-137; and Septennate for MacMahon, 130-134; propose plebiscite, 131; celebrate Prince Imperial's coming-of-age, 134-135; and Broglie (1874), 135-136; in by-elections (1874–1875), 142-143; organizational negligence and ideological rigidity, 142-143; Savary's report disastrous for, 144; divided over mode of *scrutin*, 144-147; cooperate with Gambetta against Orleanists, 147-148; tactics in National Assembly criticized, 148-151, 154; conservative instincts of, 154-157; affinities with Monarchists, 155-156; not a united voting bloc, 156-157, 218; limited effectiveness in National Assembly, 157; fail to win clergy's support, 164-167; neglect of electorate under Empire, 175; hesitations (1871) 186; cut off from electorate by "curtain" of bourgeoisie, 194-195; candidates and platforms in general elections of 1876, 195-202; in Senate elections of 1876, 203; in general elections of 1876, 207-224; distrust of newcomers, 212, 237-238; failure in 1876 analyzed, 225-229; Raoul-Duval an important recruit for, 236; leadership of (1876), 238-240; leaders meet at Chislehurst, June 4, 1876, 241-243; and Raoul-Duval's strategy, 243-248, 307-308; party discipline, 244-245; role in crisis of May 16 (1877), 248-261, 304-308; *malaise* (1878), 264-267; difficulty in accepting Republic, 265-266; and death of Prince Imperial, 268-270, 274-275; and leadership of Prince Napoleon, 274-276; "Republican," 276, 280; "Imperialist," 276-277, 280; and plan for conservative Republican party, 278-279; and Boulangism, 279-280, 286-288; membership cards and dues, 280; and right-wing Leagues, 280-281; and France's functional elites, 296-297; defective organization of, 301-303; propaganda, 303; in Parliament, 304-307
Bordeaux, 204, 210
Bouches-du-Rhône, department of, 206
Boulangism, 279-280, 286-287
Bourbaki, General, 40, 42, 45, 48, 50
Bourcart, Lieutenant-Colonel, Bonapartist candidate at Marseille, 221
Bourganeuf, 220
Bourgeoisie: change in political opinions, 80, 228; in Nièvre, 105; of Poitiers (Vienne), 105-106, 108, 198; clericalist, 116; in Aisne, 216; of La Rochelle, 185-186, 282; and Bonapartist candidates, 301
Bourgeoisie, grande, 27, 30, 155, 157
Bourgoing, Baron de, Bonapartist deputy, 138, 235

Index

Bouville, Comte de, former Prefect of Gironde, 60-61
Brittany, 163, 166, 204, 216
Broglie, Duc de: overthrown, 2; and Eure by-election, 36; on War Ministry, 47; on Bonapartist role in fall of Thiers, 121-122; and Septennate, 132; supported, then overthrown by Bonapartists, 136; on origins of Third Republic, 144; and Bonapartists, 148, 304-306; divides Bonapartists, 156; employs few Bonapartist *fonctionnaires*, 168; and Raoul-Duval, 233; and *Seize Mai*, 251, 255
"Brumairean" Bonapartists, 26, 156, 173
Brunet, "Bonapartist" minister of *Seize Mai*, 251, 255
Buffet, Prime Minister, 167, 242-245, 252

Café de la Paix, 55
Calmon family, in Lot, 211
Calumnies against the Empire, The, pamphlet, 66
Calvados, department of, 142
Cambrai, 99
Camden Place, Napoleon III's English country house, 17, 134
Camelots du Roi, 280-281
Candidacies, financing of, 88-89, 195-196
Cantal, department of, 165
Carbonari, 98, 176
Cassagnac, Adolphe Granier de, 25, 45, 212-213
Cassagnac, Paul Granier de: his *Pays* defends Empire in 1870, 10; described, 24-26; not on *comité de comptabilité*, 58; meets with Eschasseriaux, 60; in the Gers, 61, 212-213; publishes *L'Aigle*, almanac, 70-71; backs Jules Amigues, 96-97; on death of Napoleon III, 108; and alliance with Legitimists, 113-116; on fall of Thiers, 117; and extension of MacMahon's term, 131; favors *scrutin d'arrondissement*, 146; writes *The Revenge of the Polls*, 158-160; platform in 1876, 198; violent language (1876-1877), 236, 240-241, 246; undermines Rouher in *Seize Mai* crisis, 255-256; attacks Bonapartist defectors, 265-266; abandons conservative union, 267-268; attempts to block succession of Prince Napoleon, 274-275; abandons Prince Victor for "Solutionism," 277; not a proto-Fascist, 300
Cazeaux, Bonapartist deputy, 142
Center, region of France, 77, 83, 105, 143, 204-206, 216, 226-227
Chamber of Deputies, atmosphere of, 155
Chambord, Comte de (Henri V), 1, 37, 52, 112-113, 124-125, 127-128, 153, 314
Chambres syndicales, 94
Charentais, Le, newspaper, 83
Charente, department of, 14-15, 101, 146, 166, 194, 207-210, 290
Charente-Inférieure, department of: popular Bonapartism in, 6; Bonapartists elected in 1871 in, 14; editorial policy of *L'Ordre* in, 77; and death of Napoleon III, 107-108; administrative personnel after May 24, 1873, 122-124; and Septennate, 133; by-election of 1873, 160-162; Prefect of (1876), 171; role of Eschasseriaux family in, 172-173; modernization of, under Second Empire, 174-175; anti-clericalism in, 177; factors in Bonapartism of, 184-185; returns to Bonapartism (1872), 188; and *Seize Mai*, 251, 258-259; and Prince Napoleon, 271, 275; decline of Bonapartism after *Seize Mai* in, 281-286; and Boulangism, 286-287; in 1890's, 289-291; see also Eschasseriaux, Baron Eugène
Charonne, 98
Chartes, Duc de, son of Louis Philippe, 16
Cher, department of, 83
Chevreau brothers, 58, 217
Chislehurst, 17, 40, 87, 134
Church, Roman Catholic, in France, 95, 115, 246, 296-297, 300-301; see also Bishops, political views and

347

Index

Church, Roman Catholic (cont.)
 influence of, *and* Clergy, electoral influence of
Cities, Bonapartists and, 221, 300; *see also* Amigues, Jules
Clercq, deputy of Pas-de-Calais, 217-218
Clergy, electoral influence of, 163-167
"Coblence," the Bonapartist, 23-24, 30-32, 112, 115, 156, 268
Cognac, 184
Comité central de l'appel au peuple, 138
Comité central de l'Union conservatrice, 196
Comité de comptabilité, Bonapartist, 57-59, 97-98, 102, 129, 140-141, 144, 240
Comité national conservateur, Bonapartist election committee in 1876, 196-198, 214, 226-227
Communards, 92
Commune, Paris, 28, 90-91, 94-95, 119, 294
"Communists," 17
Conseillers de préfecture, 168
Conseils-généraux, 145, 185-186, 188
Conservatism, Bonapartist propaganda theme, 90, 92
"Conservative-liberal" party, 16-17, 33, 107; *see also* Orleanists
Conservative union, policy of: and Fournier in 1871, 16; demanded by *L'Ordre* (1872), 36; more important than winning working classes, 98; and bourgeoisie of the Vienne, 105-106; Magne and, 107-108, 211; after death of Napoleon III, 113-114; and fall of Thiers, 116-118; and fusion, 125-126; after failure of fusion, 128; and Septennate, 135; and Broglie, 136; criticized by Léonce Dupont, 149-150; Ollivier on, 151; in 1867–1869, 178; and Bonapartist platforms, 196-198; Eschasseriaux and, 200, 285-286; in general elections of 1876 and 1877, 200-201, 259; in Senate elections of 1876, 203; not effected in Gers, 213; in North of France, 218-219; and *Seize Mai*, 252, 256; renounced by Bonapart-

ists in 1878, 267-268; and "Solutionism," 277; and restoration of the Empire, 304-305
"Conspiracy, the great Bonapartist," 76, 138-144
Constitution: of 1852, 18-21; of 1875, 143-144
Corporatism, 94-95
Correspondance Mansard, 65, 81-83, 87, 231-232
Corrèze, department of, 221
Corsica (Corse, department of), 13, 35-36, 77, 99, 105, 164-165, 169-170, 221-223, 270-271, 283
Corsicans, in Marseille, 25, 39, 221
Côte-d'Or, department of, 36, 163
Courrier de l'Eure, Le, newspaper, 83
Creuse, department of, 220-221
Cunéo d'Ornano, Gustave, Bonapartist deputy, 207-210

Dauphiné, 206, 220
David, Baron Jérôme, Bonapartist deputy, 21, 21n.
Decazes, Duc, Orleanist leader, 139, 255
Decentralization, 18
Delafosse, Jules, Bonapartist deputy, 237, 237n.
Democracy, authoritarian, 20-21, 77, 110, 156-157, 192-193, 292, 318
Democracy, Caesarean, 26-27, 31-32, 74
Deputies, under Empire, 29-30; *see also* Bonapartists *and* Eschasseriaux
Détroyat, Léonce, journalist, 74
deux démocraties: République-Empire, Les, Léonce Dupont, 149-150
Deux-Sèvres, department of, 204, 215
Dictatorship, 19-20
Digne, Bishop of, 165
Dordogne, department of, 60, 83-86, 211
Doubs, department of, 87
Drapeau, Le, newspaper, 45
Dreyfus affair, 297
Drôme, department of, 206, 269
Drumont, Edouard, 311
Duchâtel, Comte, 192
Duclerc, Republican leader, 137
Dufaure, Republican leader, 190-191, 260

Index

Dufour, Baron, Bonapartist candidate in Lot, 198
Dugué de la Fauçonnerie, H. J., Bonapartist journalist and deputy, 66-67, 73, 75-77, 80, 90, 115, 117
Dupont, Léonce, Bonapartist journalist, 149-153, 224, 264-266
Duruy, Albert, Bonapartist journalist, 247
Duvernois, Clément, Bonapartist journalist, 56, 74-75, 77, 115

East, region of France, 12, 77, 86, 200, 206, 219-220, 226
Echo de la Dordogne, L', newspaper, 86
Ecole des Mines, 100
Education, 18, 95, 100, 115, 155, 210-211, 228
Egypt, Napoleon's return from, 37-38
Elba, reenactment of Napoleon's return from, 9, 38-45, 50-51, 296-297
Elections, 88-89, 158-164
Elections, by-: of July 2, 1871, 15, 160, 187; in 1872, 35-36; importance for Napoleon III, 38; in Aube (1873), 219, 226; in Charente-Inférieure (1873), 160-162; in Maine-et-Loire (1874), 142-143; in Nièvre (1874), 138, 141-142; (1874–1875), 142-143
Elections, general: of 1863, 176-177; of 1871, 1, 12-15, 153, 185-187; of 1876, 1, 4, 71, 89, 99, 102-103, 160, 167-171, 190-224; of 1877, 89, 254-260
Elections, to Senate (1876), 203
Elysée, rue de l', 54, 56
"Enragé," Amigues as Bonapartist, 33, 93
Empire, 20-21, 51, 97, 153-155; *see also* Second Empire
England, admired by Napoleon III, 19
Eschasseriaux, Baron Eugène: "King of the Charentes," 6; explains Bonapartist victories in 1871, 13-15; summarizes gains of 1872, 41; unflinching, 52; attends organizational meetings (May 1872), 57; named to *comité de comptabilité*, 58; criticizes *comité*, 59; responsible for organizing Southwest, 59-62; calls for more propaganda, 62; launches investigation of Government of National Defense, 67; criticizes editorials of *L'Ordre*, 77; subsidizes newspaper, 89; distrust of urban society, 100; and overthrow of Thiers, 120-121; disappointed in results of May 24, 1873, 122-124; expects defeat of fusion, 127; rejects cooperation with Republicans, 128-129; votes against Septennate, 133; proposes celebration of Prince Imperial's coming-of-age, 134; pleased by aplomb of Prince Imperial, 135; distrusts Broglie, 135; negotiates fruitlessly with Republicans, 137; astonished by Savary's allegations, 139; suspicious of Mansard, 140; summarizes Bonapartist gains in 1874, 143; calculates *scrutin de liste* better for Bonapartists, 145; rejects cooperation with Right (1875), 147; excludes Dufaure from Senate, 148; inept negotiator, 152; local preoccupations of, 154; voting record in National Assembly, 156-157; fears Bonapartist loss of peasant vote, 160; and election of Boffinton, 161-162; family history, 172-173; in election of 1849, 173; on Revolution of 1789, 173; joins party of Elysée (1851), 173; role under Second Empire, 173-174; relationship with Prefects, 174-175; consolidates position under Empire, 175-176; condemns Italian war as fatal turning point of Second Empire, 176; on Roman question, 177; estrangement from Imperial policies, 177-178; and election of 1869, 178-180; interview with Napoleon III in 1869, 179; and origins of Liberal Empire, 179-180; condemns electoral corruption, 180; builds political machine, 180-181; predicts elections, 181-182; destroys enemies, 182-183; character and personality, 183; undaunted by Sedan, 185; and bourgeoisie of La Rochelle, 185-186; and elections of February, 1871,

Index

Eschasseriaux, Baron Eugène (*cont.*) 185-187; and by-elections of July, 1871, 187-188; reelected to Conseil-général, 188; optimism, 1872, 188-189; not helped by Boffinton, 189; and elections of 1876, 190-193; believes murder a Republican campaign tactic, 192; causes of his success, 193, 225; a rarity in his party, 193; rejects placards of *Comité national conservateur*, 196; contemplates link with Legitimists, 200; not informed of new executive committee, 239; and Raoul-Duval's strategy, 245-246; and *Seize Mai*, 251-253, 258-259; on Mackau's defection, 256; criticizes Prince Imperial, 267; refuses to lead party under Prince Napoleon, 275; abandoned by son, retrenches, 282-284; and Prince Napoleon, 284; and Monarchists (in 1880's), 285-286; and Boulangism, 286-287; resigns from central Bonapartist committee, 287; advice to Prince Victor, 288-289; retires from politics, 289-291; incomplete organization of Southwest, 302; and authoritarian democracy, 309-310; limited contribution to Bonapartist party, 310-311

Eschasseriaux, Baron Joseph, great-uncle of Baron Eugène, 172-173

Eschasseriaux, René, grandfather of Baron Eugène, 172-173, 179

Eschasseriaux, René, son of Baron Eugène, 190, 193, 282-283

Espérance nationale, L', Amigues' newspaper, 93, 98, 101

Eugénie, Empress, 63, 111-112, 118, 134, 176, 178, 249, 270

Eure, department of, 36, 83, 170

Eure-et-Loir, department of, 165-166

Evreux, Bishop of, 165

Exile, psychological problems of, 37

Fascism, 7-8, 293-294, 311-312

Favre, Jules, 10

"Fidus" (Eugène Balleyguier), Bonapartist journalist, 18-19, 23-24, 38, 48, 109-110

Fleury, General, 49, 56, 58, 241, 243

Flourens, Communard leader, 96

Fonctionnaires: Imperial, after Sedan, 54; anti-Bonapartist, 123; cease subscribing to Bonapartist papers, 144; political views and action in elections of 1876, 167-170; in Charente-Inférieure, 182-183, 281; in Charente, 210; in Gers, 213; in Vendée, 215; in Corsica, 222; *attentisme* after 1870, 296-297; *see also* Prefects, Bonapartist

Fontenay-le-Comte, 215

Fournier, Charles, Imperial Mayor of La Rochelle: resists proclamation of Republic, 10-12; Bonapartist loyalty wavers in 1871, 16; on fall of Thiers, 119-120; political instincts, 154-157; describes 1873 by-election, 160-161; describes Eschasseriaux, 183; disturbed by prospect of facing universal suffrage, 190; elected to Chamber (1876), 193; and democratic politics, 225, 227; accepts support of *Seize Mai* government, 259; defeated, retires, 281-282

Fourtou, minister in *Seize Mai* government, 211, 252-255, 257

France, La, newspaper, 74

France juive, La, Édouard Drumont, 311-312

Franche-Comté, 86-87, 220

Franche-Comté, La, newspaper, 87

Franco-Prussian War, Napoleon III on, 63-64

Frankfurt, Treaty of, 66

Frohsdorf, 124

Funds, Bonapartist party: collected and allocated (1871), 65; and local journalism, 87; sources, 87-89; inadequacy criticized, 102; and choice of candidacies for elections of 1876, 195-196, 224, 238; and election costs, 202-203; and Rouher's authority, 227; limited after 1876 election, 231; as factor in *Seize Mai* crisis, 257-258; and alliance with Boulangism, 280; payment of dues instituted, 280; Eschasseriaux's recommendations to Prince Victor, 289; and oligar-

Index

Funds, Bonapartist party (cont.)
chic nature of Bonapartist party, 303-304
Fusion of Orleanists with Legitimists behind Chambord, 117-118, 124-128, 136, 233-234

Gambetta, Léon: role, 1870–1879, 1-4; and Bonapartists in 1870–1871, 11-12, 14; attacked by Bonapartist propagandists, 67-69; *La République française* his newspaper, 76; denies there is social question, 91; criticized by Amigues, 95; campaigns for dissolution of National Assembly, 115; hated by Rouher, 130; cooperation with Bonapartists in National Assembly, 144, 147-148; decrees dissolution of conseils-généraux, 186; appraised by Raoul-Duval, 233; denounces Empress, 272; task facilitated by Bonapartists, 296, 312
Ganivet, Bonapartist deputy, 146
Gard, department of, 269
Garde-champêtre, political activities of, 163
Garde Républicaine, 43
Gaulois, Le, newspaper, 73-74, 80, 96-97, 126, 130, 137, 144
Gavini, Bonapartist deputy, 13, 223, 283
Gendarmerie, political inclinations of, 43-44, 269-270
Gers, department of, 25, 60-61, 146, 166, 212-213
Gironde, department of, 15, 60-61, 83, 204, 210-211
Government of National Defense (1870–1871), 45, 67-68
Grande Armée, 46
Granier de Cassagnac, *see* Cassagnac, Paul Granier de
Guide for the Bonapartist Voter, Ernest Dréolle, 68-70
Guilloutet, Marquis de, Bonapartist deputy, 14, 14n., 212
Gudin, Republican candidate, 138

Haentjens, Alfred-Alphonse, Bonapartist deputy, 14, 14n., 34, 67, 121, 132-133, 155-156
Halévy, Daniel, 7
Hamille, deputy of Pas-de-Calais, 218, 228
Harcourt, Emmanuel d', MacMahon's secretary, 139
Haute-Garonne, department of, 163-164, 170-171
Haute-Loire, department of, 105
Hautes-Alpes, department of, 206
Haute-Saône, department of, 87
Hautes-Pyrénées, department of, 142
Haute-Vienne, department of, 220-221
Henri V, *see* Chambord, Comte de
Hérault, department of, 169
History, comparative, 2, 318-319

Illiteracy and Bonapartist voting, 210
Indre, department of, 204
Industry and Bonapartists, 100-101
International, the First, 16, 67, 90-91
Isère, department of, 105, 166, 206, 220
Italian war as turning point of Second Empire, 176
Italy, 63

Jacobins, Bonapartist, 32
Janvier de la Motte, former Prefect of Eure, 170
Jesuits, 26, 272, 276
Jews, 24; *see also* Anti-Semitism
Jolibois, Bonapartist deputy, 190, 193, 285
Jonzac, 123, 187, 190, 285, 290
Journal de Bordeaux, Le, newspaper, 83
Journal de la Vienne, Le, newspaper, 83
Journal du Cher, Le, newspaper, 83
Journal du Lot-et-Garonne, Le, newspaper, 83
Journalists, Bonapartist, 70, 75
Jura, department of, 87

Keller, former deputy of Alsace, 272

La Chapelle, Comte Alfred de, 19n., 110, 265, 278
Landes, department of, 14, 60, 83, 169, 211

351

Index

Languedoc, 206
Laroche-Joubert, Bonapartist deputy, 101, 246
La Rochelle, 10-11, 155, 174, 190, 281-282, 287
La Roncière le Noury, Vice-Admiral, 47-48
Latin Quarter, 281
Lavalette, Marquis de, 88
Lavisse, Ernest, 81, 216-217, 247, 267
Left Center, in National Assembly, 123, 132, 136-137, 167, 255
Légion Mobile, 43
Legislative Body, final session of, 10
Legitimism, 33, 108, 112-113, 153, 166, 204, 233, 314
Legitimists: attempt fusion with Orleanists to restore Chambord, 1, 124; elected in 1871, 12; elected in Sarthe, 14; Cassagnac and, 26; reject equality, 69; newspaper loses readers, 80; in Franche-Comté, 86; well-organized cadres of, 102; feared by peasants of Nièvre, 105; Napoleon III will not be satellite of, 113; give assurances to Bonapartists before fall of Thiers, 120; their regime the negation of democracy, 125-126; excused by *L'Ordre* for attempt at fusion, 128; elected to Senate with Bonapartist votes (1875), 148; and conservative union, 151; caricatured by Cassagnac, 159; among clergy, 165-167; of Poitiers, 169; and Bonapartists, in elections of 1876, 200-202; in Mediterranean coastal region, 206; and the Cassagnacs, in the Gers, 213; in Ariège, 214; win countryside in parts of western France (1876), 216; in ministry of *Seize Mai*, 251; see also Legitimism, Monarchists
Le Marois, Comte, Bonapartist deputy, 88
Lemercier, Comte, candidate in Charente-Inférieure, 178-180
Le Provost de Launay, Bonapartist deputy, 142
Le Roux, Alfred, minister of the Empire, 214-215, 228

Letter to an American, Edgar Raoul-Duval, 263
Levert, Charles, Bonapartist deputy, 35, 113, 118, 121, 132, 217, 277
Liberal Empire, 21, 30, 178, 227, 298-299, 310-311; see also Empire
Liberté, La, newspaper, 74, 88, 168, 223
Ligue de l'Enseignement, 232
Lipset, Seymour Martin, 293
Loiret, department of, 105, 108
Loqueyssie, de, Bonapartist candidate in Tarn-et-Garonne, 214
Lorraine, see Alsace-Lorraine
Lot, department of, 13, 60, 198, 211
Lot-et-Garonne, department of, 60-61, 83, 146, 166, 211-212
Lyon, 42, 45, 50, 91, 269

Machines, political, 180-184, 207, 212-214, 223, 225
Mackau, Baron de, Bonapartist deputy, 256, 256n., 280
MacMahon, Marshal: term as President of the Republic, 1-2; Bonapartists and election of, 117; and fusion, 127; Bonapartists and extension of his term, 131-134, 156-157; mentioned in Bonapartist platforms (1876), 198-199; and the Bonapartist party, 248-250, 255, 260, 307
Magne, Pierre, minister of the Empire and deputy of the Dordogne: and elections of 1871, 15-16; and Bonapartist policy (1873), 107-108; and conservative unity, 116; and fall of Thiers, 118; promised post in ministry of May 24, 1873, 121; isolated in Broglie ministry, 124; more conservative than Bonapartist, 157; enters government, 1867, to effect conservative union, 178; son organizes the Dordogne, 211; his ideas ultimately prevail, 308
Maine-et-Loire, department of, 142-143
Manche, department of, 169
Mansard, secretary of *comité de comptabilité*, 58, 82, 90, 140; see also Correspondance Mansard
Marennes, 190-191, 287

Index

Marne, department of, 166
Marseille, 25, 39, 89, 221
Massif Central, region of France, 86, 105, 166, 220-221, 226
May 16, 1877, crisis of: see *Seize Mai*, crisis of
Mediterranean littoral, region of France, 77, 206, 221, 226, 269; *see also* Midi
Mémorial, Le, of Lille, newspaper, 82
Merson, Ernest, Bonapartist journalist, 102-103, 135
Mestreau, Republican Prefect of Charente-Inférieure, 185, 187-188
Meuse, department of, 206
Midi, 104, 221, 313
Miners, of Nord, 106, 108
Missi dominici, regional Bonapartist leaders, 60-61, 102
Moissac, 256
Monarchists: and Septennate, 2, 131-132; in 1872 by-elections, 36; Bonapartist cooperation with, 108, 111, 149-151; Prince Imperial on, 110; fusion of, 118, 124; denounced by *L'Ordre*, 125; backed by Bonapartists in second *tour* of by-elections, 142-143; share Bonapartists' Assembly benches, 155; in Charente-Inférieure, 185, 282; in elections of 1876, 201; indifferent to conservative union in Senate elections, 203; strength before 1870, 204-206; in Gironde, 210; *see also* Legitimism, Legitimists, Orleanism, *and* Orleanists
Montmartre, rue, Bonapartist propaganda headquarters, 65, 72
Morbihan, department of, 165, 170
Mouchy, Duc de, Bonapartist deputy, 88
"Mountain," Bonapartist, 23, 32-33, 115
Murat, Comte Joachim, Bonapartist deputy, 13, 13n., 60, 211, 307
Murat, Prince, 187

Napoléon-Jérôme, Prince (Prince Napoleon, the Emperor's cousin "Plon-plon"): leader of Bonapartist "Mountain," 33; most Bonapartists refuse to follow, 7, 275-277; not a member of *comité de comptabilité*, 59; and the Empress, 111; ousted from France by Thiers, 116; supports cooperation with Republicans, 129; hostility toward, 269; career of, 270-271; speech of November 24, 1876, 272; outlook and character of, 272-274; view of Second Empire, 273; Bonapartist reaction to his letter of April 5, 1880, 276; views on social question, 277; retires to Switzerland, 278; death, 288; anticlericalism, 301
Napoleon III, Emperor of the French: death, 9; on return to France (1871), 17; shaken by Sedan, 17; reaction to Fidus' program, 18; basic ideas unchanged after 1870, 19; admires England, 19; constitutional ideas, 19-20; on Revolution of 1789, 20; on Republic and Empire, 20; limited understanding of social question, 20-21; ineffective arbiter among schools of Bonapartism, 21; defends Ollivier, 31; relations with Bonapartist party, 33-34; on "return from Elba," 38-40; decision expected at end of 1872, 41; rumored in Paris, 42; possible plan for return to France, 42; significance of death for Bonapartists, 51-52; orders not obeyed by Bonapartists, 57; accepts organizational plan, 57; perceives need for propaganda, 62; attacked in Republican propaganda, 63; writes pamphlets in own defense, 63-64; blamed for War of 1870, 65; regrets shortage of Bonapartist funds, 87; not wealthy, 87; refuses to create special electoral fund, 89; and conservatism, 90; dabbling in socialism criticized, 90; socialism of, 92; backs Jules Amigues, 93, 299-300; impact of death upon French public opinion surveyed, 104-107; rejects alliance with Legitimists, 113; hesitates to overthrow Thiers, 117; realizes Bonapartist parliamentary role circumscribed, 152; reported not dead, 162; un-

353

Index

Napoleon III (*cont.*)
able to help Eschasseriaux in 1869, 179; and ideas of Raoul-Duval, 238; Comte de La Chapelle declares he would have favored accepting Republic, 265; and Prince Napoleon, 274; definition of Bonapartism, 299; and socialism, 300; and failure of Bonapartism, 308, 311, 316
Napoleonic Legend, 49, 70
Nation, La, newspaper, 247-248
National Assembly, the French (1871–1875): Monarchist, enacts a Republican constitution, 1-2; nucleus of Bonapartists in, 12; declares Bonapartes responsible for ruin of France, 15; investigates Government of National Defense, 67; Bonapartists deny it has constituent authority, 69; Bonapartists and dissolution of, 115-116; results of its investigation of the Nièvre by-election published, 141-143; votes "Constitution" of Third Republic and hears Savary report, February 25, 1875, 143; Bonapartist role in, 152-153, 157; characterized, 294
National Defense, Government of, *see* Government of National Defense
Nationalists, 280
Newspapers, local Bonapartist: importance in 1871, 14; importance stressed by Lavisse, 81; location and circulation of, 82-87; precarious loyalty of, 89-90; evaluated by Merson, 103; in Charente-Inférieure, 189; in Charente, 83-86, 207; in Dordogne, 86, 211; in Lot-et-Garonne, 83, 212; in Gers, 213; in Nord, 82, 218; subsidies reduced (1876), 231; Eschasseriaux's recommendation to Prince Victor on, 289; essential to electoral success, 303
Newspapers, Parisian Bonapartist, 73-80
Nièvre, department of, 105, 108, 138, 144, 216, 269

Nord, department of, 37, 41, 106, 108, 218
Normandy, 77, 97, 204, 216
North, region of France, 77, 105-106, 143, 206, 216-218, 226, 313
Notables, Bonapartism and, 5, 298-300, 306, 309-310, 314-316
Noubel, Bonapartist deputy, 211-212

Occupations, professional, of Bonapartist politicians, 100-101
Officer corps, *see* Army
Oise, department of, 217
Ollivier, Emile, 21, 30-33, 74, 151, 221
Opportunism, 315
Opportunists, 287
Opposition, role of, under Second Empire, 63, 150
Oran, 134
Ordre, L', Rouher's newspaper: its business manager gathers intelligence, 43; established, 65; Rouher gets control of, 74-75; qualified success of, 75-76; quality of, 77; denounces Cassagnac's proposal for income tax, 96; clericalism of, 115; rejoices at fall of Thiers, 122; on monarchical restoration, 124-125; denies Bonapartist divisions over fusion, 126; excuses Legitimists, 128; on Republic, 129-130; opposes lengthy extension of MacMahon's term, 131-132; denounces, then accepts Septennate, 133-134; complains Broglie's purges ineffective, 136; subscriptions cancelled, 144; endorses *scrutin d'arrondissement*, 145; defends universal suffrage, 156; clericalism does not win clergy, 164; complains of government support for Republicans in 1876, 167; and elections of 1876, 203, 223; "reorganized" (1876), 232; absorbs *La Nation*, 248; criticized by Raoul-Duval, 248; and *Seize Mai*, 251, 260; foreswears conservative union, 267; on Prince Napoleon, 270-271
Organization, Bonapartist electoral: lacking in 1871, 14-15; propaganda

354

Index

Organization (cont.)
declares unnecessary, 53; Rouher responsible for rebuilding, 54-55; steps taken, May 1872, 57; of Southwest entrusted to Eschasseriaux, 60; failures of, criticized, 101-103; Rouher fears inertia, 142-143; in Charente-Inférieure, 177-184; local base necessary, 187; Bonapartism muted where lacking, 194; in Gironde, 210-211; in Dordogne, 211; in Lot-et-Garonne, 211-212; in Gers, 212-213; in Aisne, 216-217; in Oise, 217; in Nord, 218; in Franche-Comté, 220; in Isère, 220; compared with Republican, 224; impossible in some regions, 226; in 1890's, 280, 289; not adapted to democratic politics, 302-303; *see also* Machines, political

Orleanism, 33, 204, 228, 233, 314

Orleanists: attempted fusion with Legitimists, 1, 124; elected in 1871, 12, 14; disappoint Fournier, 16; Ollivier criticized for forming government with, 32; in Bonapartist propaganda, 69; in Franche-Comté, 86; assurances to Bonapartists before fall of Thiers, 120; on May 24, 1873, 121; hope to win over Left Center, 123; Rouher suspects of double-dealing, 125; and Septennate, 132, 135; fear of Bonapartism and acceptance of Republic, 135-139; terrified by Bourgoing's victory, 138; mount counteroffensive against Bonapartists, 139; and Bonapartist electoral victories (1874–1875), 142-143; Broglie on their unholy alliance with Republicans, 144; and Bonapartist *comité de comptabilité*, 144; Bonapartists work with Gambetta to destroy, 147-148; caricatured by Cassagnac, 158-159; among Prefects, 170; patronized by Imperial government in Southwest in 1863, 176-177; on Bonapartist slates in 1876, 202, 214; Raoul-Duval's strategy to eliminate, 242; and MacMahon, 249; in ministry of Seize Mai, 251; divisions paralyze government of Seize Mai, 255; patronage rejected by Eschasseriaux, 258; fear of Bonapartism cripples government of Seize Mai, 260; and presidential election of 1887, 286; *see also* Monarchists *and* Right Center, in National Assembly

Orleano-Bonapartists, 218, 227
Orléans, royal family of, 105, 114, 117
Orne, department of, 170

Padoue, Duc de, Bonapartist deputy, 58, 239, 241, 277
Pajol, General, 48
Palikao, General Comte de, 58
Pamphlets, Bonapartist: innumerable, 53; campaign launched May, 1872, 57; effects praised by Eschasseriaux, 62; agency created to distribute, 65; well-designed, 65-66; three chief themes, 70; importance in propaganda effort, 73; circulated by local Bonapartist paper, 189; flow diminishes (1876), 224; evaluated, 303; *see also* Propaganda
Papacy, temporal power of, 18
Paris, 9-10, 12, 50, 53, 98-99, 113-114
Paris, Comte de, Orleanist pretender, 124, 233
Paris-Journal, newspaper, 74, 88
Parliamentary government, 19-20, 27, 30, 306, 318
Pas-de-Calais, department of, 35, 44, 203, 206, 218, 228, 269
Patrie, La, newspaper, 74, 80n., 277, 289
Pays, Le, newspaper, 10, 25, 70, 73-74, 80, 144, 277
Pazzis, Comte de, 138
Peasants: Rouher on, 27-28; opinion of Republicans, 68, 129; and Bonapartist "Plain," 100; in Nièvre, 105, 108; in Vienne, 106, 196; in Nord, 106; in Aube, 106, 219; in Charente-Inférieure, 108, 160, 180, 184, 192, 282; and Prince Imperial, 109; and *scrutin d'arrondissement*,

Index

Peasants (cont.)
145; in "Pyrénées-Occidentales," 158; voting behavior of, 160-164; and Eschasseriaux, 176-180, 228; and local leadership, 187; in Southwest, 207; in Dordogne, 211; in Aisne, 216; and Bonapartist politicians, 301; Bonapartists' alienation of, 305; in French politics, 313-314

Persigny, Duc de, 26

Photographs, Imperial, 71-72, 189, 192, 303

Phylloxera, 282

Piétri, former Prefect of Police, 43, 56, 58

Pinard, Ernest, former Imperial minister, 58, 178, 199-201

Pius IX, Pope, 112, 115, 177-178

"Plain," Bonapartist: metaphor from terminology of Revolution, 23; described, 28-29; conflicting inclinations of, 32; vagaries of, 34, 301; scandalized by proposal for income tax, 97; and peasants, 100; Fournier as characteristic of, 154-155; torn between Bonapartism and conservatism, 156; and Raoul-Duval's "progressive Empire," 245; Seize Mai reveals instincts of, 268

Platforms, of Bonapartist candidates: in general elections of 1876, characterized, 194-200; of Saint Paul in Ariège, 214; in Aisne, 217; of Hamille in Pas-de-Calais, 218; of Argence in Aube (1873), 219; in East of France, 220; and problem of political classification of candidates, 223n.; of 1876, criticized by Léonce Dupont, 224; reasons for equivocations of, 226-227, 309; appeal to bourgeoisie of, 227-228; often do not offer democratic alternative to Republic, 228; in general elections of 1877, 254, 258; and electoral victories, 305

Plebiscite: of 1870, 9, 12, 204, 206-207; as means of Imperial restoration, 38; Rouher on inevitability of, 39; in Bonapartist propaganda, 69; advocated by Amigues, 96; proposed, 131; Septennate hinders appeals for, 133; Gaulois' plans for,
137; Thiers and, 149; elections as substitute for, 201; political uses of, 297-298

Poitiers, 105-106, 198

Poitiers, rue de, group of, 27

Police, 43, 72, 139

Polytechnique, Ecole, 100, 155

Prangins, Swiss estate of Prince Napoléon, 42, 278

Prax-Paris, Bonapartist deputy, 13, 213-214, 256-257

Prefects, Bonapartist, 122-125, 135, 168-171, 251; see also Fonctionnaires

Press, 10, 38; see also Journalists, Bonapartist and Newspapers

Presse, La, newspaper, 74

Prince Imperial, the, son of Napoleon III: succeeds father as pretender, 7; letters of, to an Army mess, 47; officers forbidden to attend celebration for, 47; military mentor not found for, 49; responsibility for his restoration, 51-52; not thought competent to direct his party, 58; photographs of, 71-72; no workers' delegation to celebration of his coming-of-age, 98-99; unencumbered by father's record, 107; attitude of Bonapartists toward, 109-111; and peasants, 109; political ideas of, 109-110; Chambord and, 112; Thiers on, 118; celebration at Chislehurst of his coming-of-age, 134-135; speech of, March 16, 1874, 135; receives minutes of comité de comptabilité, 141; views contrasted with those of his party, 150; Raoul-Duval finds very liberal, 235; and leadership of his party, 239; intransigence attributed to, by Cassagnac, 240-241; presides over meeting at Chislehurst June 4, 1876, 241-243; approves Raoul-Duval's plans, 242-243; apologizes Raoul-Duval, 244; abandons La Nation, 248; on Seize Mai, 249-250; Raoul-Duval criticizes, 264; and acceptance of Republic, 265; last efforts to rebuild party, 266; abandoned (1878), 267; reasons for joining expedition to South

Index

Prince Imperial, the (*cont.*)
  Africa, 267-268; death (1879), 268-270; will of, 274
Prince Napoleon, *see* Napoléon-Jérôme, Prince
Professions de foi, *see* Platforms, of Bonapartist candidates
Progrès de la Charente-Inférieure, Le, newspaper, 189, 192, 281-282, 284
Propaganda, Bonapartist: for Army, 45-46; campaign launched (1872), 57; need for, 62-63; three essential spheres of, 65; examples of, 66-71; limited by police, 72; inducements for dissemination of, 72; quantitative assessment of, 73; failures criticized, 102-103; apparatus reduced (1876), 231; evaluated, 303; *see also* Newspapers *and* Pamphlets, Bonapartist
Protectionism, 178, 188, 218, 282
Protestants, 24
Provence, 206
Prussia, 66-67, 117
Public opinion, 68, 83n., 114
Pugliesi-Conti, former Prefect of Vendée, 215
Puy-de-Dôme, department of, 27, 220, 283
"Pyrénées-Occidentales," department of, 158-160

Radicals, Republican, 36-37, 47, 151, 153, 291, 296, 312-313, 315; *see also* Republicans
Railways, 174-175, 210-211, 228
Ralliement, the, 290
Raoul-Duval, Edgar: denounces Cassagnac's proposal of income tax, 97; favors *scrutin de liste*, 146; cooperation with Gambetta, 147-148; exacts price for Bonapartist votes, 154; and Janvier de la Motte, 170; plans new efforts (1876), 231; background and political principles, 232; searches for a party (1871-1875), 232-234; skeptical of Bonapartism, 234; meets Prince Imperial, 235-236; opposes Constitution of 1875, 236; wants renovation of Bonapartism, 237-238; deplores Bonapartist indiscipline, 238; and Bonapartist executive committee, 239-240; fears influence of Cassagnac, 240-241; keeps minutes of Chislehurst meeting, 241-243; proposes parliamentary tactics, 241-242; complains to Prince Imperial of Bonapartist Senators, 243-245; on Cassagnac, 246; and *La Nation*, 247; and *Seize Mai*, 250, 262-263; abandons Bonapartism, 263-264; plan for conservative Republican party, 278-279; death (1887), 278; and *Ralliement*, 290; a "new man," 299; and Bonapartists, 307-308; design not ill-conceived, 315
Régime censitaire, 18, 147
Reille, Baron, deputy of Tarn, 223n.
Rémusat, Republican minister, 96, 113
Renault, Léon, Prefect of Police, 40, 48-49, 93-94, 116, 139
Republic: relation to Empire defined by Napoleon III, 20; durability doubted by Rouher, 39; Bonapartist attacks on, 63; blamed for loss of Alsace-Lorraine, 66; cannot be conservative, 69; not legal government, 69; and working class, 92; and bourgeoisie, 105-106; and peasants, 106; and fall of Thiers, 124; does not last in France, 153; attraction for young and ill-educated, 154; in Aisne, 216; Raoul-Duval proposes testing of, 242; the Third, 1-2, 10-11, 143, 294-295, 312-313; the Fifth, 6, 316-319
Republicanism, 33
Republicans: elected in 1872 by-elections, 36; conservative, criticized, 37; and Bonapartist propaganda in Army, 45; attacks on Imperial couple, 63; denounced by Napoleon III, 64; attacks on Empire might boomerang, 65; plotting with Prussians, 67; publish Imperial papers, 67; lies of, 68-69; as seen by peasants, 68; in Franche-Comté, 86; finding of candidates, 89; Amigues advises imitating their organization, 98; organized by secret societies, 102; advances to Bonapartists rejected, 128-129; as

357

Index

Republicans (cont.)
viewed by *L'Ordre*, 129-130; hated by Rouher, 130; and Septennate, 131; named as mayors in Bonapartist towns, 136; further advances to Bonapartists rejected, 137; Bonapartist voters support, 143; use Savary report for propaganda, 143; join with Orleanists to launch Third Republic, 143-144; tactics compared with Bonapartists', 150; caricatured by Cassagnac, 159; complain government supports Bonapartists in 1876 elections, 167; in Charente-Inférieure, 185-187; murder a campaign tactic of, 192; discipline of, 194; before 1870, 206; in Mediterranean region, 206; win towns in parts of western France (1876), 216; careers ahead of them, 227; and Prince Napoleon, 272; organization of, 309
République française, La, newspaper, 76
Restoration, the (1815–1830), 46
Réunion, 57, 306
Revenge of the Polls: A History of Nowhere and Everywhere, The, Paul de Cassagnac, 158
Revolution of 1789, 20, 25, 115, 125, 172, 184
Revue des Deux Mondes, 266
Rhône, department of, 206
Rhône, valley of, 221
Richard, Albert, leader of the International, 91-92, 97, 97n.
Richard, Jules, Bonapartist journalist, 45-46, 59, 75, 223, 279
Rigaud, Republican candidate, 162
Right Center, in National Assembly, 138, 167, 233, 255; see also Orleanists
Rochefort, town of, 193, 281, 287
Rothschilds, Paris correspondent of, 9
Rouher, Eugène, the former "Vice-Emperor": defeated in by-elections of July, 1871, 15, 187; named leader of Bonapartist party, 26; career of, 26-27; political beliefs, 27-28; leadership contested, 28; henchmen attack Ollivier, 30; criticized by Olliver, 31; and Jérômiste guerilla, 33; elected in Corsica, 35-36; believes Imperial restoration inevitable, 39; at Chislehurst (December, 1872), 40; predicts return of Napoleon III, 42; criticized by General Pajol, 48; does not take General Fleury seriously, 49; struggles to construct cohesive party, 52; must rebuild Bonapartist organization, 54; and *comité de comptabilité*, 57-59; responsible for Bonapartist planning, 59; allocates funds, 65; distributes photographs of Prince Imperial, 71; and Paris Bonapartist papers, 73-75; lacks funds for general elections, 89; and Jules Amigues, 93, 97-99; and death of Napoleon III, 107; rejects alliance with Legitimists, 113; and fall of Thiers, 117, 119, 149; and fusion, 125-127; hatred for Gambetta and Republicans, 130; opposes extending MacMahon's term, 132; counsels acceptance of Septennate, 133-134; rejects Savary's allegations, 139; conceals his papers, 139-140; on election in Maine-et-Loire, 142-143; favors *scrutin de liste*, 146; tactics in National Assembly analyzed, 149-153; and "Brumairean" Bonapartists, 156-157; conservative union as tactic of, 157; on by-elections of July, 1871, 160; undermined by Empress in 1860's, 176-178; cannot give Bonapartists orders, 189; laments rarity of men like Eschasseriaux, 193; fearful of election outcome in Charente, 194; insists on unequivocal platforms, 195; does not control candidacies in elections of 1876, 195; declares Bonapartists shut off from electorate by "curtain" of bourgeoisie, 195; on Vendée, 215; admits East of France not organized, 220; and Raoul-Duval, 236, 243, 246-247; Prince Imperial reconfirms authority of, 239; attends meeting at Chislehurst (1876), 241-243; and Bonapartist discipline, 244-245; endorses in-

Index

Rouher, Eugène (*cont.*)
come tax, 246; and *Seize Mai*, 249-250, 254-262; Raoul-Duval complains of his inertia, 264; on accepting Republic, 265; and Prince Napoleon, 270-271, 274-276; retires (1881), 283-284
Roy de Loulay, Bonapartist deputy, 133, 175, 190, 196, 281, 290
Roy de Loulay *fils*, Bonapartist deputy, 190, 193

Saint Brieuc, Bishop of, 165
Saint Denis, 98
Saintes, 123, 172, 181, 185, 190, 287
Saint-Flour, Bishop of, 165
Saint-Jean-d'Angély, 190, 281
Saint-Paul, Baron de, Bonapartist deputy, 44, 214, 218, 249, 251, 260
Saône-et-Loire, department of, 106
Sarrette, Bonapartist deputy, 121, 146, 212
Sarthe, department of, 14, 169
Sarthe, La, newspaper, 14
Savary, Charles, Orleanist deputy, 138-140
Savoy, 206
Scrutin d'arrondissement, 144-147, 189, 195, 212, 231, 257, 284, 308
Scrutin de liste, 12, 144-147, 195, 216, 238, 284, 308
Second Empire, 4, 19, 51, 294; *see also* Empire
Sedan, 9, 64, 303
Seine, department of, 204
Seine-et-Oise, department of, 206
Seine-Inférieure, department of, 204
Seize Mai, crisis of (1877), 2, 214, 230, 248-261, 305, 307-308
Senate, 147-148, 156-157, 190, 203, 242, 252, 306
Septennate, 133-135, 156-157, 234
Siècle, Le, newspaper, 168-169
Simon, Jules, Prime Minister, 186, 248
Socialism, 90-101, 300
Social reforms, advocated by Jules Amigues, 95
"Solutionism," 277
Soubeyran, Baron de, Bonapartist deputy, 74, 80n., 169

Southeast, region of France, 12, 86, 105, 199, 219-220, 226, 269
Southwest, region of France: Bonapartist victories in 1871 in, 13-14; Eschasseriaux responsible for organizing, 60; Eschasseriaux reports to Napoleon III on, 62; Bonapartist press in, 77, 83, 86, 89; Legitimists in, 166; politics of 1860's in, 176-178; *professions de foi* in, 199-200; before 1870, 204; in general elections of 1876, 207, 210-214; the only region where Empire still has widespread mass support, 224; Bonapartist organizational chain lacks links in, 302; turns from Bonapartism to Radicalism, 312-313
Stoffel, Colonel, candidate in Paris, 114, 116
newspaper, 86
Suffrage universal des Charentes, Le,

Tarbé, Edmond, Bonapartist journalist, 73, 113, 128, 130-131, 236
Tarn, department of, 223n.
Tarn-et-Garonne, department of, 13, 213-214, 256
Tax, Income, 95-96, 246, 300
Telegraph, 174
Thiers, Adolphe, first President of the Third Republic: in first years of the Republic, 1-2; seen as bulwark against "Communism," 16; fall of, and Imperial restoration, 42; reassures Army, 47; ambitions of, 69; attitude of Duvernois' *L'Ordre* toward, 74; press law under, 82; and bourgeoisie of Franche-Comté, 86; and working class, 91; and peasants of Vienne, 106; Magne advocates support for, 108; Bonapartists join with Monarchists to overthrow, 111, 116-122, 154; fall unprofitable for Bonapartists, 122-124, 168; Dupont criticizes Bonapartist policy toward, 149-150; and Radicals, 151; support for him not clearly a better Bonapartist policy, 152-153; return to protectionism of, 188; Raoul-Duval **distrusts, 233**

359

Index

Toulouse, 163, 204
Treasury, Bonapartist, *see* Funds, Bonapartist party
Treaty, commerical, of 1860 with England, 184-185, 187, 210
Trochu, General, 67, 186

Union bretonne, L', newspaper, 23n., 83
Union des Droites, 280, 286
Union nationale du commerce et de l'industrie, 94
Universal suffrage, 18, 155-156
Uzès, Duchess d', 280

Vannes, Bishop of, 165
Var, department of, 104, 166, 221
Vast-Vimeux, Bonapartist deputy, 175, 186, 190, 225, 252
Vendée, department of, 204, 214-215, 228
Verney, distributor of Bonapartist propaganda, 72-73
Versailles, 52
Veuillot, 18
Victor, Prince, son of Prince Napoleon, 269, 274, 276-278, 284, 288-290
Vienne, department of, 80n., 83, 105-106, 108, 169, 196, 198, 204, 215

Wallon Amendment, 2
War, Ministry of, 47, 63
Weavers, hand-loom, 99
West, region of France, 83, 105-106, 143, 200, 204, 214-215, 226, 313
What September 4 Cost, Dugué de la Fauçonnerie, 66, 73
Wimpffen, General, 67
Workers, railway, 185, 193, 228
Working classes: Napoleon III on, 20-21; Fidus' plans for, 24; Rouher on, 28; Ollivier and, 31-32; Emperor condemned for his sympathy for, 90; under the Second Empire, 91, 204, 206; and Bonapartists, 91-101; in Nord, 106; in Aisne, 216; *see also* Amigues, Jules

Yonne, department of, 166

Zululand, 109

Augsburg College
George Sverdrup Library
Minneapolis, Minnesota 55404